THE POETRY OF LIFE

UNDERSTANDING HUMAN CONTROL SYSTEMS AND THE BRILLIANCE OF THEIR DESIGN AND FUNCTION

ALAN ST CLAIR GIBSON

Typeset in Book Antiqua

Editing, design, typesetting and publishing by UK Book Publishing

www.ukbookpublishing.com

ISBN: 978-1-915338-05-1

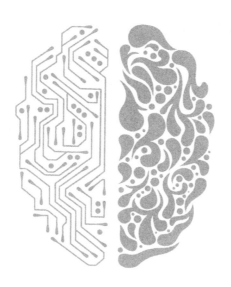

About the Author

Professor Alan (Zig) St Clair Gibson is currently the Associate Dean (Research) in the Faculty of Health Sciences at the University of Hull. Prior to this he was the Deputy Dean (Research) in the Faculty of Science and Health at the University of Essex. He has previously been Dean of the Faculty of Health, Sport and Human Performance at the University of Waikato, New Zealand, and Head of the School of Medicine at the University of Free State, South Africa. Prior to this he was first Director of Research / Chair of Integrative Neuroscience and then Head of Department in the Faculty of Health and Life Sciences at Northumbria University. He graduated from the University of Cape Town with an MBChB in 1990, a PhD in 1997 and a MD in 2002. He has previously been an Associate Professor in the MRC/UCT Research Unit of Exercise Science and Sports Medicine at the University of Cape Town, and a Research Fellow at the Human Motor Control Section, National Institute of Neurological Disorders and Stroke, at the National Institutes of Health, Washington DC, USA. He has published more than 150 research publications, and is a world-leading expert in the field of control system theory. He publishes a monthly blog (ziggibson. wordpress.com) of academic and research interest which has attracted more than 50,000 readers, the core of which have been brought together in this book. His wife, Kate, and he have two children, Luke (16), and Helen (13), and he enjoys spending time with his family, walking his dogs, reading history, walking, cycling, kayaking, and doing any other sport when he has the time to do so.

Dedication

Dedicated firstly to my family, Kate, Luke, and Helen. Thanks for your tolerance of all the days on weekends I worked on writing this in the garden office shed, or other home offices during our life together in the United Kingdom, New Zealand, and South Africa.

Dedicated secondly to Philip Hugh Lloyd, great friend and man of peerless integrity, humour, and a constant searcher for meaning and understanding of life and its limits, who died all too soon on the Mountains of Patagonia searching for his own truth.

Dedicated thirdly to two great science mentors who taught me how to be a scientist and study and understand the poetry which is life and its living. Firstly Mike Lambert, my PhD supervisor at the University of Cape Town and later colleague and great friend, who was always the example of what a true scientist and academic should be – interested in all things scientific, dispassionate about study outcomes, absolute integrity and honesty as first principles, and always supportive with no self-ego like so many other successful academic Professors. Mike was and is a fantastic role model in the early years, and to this day. Secondly, Kit Vaughan, my Head of Department at the University of Cape Town and later colleague and good friend, who taught me about the business of science, academic leadership, and how to manage teams to get the best out of them, and also someone with complete integrity, honesty and always wide smile and wicked sense of humour. To both of these great men, along with many other folks, I owe a huge debt of gratitude. Hopefully they will smile at and be pleased with the contents of this book as a product of the life work of their protégé.

Preamble

'When I heard the learned astronomer,
When the proofs, the figures, were ranged in columns before me,
When I was shown the charts and diagrams, to add, divide, and measure them,
When I sitting heard the astronomer where he lectured,
With much applause in the lecture room,
How soon unaccountable I became tired and sick,
Till rising and gliding out I wandered off by myself,
In the mystical moist night air, and from time to time,
Looked up in perfect silence at the stars.

Walt Whitman

Sections and Essays

General Introduction

This book describes the science behind the workings of the body, mind, and life around us in a way that is hopefully easily readable for everyone. It is composed of a series of 'Essays' where each Essay is about one specific scientific topic, in a way that hopefully will enlighten the reader about complex issues and behaviour in a simple, easy to understand manner. The Essays are linked with explanatory text and are divided into sections of similar topics of interest. The book can be read from beginning to end, or by section, or if the reader wishes, by individual Essay in no particular order, other than that of what interests the reader.

Thirty years of being a scientist made me aware that life and its control process have a rhythm and structure underpinning all activity, which takes time to be seen and understood, and there is a beauty to these rhythms and structures similar to that of great poetry, which I have tried to put into words in each of these Essays. I hope that the reader will find some understanding of how beautiful the poetry of life is, with its extraordinary complexity yet also perfect simplicity of design, from reading them. Enjoy!

Foreword

To the general public science can seem an abstract pursuit: dry, mundane, overly meticulous and monotonous with messages that are often nebulous, inconsistent or contradictory. But this perception obscures the truth – the initial wonder; the thrill of the chase; the exultation when a research study is complete and something 'new' has been discovered; the knowledge that some contribution has been made to better understanding the magical life that we lead. Above all else, it is this wonder, passion and excitement that Alan St Clair Gibson ('Zig' to his friends) has captured so astutely in "The Poetry of Life".

I can trace my own interest in 'life' and 'science' to pondering, as a small boy growing up in Chepstow in South Wales, the following questions: "Why am I here?", "What is this all about?", "What if I vanish without trace and without leaving behind something that my presence on earth can be remembered by?" Indeed, these are my earliest memories and I still have the same questions today! Maybe some questions will and should always remain philosophical and metaphysical. In primary school, I became fascinated by space: planets, stars, galaxies, black holes, creation, time, the unfathomable size of the universe, and our puny temporal and spatial significance within it. The notion of infinity is difficult for the human mind to comprehend. I still remember a line from a 1970s science magazine or TV programme: "There are many, many more stars in the universe than all the grains of sands on all the world's beaches." That takes some thinking about!

Back in the '70s, I combined membership of the Junior Astronomical Society with a fascination for science fiction. I particularly enjoyed reading the novels of Isaac Asimov and Philip K Dick and watching the brilliant TV programmes 'Tomorrow's World' and 'Dr Who' (when Tom Baker was 'The Doctor'). My obsession with Dr Who stretched to me wearing, in all weathers, a long multi-coloured scarf (à la Baker) that my Nanny Elsa had knitted for me, and using my pocket money to buy multiple packets of Weetabix from the mobile shop that frequented our street just so I could collect the promotional Dr Who stickers they occasionally contained. Eventually, my mum asked the shopkeeper not to sell me any more Weetabix! I believe the haunting, synthesised theme tune of Dr Who was the initial stimulus for my ongoing love of electronic music (particularly Gary Numan).

Growing up in the '70s and '80s was exciting and there seemed to be so much science around us. I vividly remember our class at primary school watching – on the huge box-like TV that was wheeled in on a trolley – the Space Shuttle's first launch in April 1981. Possibly that inspired my first career choice – to be an astronaut. I even joined the Air Training Corps after reading that most astronauts start their careers as military pilots though the connection between spaceflight and polishing my boots often seemed tenuous.

Then something else came along that derailed my (literally) lofty ambitions: sport. I was fortunate to have charismatic and truly inspirational physical education teachers at Chepstow Comprehensive school. They were hard but fair and valued effort and determination over outright talent. Perhaps they noticed something in me, though I think it's more likely I wanted to be noticed by them, and slowly, but surely, I discovered an ability for middle and long distance running. Encouraged by my teachers, over the course of my teenage years, I first made the school cross-country and athletics teams, and then the Gwent county team, then the Welsh team, and eventually I represented Great Britain and Northern Ireland juniors, and even set a couple of UK age records for 10K and the half marathon. Posters of new heroes, like Steve Ovett and Steve Jones, joined those of Gary Numan on my bedroom wall. Forget becoming an astronaut, I wanted to be the Olympic champion and world record holder!

I was self-coached and devoured all the sports physiology and training literature I could get my hands on in order to construct, for myself, the 'perfect' training programme. My new burning questions became: "What are the determinants and limitations to endurance exercise performance?", "Why are some runners better than others?", and "What can a person do to get faster?" I have asked, and been fortunate enough to address, exactly these same questions over the last 30 years as a researcher, lecturer and university professor. I never achieved my ambition of becoming the Olympic champion or world record holder – I sadly discovered my own limitations – but I have had the incredible opportunity to help more talented athletes than myself to achieve those same things.

I guess my scientific focus shifted from pondering the place of a human in the universe to how that human coordinates the many millions of cells in his or her body to achieve everything from the apparently prosaic to the superlative. Like Zig, I'm interested in the following: "How do we move?", "How do we produce the energy and at the right rates?", "How do we shift oxygen from the air around us to our cells?", "How is all of this affected by extreme exercise?" and "What is fatigue and what can we do about it?" To address these questions, we need to know about anatomy, physiology, biomechanics and psychology, not only separately, but in combination. When we exercise, we become exquisitely aware of life: of our breathing, our circulation, our muscles and our movement, the existence of discomfort and pain, and our motivations to have started and to continue exercising.

I tell my own story here, partly because Zig asked me to, but also because I see clear parallels in Zig's life and career and his inspirations for writing "The Poetry of Life". While the scientific method is the necessary means by which we test our hypotheses, it is the sheer wonder of the question itself that continues to fascinate and inspire us. The opportunity to simply ask the question, to consider the mechanisms by which things work, and occasionally to make tiny contributions to the way in which we understand life and the world, is a privilege and a joy.

"The Poetry of Life" is a collection of linked scientific essays that review many of the key psychobiological issues that life scientists are presently wrestling with – and yet it doesn't feel like a science book. When I read Zig's words, I also hear his voice, and it conveys the wonder and excitement about science and discovery that I know he feels so passionately. Zig has the knack of articulating highly complex and sometimes discordant concepts from various strands of science in a refreshing and highly engaging way. He speaks from his experiences as a medical doctor, a researcher in physical and psychiatric disorders, and an expert in exercise science and fatigue. It's a unique combination and it has led to a tour de force of a book that not only informs but simultaneously entertains. It demystifies science, strips out the jargon and makes the 'story of life' accessible.

After reading the book, I fully understand why Zig included the word 'poetry' in the title. The book is an ambitious undertaking, covering the entire gamut from basic physiology to abstract theory of motor control. Yes, it's comprehensive; sure, it's detailed; too right, it's sometimes challenging – but it's held together by joie de vivre and a humble appreciation for the orchestrated harmony of living systems and their relationship with the environment they inhabit.

"The Poetry of Life" reminds me that I should be grateful that, like Zig, I found a career that enables me, every day, to marvel. The book catapulted me back to Chepstow and my earliest memories as I examined my place in the world. My hope is that we never lose our child-like awe for the wonder and magic of life. Life is surely a journey of discovery and "The Poetry of Life" may be our aide memoire.

Andy Jones

Professor Andrew Jones, PhD, is one of the UK and world's leading applied physiology and sport science researchers, and is currently in senior university management at the University of Exeter. He has published more than 300 scientific articles, which have received more than 30,000 citations, and he is one of a very rare group of scientists with an H-Index of more than 100. Apart from his scientific and leadership work, he does significant outreach work, assisting Olympic athletes, Welsh Rugby and Football, and other sports folk achieve higher performance, and works with several companies developing health products and ergogenic aids. He is regularly invited as a keynote speaker to international conferences, and to give lectures at universities and companies all around the world. He is also a talented athlete, achieving a number of middle-distance running record performance in the days of his youth in his beloved Wales. Most importantly, Andy also immerses himself daily in understanding more deeply the poetry of life at his laboratory bench.

Section 1.
Introduction

As I write this in my garden shed, which became my person cave and home office a few years ago, I can see through its dusty windows birds, bees and insects flying around the garden in the warm late afternoon, early summer North-East England air. On trees and bushes, flowers are coming into full bloom, and appear to reach hungrily up towards the blue sky and warm sun, whilst swaying in the light breeze which takes the edge off the heat of the afternoon. At my feet our family Labrador sleeps peacefully, and beyond the fence bordering one side of our garden where a walkway runs, occasionally I can hear the laughter of children and older folk talking to each other while walking past. All around me life is happening in all its forms and glory, and life as a concept has always fascinated me and been at the core of my thoughts, lifestyle, and career choices since I was young and first took note of it.

This interest in life and what life meant interested me from when I was a child. My first choices as school subjects were Biology, Chemistry, Physics and History, and if I had been able to take it as a further subject, I would have chosen Geography too. I remember most clearly being fascinated by the cycles of nature and learning how science taught us new things over historical time, such as the Earth was round and not flat, that the Earth flew round the sun, and not vice versa, and that a strange force called gravity kept us all standing up straight and with our feet on the earth. My parents kept picture books of the first moon landings, and being born in 1966, some of my first memories were of paging through these photographs and news stories of the moon landings, being astonished by the pictures of the moon surface, and the astronauts bouncing high in the air at every step in the gravity-free environment. Equally interesting were chemistry experiments, where the teacher encouraged us kids using 'recipe pages' to mix up materials or gases and view the resultant changes in colour in test tubes, or increased heat generated by the reaction between them, or the terrible smells that could be created by sulphur-related and other experiments. While I was never good at either maths or physics, for reasons which are still beyond me, I was both astonished and fascinated by equations, and that they could predict numbers or scenarios in a predictable or iterative way. All these interests surely grounded my life and interests in the physical sciences, which were to be and have been the 'playthings' which have occupied my mind since then in both my work and creative life.

Perhaps recognizing this interest in the natural and physical world as a young child, my parents from a very early age in a not too subtle way suggested that a career in medicine would be a good choice for me. This was quite a big thing to contemplate, as neither my parents had studied at a university, nor did either of my siblings. When I was 12 or 13 my parents sent me up from Durban, where we lived, to Pretoria to stay with one of my father's best friends, who was an accomplished Orthopaedic Surgeon, so I could watch him both operate and do ward rounds in the hospital where he worked. I can't deny the trip had a big impact on me. I was allowed to stand in the corner of the operating theatre and watched our family friend do hip replacement operations, femur fracture repairs, and a whole host of other operations everywhere, which were each accompanied by a lot of blood and gore, and a new and unseen view of muscle and bones as active entities rather than just suggestions below the skin of my own body and those of others around me in my childhood. I was fascinated, not just by the operations themselves, but by the high energy level in the operating theatre itself, with roars of rage being emitted whenever something went wrong, and a lot of banter and flirting with the nurses when things were going right by the surgeons and anaesthetists in the operating room. I went back to Durban a changed person, knowing what I wanted to do as a career, or so I thought, and as when a child, deeply fascinated by the life processes evident during the operations, including body organs and anatomical structures which made us function as humans.

I would like to say that all went rosily for me from then on at school until I started my medical training, but this was unfortunately not the case. For three generations, the male offspring of our family had gone to a prestigious boarding school in South Africa for our senior and final four years of schooling. I was both expected, and indeed welcomed, the opportunity to follow the tradition of enrolling in this boarding school, and worked hard enough in preparation for the entrance examinations that I was awarded a Scholarship to study there, which pleased my parents as it meant a substantial reduction in the fees that needed to be paid each year, even if they were wealth enough to have a disposal income and few financial worries. However, not long after arriving at the boarding school, I realised that despite its excellent teaching programme and facilities, boarding school was not for me, given that like most boarding schools, it was run with military precision and perhaps discipline too, and each hour of our day was planned out and we were required to perform the routine set out for us with no chance of deviating from the requirements of the said routine. I very quickly realised my personality was not suited at all to such a controlled way of life, and I survived, but did not thrive, in the rigid boarding school environment. The problem though was telling my parents I was not happy and wanted to move to a day-school, or perhaps try any different environment. I knew how much it meant to my parents not only that I was a third-generation attender, but I had won a scholarship to go there. Instead of discussing it with them, I stopped eating and basically starved myself for a few months, as a silent, and in the initial stage probably a subconscious, protest at being at a boarding school. After a while both my teachers and parents noted an alarming drop off in my weight, and I was sent to doctors and psychologists, who worked out very quickly that I did not want to be at the boarding school and suggested to my parents that I change school to see what the effect of this would be on me. As soon as I was in a day school, with much less rigid discipline at school, and with almost total freedom to do what I wanted to do out of school hours, I immediately started eating again and my weight returned and stabilised.

The fascinating thing about this episode, which must have been very challenging to my parents, family, and friends, was that during the time of starving myself, I felt perhaps paradoxically completely in control of my activity and surroundings and gained a sense of power and confidence which I had not felt to such a degree before. Being interested as described above in life, human and biological processes, this got me thinking and wanting to learn about psychological processes, and in time I enjoyed learning about the subconscious, drives, the need for freedom of expression, and the effect of civilization, so necessary for ensuring order and structure to societies, worked by curtailing those individual freedoms that appeared to be more important, or necessary for my survival and personal growth, than the other folk who attended the same good boarding school I attended, and thrived and did well there in its ordered and structured environment. Clearly, the personality, or characters of those folk needed externally set boundaries to grow and thrive, whereas folk like myself were stifled by externally set boundaries, and preferred setting and living by my own internally set boundaries and drives to be able to thrive and be most productive. It is perhaps not surprising with a history that included episodes like this in my teenage years, that I became an academic, with an interest in psychophysiology and both internal and external control systems.

When the time came to choose a career, it seemed a no-brainer to choose medicine, given my interest in and curiosity about life processes. I was also interested in law, and fancied myself one day being a judge, or working at high level financial control companies, or being a historian, but medicine was eventually the chosen career, and six fascinating years of study followed at the University of Cape Town, in Cape Town, South Africa. For someone interested in the life sciences, I could not have asked for a better course curriculum to learn about every aspect of the human body and human behaviour in both health and disease. In our first years, we learn about basic life processes in courses such as human biology, animal biology, physics, and chemistry, and in the second year we learnt basic anatomy and physiology, in minute detail. As probably occurred for hundreds of years in medical school training, six of us in a group had our own cadaver, and we spent a year dissecting it from a completed corpse to the point where it was almost unrecognisable as a human body, given the dissecting we had done on it, albeit in a respectful manner, to see and learn the names of every single organ, vessel and nerve in the body and brain. For someone interested in the life force, the cadavers were interesting, as they were 'human bodies', but no life force was visible in them, and to me they may have been made of plasticine or leather, for all they were real flesh and blood. I was never great on list learning, preferring concepts to absolutes, and hence was never great at learning anatomy, but I absolutely loved physiology, learning about how blood was pumped around the body, how the lungs worked, and more general control concepts, like the negative feedback loop, and other such concepts, which will be investigated in more detail in several of the essays that follow this introduction. In our third year we learnt about the different diseases and pathology which affected the human body, and could kill it, in disciplines including microbiology, chemical pathology, and general pathology. The final three years were clinical teaching years, where each year we learnt successively more in depth and challenging disorders in neurology, cardiology, paediatrics, obstetrics and gynaecology and the surgical disciplines, gradually being introduced to real patients, and in our last year actively managed them under the strict guidance of Interns and qualified medical practitioners in the different specialties.

Two significant things about my medical training became clear to me only many years after I had qualified as a medical doctor. Firstly, while our degree was excellent at 'setting one up' to be a specialist in medicine, or surgery, or pathology, or whatever, we had very little training in general practice work, almost zero training in community social work, and no training in financial or business management practice, all of which would prove to be crucial to most doctors who went into their own practice or chose the general practitioner route. These absences were picked up by clinical trainers of the next few decades, and by the time I became Head of a Medical School in

Bloemfontein, South Africa, 25 years after completing my own medical training, all these requirements were part of the curriculum, in the form of community based education, general practice being recognized as a specialty in its own and requiring a further five years training, and inter-professional education techniques, where medical trainees teamed up with social workers, physiotherapists, nurses, nutritionists, sports scientists, and occupational health workers, amongst others, once a week where they as a team worked on a simulated patient with a chronic disorder such as diabetes, with the aim of managing their care holistically rather than just with prescribed drugs or surgical operations. In contemporary times, the focus has moved even more to developing medical schools focussed specifically at training general practitioners – such was the aim of the University of Waikato in New Zealand, where I was a Foundation Dean of a new Health Sciences Faculty which would incorporate a medical school with this approach, although such an approach did raise concerns in some 'old-school' trained medical academics, who wondered how GP focussed training could in effect differ from the older, more conservative methods of medical training, a debate which is still ongoing, and is the subject of several of the Essays also following later in this book.

The second 'realisation' that only hit me several years after I completed my medical training was how important certain key figures had been in my knowledge growth during my six years as a medical student. These were the folk who as trainers and academic clinicians had made a significant impression on me, either good or bad, and who had by their example and enthusiasm for their subject engendered a similar passion in me for their fields of interest, or for study of life activities and function in general. Professor Johan Koeslag was foremost on this list. He lectured us in physiology in our second year, and was a real iconoclast and lateral thinker, publishing theoretical articles such as 'what is normal' (which is a key theme of one of the Essays in this book) and 'what is life'. He also gave me a real wake-up call about weak arguments and sloppy thinking, when he gave me ten percent for an essay he had asked us to write on what the Venus of Willendorf statuette told us about women's body shapes in pre-historic times. I reasoned that woman must have all been superbly fit and slim due to having to constantly gather food and move around, which was obviously foolish given the Venus of Willendorf statuette depicted a round, overweight, solid women, rather than a lithe, fit one. Others included Professor David Dent, a remarkably talented surgeon, and Prof Ralph Kirsch, a Professor of Medicine and Head of a Liver Research Unit, both of whom took great care of us students and treated us as 'equals' rather than requiring obsequiousness, which was interesting given that both were perhaps the most successful senior clinicians in the faculty from an international recognition perspective. Of course, these were only a few of many excellent teachers and academics who had a profound effect on me, and whose teaching I still remember to this day, and whose knowledge created a vast pool of information in each of us medical students' brains which would be helpful later in life in whichever vocation we each chose for our future careers.

It must be noted that my medical training was only a small part of my life and learning in those critical post-adolescent six years at university, to a degree where I perhaps let my marks and training suffer due to other interests and influences during my time at the University of Cape Town. Sport became a major interest of mine during this period. I was never hugely interested in team sports at school, but watching my uncles paddle in a famous canoe race in Natal, the Dusi Canoe Marathon, each year in January when I was a child stimulated an interest in kayaking and water sports that I still find enjoyment in four decades later. While I paddled a bit in my last year of school, with good friend Spook Rowe, whose brother Brad kindly drove us down to the harbour to train at 5.00 most mornings before school, it was only at university that my own sports career took off. In my first few years at university, I mixed up paddling, running, and cycling, and did many marathons and ultramarathons, in particular kayaking and running, but also triathlons and a few cycling races, often running a marathon race on Saturday early morning, and a canoe marathon which started late morning, rushing to drive between the end of one and the start of another. I was never good in the early morning, so ran most lunchtimes, and paddled in the later afternoon, and often used to, in the later evening, go to the gym or play squash against folk I stayed in residence with. Clearly this was way too much, and I broke down physically from over-training on several occasions, but absolutely loved the lifestyle (with my medical training fitted around this sporting activity). In my last few years, I focussed mostly on paddling, as my physique and frame were always too large to be much good as a runner, and it was gratifying each year to find my results improving, until I was regularly in the front bunch of races, and won one or two races, usually shorter distance races, and sprints, represented my province at national sprint events, and was awarded my University Full Blues for canoeing. I lived in digs with some phenomenally good paddlers and athletes, including Philip Lloyd, Tony Hansen, Margi Alford, Andrew Schulze, David Ketley, and Henri Van Der Merwe, amongst others, some of whom went on to achieve Springbok (national colours) in different types of kayaking events, and many visitors to our digs like Mark Perrow, Bruce Yelland and Jerome Truran went on to win many South African titles and major races. While most of us enjoyed the pain and challenge of racing, some of my peers like Phil Lloyd, Tony Hansen and others slowly changed their interests to more dangerous challenges, firstly in big river white water kayaking, in huge and dangerous, often flooded rivers, and then into mountain climbing. Phil Lloyd was particularly 'bitten' by the latter, and eventually after graduating spent several years climbing some of the most challenging mountains in Yosemite, the Himalayas and in Patagonia. Sadly, a few years into his mountaineering career, where he very quickly became internationally respected and famous for his achievements doing complex routes on big mountains, while descending one day on the central Tower of Paine in Patagonia, his 'support' rope embedded into the rock face came loose and he fell down the mountain slope to his death, a tragic end to a frenetically lived and well-filled life. One of the essays is about him, and the 'drives' that led him and folk like him to push the limits in such dangerous pursuits. For me, personally, this sport-focussed lifestyle was important from a self-confidence perspective, and I loved the actual training and 'doing' of the sport, but my 'all-embracing' approach to it ended a year or two after a holiday trip to the United Kingdom and Europe with my good friend and fellow medical student Simon Anderson, during which at a random book shop in Notting Hill I had picked up a book on Existentialism

– The Fall, by Albert Camus – and as it goes was completely hooked by its contents, and read it eight times during the three weeks of our trip there, and several more times subsequently. The concept of existential philosophy hit some chord in me deeply, and a year or two after reading this book, as well as a whole lot of others by Camus, Jean Paul Sartre, and other existentialist writers, I was paddling one evening in a kayaking time trial and straining hard to stay with the front bunch, and it suddenly struck me that I was spending all this time and effort doing something which in the broad perspective of life was almost completely pointless – namely trying to 'beat' other folk in kayaks on a lake by rotating my arms as hard as I could whilst holding a paddle – the results of which no-one except for those that did it would ever know, and which served no purpose except comforting a somewhat weak young man's ego. After this revelation it became very difficult for me to sustain high levels of training and racing, and something in me wanted to 'smell the roses' rather than rushing past them and see other aspects of life and understand everything better than I would or could if I spent the rest of my life blindly paddling and racing all day. It was the end of an enjoyable part of my life, but also time to move on to other things.

After completing my medical training and spending a few months focussing on paddling for some sprint trials I was set on competing in, it was time for my internship, after which I chose to do a short stint as a Surgical Medical Officer, with the thought that this would be the start of specialising in some sort of Surgical discipline. It's strange to me now, when if I chose to go back to practising medicine I think I would focus on either neurology or psychiatry disciplines, that I chose surgery, and it could only have been the influence of watching my father's Orthopaedic friend operate, and having an expectancy both for myself, and from my parents and friends, that this would be the natural course for me – and of course, most Orthopaedic Surgeons in particular are retired sports folk, even if this is a grand generalisation. Given that I was starting my Internship year late due to paddling full time for a few months after completing my medical training, not many 'choice' hospitals had places available for me to do my final required bit of training, and I was indeed fortunate that a good friend and colleague of mine, Dr Larissa Cronje, managed to organize me a place at a small rural hospital in the central Natal town of Pietermaritzburg, Edendale Hospital, which was situated in the middle of a township where violence – both political and social – were endemic, and one was guaranteed to have to do a lot of surgical work 'at the coalface' where the learning curve was steep but surgical experience easy to come by. I had a number of 'firsts' during my time working there and later at Grays Hospital, also situated in Pietermaritzburg, and a steep learning curve, not just in surgery but in a number of different life skills and my own shortcomings (perhaps shortcomings is harsh, and I should rather say work and life preference and way of doing things) too. I did indeed learn a lot about the practical nature of healing folk, which is the clinicians life calling and role, and I did do and learn a lot about surgery, performing a whole lot of appendicectomies; laparotomies (opening up the abdomen), most often to fix bowel, stomach or other abdominal wounds after gunshot or knife wounds, given that violence was endemic in the township which the hospital served; limb removals mostly for diabetic-related chronic wound sepsis and associated gangrenous limbs; and other similar relatively easy surgical procedures, which are the stock in trade operations for a peripheral rural hospital. I also acted as assistant to some very good surgeons who worked at the hospitals, including Offie Pherson, Bernie Little, Mahomed Gafoor and several others, and enjoyed learning about more complex surgery, such as thyroid procedures, bowel, and breast cancer resections, and even some laparoscopic gall bladder and liver work, which was fascinating to watch and be involved with, even as assistant rather than first surgeon. I also did spells as part of my internship requirements in Medicine and Paediatrics, and found while Medicine (treating medical disorders like diabetes, TB, HIV, and cardiac failure) was interesting, I could not relate to Paediatrics at all from an interest perspective, and even less to Obstetrics and Gynaecology, which was noteworthy in itself, given that several of my colleagues really enjoyed these disciplines and have gone on to be world experts in these fields. To my surprise I found I was also very interested in intensive care work, which involved keeping alive very sick folk who needed constant respiratory, kidney, and heart support either after operations or due to the illnesses which had damaged these organs in the patients we looked after. We were allotted night calls to either ICU, the trauma unit or ward cover, and I found I was happy to swop out my trauma and ward cover calls to work in ICU, even if they were usually the most work intense, and there was not much chance of getting any sleep on ICU call, as one usually had to take bloods on patients every hour, and monitor and change their drug dosages or respirator setting every few minutes in some patients. I enjoyed the complex technology involved with the ICU work, and also having to work out complex treatment algorithms for each patient, which as I say surprised me, but was perhaps a portent of my later strong interest in research and the complex technology used in brain science work, which I was involved with for the large part of my academic career.

Medical work made me find out things about my personality that were not all positive, or indeed reconcilable with medicine or the daily life of a medical doctor. I found myself frustrated with the rigid time prescriptions and hospital rigid rules in place to make the hospital work efficiently and to optimize treatments of patients. Similar to my time at boarding school, I did not enjoy having each day rigidly controlled – for example one had to be in the hospital at a specific time, and if you were on call you had to stay in the hospital environment often for 36-hour cycles, and the environment where I most thrive in is where I don't have too many rules or time constraints or requirements, and where I have ample 'space' to be creative and 'ponder' how to do things best. This does not mean I don't like hard work, and in fact I probably have in my life worked harder and longer hours than most folk, but they happen on my own terms, and long hours are usually more than fine when the creative 'juices' are flowing, or a problem in the work environment needs sorting out. I also didn't like the hierarchy of hospitals, and the fact that senior folk were always 'right' and could not be challenged without threat to one's career in the hospital environment. Whether as a student or Professor or Executive Dean, I have always encouraged everyone to call me Zig, yet most folk in hospitals like to be called by their title, and do not appreciate being challenged on their knowledge by junior staff. Many personality assessments from a number of leadership courses I have attended have routinely shown me to be generally an extrovert as my dominant personality type, but with a large 'quantity' of the introvert in me too, and a need to recharge my batteries and be on my own for long periods after intense episodes or time with other folk, and again, if one works in a hospital environment, with rigid time rules, there is no place or hardly ever the correct time to get those important periods of solitude introverts and hypersensitive folk need (there are essays on all these topics in the book itself). So after less than two years of clinical medicine, I decided to take a year off hospital work and do some research, and 27 years later I am still doing research, or at least managing / leading the research endeavour, and with the less rigid lifestyle which is academia, absolutely loved this 'second career' of mine, thought I often miss doing clinical work, and the instantaneous gratification one gets in the trauma surgery environment where one's quick and successful intervention is often the only difference between a patient dying or living. Ironically, when my whole life had been planned as a clinical medicine one, as described above, it was an 'on the spot' decision after a challenging few months in the hospital to do some research, that changed my career, or allowed me to have a 'second career', which has been hugely enjoyable and transformational for me, and allowed me to develop many of the thoughts and concepts that make up a number of the essays described in this book.

For the next 14 years I had the most fantastic time possible doing basic and applied research and thinking about research and related philosophical problems 'morning, noon and night'. There were two outstanding researchers in the clinical world at the University of Cape Town that I knew and pondered working with in my planned 'year' sabbatical from clinical medicine – the first was Professor Ralph Kirsch, who led the highest ranked South African Medical Research Council Group examining liver disorders and pathology, and the second, Professor Tim Noakes, who led the Bioenergetics of Sport Research Unit (sport and exercise science focussed) and with whom I had interacted during my sports career whenever I was injured, and who also had a highly rated Medical Research Council group. I eventually chose the latter, as I did not have much interest in liver work, and sport then was and is still a big thing in my life. This was a huge career risk, as in Tim's own words, Sport and Exercise Science

/ Sports Medicine was still regarded as a 'Cinderella' discipline in Medicine, and always had to, and in many ways still does, struggle to 'own' its place at the medical table of specialties, and is also perceived as a threat to Physiotherapy and other Allied Health disciplines, so joining a research team in such a discipline was not often looked on enthusiastically by some folk who followed more traditional research career routes, such as cancer or cardiac research. Despite all this, it turned out to be a good decision for me, as it is a discipline that has components of all the other more specific disciplines in it, and being in the discipline, for all its 'Cinderella status', allowed me to develop my knowledge and ideas to a far greater degree than would have been the case in a liver, or other medical specific research unit.

Not having a topic to start that I was at that stage interested in, Tim Noakes suggested I look at tourniquet ischemia effect on the lower limb muscles during knee operations, given that it was a concern back then (and still is now) and knowing that I came from a past background of doing surgical work. I registered for a master's degree in science and spent a year reading hundreds of research papers on the subject, and I quickly came to realise that the real problem was not the tourniquet, but neural pathway changes coming down from the brain, which after knee surgery inhibited the muscles around the knee as a paradoxically protective mechanism. As a result of these observations, I changed my degree registration to a PhD, and over the next five years grew more and more interested in the brain and its function, while completing my PhD. After finishing my PhD, in a somewhat masochistic manner I immediately registered for an MD degree, examining chronic fatigue in athletes who had pushed themselves too hard and too long, and became exercise intolerant. This fascinating topic introduced me also to psychology, and the concept of biological and psychological drives, and the work of Jung, Freud, Adler, Rank and others from the glory days of psychology at the turn of the nineteenth century, and again changed my way of thinking and research interests. My MD was completed five years later, when I was 35, which meant I had been studying and learning for what would be half of a lifetime, if I were to reach the age of three score years and ten, but it was this long, long, period of learning and performing research which led to a number of the ideas, which turned into essays, and which are presented in this book.

On a personal level, apart from scientific knowledge, this long period as a scientist taught me further insights into my own personality and way of working / approaching problems. My very able colleague and good friend at the University of Cape Town, Professor Vicki Lambert, describes three 'types' of scientists, namely 'moles', 'mutts' and 'mappers'. Moles are scientists who remain focussed on one problem or area of science all their life – enzymes in a cell, or a gene and how it functions, or on neurons in a brain – and these folks have made many great breakthroughs and probably received the lion's share of Nobel prizes for making breakthroughs in our understanding of components of systems in the body and how they work. Mutts are scientists who like to do studies in several different areas of science, moving across boundaries and silo-thinking. Mutts will, of course, never be as expert in a specific field as moles are, but they do see more of the bigger picture or at least understand that you will not find answers to the complex problems which humans have to engage with as part of life by looking at one system or process, but need to look at different systems and be more integrative in one's thinking to solve 'real life' problems. While physiology is the discipline which mutts were generally attracted to, given it allowed the examination of whole-body systems like the blood circulation and heart and lungs, or Musculo-skeletal system of the entire body, as examples, physiology as a discipline has unfortunately languished and now most mutts do work in areas such as systems biology, or integrative neuroscience (which studies brain and body interactions) and suchlike areas of science. The third category Vicki described are 'mappers' – folk who try and put it all together and see the entire landscape of a problem or behaviour or function, Mappers look at human behaviour in its entirety, or regulatory rules that govern systems entirely, or at entire human and social 'maps' of human daily behaviour, and do work that borders on the philosophical side of science. I have never remotely been a mole, somewhat sadly as this is the easiest way of doing science to get grant funding for projects, and Nobel prizes for specific medical or physiological breakthroughs, and at the start of my career was probably a mutt, but I have become very much a mapper as time progressed and my science-based knowledge increased over the years. This is evident in my self-chosen Twitter handle – Jack of all Trades, Master of Some – and in the publications through my career, which tended to have a spate of data papers, then a theoretical review paper that brought all the data together as new conceptual ideas, which are probably my most cited academic work, and of course hopefully in these Essays which make up this book, which covers my thinking and development section wise from 'mutt' type work explaining, or attempting to explain, complex activity and behaviour across multiple human systems and activities, to control system theories, to the final section, which are my favourite pieces, and describe general control theories, and attempt to explain how intangible 'rules' govern life processes, which is where my life as a career scientist ended, and about which I think of in my third and probably final career as an academic leader and manager.

This period also taught me the value of mentors. There are a lot of definitions of mentor, but to me mentors are older role models, who becomes a trusted adviser, and who helps one 'know the ropes' of one's current role, and often advises one not just about work but also pastorally, and on one's future work and life plans. As a great mentor at the University of the Free State, then Vice-Rector, Nicky Morgan reminded me, one has to be careful about not putting one's mentors on too high pedestals, as all of them, or at least most of them, have in his words 'feet of clay', meaning that they have their own faults and shortcomings, which one tends to be blind about when one is younger and looking up to them as a role model of how one would like to be as one got older and one's career matched where they were when they were perceived as a mentor. One also has inspirational figures in one's career, often folk who one does not know personally, but who one 'wishes to be like' in one's life due to what they have achieved, or how they approach life. There as so many I could and perhaps need to name who in my life have been mentors and role models, and I have tried my best to do these folks justice in the acknowledgments section at the end of the book.

As I approached my forties, a lot of life changes happened to me, as they do to most folk. I got married and had children, and due to concerns about high crime and violence in South Africa, decided with my wife that it was time to move away permanently from that country and make a new one as my young family's home and base. To date I have lived for prolonged periods in four countries on four continents – South Africa, the USA, New Zealand, and the UK. One of the perks of being an academic is that universities are fairly similar institutions worldwide, so it is easy to move to similar roles in different countries, and academics and doctors are always high on the list of 'wanted' immigrants in most countries. I also found that I was 'burnt out' academically after nearly 15 years working seven-day weeks as a researcher and thinking about research (which led to the contents of most of the Essays in this book), and felt I needed a new challenge and focus. I thought briefly about going back into clinical medicine, but was encouraged by several colleagues to think of a career in university management / leadership, and to be honest, I had been increasingly interested in doing this, after being 'burnt out' academically, having the desire to move away from the country I had lived in for most of my life and the laboratory environment at the University of Cape Town which I had worked on for nigh on 15 years. Hence, my approaching forties proved to be an apt time to make a change into academic leadership roles and move the focus of my day away from the research bench and my own specific career goals to more of a big-team leadership role. While in my early life I was self-focused and enjoyed my own time, and did not feature much in school leadership roles, in my twenties and as I have aged, a natural tendency to lead teams and discussions became evident in me, and this was, and is, helped by being both a 'large' personality and large in body and frame (keeping my weight in check is my greatest challenge that I mostly lose on a daily basis!). As I described earlier, as part of several leadership courses I was lucky enough to be put on by my line managers in the early stage of my management career, I was found to have an 'ENTJ' personality using the Myers-Briggs assessment test (High Scores for Extraversion, Intuition, Thinking and Judgement – also known as the Commander personality), which is apparently the profile most frequently found in big team leaders in all aspects of life, from business, to health, to politics. While a large number of Psychologists have questioned the validity of this scale, every leadership course I have been on, where leadership capacity has been assessed, I come out as a natural leader, and I guess the proof is in the pudding, as in the last 15 years I have had numerous leadership roles, and while making several mistakes particularly earlier in my leadership career, most folk would say I have done pretty well in these leadership roles, and have left them with the environment I managed being in a better place after my time working there than it was before I started, which is perhaps the only real indicator one can have of leadership success or failure. I have chosen to work slowly up the academic ladder, after seeing so many folks, particularly in South Africa, who were fast-tracked up the leadership ladder to top positions which they did not have adequate experience in to fulfil, fail miserably in their leadership roles, and indeed, make life a misery for all those around them and those they managed and led. Thus, over the years I have been fortunate to have been offered and undertaking a diverse array of leadership roles including as a Director of Research in an academic Department, then Head of Department, then Head of a Medical School, then a Foundation Dean of a new Faculty, and in the last two roles, a Deputy Dean of Research operating at the Faculty Management level. I hope to have two more jobs before I retire, firstly a Deputy Vice Chancellor role and then a Vice-Chancellor role running an entire university, and if the gods smile on me hopefully this will happen, and my experience at the different steps along the way will help me in the following larger leadership job levels. Interestingly though, my hardest leadership roles were those at the more operational (lower) level of an institution, where one has to manage things like daily work routines, timetables, and staff human resource issues, and each time I have gone up a level leadership wise, and the jobs become more strategic and less operational, I have paradoxically found them easier, rather than harder to fulfil, perhaps due to the fact that I am a mutt-turned-mapper, and control system theory became my major work and life interest in the second half of my academic career. Either way, I have learnt that leadership has several specific requirements, and paradoxically the higher one goes, the more generic rather than specific they become, and I feel I would if asked not do a bad job managing a company of any size, or running a country as a politician, or whatever big leadership role is needed, and this is not arrogance saying this, its seeing and understanding things and how they work after 15 years being a leader and manager, and reading a lot about it over the last few years. These experiences of management and leadership are described in several of the Essays in the later sections of this book.

In summary, therefore, this overview of my life history is written so the reader has some understanding of the development of ideas and concepts that these Essays are the final product of. I have not dwelt much on my own personality and its many flaws, but for those interested I am what is known as a 'hypersensitive' person, who picks up everything around one to a greater degree than most folk, and this is good for helping me 'seeing' and understanding 'life and how it happens' more quickly perhaps than most, but it has a great downside in that folk who have hypersensitivity (see Essay on this) have high stress and anxiety levels, that in my life have led to the development of things like perennial high blood pressure and other such health issues that need constant work on. For what it's worth knowing, I have always been a very emotional person, rather than a detached, introspective type, yet paradoxically spend most of my days thinking about things and trying to work out and understand all around me and all that happens, even while I am immersed in living and 'feeling' life as it happens to me. For good or bad, I have always had great love of 'wine, women and song', have always had a fiery temper, and have for most of my life lived hard, worked hard, loved hard, and done all I have done to the utmost it can be done. As I have aged, thankfully, all these parts of my personae have 'calmed' somewhat, and perhaps because of this, and because a lot of the thoughts I have had have taken a long time to digest and work through, all these Essays were written in the time period from my later forties to mid-fifties, with the content of some, as will be obvious, coming to my attention in my twenties or earlier, but which needed a long time to process and make sense of. I hope you as the reader find them interesting and enjoy them, and I am sure you will find synchrony with some if not all of them, or at least will be stimulated to think about some of the concepts described in them. I would like perhaps to have written a few more, but equally,

I found myself at peace with getting most of my 'thoughts' on life out on paper by the time I had written the sixtieth one, as if a life project of thinking had been completed. They are all written for a general rather than scientific audience, and as such are full of anecdotes and personal stories to try and explain difficult scientific concepts to the everyday person who hopefully will enjoy these. I have also not cross-referenced any of the points raised in the text, but rather have put a few 'further' reading books or sources in for those interested at the end of the book. Happy reading, and I hope my life's work and thinking which went into creating this book is of some interest to you and will in some way 'touch you' and perhaps help you understand 'life' and the beautiful poetry of its rhythms, cycles and changes a little more after reading the Essays in it.

Section 2.
Understanding basic human physical and mental function

Section 2.1. Introduction

In this first section, in a series of 16 Essays examining a specific topic, we will explore the basics of bodily control and mind function, to be able to understand the physical and mental control processes which govern our daily functions and activity. From genes to muscle and bones, from brain processes to external social drives and requirements, we examine the many different exquisite control processes which either are a part of the structures of the body and mind itself, or act on the body and mind as external agents requiring reaction to, and by doing so produces planned activity and function. As each essay develops, we see that at every level, from the single cell to a specific organ or body control system such as the vascular or nervous system, to the entire body and mind, exquisite control processes are at work controlling every single component of our bodily function, from the single cell enzyme activity level to us picking up a glass to drink, to running a marathon. There also appears to be a sequential planning to every activity in the body, to each phase of our life, from childhood to young adult, to mature member of society, to ageing veteran of life, and finally to our death, the knowledge of which as an eventual outcome to our lives paradoxically programs and regulates a lot of our life activities and functions across the life span. Hopefully, through the medium of each essay, you as the reader will see how brilliant, and beautiful the human body and mind are, and how exquisite the control processes that govern our life are too. Whoever or whatever made us, and all the creatures and life forms around us, surely did a brilliant job, with an attention to detail that is astonishing to understand and see as a scientist, clinician and a person interested in life and its mysteries. The function of these 'building blocks' of the human body and life are, indeed, poetry in motion, to those of us who research them, and hopefully to you all to see and understand as they are described in the Essays in this section.

Essay 1. Memes and genes - Transition of cultural and social identities beyond the physical realm

---

One of the key questions in science is where the 'code' for life is held, and for a long period of time it was thought that the genes contained the 'code' for all life, both physical and mental. But this theory has been questioned, and it has been suggested that mental, and even more so social, characteristics of any person are not controlled by genes, but are passed down by family and social interactions, and this 'passing down' of non-physical behaviour and function is described as meme transition. In this first Essay we examine the concept of memes as opposed to genes.

On holiday the last few weeks in the town of my birth with my young children got me reflecting on memes and their role in maintaining personal and cultural attributes across generations and time. We have lived through more than half a century where in science the 'gene era' has dominated, perhaps because of the remarkable breakthroughs that have occurred in genetics and molecular biology, since the discovery of the nature of DNA and how it replicates, in the last half of the previous century. In the gene model of life, everything we are and do is encoded in our genes, and these genes are physically transmitted to our children, who become a copy of ourselves (blended of course with our partners genes) and who propagate our DNA further through their own children and then on to future generations of offspring.

This gene model mostly makes sense for our physical makeup, but the problem with it, of course, lies in the behavioural and social realm, which are intangible and cannot be directly related to specific genetic activity, and which also appear to be both propagated and 'passed down' through generations in a manner similar to genes transmission. In the last few decades such 'heritable' social behaviours have been described as memes (also described in the past as 'culturgens'), which are defined as an idea, behaviour or style that spreads from person to person within a culture, and which act as a unit of culture, idea, or practice that can be transmitted from one mind to another through writing, speech, gestures, rituals or other imitable or mimicked behaviour. So, in the analogy of my children, looked at from a meme perspective, it would be that they pick up behaviour I am exhibiting, or have exhibited in the past and exhibit it themselves in their own future lives. In the analogy of my old hometown, social routines or behavioural actions and potentially prejudices that occur in the time of one generation who lived there will continue to occur in the following generations – for example having Christmas lunch with ones extended family, singing Christmas songs each year on Christmas Day, and even taking a holiday break at this time of year as a regular occurrence – all of these behaviours we do as 'routine' were done by our parents before us, and will likely be done by our children after we are gone, given they are experiencing these activities as seminal occasions of their early youth and are therefore memes. Therefore, memes such as these are in effect 'propagated' across generations in a similar manner to how DNA is propagated, but exist as a social entity, or as behaviours, which are external to our own existence and have a 'life' of their own. In extreme versions of meme theory, humans don't exist to propagate their own DNA, but rather to ensure the propagation and maintenance of the memes of which they engage with, although of course social and behavioural memes cannot exist without human life and interactive activity. There are also, of course, different 'sizes' or levels of complexity of memes – for example Christmas lunch would be a relatively simple meme, while religion in its entirety would be an example of a complex meme.

Like physical genetic based evolution, where advantageous traits are maintained and develop while negative traits eventually disappear, memes that survive for long periods of time and over multiple generations surely are advantageous to the communities where they exist. However, some memes, such as innate cultural prejudices which exist in communities or cultures over many generations, such as racism or jingoism, can of course be self-defeating and damaging, and one can even argue a case that patriotism for a particular cause or country, which is another example of a complex meme, can lead to conflict with other countries or cause, and perceptions of superiority in those that are patriotic. Therefore, memes like patriotism, let alone jingoism and other prejudicial memes, need to be examined carefully by those who have the power to encourage or enhance their propagation.

Memes are, of course, of particular interest and relevance to those who move to different places or live in populations with diverse cultures, where one's own meme experiences may be very different to those around one in a new or culturally diverse environment, or those whose job it is to try and change a particular culture or way of life which is perceived to be 'out of step' with either the ethos of more general / universal social environments, for example society memes which are prejudicial to some of its own society or those of others around them, given that memes by the definition above are self-propagating and potentially conservative / resistant to change.

So, going back to the holiday thoughts – when seeing my son or daughter behaving in a way that I recognized was a 'mirror' of my own behaviour, made me realize how important it is to be aware of memes, and how one's actions and behaviours can be transmitted across generations. Equally, being in the hometown of my birth made me realize how the more complex social memes are 'alive and well' in that place of my youth, and continue of their own will, for good or for bad. Despite many years living in different places and continents, the memes which I noted were still strong and ongoing there had a magnetism of their own, given the memories they evoked of times past from the halcyon days of my own youth, and I realized again therefore how important it is to sift through each meme carefully, in order to determine which memes are positive and which are potentially negative, both for one's own life and wellbeing, and perhaps more importantly, for those around us and in society in general. There is perhaps a need to try and curb the negative both in one's own behaviour, and in one's social environment in which the memes exist and propagate, in order to attenuate the propagation of the potentially negative memes, either behaviourally or socially. Of course, whether one as an individual has any real control over them, is another story.

Essay 2. Testosterone and its androgenic anabolic derivatives - One small drop of liquid hormone that can a man make and can a man break

Almost as important as the genes and memes in controlling human behaviour and function are the hormones, in particular the sex hormones. The male hormone testosterone is secreted in a pulsatile manner in different quantities throughout life, and its presence stimulates the growth of physical male attributes. It also appears to increase aggressive behaviour. In the last 50 or so years, testosterone has been used by bodybuilders and athletes to increase muscle strength, speed and athletic performance. In this Essay, we look at testosterone and how it affects and controls the human body.

I watched a great FA Cup football final last night and was amused as always when players confronted each other after tackles with aggressive postures and pouting anger-filled stares – all occurring in front of a huge crowd looking on and under the eyes of the referee to protect them. On Twitter yesterday and this morning I was engaged in a fun scientific debate with some male colleagues and noted that each time the arguments became 'ad hominem' the protagonists became aggressive and challenging in their responses, and only calmed down and became civil again when they realized it is banter. I have over many years watched my wonderful son grow up daily, and now he is ten have observed some changes occurring in him that are related to increasing development of 'maleness' which occurs in all young men of his age. In my twenties while completing my medical and PhD training, I worked part time as a bouncer, and it was always fascinating to see the behaviour of males in the bars and clubs I worked in then change when around females 'dressed to kill' and out for the evening. With the addition of alcohol this became a dangerous 'cocktail' late in the evenings, often with violence breaking out as the young men tried to establish their dominance and 'turf', or as a result of perceived negative slights which 'honour' demanded they respond to, and which resulted in a lot of work for me in the bouncer role to sort out. All this got me thinking of the male hormone testosterone and its effect on males through their lifetime, both good and bad.

Testosterone is the principal male sex hormone that 'creates' the male body and mind from the genetic chromosomal template supplied at conception. It is mostly secreted by the testicles in men, and to a lesser degree from the ovaries in women, with some secretion also from the adrenal glands. There is approximately seven-eight times higher concentration of testosterone in males than females, but it is present also in females, and females are susceptible to (and may even be more sensitive to) its actions. Testosterone is a steroid-type hormone, derived originally from cholesterol-related chemical substances which are turned into testosterone through a complex pathway of intermediate substances. Its output from the testes (or ovaries) is stimulated by a complex cascade of neuro-hormonal signals that arise from brain structures (gonadotrophin release hormone is released by the hypothalamus structure in the brain and travels to the pituitary gland, which in turn releases luteinizing hormone and follicle stimulating hormone, which travels in the blood to the testicles and in turn cause the release of testosterone into the bloodstream) in response to a variety of external and internal stimuli (though what controls testosterone's release, and how it is controlled, in this cyclical manner over many years is almost completely unknown). The nature of 'maleness' has been debated as a concept since antiquity, but it was in the 1800's that real breakthroughs in the understanding that there was a biological basis to 'maleness' occurred, with hormones being identified as chemical substances in the blood, and several scientist folk such as Charles Brown-Sequard doing astonishing things like crushing up testicles and injecting the resultant product into their own bodies to demonstrate the 'rejuvenating' effect of the 'male elixir'. Eventually, in the late 1800s, testosterone was isolated as the male hormone – it was named as a conglomerate derivative of the words testicle, sterol and ketone – and in the 1930s, the 'golden age' of steroid chemistry, its structure was identified, and synthetic versions of testosterone were produced as medical treatment analogues for folk suffering from low testosterone production due to hypogonadism (reduced production of testosterone due to testicular function abnormality) or hypogonadotropism (reduced production of testosterone due to dysfunction of the 'higher' level testosterone release control pathways in the brain described above).

Testosterone acts in both an anabolic (muscle and other body tissue building) and androgenic (male sex characteristic development) manner, and one of the most fascinating things about it is that it acts in a 'pulsatile' manner during life – increasing dramatically at very specific times in a person's life to effect changes that are essential for both the development and maintenance of 'maleness'. For example, in the first few weeks after conception in males there is a spike in testosterone concentration in the foetus that results in the development of genitals and prostate gland. Again, in the first few weeks after birth, testosterone concentrations rise dramatically, before attenuating in childhood, after which a further increase in the pre-puberty and the pubertal phases occurs, when it is responsible for increases in muscle and bone mass, the appearance of pubic and axillary hair, adult-type body odour and oily skin, increased facial hair, deepening of the voice, and all of the other features associated with (but not all exclusive to) 'maleness'. If one of these phases is 'missed', normal male development does not occur. As males age, the effects of continuously raised testosterone associated with adulthood become evident as loss of scalp hair (male pattern baldness) and increased body hair, amongst other changes. From around the age of 55, testosterone levels decrease significantly and remain low in old age. Raised testosterone levels have been related to a number of clinical conditions that in the past have been higher in males than females, such as heart attacks, strokes and lipid profile abnormalities, along with increased risk of prostate (of course it's not surprising that this is a male specific disorder) and other cancers, although not all studies support these findings, and the differences in the gender-specific risk of cardiovascular disorders in particular is decreasing as society has 'equalized' and women's work and social lives have become more similar to those of males in comparison to the more patriarchal societies of the past.

More interesting than the perhaps 'obvious' physical effects are the psychological effects of testosterone on 'male type' behaviour, though of course the 'borders' between what is male or female type behaviour are difficult to clearly delineate. Across most species, testosterone levels have been shown to be strongly correlated with sexual arousal, and in animal studies when an 'in heat' female is introduced to a group of males, their testosterone levels and sex 'drive' increases dramatically. Testosterone has also been correlated with 'dominance' behaviour. One of the most interesting studies I have ever read about was one where the effect of testosterone on monkey troop behaviour was examined, in which there are strict social hierarchies, with a dominant male who leads the troop, submissive males who do not challenge the male, and females which are 'serviced' only by the dominant male and do not challenge his authority. When synthetic testosterone was injected into the males, it was found that the dominant male become increasingly 'dominant' and aggressive and showed 'challenge' behaviour (standing tall with taught muscles in a 'fight' posture, angry facial expressions, and angry calls, amongst others) more often than usual, but in contrast, there was no effect or change of the testosterone injections on non-dominant male monkeys. When the females were injected with testosterone, most of them became aggressive, and challenged the dominant male and fought with him. In some cases, the females beat the dominant male in fighting challenges, and became the leader of the troop. Most interestingly, these 'became dominant' females, when the testosterone injections were discontinued, did not revert to their prior submissive status, but remained the troop leader and maintained their dominant behaviour even with 'usual' female levels of testosterone. This fascinating study showed that there is not only a biological effect of testosterone in social dominance and hierarchy structures, but that there is also 'learned' behaviour, and when one's role in society is established, it is not challenged whatever the testosterone level.

Raised testosterone levels have also been linked with level of aggression, alcoholism, and criminality (being higher in all these conditions) though this is controversial, and not all studies support these links, and it is not clear from the 'chicken and egg' perspective if increased aggression and antisocial behaviour is a cause of increased testosterone levels or is a result of it. It has also been found that athletes have higher levels of testosterone (both males and females) during sport participation, as have folk watching sporting events. In contrast, both being 'in love' and fatherhood appears to decrease levels of testosterone in males, and this may be a 'protective' mechanism to attenuate the chance of a male 'turning against' or being aggressive towards their own partners or children. Whether this is true or not requires further work, but clearly there is a large psychological and sociological component to both the functionality and requirements of testosterone, beyond its biological effects. One of the most interesting research projects I have been involved with was at the University of Cape Town in the 1990's, where along with Professor Mike Lambert and Mike Hislop, we studied the effect of testosterone ingestion (and reduction of testosterone / medical castration) on male and female study participants. We found not only changes in muscle size and mass in those taking testosterone supplements, but also that participants ingesting, or injecting, testosterone had to control their aggression levels and be 'careful' of their behaviour in social situations, while women participants described that their sex drive increased dramatically when ingesting synthetic testosterone. In contrast, men who were medically castrated described that their libido was decreased during the period of time of the study when their testosterone levels were reduced by testosterone antagonist drugs to very low levels (interestingly they only realized this 'absence' of libido after being asked about it). All these study results confirm that testosterone concentration changes induce both psychological and social outcomes and not just physical effects.

Given its anabolic effects, testosterone and its synthetic chemical derivatives, known commonly as anabolic steroids, became attractive as a performance enhancing drug by athletes in the late 1950's and 1960's as a result of it being mass produced synthetically from the 1930's, and as athletes became aware of its muscle and therefore strength building capacity after its use in clinical populations. Until the 1980's, when testing for it as a banned substance meant it became risky to use it, anabolic steroids were used by many athletes, particularly in the strength and speed-based sporting disciplines. Most folk over 40 years old will remember Ben Johnson, the 1988 Olympic 100m sprint champion, being stripped of his winner's medal for testing positive for an anabolic steroid hormone during a routine within-competition drug test. Testosterone is still routinely used by bodybuilders, and worryingly, a growing number of school level athletes are being suggested to be using anabolic steroids, as well as a growth of its use as a 'designer drug' in gyms to increase muscle mass in those that have body image concerns. An interesting study / article pointed out that boy's toys have grown much more 'muscular' since the 1950's, and that this is perhaps a sign that society places more 'value' on increased muscle development and size in contemporary males, and this in a circular manner probably puts more pressure on adolescent males to increase their muscle size and strength due to perceived societal demands, and thereby increases the pressure on them to take anabolic steroids. There is also suggested to be an increase in the psychological disorder known as 'muscle dysmorphia' or 'reverse anorexia' in males, where (mostly) young men believe that no matter how big they are muscle size wise, they are thin and 'weedy', and they 'see' their body shape incorrectly when looking in the mirror. This muscle dysmorphia population is obviously highly prone to the use (perhaps one should say abuse) of anabolic steroids as a group. There appears to be also an increase in anabolic steroid use in the older male population group, perhaps due to a combination of concerns about diminishing 'male' function with increasing age, a desire to maintain sporting prowess and dominance, and a perception that a muscular 'body beautiful' is still desirable by society even in old age – which is a concern due to the increased cardiovascular and prostate cancer risks taking anabolic steroids can create in an already at-risk population group. There is also a growth in the number of women taking anabolic steroid / synthetic testosterone, both due to its anabolic effects and its (generally) positive effects on sex drive, and a number of women body builders use anabolic steroids for competitive reasons due to its anabolic effect on muscles, despite the risk of the development of clitoral enlargement, deepening voice, and male type hair growth, amongst other side effects, which potentially can result from females using anabolic steroids. Anabolic steroid use therefore remains an ongoing societal issue that needs addressing and further research, to understand both its incidence and prevalence, and to determine why specific population groups choose to use them.

It has always been amazing to me that a tiny biological molecule / hormone, which testosterone is, can have such major effects not only on developing male physical characteristics, but also on behavioural and social activity and interactions with other folk, and in potentially setting hierarchal structures in society, though surely this 'overt' effect has been attenuated in modern society where there are checks and balances on male aggression and dominance, and females now have equal chances to men in both the workplace and leadership role selection. Testosterone clearly has a hugely important role in creating a successfully functioning male both personally and from a societal perspective, but testosterone can also be every male's 'worst enemy' without social and personal 'higher level' restraints on its potential unfettered actions and ways of working. It has a magic in its function when its effects are seen on my young son as he approaches puberty and suddenly his body and way of thinking changes, or when its effects are seen (from its diminishment) in the changes of a man in love or in a new father. Perhaps there is magic also in the reduction of testosterone that occurs in old age, as this is likely to be important in allowing the 'regeneration' of social structures, by allowing new younger leaders to take over from previously dominant males, by this attenuation of testosterone levels perhaps making older males 'realize' / more easily accept that their physical and other capacities are diminished enough to 'walk away' gracefully from their life roles without the surges of competitive and aggressive 'feelings' and desires a continuously high level of testosterone may engender in them if it continued to be high into old age. But testosterone has an ugliness in its actions too, which was evident in my time working as a bouncer in bars and clubs, when young men became violent with other young men as a way of demonstrating their 'maleness' to the young females who happened to be in the same club and were the (usually) unwitting co-actors in this male mating ritual drama which enacted itself routinely on most Friday and Saturday nights, usually fuelled by too much alcohol. Its ugliness is also evident on the sporting field when males kick other men lying helpless on the ground in a surge of anger due to losing the game or for a previous slight, despite doing so within the view of a referee, spectators, and TV cameras. Its ugliness is also evident in the violence that one sees in fans after a soccer game preying on rival fans due to their testosterone levels being high through watching the game, and in myriad other social situations where males try to become dominant to lever the best possible situation or to attract the best possible mate for themselves, at the expense of all those around them – whether in a social or work situation, or a Twitter discussion, or even a political or an academic debate – the 'male posturing' is evident for all to see in each situation, whether it is physical or psychological. Perhaps it was not for the sake of a horseshoe that the battle was lost, but rather because of too little, or too much, testosterone coursing around the veins of those directing it. There are few examples as compelling as that of the function of the hormone testosterone in making male behaviour what it is which demonstrates how complex, exquisite and essential the relationship between biological factors and psychological behaviour and social interplay is. What truly 'makes up' a man and what represents 'maleness' though, is of course another story, and for another debate.

Essay 3. Energy flow in the body - Do components of Vitalism theory still offer something for our understanding of life

While in the last few centuries it has drifted out of mainstream science as a concept, in the past what was thought as crucial for the human (and animal) existence was the 'elan vital', or bioenergy which 'activated' and maintained the cells of the body, and which made a moving, interacting human so different from inanimate objects like stones, rocks and trees. It was also thought that this energy flow in the body was related to the soul and spirit, as when someone died it was clearly evident that the energy force left the body and it subsequently decomposed, and it was thought that the spirit left with it. In this Essay we will examine the old theory of Vitalism, or 'elan vital', and assess whether it still needs to hold a place in the pantheon of 'activities' which are required to make us 'human', including genes, hormones, brain activity and all those described previously and below in these essays.

I was watching a wonderful Open Day introductory session for potential students at our university and was struck by the almost tangible energy emanating from a huge gathering of the young final year school attendees, particularly when a band played some current chart-topping music for them as part of the festivities. This 'feeling' of 'energy' in the mass of young folk got me thinking again of the old concept of Vitalism, and the more recent concept of Bioenergetics, both of which I have thought about often and have studied on and off during my career to date, though I feel never to a satisfactory degree or level of attention. Vitalism is the theory that living organisms are different to non-living organisms because they have energy / a vital spark / 'élan vital'. Perhaps unfortunately for the theory of Vitalism, this idea of 'élan vital' was related by some to be representative of or associated with the soul, whatever the soul of a human is or where or how it resides in the material body. In the Western scientific world, the concept developed in part as a reaction to more mechanical theories of the body such as that of the philosopher Descartes, who proposed that the body was simply a machine which performed mechanical functions when interacting with the environment in a mechanically generated way. Proponents of Vitalism theory believed that such mechanistic interpretations were not able to account for the characteristic of life which we 'feel' and 'know', and which manifestly 'disappear' when anyone dies and the 'life force' is no longer part of the body, which becomes a non-living entity we call a corpse when we shuffle off this mortal coil. In the last century, with the dawn of the reductionist era of science, and the primacy of genetic and biochemistry based research, the theory fell into disrepute, due to scientist folk saying that its concepts could not be tested (with the current laboratory test available), and that Vitalism was therefore a 'pseudoscience', believed in and used as the basis for clinical interventions only by alternative medicine practitioners, and should therefore be 'relegated to the trash heap of science', as it pretty much has as a scientific belief and discipline.

The concept of 'energy as a life force' is of course not exclusive to the Western scientific world, nor did it originate in the West, with Chinese and other Eastern cultures developing similar concepts thousands of years ago, which are still believed in and used as the basis for clinical practice today. For example, in traditional Chinese culture, Qi (also known as Chi) is perceived to be the central underlying principle of traditional Chinese medicine, and describes natural 'energy', life force and energy flow. In order to enhance or heal patients with illnesses, Chinese medical practitioners believe that by enhancing the energy systems and flow, using techniques for example such as Feng Shui (arrangement of energy 'space') or Qigong (coordinating breathing, movement and awareness) and acupuncture, most illnesses can be healed. In the Hindu religion and culture, Prana describes similar energy forces, and the concept of Chakras suggest that energy points or nodes occur through the body in distinct regions and 'lines'. These beliefs are underpinned by the idea that there is a 'life force' that is likened to, or is, an energy flow around and through the body, which forms a cohesive, functioning entity. Practitioners believe that by understanding its rhythm and flow, and treating imbalances in these energy systems, allows for the healing of illnesses and leads to enhanced 'stability' and longevity. Interestingly, unlike Vitalism, the Eastern practitioners of these fascinating healing techniques are generally unwilling to define terms such as Qi with reductionistic, 'Western' concepts such as 'energy' per se, though this is the best description of it. Like how Vitalism is viewed by most contemporary scientists, most of these concepts are generally given short thrift by most Western scientists.

This negation of bio-energy concepts by most 'hard core' Western scientists is both paradoxical and puzzling, given that several classical research techniques, particularly in neuroscience and psychophysiology, use bio-energetic principles as their core. For example, the electroencephalograph (EEG) clinical and research device is a non-invasive technique which measures electrical activity of brain tissue and neurons in the brain at a distance from the brain tissue itself (the measuring electrodes are placed by necessity on the scalp). Transcranial magnetic stimulation (TMS), is a non-invasive technique used to stimulate different regions of the brain, using a magnetic coil which sends electromagnetic impulses into the brain tissue that creates physical outcomes in the peripheral muscles. I will never forget the first time I watched a TMS device in action in the laboratory I worked in at the National Institutes of Health Research Centre in Washington DC in the USA, where with my great colleague and friend from Austria, Dr Bernhard Voller, we were using TMS to stimulate the motor cortex, and by doing so controlling and manipulating movement in the fingers and other peripheral muscles. I had the distinct feeling I was watching 'magic' happening each time the finger moved in response to the TMS impulse being delivered by Bernhard to the brain using the magnetic coil placed on (or just above) the participant's scalp. Yet we have subsequently published several research articles in respected international journals of our findings using these two brain examination techniques, which 'tap into' non-physical bio-energetic / electromagnetic activity in, and emanating from, the brain tissue, in contrast to what would happen if we tried to get a research paper published that examined Chakras or Qigong

51

energy practices. Even more interesting is what is seen when using a galvanic skin response (GSR) research testing device in the laboratory, which picks up electrodermal activity (electrical activity of the skin), and which shows drastic changes in activity when emotionally charged interventions are shown or given to participants in trials. The GSR device is what is basically used in lie detector tests – your bio-energetic activity changes when one lies or are required to answer questions which are emotionally charged (interestingly psychopaths, who show very little emotional lability or affect changes, are able to 'fool' lie detector tests given that they show no response to such tests, as easily as they are able to demonstrate anti-social behaviour).

So why do concepts like Vitalism and 'alternate' therapies such as Feng Shui and Qigong produce a usually hostile response in so many 'Western' / classical scientific folk? Perhaps it is because such theories often become conflated with, or are discussed as being related to, issues such as the 'soul', which conceptually is beyond basic bio-energetic force theory principles, and usually brings in non-secular beliefs and religion into the debate, even if the body's energy / life force and the 'soul' (if there is such a thing) can perhaps occur separately and / or be discussed as non-religious entities. It may be because of the predominant reductionistic view of life and science which currently occurs, in which gene theory (which is still very relevant, though surely cannot explain completely what 'life' is), biochemistry and mechanical explanations for phenomena and all behaviour in life still very much 'hold sway' in both scientific and general folks' s life view. Perhaps because of this, alternate energy related body control paradigms are often regarded with disdain by 'classical' scientists / research folk. It may be a result of not having the research techniques available still to adequately explore concepts like Bioenergetics, Qi and Prana. It may be that most scientists are scared to research these concepts, given the risk of being labelled a 'crank' for not staying in 'mainstream' academic research, no matter how contrary it is/ paradoxical from a scientific exploration perspective, for academic folk to denigrate colleagues who choose to spend time examining these very interesting, but perceptually 'lateral', and very academically challenging concepts.

What I do know though, after more than 20 years working in science and medicine, is that I still have not read or heard one theory or idea that adequately explains what 'life' is, or how our body's energy is maintained, or what is 'extinguished' in the body when we die. I do know that I feel 'energy' as part of my life and how life 'feels' to me, and that this energy waxes and wanes depending on how tired I am and my emotional state. I do know that when someone who is caring and kind gives me a hug or puts their hands on me, I feel a calming presence and a change in my own 'energy' and 'feelings'. I do know that when I am sitting quietly, I often 'know' that someone I can't see is looking at me or directing energy at me, and when I look around, indeed someone is doing so. I do know that I 'feel' the energy of people whom I meet in a negative or positive way, and those who I have 'positive energy' with usually become friends, and those who I feel 'negative energy' from generally remain challenges to me from an interactive perspective no matter how long I know them and try and warm to them (and probably vice-versa too). Us scientists have a long way to go to understand such phenomena and activities and behaviour, and instead of negating them or dismissing them as not existing, will probably find that the next major breakthrough in understanding life's regulatory processes, and life itself, will come through from examining and understanding these concepts. As for watching the 'group energy' of the young folk whom I saw dancing and clapping along to the music and enjoying the wonderful ambience of yesterday's Open Day welcoming event, well, maybe for now I'll just enjoy observing the 'energy' of all of them, revel in its positivity, and hope in the future that we can harness such 'group energy' for the greater good, not just from a scientific understanding perspective, but also from the perspective of using it as a method / potential 'group' gestalt healing tool in the future for challenging social and community interactions and behaviour. But as for understanding it, that is surely for another day / another epoch / another time way in the future.

Essay 4. The brain, the mind, and me - Where are 'we' in the convoluted mass of neurons we call the brain

---

The brain is both the most imperious and currently most mysterious organ in the body. It supposedly contains 'us' — our thoughts, personality, emotions and memory — as well as controlling all the functions of the body through the peripheral nerves and autonomic hormone releasing nervous system. But we sadly still know very, very little about its basic function, and there is currently no satisfactory unifying theory of the brain that solves how 'it' works. In this Essay we examine the brain and what we know of how it works, and what we still need to 'do' to find out all its mysteries and overall function.

This week I had some fun time getting some basic research projects on the go, a welcome break from my now almost full-time management life, as much as I enjoy it. I was asked to comment on a theoretical article that suggested that the prefrontal cortex is important in pacing and fatigue processes, and to write a review article on brain function regulating activity, by my good friend and world leading physiologist and exercise scientist, Professor Andy Jones, and both of these got the neurons firing in a pleasant way. For most of my career I have been a researcher, and while I describe my main research interest as understanding generic regulatory control mechanisms when asked about it, my research passion has always been the brain and how it functions, and creates 'us' and what we see, feel and experience as 'life'. I will never forget the 'buzz' I got when working at the NIH in Washington DC, with Austrian neurologist without peer, Dr Bernhard Voller, when we put a needle electrode into one of the muscles controlling eye movement of a subject and heard the repetitive 'clicks' of each action potential as it fired in order to control the muscle's movement, or when we used transcranial magnetic stimulation to stimulate the motor cortex (basically a magnet placed on the skull which 'fires' electromagnetic waves into the brain) and saw muscles in the finger or foot twitching when we selectively targeted different regions of the motor cortex. I will never forget the feeling of excitement when with Dr Laurie Rauch at the University of Cape Town we first got good quality EEG traces from folk and saw the EEG change frequency and complexity when someone put their hands on the folk being tested. I will also remember the wonder I felt (tinged with a degree of sadness for the rats which were sacrificed) working with Professor Viv Russell and Dr Musa Mabandla when we saw quantitative differences in neurotransmitter levels in areas of the brain of rats associated with motivation and drive that had run to exhaustion compared to more 'lazy' ones that simply refused to run as much as others did. Having said all this, it's amazing that after all these years, and so much research performed on the brain by so many top quality folk all round the world, we still have almost no idea of how the brain functions, how and where the mind is and how it relates to the physical brain structures and processes, and where 'we' and our 'soul' are in relation to this most complex organ in our body.

As everyone knows, the brain is an odd-shaped organ situated in the skull which consists of billions of neurons which connect with each other and with nerve fibres that 'flow' out to the body and which regulate all our body systems, processes and functions. Information is sent through neurons via electrical signals (called action potentials) which create 'coded' messages and commands. In a somewhat strange organizational structural process, there is a gap between each neuron where they connect to each other (called a synapse) and chemical substances called neurotransmitters fill the gap when electrical activity comes down the neuron and allows the 'message' to be transferred to the next neuron with great fidelity, though the synaptic neurotransmitter activity can also amplify, moderate or attenuate the signal passing through it, in a manner which is still not well understood, but related to the type of neurotransmitter that is secreted at the synapses. The brain also 'secretes' chemical substances such as hormones and regulatory factors that go via the bloodstream to various peripheral organs in the body and can control their function in a slower but longer acting way.

Though we do have some knowledge of basic output and input functions of the brain, such as vision and hearing processes, and sensory inputs and motor outputs from and to the body, there is currently no unifying theory of how neural activity in the brain works in its entirety to control or create the complex activities associated with life as we know it, such as thinking, memory, desire, awareness or even basic consciousness. Before the 1700s it was assumed that the brain functioned as a type of 'gland', based on the theories of the Greek physician Galen. In his model, the nerves conveyed fluids from the brain to the peripheral tissues (so he was right at least about the 'secretory' function of the brain). In the 1800s, using staining techniques and the (then) recently developed light microscope, Cayal and Golgi showed that neural tissues were a network of discrete cells, and that individual neurons were responsible for information processing. Around the same time Galvani showed that muscles and neurons produced electricity, and von Helmholtz and other German physiologists showed that electrical activity in one nerve cell affected activity in another neuron it was in contact with via a synapse in a predictable manner. Two conflicting views of how the brain uses these electrical-based neuronal systems to send commands or information were developed in the 1800s. The first was reductionistic, suggesting that different brain regions control specific functions. This concept was based on the work of Joseph Gall, who also suggested that continuous use of these different brain regions for specific tasks caused regional hypertrophy (increased size). Gall suggested that this regional brain hypertrophy created bulges in the skull, which could be associated with the specific function of the underlying brain tissue. While the skull theory of his has 'fallen by the wayside', in later years Brodmann described 52 anatomically separate and functionally distinct regions of the cortex, and Hughlings Jackson showed that in focal epilepsy, convulsions in different parts of the body were initiated in different parts of the cerebral cortex. These findings were supported by the work of Penfield, who used small electrodes to stimulate different areas of the motor cortex in awake neurological patients and induced movements in different anatomical regions of the body (similar to the work we did at the NIH, albeit we did it in a more indirect / less invasive way).

The second and opposing view was that all brain regions contribute to every different mental task and motor function in an integrative and continuous manner. This theory was based on the work of Flourens in the 1800's and was described as the aggregate field theory. Recent research has shown that large areas of the brain communicate with each other continuously using electromagnetic waves of different frequency during any task. Further support for the aggregate field theory comes from the concept that no activity is ever simple, and even a 'simple' motor task such as moving the hand to get something is the final common output of multiple behavioural demands such as emotional context, prior experience, sensory perception and homeostatic requirements, and therefore cannot be attributed solely to any specific / single region, except from a final output perspective. While the aggregate field theory fell into disfavour in the late 1900's, due to the development of MRI, CT and PET scanning of the brain and these techniques' ascendancy to being 'the in thing' in neuroscience / brain research over the last few decades, the 'snapshot' methodology associated with brain scanning using MRI and these other image-based techniques have contributed very little real understanding of how the brain functions, apart from creating 'pretty' pictures that show that certain brain regions 'light up' whenever a task is performed. Unfortunately, often the same areas of the brain are shown to be active when using these techniques during very different testing protocols, which creates a confusing and complex 'picture' of what is happening in the brain during even simple tasks.

Incredibly, therefore, we still know so little about how the brain works that this basic argument between 'regional' versus 'general' brain functionality has not been resolved, despite all the technological development in the last few decades, such as those described above. Even more mysterious is how the 'mind' works, and there is still active debate of what the 'mind' is, and how it relates to physical brain structures. The mind is defined as the cognitive faculties that enables consciousness, perception, thinking, judgement, and memory. As will be obvious, this definition of the mind can at best be described as a conceptually 'hazy' one and does not help much clarify things, but basically the mind is what 'we' are – the 'me' that makes our life feel as if it is 'ours' and that we are unique, and our experiences and thoughts are 'our own'. The debate still rages about whether the mind is 'in' – the monist or materialist doctrine – or 'out' of the brain tissue – the 'dualist' doctrine. The monist / materialist doctrine posits that everything we think, feel and 'are' can and is found in the functioning and activity of the neural cells and neurons in the brain. The dualist theory posits that 'we' are an immaterial 'spirit', as described by Rene Descartes, that is related to but exists 'out' of the brain and body – a more spiritual interpretation of what 'we' are and a theory which allows for concepts such as 'soul'. The clearest evidence for a strong relationship between physical brain matter and the mind is the effect of physical agents such as psychoactive and anaesthetic drugs and alcohol on the 'mind', and the effect of traumatic brain injury in certain areas of the brain on mental function and the mind. But, given that we have absolutely no idea where memories are stored in the brain or how they are stored, how 'thought' happens, or even what consciousness 'is', it is difficult to completely refute the dualist approach, even as a hard-nosed scientist, although it is the 'death sentence' for many a neuroscientist's career for one of us to suggest a belief in dualism is a scientifically possible entity. Religion is perhaps in many ways a derivative of this 'explanatory gap' between mind and brain function and will continue to flourish until science eventually (if possible) proves the materialist / monist theory to be true or refutes the dualist theory with more evidence than we currently have.

So, what do we know of the brain, the most brilliant and puzzling organ in the body, and how it functions? Sadly, after 25 years studying it, I must be honest and say almost nothing, and anyone who says differently, is not being honest or is deluding themselves (which of course would be an irony of note). Us neuroscientists are in many ways beholden to and 'straitjacketed' in developing our brain and mind theories by the laboratory investigative techniques that are currently available which allow us to examine whatever our area of interest is, and unfortunately in the brain research area, these techniques are just not subtle enough, or conversely not complex enough, to allow us to have any more understanding today of how the brain works than in many ways was known one or two hundred years ago. It's amazing that we know so much about heart, liver, and muscle function – indeed any organ of the body – and so little about the brain, which is such a seemingly impenetrable mystery. Most neuroscientists like myself eventually focus on examining specific areas of brain or mind function, perhaps to protect ourselves from a sense of being abject failures in our chosen discipline – which is why I describe my main area of interest as control theory rather than 'brain function' research to those that ask. But, it surely will be some scientist, working with some new recently developed piece of equipment that we are not yet aware of, that will have the 'eureka' moment for neuroscience similar to what occurred with genetics / molecular biology in the 1950s with the breakthrough in the understanding of the structure of DNA that in turn led to how quickly molecular biology developed in the subsequent 60 years to its current status and we will have a clear understanding of how the brain works and how the mind fits in to the puzzle. Whoever does have this 'eureka' moment will very much deserve their Nobel Prize. Until that time, I, and probably most research folk who are interested in basic brain function, will keep on telling our new neuroscience / physiology / exercise science students each year that as scientists us neuroscientists are dismal failures / the least successful of all the research folk working in academia, given how little of brain and mind function we know and understand, despite all our valiant endeavours and countless hours in the lab, trying to work it all out.

But, having said this, I will also continue to marvel at the brain and mind, and be thankful that I had, and have, the career from a research perspective that I do, trying to work out and understand something as truly amazing as the brain, which is the 'root of all life as we know it', whatever life and our part of it is. In the mass of neurons in our brains, which work in some mysterious way and using codes we still need to 'crack', 'we' exist, feel, live and die. Unless of course the dualists are right, and us research folk have been fooling ourselves for a long time, and 'we' are just spirits that exist in our bodies for the length of time we are alive, before heading off for another adventure, either in another body, or in another world. Time, hard work, and perhaps a good dose of luck, will allow us neuroscience folk to eventually have a definitive opinion either way – however, now, the mind is willing, but the contemporary brain appears to be too 'weak' to make or find that elusive 'eureka' breakthrough and know what itself, and indeed 'we', are all about.

Essay 5. The Libet awareness of initiation of action study - Do we have free will or are we slaves to our subconscious

Most activity we do 'feels' as if it is being done by 'ourselves', and in response to our conscious demands of our body to perform an act. This is known as agency, and is linked to the concept of free will, which suggests that we have choices in the decisions we make. More than a hundred years ago, the presence of the unconscious, also known as the subconscious, an impenetrable mass of childhood desires, fears and complexes, was suggested by an excellent group of first-generation Psychologists, and that any actions were actually set in motion by the unconscious, and only 'seemed' to be conscious. Free will in this model could not exist, as although we 'feel' as if we are in charge of a decision, in effect the unconscious controls and both 'orders' and 'organises' all of the feeling of wanting something, the feeling as if we are making a choice about it, and the acting out of that choice. These concepts are difficult to 'get one's' head around, and in this Essay, we examine them, and the experiments which were done to prove or disprove the theories of free will and determinism.

At a meeting of the South African Council of Deans, which I attended earlier this week, what struck me most about the day, apart from the great discussions and wisdom of the wise folk I interacted with, was a bowl of popcorn on the table in front of me and my reaction to it. After having a few pieces of popcorn, I said to myself that that was enough, and I focussed back on the erudite discussion going on around me. But, seemingly without any control from me, my hand reached out and picked up more popcorn for me to eat on several occasions, and it felt like my hand was acting in a disembodied way and against my wishes. This reminded me of a great article by my mentor during the time I worked at the National Institutes of Health in Washington DC a few years ago, Dr Mark Hallett, one of the most highly cited and world-renowned neurologists and motor control researcher, in which he described a similar scenario (in his case it was a bowl of peanuts). In his article, Mark proposed that ground-breaking research work by Dr Benjamin Libet performed a few decades ago perhaps explained what was happening in such examples where we feel that we are not in control of our body's actions, and whether we ever have free will in any of the activities which we initiate and perform during our daily lives.

Benjamin Libet was a neuroscientist who worked in the Physiology Department at the University of California in San Francisco, and was interested in brain function, particularly the neural activity and sensation thresholds associated with the awareness of intention to act during motor (muscle controlled) tasks. He performed a classic experiment in the 1970s where he used an electroencephalogram (EEG), which monitors electrical activity emanating from the tissues of the brain, an electromyogram (EMG), which monitors electrical activities of muscles when they move, and timing devices to assess when participants in his trial became aware of their intent to move their finger, when brain activity in the motor cortex and other areas of the brain changed associated with the planned finger movement, and when the finger actually moved after the participant initiated the movement. Libet asked the study participants to decide themselves when to move their finger, so they would be in control of the initiation of the finger movement, rather than telling them when to move their finger, which was crucial to the trial's outcome from an agency / control perspective, which was what the study was all about.

The participants became aware of their intent to move their fingers approximately 300 milliseconds prior to the movement of the fingers occurring, as objectively measured by the onset of EMG activity in the muscles of the fingers. Two further findings of the study were firstly that electrical brain activity, as measured by EEG activity in the motor and pre-motor areas of the brain, started changing approximately 1050 milliseconds prior to the actual movement of the finger (this early EEG activity prior to a muscle movement is generally known as a Bereitschaftpotential, which is the German word for 'readiness potential'), which was well before the participants became 'aware' of their intention to act / decision to move their finger; and secondly that the 'awareness' of the finger movement itself, as opposed to the awareness of the intent to move it, was described by the participants to have occurred approximately 90 milliseconds prior to the finger actually moving. The first finding that there was brain activity in the movement control areas of the brain even before the participants became aware of the decision to move their finger indicates that subconscious brain activity occurred that controlled the finger movement before conscious 'intent to act' decisions occurred. Even more astonishing, the second finding that the 'awareness' of movement of the finger occurred prior to the movement actually occurring suggested that this 'awareness' of finger movement was 'pre-dated' by the brain to this time point and was not related to the actual physical movement of the finger itself – in other words the conscious awareness of the movement was 'painted in' by the brain to the time when the brain 'thought' it was the appropriate time. This finding indicates that our conscious awareness of movement appears to be a 'figment of our imagination', or more specifically, an artificial construct generated by unconscious regulatory processes.

Libet and his colleagues concluded from his experiments that unconscious control processes regulate most of our activity, and that conscious awareness of intent is a derivative of these unconscious control processes, and further that free will is an illusion created by them. This study and its conclusions generated a huge amount of interest, and does so to this day, given it was the first time the concept of 'free will' had been assessed in an objective way, and had been shown to not occur during the testing conditions of the trial. While a number of research folk, and in particular a number of philosophers (philosophers love to argue about free will, and believe concepts such as free will and consciousness to be very much in their domain of study, even if they don't often do any objective research on these topics themselves), have attempted to negate or pick holes in the study design, the findings have been replicated on a number of occasions, with further studies showing that brain activity in other brain areas such as the frontal cortex can occur even earlier than that which Libet demonstrated in the motor and pre-motor cortex prior to movement. These findings suggested that free will appears to be the 'slave' of the unconscious, or even further that it does not occur in activities we believe we 'control'. While this study examined simple finger movement, there are a number of other 'physical' examples of unconscious control activity which Mark Hallett suggested support Libet's finding, such as patients with chorea (a movement disorder) not perceiving their limbs are moving when in reality their limbs move around in wild patterns in a continuous manner, and in motor activities such as automatic responses to tasks, sleepwalking, and neurological disorders like alien hand syndrome, where after damage to certain parts of the motor control area of the brain, patients' limbs can move, but the patients do not feel they have control or agency over these movements, and that the limbs are moving as if controlled by 'another'.

If our movements and actions are not controlled consciously or in a free willed way, where and how does the control of movement occur? Of course, to answer this brings in the notion of the unconscious, and that control mechanisms occur in some manner and in some brain structures that occur automatically at a level which is 'not available to introspection' (if they were we would be consciously aware of this), which to most scientists is problematic given that such a concept would therefore be impossible to understand with the research techniques we currently have available. The concept of the unconscious is also unfortunately a controversial one for 'political' / moral reasons, because it is related to the work and ideas of Sigmund Freud, who suggested that unconscious sexual urges, and the gratification of these, was the basis of all planned human movement and actions. These suggestions perhaps unsurprisingly generated abhorrence for his theories from both colleagues and society after they were published, although the unconscious was described and discussed as a concept long before Freud theorized about its actions and existence. Unconscious processes such as memory storage and automated movement are routinely accepted as fact, but when intent, agency, motivation, phobias, complexes and desires are discussed, controversy rages regarding whether these do exist at an unconscious level, or which are purely conscious entities. Libet's study was the first objective study which showed that, at least from a physical / electrical brain activity perspective, action was indeed controlled by these unconscious processes, which were for so long theorized about, yet were essentially unproven until his seminal work.

So, going back to the popcorn episode in my case, and that of the peanuts in Mark Hallett's article, it would appear from Libet's experiment that Mark and I, and surely all folk, are not completely 'in control' of our actions as much as we would like to be. While this is a worrying concept if one believes in free will, and that we are masters of our own destiny from a conscious, 'choice' perspective, it is helpful to all folk in explaining why one does things that seem contrary to what one's conscious wishes, or occasionally moral wishes, are. There clearly is an 'agency' that 'drives' what we do and what we want (dare I say desire), that occurs at an unconscious / subliminal level, and which often appears to create discordancy with our conscious desires and wishes. We currently have no idea where in the brain this unconscious 'agency' exists or how it 'works' – psychologists use dream assessment as one technique of understanding them, and neurophysiologists techniques like galvanic skin responses to psychological suggestion (saying something to a person which might make them feel uncomfortable, and monitoring their skin conductance changes as a measure of their discomfort – similar to what happens in a lie detector test), but these are all very nebulous measures of the function of unconscious processes. Perhaps even if we cannot at this point understand 'where' or 'how' unconscious agency occurs, an understanding that it surely exists in all of us, and that free will may be an illusion created by it, is helpful at least in assuaging the guilt most of us feel when 'succumbing' to our 'desires', such as those that I felt for the popcorn this week that led to my hand reaching out for more almost 'without control'. Of course, most folk perceive that the danger exists, when accepting a potential lack of conscious control as part of our routine existence, of losing the capacity for 'self-discipline' and our life sustaining healthy habits and social structures, if we 'agree' to use this information as an 'excuse' to not worry about succumbing to each of our unconscious desires. However, whether one worries or not appears to make not much difference to the actions of our unconscious agency, and the question perhaps should be why there is so often a 'dissonance' between what our conscious thoughts 'tell us' what we should want or what we should do (or more often not do!), and what our unconscious agency insists on, as in the case of the popcorn incident. The concept of a lack of free will is also of course troubling to our sense of self identity, and the confidence we feel because of perceiving we are in control of most situations and our own destiny, at least on a personal level. As Freud put it, there have been three severe 'blows' dealt to human vanity by science (as Paul Ferris well described in his biography of Freud) – the first 'blow' being the cosmological one, which removed humans from their perceived position as the centre of the / their universe; the second being the biological one, when Darwin's work showed our animal origins; and the third, and in Freud's words, the 'most wounding', being the psychological, which 'rearranged the mind to make it subject to a dilatory unconscious, and so demonstrated that the ego is not master in its own house'. The classic study performed by Libet was the first objective study to give us evidence that Freud may indeed have been right about the third 'blow', or at least about the presence of unconscious agency. So, I guess that at least until scientist folk work out how unconscious agency works, and I can perhaps better control and prevent my hand from reaching out for it after the scientists work out its mechanism of action, the only solution to the popcorn issue is in future to please hide that bowl of popcorn from me, to protect me from my own unconscious drives.

Essay 6. Self-talk and mentors - Our inner soliloquies tell what we want and who we are

As described in an earlier essay, it is currently impossible to 'view' the subconscious or even know where in the brain it resides. But, we can perhaps 'hear' the subconscious, with it being suggested that our inner voices, also known as self-talk, are a way into 'hearing' the subconscious. Many folk don't realise that they have a continuous conscious inner dialogue going on in their head, which usually consists of two voices, an 'I' voice, which has been suggested to be primordial needs or concerns arising from the subconscious, and the 'me' voice, which tries to explain, or reassure, the 'I' voice, that all is okay, or whether one needs to take action based on the concern or not. In this Essay we examine self-talk, and assess its potential relationship to the subconscious, and what contributes to its make-up as its component parts.

Doing some work initiating both mentorship structures and leadership courses in my work environment got me thinking about self-talk in a circuitous way. Self-talk is the dialogue between the voices that we hear 'in' our mind throughout most of our waking lives. It has also been described as private speech, inner dialogue, soliloquy, or sub-vocal speech, amongst other definitions. Different categories of self-talk have been described. Regressive self-talk occurs where there is the release of emotional energy, which is not directed at any specific target or person, as when one hurts oneself and curses to oneself because of the pain. Intrapersonal self-talk is related to structuring and sustaining cognitive capacity, such as repeating a telephone number or reminding oneself to remember someone's name after meeting them. Interpersonal self-talk is self-talk which is directed towards communicating with others in the future, such as researching a speech for future delivery, or planning what one will say in a future meeting.

While these categories provide structure in describing our self-talk, a lot of time our own self-talk seems to be idle chatter, which 'bounces' between topics, and crucially usually 'sounds' like a dialogue between two, or occasionally more voices when one is consciously focussing on / listening to the discussions in one's own mind.

It has also been suggested that self-talk may be a crucial component of conscious perception of one's environment and self-awareness, by alerting the 'mind' to changes in emotional and physical state and creating an understanding of whether these changes and the cause of them are relevant or are of concern to the individual, by allowing the individual to take the 'perspective of the other' in their own mind. Associated with this concept, it has been pointed out that self-talk cannot occur as a single voice, but rather is, by definition, a soliloquy that occurs between at least two inner voices. There is an 'I' voice, representing the voice urging one to act or describing a current activity, and a 'Me' voice which takes the perspective of the 'other' and with which the 'I' voice is assessed.

It has been suggested that previous social interactions with other individuals allows one to gain a viewpoint of oneself by becoming aware of that person's perspectives of our actions or thoughts. Therefore, taking the perspective of the 'other' is the ability to understand that a person's viewpoint may be different to one's own, and potentially to use this information to change one's behaviour or viewpoint. Self-talk allows, or is, the result of the internalization of this mechanism of taking another person's perspective, as one can describe to one's 'Me' voice (a real or imagined person) in one's own mind the reasons for behaving in a certain manner during a previous experience, or for planning behaviour in future similar based on how the 'other' would respond to it. When one engages in self-talk with the 'Me' voice, therefore, which takes the perspective of the other, we can tell ourselves what others expect of us. This 'Me' voice can be the opinion of a single individual who has had a positive impression on us as a wise counsel in the past, or of a 'generalized other', which would be the perceived expectations of what the person believes their community would do in the situation being described by their

'I' voice. These different perspectives may have been learnt or adapted from previous social interactions with other individuals, groups of individuals, or from writings and media excerpts that describe community values or expectations that are internalized and become the content of the 'Me' voice. Therefore, we have a soliloquy going on in our minds the whole time, and this self-talk is a discussion between the desires of the individual during a particular experience, and the learned social expectations derived previously from external discussions or interactions with an individual, group or community.

So how does all this relate to mentorship and leadership as I described earlier was occurring in my own thoughts the last while (personal self-talk!). Well, clearly mentors are crucial for supplying the information that has the potential, if they are respected, to become the 'Me' voice in our minds. I have noticed from my own experiences and becoming aware of my own self-talk (and doing some research and reading on it) that my inner soliloquies often occur with mentors from the past that I have respected – for example my PhD supervisor, a wise family friend, a senior leader at the University I work at – and when I am confronted with a situation that angers or concerns me, I find myself in my mind 'communicating' with these respected folk from my past, and by doing so come to a way forward through the problem I am facing. As I grow older, more respected folk are added to my community of 'others', and situations seem to become easier to deal with as I age, as they generally do for most folk as they get older and who all are going through a similar process of incorporating mentors as "Me' voices as is happening to me. So obviously, getting the right mentors, and right potential folk to supply the text for one's 'other' perspective (the 'Me' voice in our head) is crucial, and perhaps our best chance, of moderating our own behaviour in a way that will make ourselves leaders and role models for those around us and for the next generation following us, who look to us to provide their own 'perspective of the other'.

Of course, a person can have a problem if their 'Me' voice is not wise but is rather self-damaging or is generated from a negative role model that becomes unwittingly introduced into one's panel of 'others' which one uses as an action frame of reference. Whether these voices can be consciously altered over a short period of time is not clear either. Obviously with time given that 'Me' voices are added means that our self-talk protagonists can be altered, but in many ways self-talk and the outcome of the dialogue create our personality / view of life (however one wishes to define our core way of viewing and interacting with life), and to alter completely all the voices one has accumulated would create a completely different personality or way of thinking. Such major self-talk does not seem to occur unless there are catastrophic changes in one's environment or personal life, such as divorce, death of a loved one, or natural disaster, which one's 'Me' voices cannot provide a frame of reference or good advice for. When this occurs the inner 'Me' voices can become fragmented and in the end be replaced by other 'Me' voices which are able to make sense of the current crisis or trauma, and therefore would potentially create a very different personality as an outcome to the catastrophic trauma. But for most folk, as the old saying goes, the passing of time is the only healer and thing that will change a damaging 'Me' voice.

So, we need to be aware that we have the potential as parents, mentors, or leaders to end up as 'voices' in those we interact with and take an interest in what we say and do. To be successful we surely need to manage the 'I' voice – psychology folk would find resonance with these concepts described above with those of Freud's 'Id and Ego' theory or Steve Peters' classic description of our 'Inner Chimp' which the 'Human' in us needs to control to be successful – but also we need to get the right blend of 'Me' voices (the 'others') which are generated by mentors of our past, which will see us through all the complex situations we face in our daily life. Being aware of our own self-talk, and the make-up of it, is perhaps crucial for the success or failure we make of our lives, and of course, the mentors we choose and who become ingrained in minds as 'Me' voices surely make all the difference.

Essay 7. Control of movement and action - Technically challenging conceptual requirements and exquisite control mechanisms underpin even lifting your coffee cup

While the function of the brain itself is still mostly a mystery to us, we do have more information on and understanding of the outputs of the brain which control the body, which it does through nerves to the muscles of the body, or to the visceral organs in the gut, or due to release of hormones into the blood stream from the pituitary gland at the base of the skull. This increased knowledge of function of peripheral outputs is perhaps due to the fact that we can relatively easily measure outcomes of these 'commands' by recording the movements they create, or changes in the gut they induce. However, with millions of muscle fibres and hundreds of different muscles to coordinate, the control of even simple movements is complex, and must require multiple computations of control choices and harmonious sequential firing of many different nerve fibres. In this Essay we examine the work done in this field of control of movement, and action and examine its complexities.

During the Christmas break we stayed in Durban with my great old friend James Adrain, and each morning I would, as usual, wake around 5.00 and make a cup of coffee and sit outside in his beautiful garden and reflect on life and its meaning before the rest of the team awoke and we set off on our daily morning bike-ride. One morning I accidentally bumped my empty coffee mug, and as it headed to the floor, my hand involuntarily reached out and grabbed it, saving it just before it hit the ground. During the holiday I also enjoyed watching a bit of sport on the TV in the afternoons to relax after the day's festivities, and once briefly saw highlights of the World Darts Championship, which was on the go, and was struck by how the folk competing seemed, with such ease, and with apparent similar arm movements when throwing each dart, to be able to hit almost exactly what they were aiming for, usually the triple twenty. When I got back home, I picked up from Twitter a fascinating article on movement control posted by one of Sport Sciences' most pre-eminent biomechanics researchers, Dr Paul Glazier, written by a group of movement control scientists including Professor Mark Latash, whom I regard as one of the foremost innovative thinkers in the field of the last few decades. All of these got me thinking about movement control, and what must be exquisite control mechanisms in the brain and body, which allowed me in an instant to plan and enact a movement strategy which enabled me to grab the falling mug before it hit the ground, and enabled the Darts Championship competitors to guide their darts, using their arm muscles, with such accuracy to such a small target a fair distance away from them.

Due to the work over the last few centuries of several great movement control researchers, neurophysiologists, neuroscientists, biomechanists and anatomists, we know a fair bit about the anatomical structures that regulate movement in the different muscles of the body. In the brain, the motor cortex is the area where command outflow to the different muscles is directly activated, and one of the highlights of my research career was when I first used transcranial magnetic stimulation, working with my great friend and colleague Dr Bernhard Voller, where we were able to make muscles in the arms and legs twitch by 'firing' magnetic impulses into the motor cortex region of the brain by holding an electromagnetic device over the scalp above this brain region. The 'commands for action' from the motor cortex travel to the individual muscles via motor nerves, using electrical impulses in which the command 'code' is supplied to the muscle by trains of impulses of varying frequency and duration. At the level of the individual muscles, the electrical impulses induce a series of biochemical events in and around the individual muscle fibres which cause them to contract in an 'all or none' way, and with the correct requested amount of force output from the muscle fibre which has been 'ordered' by the motor cortex in response to behavioural requirements initiated in brain areas 'upstream' from the motor cortex, such as one's eyes picking up a falling cup and 'ordering' reactive motor commands to catch the cup. So while even though the pathway structures from the brain to the muscle fibres are more complex than I have described here – there are a whole host of 'ancient' motor pathways from 'lower' brainstem areas of the brain which also travel to the muscle or synapse with the outgoing motor pathways, whose functions appear to be redundant to the main motor pathways and may still exist as a relic from the days before our cortical 'higher' brain structures developed – we do know a fair bit about the individual motor control pathways, and how they structurally operate and how nerve impulses pass from the brain to the muscles of the body.

However, like everything in life, things are more complex than what is described above, as even a simple action like reaching for a cup, or throwing a dart, requires numerous different muscles to fire either synchronously and / or synergistically, and indeed when catching a falling cup, just about every muscle in the body has to alter its firing pattern to allow the body to move, the arm to stretch out, the legs to stabilize the moving body, and the trunk to sway towards the falling cup in order to catch it. Furthermore, each muscle itself has thousands of different muscle fibres, all of which need to be controlled by an organized 'pattern' of firing to even the single whole muscle. This means that there needs to be a coordinated pattern of movement of a number of different muscles and the muscle fibres in each of them, and we still have no idea how the 'plan' or 'map' for each of these complex patterns of movement occurs, where it is stored in the brain (as what must be a complex algorithm of both spatial and temporal characteristics to recruit not only the correct muscles, but also the correct sequence of their firing from a timing perspective to allow co-ordinated movement), and how a specific plan is 'chosen' by the brain as the correct one from what must be thousands of other complex movement plans. To make things even more challenging, it has been shown that each time one performs a repetitive movement, such as throwing a dart, different synergies of muscles and arm movement actions are used each time one throws the dart, even if to the 'naked' eye it appears that the movement of the arm and fingers of the individual throwing the dart seems identical each time it is thrown.

Perhaps the scientist that has made the most progress in solving these hugely complex and still not well understood control processes has been Nikolai Bernstein, a Russian scientist working out of Moscow between the 1920s and 1960s, and whose work was not well known outside of Russia because of the 'Iron Curtain' (and perhaps Western scientific arrogance) until a few decades ago, when research folk like Mark Latash (who I regard as the modern day equivalent of Bernstein both intellectually and academically) translated his work into English and published it as books and monographs. Bernstein was instructed in the 1920s to study movement during manual labour in order to enhance worker productivity under the instruction of the communist leaders of Russia during that notorious epoch of state control of all aspects of life. Using cyclographic techniques (a type of cinematography), he filmed workers performing manual tasks such as hitting nails with hammers or using chisels and came to two astonishing conclusions / developed two movement control theories which are astonishingly brilliant (actually he developed quite a few more than the two described here), and if he was alive and living in a Western country these would or should have surely led to him getting a Nobel prize for his work. The first thing he realized was that all motor activity is based on 'modelling of the future'. In other words, each significant motor act is a solution (or attempt at one) of a specific problem which needs physical action, whether hitting a nail with a hammer, or throwing a dart at a specific area of a dartboard, or catching a falling coffee cup. The 'act' that is required, which in effect is the mechanism through which an organism is trying to achieve some behavioural requirement, is something which is not yet, but is 'due to be brought about'. Bernstein suggested that the problem of motor control and action, therefore, is that all movement is the reflection or model of future requirements (somehow coded in the brain), and a vitally useful or significant action cannot either be programmed or accomplished if the brain has not created pre-requisite directives in the forms of 'maps' of the future requirements which are 'lodged' somewhere in the brain. So, all movement is in response to 'intent', and for each 'intent' a map of motor movements which would solve this 'intent' is required, a concept which is hard enough to get one's mind around understanding, let alone working out how the brain achieves this or how these 'maps' are stored and chosen.

The second of Bernstein's great observations was what is known as motor redundancy (Mark Latash has recently suggested that redundancy is the wrong word, and it should have been known as motor abundancy), or the 'inverse dynamics problem' of movement. When looking at the movement of the workers hitting a nail with a hammer, he noticed that despite them always hitting the nail successfully, the trajectory of the hammer through the air was always different, despite the final outcome always being similar. He realized that each time the hammer was used, a different combination of arm motion 'patterns' was used to get the hammer from its initial start place to when it hit the nail. Further work showed that each different muscle in the arm was activated differently each time the hammer was guided through the air to the nail, and each joint moved differently for each hammer movement too. This was quite a mind-boggling observation, as it meant that each time the brain 'instructed' the muscles to fire in order to control the movement of the hammer, it chose a different 'pattern' or 'map' of coordinative muscle activation of the different muscles and joints in the arm holding the hammer for each hammer strike of the nail, and that for each planned movement, therefore, thousands of different 'patterns' or 'maps' of coordinated muscle movement must be stored, or at least available to the brain, and a different one appears to be chosen each time the same repetitive action is performed. Bernstein therefore realized that there is a redundancy, or abundancy, of 'choice' of movement strategies available to the brain for each movement, let alone complex movement involving multiple body parts or limbs. From an intelligent control systems concept, this is difficult to get one's head around, and how the 'choice' of 'maps' is made each time a person performs a movement is still a complete mystery to movement control researchers.

Interestingly, one would think that with training, one would reach a situation where there would be less motor variability, and a more uniform pattern of movement when performing a specific task. But, in contrast, the opposite appears to occur, and the variability of individual muscle and joint actions in each repetitive movement appears to maintain or even increase this variability with training, perhaps as a fatigue regulating mechanism to prevent the possibility of injury occurring from potentially over-using a preferentially recruited single muscle or muscle group. Furthermore, the opposite appears to happen after injury or illness, and after for example one suffers a stroke or a limb ligament or muscle tear, the pattern of movements 'chosen' by the brain, or available to be chosen, appears to be reduced, and similar movement patterns occur during repetitive muscle movement after such an injury, which would also be counter-intuitive in many ways, and is perhaps related to some loss of 'choice' function associated with injury or brain damage, rather than damage to the muscles per se, though more work is needed to understand this conceptually, let alone functionally.

So, therefore, the simple actions which make up most of our daily life, appear to be underpinned by movement control mechanisms of the most astonishing complexity, which we do not understand well (and I have not even mentioned the also complex afferent sensory components of the movement control process which adjust / correct non-ballistic movement). My reaction to the cup falling and me catching it was firstly a sense of pleasure that, despite my advancing age and associated physical deterioration, I still 'had' the capacity to respond in an instant and that perhaps the old physical 'vehicle' – namely my body – through which all my drives and dreams are operationalized / effected (as Freud nicely put it) still works relatively okay, at least when a 'crisis' occurs such as the cup falling. Secondly, I felt the awe I have felt at many different times in my career as a system control researcher at what a brilliant 'instrument' our brains and bodies as a combination are, and whatever or whoever 'created' us in this way made something special. The level of exquisite control pathways, the capacity for and of redundancy available to us for each movement, the intellectual capacity from just a movement control perspective our brain possesses (before we start talking of even more complex phenomena such as memory storage, emotional qualia, and the mechanisms underpinning conscious perception) are staggering to behold and be aware of. Equally, when one sees each darts player, or any athlete performing their task so well for our enjoyment and their success (whether darts players can be called 'athletes' is for another discussion perhaps), it is astonishing that all their practice has made their movement patterns potentially more rather than less variable, and that this variability, rather than creating 'malfunction', creates movement success and optimizes task outcome capacity and performance.

It is in those moments as I had when sitting in a beautiful garden in Durban in the early morning of a holiday period, reflecting on one's success in catching a coffee cup, that creates a sense of wonder of the life we have and live, and what a thing of wonder our body is, with its many still mystical, complex, mostly concealed control processes and pathways regulating even our simple movements and daily tasks. In each movement we perform are concealed a prior need or desire, potentially countless maps of prospective plans for it, and millions of ways it can be actualized, from which our brain chooses one specific mechanism and process. There is surely magic in life not just all around but in us too, that us scientist folk battle so hard to try and understand, but which are to date still impenetrable in all their brilliance and beauty. So with a sigh, I stood up from the table, said goodbye to the beautiful garden and great friends in Durban, and the relaxing holidays, and returned to the laboratory at the start of the year to try and work it all out again, yet knowing that probably I will be back in the same place next year, reflecting on the same mysteries, with the same awe of what has been created in us, and surely still will be no further to understanding, and will still be pondering, how to work it all out – though next year I will be sure to be a bit more careful where I place my finished coffee cup.

Essay 8. Information processing in the brain and body - Are we managed by and do we regulate our lives using discrete units of information rather than a continuous flow of knowledge?

One of the most interesting things one gets to see (or hear) when measuring neural output from the brain along peripheral nerves to the different muscles in the body, is that the 'message' relayed down the nerve occurs in discreet units of firing, and the pattern of this firing creates the 'code' by which this message is transported to the muscles, which makes them move in the way the brain wanted, in a coordinated way with multiple other muscles and with the right amount of force generated for the right amount of time it is needed. In this Essay we examine how this 'code' is created, how it 'jumps' or 'flows' across different structures such as a chemical nerve synapse, and whether there is a universal code in the brain and body we can 'tap into' and use perhaps as a way of understanding how the brain works to create and distribute information and commands.

I have been spending quite a bit of time at work since I started my current role as a Head of a Medical School two years ago trying to get data 'dashboards' together of all aspects of our business profile, so I can better understand our strengths and weaknesses, and make informed decisions on how to strategically improve what we do and how we do it. On the home front we are making some plans to change our living environment and are gathering data to make the best possible decision before doing so with the information we have available to us. Most of my life I have been a research scientist and generating and understanding data has been the 'trademark' of my working life. One of the major challenges left for science and us scientists to solve is the understanding of basic brain function and the brain's capacity for dynamic regulation of the body's activity. A major component of this endeavour is understanding how the brain responds to information flow from the body, how it analyses this information it receives, how it comes to a decision to act (or not act) based on this information analysis, and how it generates information flow back to the body for it to respond to and / or make changes as a consequence of these decisions. Most of the time life 'feels' as if it occurs in an 'always happening', linear, continuous manner, and there are no apparent 'gaps' in our conscious awareness of activities occurring either around us or in which we are ourselves functioning and required to make decisions about. But, us scientists when examining brain and body function, 'break up' the information we record from a research participant we are observing into discrete data units, using a variety of physiological laboratory assessment equipment, which are recorded and stored as such, and we later print these data out or put these recordings into spreadsheets as numerical data, and create line or bar graphs in order to understand and explain what we have observed. The question therefore arises if, as part of the inherent brain and body regulatory mechanisms which manage our daily life activity, do we similarly understand and assimilate an understanding of activity occurring in and around us in such an information processing / discrete data-based way?

One of the most pivotal moments of my research life was working with the peerless Neurologist Dr Bernhard Voller as a Research Fellow at the National Institutes of Health in Washington DC, 15 years ago, when he showed me how to perform the technique of fine wire invasive recording of skeletal muscle activity (known as electromyography). When we had placed the electrode in a muscle (we examined the nerve firing in eye muscles for the specific experiment), and the subject blinked, one heard the firing of the nerves controlling the muscle via a speaker attached to the electrode recording device, and the rate of firing increased rapidly each time the subject blinked with greater force. What was such a 'wow factor' for me, was that what we were listening to was the information 'code' going down from the brain to the specific muscle we were studying, in order to make it contract with the required force production. If you put a similar electrode into any nerve in the brain or travelling from the brain to the body, you will see or hear a similar firing rate change happening, which is the 'code' used by the brain to generate commands and induce changes in function of any organ the nerves target. One of the most interesting studies I have ever read looked at single neuron firing in the motor cortex of a monkey's brain when its arm was being moved in different directions around its elbow joint. Each movement created a different 'code' of firing that was unique to each specific movement, and if one looked at the graph plots of the generated data after learning the different 'codes' for each movement, one could predict with a high degree of certainty which arm movement had occurred to produce each specific trace. So, certainly at the physical nerve firing level, information is generated, and function regulated, by discrete coded information that was evident and could be 'decoded' when examining the firing rate of a particular nerve.

This numerical coding of information is also evident across a variety of body systems. For example, heart rate is a measure of how fast the heart beats, and we know that when the heart beats faster it is working harder in response to a greater need for blood flow around the body, such as when doing exercise, or during a hot day, or when one is sick and has a fever. Therefore, if we examine a heart rate trace collected during a 24-hour period of time from someone, without being told what the person whose heart rate we were retrospectively examining had been doing, we could make a good guess of what activities the person had been involved with at different stages of the time period their heart rate was assessed. For example, if the heart rate is very high for an hour or two in the early morning or evening period, one can assume with a high degree of certainty that this is probably caused by the performance of a bout of exercise. In contrast, if heart rate is very low for an extended period of several hours in the evening time, one can guess that this would be associated with a time period when the participant was sleeping. Another very interesting study for me was one that examined the output of neurotransmitters (a chemical substance) when a varying change in firing rate was artificially induced in a neuron 'upstream' of the synapse where the neurotransmitter was released, and it was found that the release of neurotransmitter occurred in a discrete pulsatile manner that was directly correlated with the 'upstream' induced firing rate. This indicates that the 'fidelity' of the rate coded neural message was maintained even by chemical substances, and that regulatory information is not confined in complexity or content only to neuronal firing mechanisms but occurs also in blood borne / neurochemical substrates.

To ensure this 'rate coded' information be created and interpreted, some yet unidentified algorithmic processes in the brain needs to break it up into 'useable' bits or chunks of information of a certain length or period of time, and the interpreting algorithm needs to have a 'pause' in order to both make sense of this information and respond to it, before 'receiving' and responding to further information from the same source. If information arrived in a continuous stream that was not 'broken up' into 'bits' of information, no interpretative sense could be made of it, and no logical response based to the information encoded in it could be initiated. We have previously suggested that information must occur as, or be broken up by the brain into, 'quantal packets' of information, and each 'quantal packet' of information is used by the brain to make sense of what is required by whatever initiated the perturbation that led to the generation of the information flow, and how the brain needs to respond to the information. There is surely always alternating periods of 'certainty' and 'uncertainty' occurring related to the flow of information in the brain and body - certainty when a coherent quantal packet of information is received and 'understood', and uncertainty in the periods prior to the full required quantal packet of information being received, or during the period after the full quantal packet of information was received and a response to it enacted, during which time and after which further information from the original source will be required to assess whether the response was satisfactory and / or fulfilled the need that caused the original information to be generated. So, the passing of time is a fundamental requirement of information flow and the understanding of it, and there will always be alternating time periods of certainty and uncertainty related to the information flow. What length of period of time or quantity of information is required to create a period of certainty in any brain or body system is likely to be a product of the type of substance which creates the information (i.e.

shorter in nerve tissue and longer in humoral / blood substance), what purpose the information is created for, and the complexity of the issue the information is associated with.

Clearly from the above examples, a strong case can be made that information coding underpins the regulation of physical brain and body function. However, it is more difficult to understand how cognitive (mental) information we receive from the external world is 'managed', and if and how we 'break it up' into useable 'bits' of discrete information that can be made sense of by our algorithmic information processing functions of the brain. Most data would suggest that we do indeed break up information of social or environmental situations into at least categorical (for example need to respond / not respond) information. My esteemed colleague at the University of Worcester, Andy Renfree, has looked at decision making theory in relation to physical activity and shown that we make cognitive decisions on future levels of activity or plan for future activity based on either rational (taking all factors into account) or heuristic (using past experience to attenuate the complexity of decision making requirements) information and cognitive decision making, using differentiated information about one's own current physical capacity and performance level, environmental factors, and the capacity of other individuals one is competing against, amongst a number of other factors. Knowledge of all possible behavioural outcomes, and an assessment of the potential risks to oneself of all the potential outcomes, as well as their potential rewards, are surely also individually assessed as part of any action related decision-making process. However, cognitively, and consciously it never 'feels' that all such factors are so individually and discretely assessed, but rather that life occurs as a 'smooth', continuous activity, with no perceptual 'gaps' occurring when decisions are being made or when cognitive uncertainty must be occurring. This 'smooth' conscious perception of life with no 'gaps' in it may occur because we do not focus on a specific thought, activity or sensation for any extended period of time, and rather 'switch' our attention continuously between different issues we are 'working through'. Therefore, as a number of different thoughts related to different issues 'intrude' sequentially on our consciousness, this may 'fill the cognitive gaps' which would occur as a necessity when making cognitive decisions on any one specific issue or requirement, in the time periods of uncertainty before a cognitive 'decision' is made about any one 'issue' one is dealing with. It is obviously very difficult to research this area of cognitive information processing, given our lack of knowledge of core brain function, and the difficulty of being able to objectively assess one's continuous real-time thought processes with the current laboratory research techniques available to us, which are still very crude and retrospective / mostly qualitative in nature.

While life as we know it may thus appear to occur as a continuous flow of activity and events which we respond and react to, how we interpret these activities and events and regulate our responses to them may indeed occur in a discrete information-based numerical manner, replete with information 'gaps' and periods of uncertainty interspersed with 'quantal packets' of information rich certainty time periods, that each vary in length dependent on the complexity of the situation being assessed, the processes being used to assess it, and the physical substances in the brain and body used to assimilate and understand them. Information processing and decision making underpins all regulation of our brain and body functions and our successful interaction with the socially and environmentally challenging external world in which we exist. Our successful reaction to changes in either external environments or our internal physiological milieu depends on the successful generation of information describing these changes, the successful interpretation of this information, and the successful generation of actions in response to this information. At the neuronal level simple firing rate and rate coding underpins all information flow, and our physical responses are related to changes in this 'code' and the information encoded by these firing rate changes. To better understand the manner how this information processing occurs in more complex issues is a lifetime of work in the time ahead for us neuroscience and information science folk. But, perhaps us scientists use discrete numbers and data to makes sense of how things work, because at the level of brain and body regulation and control, information flow and discrete data generation and assessment are the conceptual requirements underpinning all successful life activity, and us scientist folk are merely copying the 'instruments and methods' of the master designer who created us in the way we have been created when we do such work, whatever that master designer is or was. Time will tell if this is true or not, but, pertaining to our domestic decision-making requirements relating to whether we should stay in our current environment or move to another – brain neurons, was that one click or two I heard when you fired as I was thinking on this issue a moment ago?

Essay 9. Cell function and metabolic flux control - The puzzle of regulation of massive numbers of continually occurring processes in a spatially challenged environment

Beyond even the complexity of controlling nerve firing rates, is the complexity of managing the activity in the individual cells of the body, which are thought to be 10 trillion in number, and all of which are required to act synergistically and with functional 'purpose' when a task is being performed. An individual cell is also tightly packed with enzymes and proteins which are designed to create energy for the cell, or to be part of a moving, dynamically flexible organ like a muscle, to have metabolic fuels continuously arriving in the cell at the correct concentration required for the current level of activity the human in their entirety is performing and must excrete by-products of energy generation at the same time. How this is all done in one space, and how the different processes occurring concurrently in each cell occur without compromising each other, is still not well known. In this Essay we will therefore examine control of cell function and metabolic flux, and what is known, and what is still to be discovered, about it.

In the early years of my medical training, many years ago, it was hugely exciting to learn the basic science of how the body functioned, before we learnt about the pathological processes affecting body function, and how to treat these. Two visual memories have always stuck in my mind from the lectures I attended back then. These were both of some brilliant diagrams drawn on the blackboard during these basic physiology and anatomy lectures by two charismatic teachers. The first was of the neural pathways flowing to and from the brain, and these complex but organized information directing structures were drawn with such clarity that they entranced me, to the extent that they perhaps in part led to me becoming an integrative neuroscience and system regulation researcher for much of my career. The second blackboard drawing I remember was of the metabolic pathways of a cell, which made me feel a sense of awe regarding the complexity and sheer volume of processes and structures present in a cell when I saw them for the first time as line drawings on the blackboard way back then. Being throughout my life more of a systems and processes, rather than a specifics and detail, type of thinker and person, these cell pathway pictures made me feel a touch 'queasy', no matter how beautiful they were drawn, and this 'queasiness' I felt then perhaps moved me 'away' from molecular or cellular biology as a career choice, because intuitively I knew even then I would never have the capacity, or interest, to learn each different enzyme or DNA or protein structure in the cell, and how each of these 'worked' to provide the basic energy needed to sustain life as we know it. A couple of days ago, Professor Craig Sale, one of the UK's foremost Physiology and Exercise Science researchers, and surely one of the nicest persons on the planet, posted a fascinating review article on Twitter examining basic cellular metabolism changes related to exercise to rest transitions, and reading about the associated changes in ATP, NADH, and CrP, amongst other cellular substrates and enzymes described in this review article, reminded me of those flow diagrams of my medical training days, and got me thinking about the basic function of the cell, and how the flux of all these basic cellular substrates is managed in the microscopic cellular environment.

The cell is the basic structural and functional unit of any organism, including us humans. One's entire body is made up of cells, and it is thought that each person consists of around 10 trillion cells (a number so vast I can't get my head around it). While the cells making up different structures in the body like skin, muscle, bone have some differences in their structure and function, the basic 'makeup' of all cells is almost identical, and fascinatingly from an evolutionary perspective works similarly across all species and indeed most living structures. Each cell is surrounded by a cell membrane and has many organelles in it that are important for its survival and optimal function, including a nucleus (where the cell's DNA is stored which is important for replication), mitochondria (the energy creating 'powerhouses' of the cell), and several storage and structure creating entities known as the Golgi apparatus and endoplasmic reticulum, amongst others. The cell membrane is important not just for structural integrity, but also for controlling the movement of substrates, fuels, metabolites and signalling molecules into the cell, using enzyme related receptor mechanisms. The cell's interior consists of a fluid substance known as cytoplasm, in which enzymes and cofactors either break down carbohydrates, fats and proteins into basic energy products (the basic energy molecule in the cell is adenosine triphosphate – ATP) in a process known as catabolism (this process also occurs at a rapid, energetically efficient process in the mitochondria), or builds up structural components required to repair damage in the cell, or to create a second cell when the cell replicates, in a process known as anabolism.

In either the cytoplasm of the cell, or the mitochondria, are the numerous metabolic 'pathways' which were so elegantly drawn for us in our student days, and as a 'cascade' through numerous sequential intermediary products in a process managed by sequential enzymes and co-enzymes, fuels such as carbohydrates and fats are catabolised into basic energy products such as ATP. For example, in the cytoplasm of the cell, the 'glycolytic' pathway occurs, while in the mitochondria the 'Krebs cycle' and 'citric acid cycle' are different catabolic pathways. Oxygen is a necessary requirement of the mitochondrial basic energy producing processes which are therefore defined as 'aerobic' pathways, while the cytoplasmic glycolytic processes do not require oxygen, and are defined as 'anaerobic' pathways. The anaerobic glycolytic pathways are not as efficient in producing basic energy as the aerobic pathways and produce metabolic by-products which need to be removed from the system, such as lactic acid. Because lactic acid builds up during high intensity exercise like sprints or other ballistic / maximal activity, it is thought that during high intensity exercise the cells become oxygen deprived or 'anaerobic', and the glycolytic pathways are used preferentially and as a final energy 'reserve', though whether cells are ever completely oxygen deprived and therefore rely on 'anaerobic' mechanisms to produce fuel during activities of daily living or during exercise is still controversial. There are an enormous number of different pathways in a cell, and seemingly each month, a new enzyme, co-factor, intermediate product, or metabolic by-product is discovered, which creates an even more complicated 'picture' of the working environment in each cell.

The regulation of these complex cellular activities and structures has focussed principally on metabolic flux and enzyme kinetic processes. Metabolic flux is defined as the rate of turnover of molecules through a specific metabolic pathway and describes the 'movement' of substrates or intermediary products 'through' a specific pathway. Metabolic flux is related to the 'need' of both the general body and specific cell environment for energy and is increased when there is greater need (for example when one exercises), or when there is greater substrate present (for example after a meal). One of the most amazing things in science is how each of the different 'steps' of each pathway increases sequentially and in a temporally co-ordinated way when increased need or increased substrate availability occurs, to ensure that the pathways work correctly and are not 'overwhelmed' whenever there is the need for increased activity in all its component parts. This coordinated increase in activity in an entire metabolic pathway is thought to be controlled by increased and optimized enzyme function at each step of the specific pathway's processes. Enzymes are protein molecules that can 'manipulate' and therefore control other molecules and substrates, and enzyme kinetics is defined as the study of the chemical reactions that are regulated by enzymes. When there are increased energy requirements, the function of the pathway's enzymes is up-regulated, in order to 'deal with' the increased demand. The function of an enzyme can be plotted (for those technically minded folks an example of this is the Michaelis-Menten function equation) as substrate concentration increases, and generally at the start of a period of increased 'need', enzyme activity at each different step of a metabolic pathway is rapidly increased to compensate for the increased requirement. After this initial rapid increase in enzyme activity, enzyme activity 'levels out' as the maximal activity capacity of the enzyme is reached. The enzyme kinetic / cell regulation researcher folk suggest that the rate limiting capacity of any pathway (and therefore the energy creating 'controller') is that of the enzyme with the 'lowest' functional capacity – in other words, the enzyme in a pathway that can least up-regulate its function in a time of increased energy demand or increased energy fuel supply, is the factor that controls the metabolic properties and activity of that particular cell. In this paradigm, therefore, the human body's physical functional capacity is related to these cellular-level rate limiting enzymes, together with the quantity of energy fuels available that can be used by the enzymes.

All this knowledge of basic cell structure and function, that is still increasing incrementally (perhaps even exponentially) as yet another cellular regulatory molecule, enzyme or membrane signalling / transduction regulatory protein is discovered, still fills me with as much awe today as it did nigh on 30 years ago when I first learnt about it as a first-year medical student. However, I do believe that a lot more research is needed in the field of cellular metabolic regulation for us to have a clearer understanding of its regulatory processes. Indeed, the wonderful 'pictures' drawn of the metabolic pathways may, in a paradoxical way given that they are so complex, be describing cellular regulatory mechanism in a too simplistic manner, and we perhaps have a long way to go still to fully understand regulatory control mechanisms at the cellular level. For example, hundreds, if not thousands, of different metabolic pathways are actively catabolizing substrate fuels, or synthesizing new structural molecules, at any one point in time. Likewise, thousands, if not millions of different individual molecules are being acted upon, or are acting upon other molecules, in any one cell at any single point in time. How the integrity and fidelity of each metabolic pathway is maintained in the face of all this co-existing 'other' metabolic activity has still not been determined. How each molecule 'knows' where it 'has to go', and where in the cell it will be acted upon, at a single point in time, let alone in the required temporally appropriate manner, is still pretty much unknown. Equally, how the function of individual cells is harmoniously regulated as a component of the gestalt millions and billions of cells in a specific organ, which all must be similarly up-regulated in time of need or increased substrate concentration, and then down-regulated at time of work-rest transition, is not understood at all. Whether different specific cells have different efficiencies and metabolic milieus compared to that of their neighbours, has also not been determined, and for us to have knowledge of this conundrum will need spectacular new laboratory techniques to be developed. How the afferent 'messages' from each cell become a gestalt 'message' to the brain which 'suggest' a requirement for an initiation of behavioural change, when for example fuel supplies are depleting, is also completely unknown, as is how each different cell receives similar efferent information to either increase anabolic or catabolic need as it is required. Furthermore, the relationship between the 'physical' control processes such as enzyme kinetic control process or metabolic flux determinants, and electrical / electromagnetic energy, is not clear. All active metabolic control mechanisms are underpinned by electrical activity changes, or at least electrical activity can be detected in cells whenever physical chemical changes occur in the cell. One of the most interesting research papers I have ever read described a study of NADPH activity in macrophage cells. When Interleukin-6, a humoral (blood / fluid related) signalling / regulatory molecule was added to the cells, the concentrations of NADPH increased. When an electrical current was supplied to the cells along with interleukin-6, the concentration of NADPH increased even more than when just the interleukin-6 was added. How this 'piezo-electric' electrical / chemical interaction works at the cellular level is still not clear, as is whether electrical, or electromagnetic activity, are subsidiary or integral components of cells and their metabolic regulation.

A beautiful picture or line drawing of a particular metabolic pathway of a cell gives us, therefore, a 'snapshot' of the processes involved in that specific pathway but does not give us the full picture of what must be 'dizzying' real life / real time activity occurring as a hugely complex, interactive, always changing, process and environment in any one cell, let alone in an aggregation of cells. How control processes occur in not just one cell but similarly in many cells is another problem of an order of magnitude greater than we can perhaps currently understand with our available research techniques and conceptual frameworks we use to understand such function, which usually involve breaking down such dynamic processes into its composite parts to allow easier explanation. By reducing the complexity such so we are to do so, we perhaps lose our capacity to understand the 'gestalt' control processes and mechanisms in the cell. A good scientist will always be humbled by the awareness of how much activity, and how much regulatory control, is required for even a single, 'simple' cell, which is the basic building block of all physical life processes and structures we know of and are made of. An integrative systems scientist like myself will always admire and respect the work done by the scientist folk who work at solving the 'detail' that exists in each cell and its individual component. But the big questions of cellular function and metabolic regulation are still surely ahead of us to be answered, and beautiful flow diagrams of cellular metabolic regulatory pathways, as those which will always be engraved in my mind from those seminal days of my academic youth were, will never be sufficient to allow understanding of the 'place' of the regulatory processes in the cell in the bigger picture of the regulation of life as we know it.

Perhaps using a three-dimensional high-tech video clip of real time cellular activity, some charismatic lecturer, way in the future, will be able to explain to some young medical students how it really does all work, when I have long been resting in my pine box, and my cells are of the earth and being used as energy for another generation of cells in another future scientist's body. Time will tell. But, for now, I will have to be satisfied with the memory of those beautifully drawn cellular pathways and keep trying to remember the names of each substrate, enzyme and intermediate metabolite associated with them. And if I could go back in time, I would tell those two great lecturers that their drawing skills and passion for their subject matter were still remembered 30 years down the line and inspired a career choice for me.

Essay 10. The core requirement and skill of decision-making in life - Removal of uncertainty is usually positive and cathartic but is also an ephemeral thing

---

When we make a movement or change our activity or behaviour, this is generally in response to some change in something in our surrounding environment, or internal body, that we respond to by changing our own activity, either to compensate for the external or internal changes, or to resist them. At the core of any altered activity is decision making. We usually have an array of response options we can choose from, and we choose what we think the best of these are. In this Essay, we look at factors involved in decision-making, and how our brain uses information and prior experience to come to decisions either quickly or after a long period of thought, dependent on the situation we find ourselves which requires a response.

This week, for the first time since moving to New Zealand and starting a new job here, I cycled in to work, and in the early afternoon faced a tough decision regarding whether I had the level of fitness capacity to cycle back home at the end of the day. Three-quarters of the way through the ride home, I felt very tired and stopped by the side of the road, and I considered phoning home and asking them to pick me up. This morning I opened the fridge and had to decide whether to have the routine fruit and yogurt breakfast or the leftover piece of sausage roll. We have been six months in our new life and job here, and we have come to that period of time of deciding whether we have made a good decision and to continue, or whether we have made a disastrous error and need to make a rapid change. As I write this my wife asks me if I planned to go to the shop later, and if so whether I could get some milk for the family, and I had to stop writing and decide on whether I was indeed going to do so as part of the weekend post-writing chores, or not. All these activities and issues required me to make decisions, and while some of them appeared to be of little consequence, some of them were potentially life and career changing, and, even if it seems a bit dramatic, potentially life-ending (whether to continue cycling when exhausted as a fifty-something). Decisions like these must be made by everyone on a minute-by-minute basis as part of their routine daily life. The importance of decision-making in our daily lives, and how we make decisions, is still controversial and not well understood, which is surprising, given how much our optimal living condition and indeed survival depends on making correct decisions, and how often we must make decisions, some of which are simple, some of which appear simple but are complex, and some of which are overtly complex.

Decision-making is defined as the cognitive process (which is the act or process of knowing or perceiving) resulting in the selection of a particular belief or course of action from several alternative possibilities, or as a problem-solving activity terminated by the genesis or arrival of a solution deemed to be satisfactory. At the heart of any decision-making is the requirement to choose between an array of different options, all of which usually have both positive and negative potential attributes and consequences, where one uses prior experience or a system of logical 'steps' to make the decision based on forecasting and scenario-setting for each possible alternative choice and consequence of choosing them. One of the best theoretical research articles on decision-making I have read / been involved with is one written by Dr Andy Renfree, an old colleague from the University of Worcester, and one of the Sport Science academic world's most creative thinkers. At a systems level, he suggested that decisions are made based on either rational or heuristic principles, the former working best in 'small world' environments (in which the individual making the decision has absolute knowledge of all decision-related alternatives, consequences, and probabilities), and the latter best in 'large world' environments (in which some relevant information is unknown or estimated). As described by Andy, rational decision-making is based on the principle that decisions can only be made if certain criteria are met, namely that the individuals making the decision must be faced with a set of behavioural alternatives and, importantly, information must be available for all possible alternatives of decisions that can be made, as well as of the statistical probability of all the outcomes of the choices that can be made. This is obviously a large amount of requisite information, and a substantial period of time would be required to make any decision based on such 'rational' requirements. While using this method would likely be the most beneficial from a correct outcome perspective, it would also potentially place a high demand on the cognitive processes of the individual making the decision. Bayesian decision-making is a branch of rational decision-making theory, and it suggests that decision-making is the result of unconscious probabilistic inferences. In Bayesian theory, a statistical approach to decision-making is made based on prior experience, with decision making being moderated (and therefore speeded up) by applying a 'bias' towards information that is used to make the decision which is believed to be more 'reliable' than other information, and 'probability' of outcomes being better or worse based on prior experience. Therefore, in the Bayesian model, prior experience 'speeds up' decision-making, though all information is still processed in this model.

In contrast, heuristic decision-making is a strategic method of making decisions, which ignores information that is available but is perceived to be less relevant to the specific decision being made, and which suggests that decisions are made based on key information and variables that are assessed and acted upon rapidly, in a manner that, as Andy suggests, incorporates 'rule of thumb' or 'gut feel' thinking, which places less demands on the cognitive thinking processes of the individual. As described above, rational decision-making may be more relevant in 'small world' environments, in which there are usually not a lot of variables or complexity which are required to be assessed prior to making a decision, and heuristic thinking in 'large world' environments, which are complex environments where all information, whether relevant or not, cannot be known, due to the presence not only of 'known unknowns' but also 'unknown unknowns', and where an individual would be potentially immobilized into a state of 'cognitive paralysis' if attempting to assess every option available. The problem of course is that even decisions that appear simple often have multiple layers of complexity that are not overt and of which the individual thinking about them is not aware, and it can be suggested that the concept of both rational and 'small world' environments are potentially abstract principles rather than reality, that all life occurs as part of 'large world' environments, and that heuristic processes are what are used by individuals as the main decision-making principles during all activities of daily living.

Of course, most folk would perceive that these rational and heuristic models are very computational and mathematical based, and that perhaps 'feelings' and 'desires' are also a component of decision-making, or at least these are how decision-making is perceived to 'feel' to them. As part of the Somatic Marker hypothesis, Antonio Damasio suggested that 'body-loop' associated emotional processes 'guide' (and have the potential to bias) decision-making behaviour. In his theory, somatic markers are a specific 'group of feelings' in the body and are associated with specific emotions one perceives when confronted with, and are related to, the facts or choices one is faced with and need to decide about. There is suggested to be a different somatic marker for anxiety, enjoyment, or disgust, among other emotions, based on an aggregation of body-related symptoms for each, such as heart rate changes and the associated feeling of a pounding chest, the sensation of breathing changes, changes in body temperature, increased sweat rate, or the symptom of nausea, some or all of which together are part of a certain somatic marker group which creates the 'feeling' of a particular emotion. Each of these physiologically-based body-loop 'states' are capable of being components of different somatic marker 'groups', which create the distinct 'feelings' that are associated with different emotions, and which would valence decisions differently depending on which somatic marker state / emotion is created by thinking of a specific option or choice. This hypothesis is based on earlier work by William James and colleagues more than a hundred years ago, which became the James-Lange theory of emotion, which suggests there is a 'body-loop' required for the 'feeling' of emotions in response to some external challenge, which is in turn required for decision-making processes related to the external challenge. The example used to explain this theory was that when one sees a snake, it creates a 'body loop' of raised heart rate, increased sweating, increased breath rate and the symptom of nausea, all of which in turn create the 'feeling' of fear once these 'body-loop' symptoms are perceived by the brain, and it was hypothesized that it is these body-generated feelings, rather than the sight of the snake itself, which induces both the feeling of fear and the decision to either rapidly run away, or freeze and hope the snake moves away. While this model is contentious as it would make reactions occur slower than if a direct cognitive decision-making loop occurred, it does explain the concept of a 'gut feel' when decision-making. Related to this 'body-loop' theory are other behavioural theories about decision-making, and it has been suggested that decisions are based on what the needs, preferences and values of an individual are, such as hunger, lust, thirst, fear, or moral viewpoint, but of course all of these could equally be described as components of either a rational or heuristic model, and psychological / emotional and cognitive / mathematical models of decision-making are surely not mutually exclusive conditions or theories.

These theories described above attempt to explain how and why we make decisions, but not what causes decisions to be right or wrong. Indeed, perhaps the most relevant issue to most folk is why they so often get decisions wrong. A simple reason may be that of 'decision fatigue', whereby the quality of decision-making deteriorates after a prolonged period of decision-making. In other words, one may simply 'run out' of the mental energy, which is required to make sound decisions, perhaps due to ongoing changes in 'somatic markers' / body symptoms each time a decision is required to be made, which creates an energy cost that eventually 'uses up' mental energy (whatever mental energy is) over the period of time sequential decisions are required to be made. Astonishingly, judges working in court have been shown to make less favourable decisions as a court session progresses, and the number of favourable decisions improves after the judges have had a break. Apart from these data suggesting that one should ask for a court appearance early in the morning or after a break, it also suggests that either physical or mental energy in these judges is finite, and 'runs out' with prolonged effort and the use of energy focusing on decision-making related to each case over the time period of a court session. There are other, more subtle, potential causes of poor decision-making. For example, confirmation bias occurs when folk selectively search for evidence that supports a certain decision that they 'want' to make, based on an inherent cognitive bias set in their mind by past events or upbringing, even if their 'gut' is telling them that it is the wrong decision. Cognitive inertia occurs when folk are unwilling to change their existing environment or thought patterns, even when new evidence or circumstances suggest they should. People tend to remember more recent information and use it preferentially, or forget older information, even if the older information is potentially more valid. Repetition bias is caused by folk making decisions based on what they have been told, if it has been told to them by the greatest number of different people, and 'groupthink' is when peer pressure to conform to an opinion or group action causes the individual to make decisions they would not do if they were alone and not in the group. An 'illusion of control' in decision-making occurs where folk display a tendency to under-estimate uncertainty because of a belief that they have more control over events that they have. While folk with anxiety tend to make either very conservative or paradoxically very rash decisions, sociopaths, who are thought to have little or no emotional 'body-loop', are very poor at making moral-based decisions or judgments. Therefore, there are a whole lot of different factors which can impact negatively on decision-making, either because one's upbringing or prior history impacting on the historical memory which is used to valence decisions, or because one's current emotional or psychological state having a negative impact on decision-making capacity, and even simple fatigue can be the root cause of poor decision-making.

At the heart of decision-making (excusing the pun, from the perspective of the somatic marker hypothesis), is a desire of most folk to remove uncertainty from their lives, or change their life or situation to a better state or place as a result of their decision, or to remove a stressor from their life that will continue unless they make a decision on how to resolve it, remove it, or remove themselves from whatever causes the stressor. However, during my days as a researcher at the University of Cape Town, we suggested that conditions of uncertainty and certainty associated with information processing and decision-making are cyclical (we called it the 'quantal packet' information processing theory, for those interested). A chosen decision will change a position or state of uncertainty to one of certainty as one enacts changes based on the decision (or if one chooses to 'wait and see' and not alter anything) from the context that one is certain a change will occur based on what one has decided to do, even if one cannot be sure if this difference will be positive or negative while the changes are being enacted. However, with the passing of time, the effects of the decision made will attenuate, and uncertainty will eventually re-occur, which require a further decision to be made, often with similar choices to which occurred when the initial decision was made. Underpinning this attenuation of the period of 'certainty' is the concept that although one will have factored in 'known unknowns' into any decision one makes using either rational or heuristic principles, 'unknown unknowns' will surely always occur that will cause even the best strategic decisions to require tactical adjustments, and those that are proven to be an error will need to be reviewed and changed. One can also 'over-think' decision-making as much as one can 'under-think' it, as well as being kept 'hostage' to cognitive biases from one's past which continuously 'trip one up' when making decisions, despite one's best intentions. Having said all of this, it often astonishes me not that folk get decisions wrong, but rather that they get so many decisions right. For example, when driving along a highway, one is reliant on the correct decisions of every driver that passes for one's survival, from how much they choose to turn their steering wheel, to how much they use their brake for a corner, to an awareness in each of them that they are not too tired to be driving in the first place. It's amazing when one thinks of how many decisions we make, either consciously or unconsciously, which so often turn out right, but equally it is the responsibility of each of us to work on the errors created by our past, or by our emotional state, or by 'groupthink', which we need to be vigilant about and remove as best possible from the psyche.

Making any decision is usually cathartic due to the removal of uncertainty and the associated anxiety which uncertainty often causes, even if the certainty and feeling of goodwill generated by making any decision is usually ephemeral and lasts only for a short period of time before other matters occupy one's attention that require further decision-making. Pondering on my decision-making of the last week retrospectively, I think I made the right decision when choosing to cycle home after work, and to do so all the way home, even if I was exhausted when I got there, given that I did not collapse or have a heart attack when doing so, and there will surely be long term health benefits from two long cycles (though of course long is relative at my age!) in one day. I did choose the healthy food alternative for breakfast this morning, even though often I don't, particularly during meals when I am tired after a long day's work. I will get the milk my wife asked me to get this afternoon, in order to both get some fresh air after a creative morning of thinking and writing, and to maintain the harmony in our house and life, even though it is raining hard and I would prefer to be writing more or reading a good book this afternoon. The 'jury is still out' about whether this move to New Zealand and a new work role has been a good career and country move, and my current decision on this is to let more time pass before making an action-generating reasoned decision on it, though of course we have already moved several times to new places round the world in the last two decades, and the family is looking forward to some lifestyle stability in the next few years, and these factors need to be part of any reflection on a current-environment rating decision. Each of these decisions seemed ostensibly relatively simple to make when I made them, yet each surely had an associated entire host of different reasons, experiences, memories, and requirements which were worked through in and by my mind before making them, as will be so for all folk making decisions on all aspects of their life during a routine day. What will I have for lunch now I am finished writing this and am now tired and in need of a break and sustenance? Perhaps I will leave off that decision and relax for a period of time before making lunch-related choices, so as not to make a fatigue-induced bad decision, and reach for that sausage roll, which still is in the fridge. And I need to get going and enact that decision I made to get the milk and head off to the shops in order to do so as soon as possible, before lethargy sets in and I change my mind, otherwise I will surely be in the 'dog house' at home later this afternoon, and my sense of cathartic peace resulting from having made these decisions will be even more ephemeral than usual!

Essay 11. Passion and desire - The wild horses demand freedom but cause chaos when their halter is let slip

Perhaps one of the most important types of decisions one faces in life is whether to react, or not react, to a stimulus, whether external or internal, which induces an emotional response in one, whether it be anger, or desire, or fear. Emotions are important for 'telling' oneself how some information one receives is 'felt', and clearly have an evolutionary role of indeed creating a response or an action to either welcome or become hostile towards the stimulus. Equally, we know that emotions are often 'treacherous' and can hijack one's state of mind and being and predispose one to perform acts which can cause offence or personal harm after the emotionally-driven actions are performed, such as losing friends or even being in trouble with the law for assault or suchlike excessive behaviour. In this Essay we examine emotions and emotional responses, and furthermore attempt to understand what triggers them and how they are generated.

'Travellers at least have a choice. Those who set sail know that things will not be the same as at home. Explorers are prepared. But of us, who travel along the blood vessels, who come to the cities of the interior by chance, there is no preparation. We who were fluent find life is a foreign language. Somewhere between fear and sex. Somewhere between the swamp and the mountains. Somewhere between God and the Devil passion is and the way there is sudden and the way back worse.' Thus did Jeanette Winterson, in her written masterpiece, The Passion, describe and define passion and desire. In my youth as a twenty-something, this book was given to me by a good friend, Wendy Sanderson Smith, after she thought it would synchronize with my own temperament and approach to life back then (as I guess most folk in their twenties 'lived' and 'loved' in their own halcyon early adult days), and indeed it did. I have noticed that a lot of folk post pictures on Facebook (including myself) of their late teenage / early adulthood days, and often these include friends or activities from University or College times. My brother, John, sent me a video clip of some young folk doing extreme sports such as skydiving, bungee jumping and aerial cycling tricks, which led to a fun discussion of whether we still had the passion and desire to do such activities (or are physically capable of doing them) as our fifties fast approach, or as quaintly suggested in the film the Big Lebowski, 'our revolution is over'. All these got me thinking of passion and desire, and what the teleological reason for their existence is, and whether losing our passions and desires as we get older, or at least refining, sublimating or managing them is a good or bad thing, or at least a necessary 'evil' allowing us to maintain the order and structure which is required to us to be successful in most facets of adult life.

Passion is defined as a very strong feeling about a person or a 'thing', and desire as a sense of longing for a person, object or outcome. Some research folks classify both passion and desire as emotions, which itself is defined as 'relatively brief' conscious experiences characterized by intense mental activity that results in a high degree of either pleasure or displeasure. But others perceive extreme passion and desire to be part of the spectrum of obsessive disorders, and to have a degree of psychopathology underlying them. Passion and desire have through history been contrasted with reason, which together engage in a constant 'battle' to control one. Mostly passion has been given a 'bad rap', with Plato suggesting that individual desires must be 'postponed' in the name of 'higher' rational ideals, Baruch Spinoza suggesting that 'the natural desires are a form of bondage', and Dave Hume suggesting that passions and desires are 'non-cognitive, automatic, bodily responses. To most religious doctrines, passion and desires are very much feelings and sensations to be resisted, unless that desire leads one towards 'God', when it can then become a mechanism for good and positive advancement of a 'higher' moral functioning and way of life, without the sinful desires of 'the flesh'.

However, passion and desire have also been suggested to be (unless extreme) an important component of human bonding and the establishment of a sexual relationship with a mate, without which there would be potentially no propagation of the human species. Sexual attraction is based on the capacity of someone to arouse the sexual interest of another, and the requirement of someone else to respond to that capacity. Folk can be sexually attracted to physical qualities in another, or how they move, their voice, smell or what they wear and how they interact (flirting is a mechanism of triggering arousal in another), or their social status, but it is generally always a two way 'thing', with both individuals needing to find the prospective partner sexually attractive to each other. There is a strong brain-body 'loop' and physical sensations associated with desire and the feeling of 'passion' generated by another, including trembling, pallor, flushing, heart palpitations, pupil dilatation and general feelings of 'weakness'. Folk in the throes of passion also describe 'feelings' and symptoms such as awkwardness, stuttering, shyness, confusion, and even insomnia and loss of appetite. Current research is working on trying to understand the mechanisms related to the development of these 'symptoms', and it is thought that perhaps acute hormonal (cortisol and pheromones for example) changes or components of the hypothalamic-pituitary-adrenal gland axis are involved in linking psychological 'desire' to physical body structures and physiological systems which generate these symptoms. Interestingly, a relationship between sexual attraction / desire and anxiety has been suggested, and when folk are more anxious, or are put in situations where they have heightened anxiety (for example generated by physical danger) they appear to experience increased sensations of desire and passion.

While as described above there are teleological (purposively beneficial) reasons why desire and passion exist, passions and desires can become pathological, particularly when they are unidirectional or unrequited. Limerence (also known as infatuated love) is the state of mind which results from an attraction to someone else in which there are obsessive thoughts and fantasies about that person and strong / overpowering desire to have one's passion / love reciprocated. Obsessive love is defined as an obsessive desire to 'possess' another person towards whom a strong desire is felt, together with an inability to accept rejection of their desire by the person towards whom it is felt. Limerence involves intrusive and often intolerable / painful 'thoughts' of the person who is the 'limerent' (person towards whom the 'crush' is directed), an acute longing for reciprocation and fear of rejection, and periods of fantasizing about ideal circumstances where there is cohabitation with the limerent in an intimate way (sexual fantasy is a usual but not an absolute requirement of the limerence state). Interestingly, in this obsessive state there is always a 'balance' between hope and uncertainty, or indeed a requirement for both, and the uncertainty component results in constant analysis by the individual suffering from limerence levels of desire or passion, with every utterance or perceived body language of the limerent being pondered about endlessly and analysed for meaning. Folk can remain in this limerence state for a prolonged period of time if their desires and passion are not requited, but if the limerent returns their affections, a 'normal' relationship can develop. If there is absolute rejection by the limerent, after a period of time the desires eventually become attenuated and the individual 'moves on' to another potential limerent and 'transfers' their extreme passions and obsessive desires to this next unfortunate soul. It is thought that early childhood trauma or a failure of childhood attachment bonding to their primary carer may be associated with this extreme level of passion or desire in folk with obsessive levels of passion and desire, though this theory is still controversial and not completely accepted by research folk in the field.

As one gets older, several changes occur which attenuate the extreme passions that are associated with youth, and in most folk, they are either assuaged by involvement in a healthy / mature relationship with the person one is attracted to (had a crush on), or one's passions are sublimated into other 'pursuits'. These can be work related, or a hobby, or sporting endeavours. This 'sublimation' can be healthy and lead to a sense of satisfaction and success in a chosen career or hobby or sport if there is genuine enjoyment of whatever is being done that one is passionate about, and in a circular way if one is successful in the field one chooses to focus the attenuated drive in, it can potentially bring about an attenuation of the sublimated drive itself. However, if one does not enjoy work, or a hobby, but continues to do it obsessively and as a compulsion, as what happens in the case of attraction limerence, this can lead to workload related stress, burnout and a sense of dissatisfaction / psychological 'pressure' that is not assuaged no matter how hard one works. Perhaps, therefore, many folks who work extremely hard, or are involved in hobbies or sports in an extreme manner in their middle or old age, may have sublimated drives related to unrequited passions and desires in their young adulthood (though the causation of this is very complex and several factors may be involved). Equally, some folk may never adequately sublimate their limerence related desires, passions, and obsessions, and engage for most or all of their lives in unrequited, or requited but unfulfilling, obsessional relationships in a serial manner. It must be noted that while most folk at some stage of their youth develop a 'crush' on someone or at least feel a sense of passion or desire for someone they meet or interact with, not all folk feel extreme desires, passions or limerences for other folk at any stage of their lives, and rather choose a mate and settle into life routines using cognitive / rational decision-based processes, without feeling any substantial passion. Whether these folk perhaps have an abstract notion of romantic 'love' they 'feel' for their chosen partner, or genuinely feel no passion or emotional bond with their partner, and merely co-exist without any overt or covert show or feelings of passion and desire, is still not clear / well determined – though they clearly would need to choose a partner who is satisfied by such a 'passionless' but functional arrangement if it has a chance to be a success and a long-lasting relationship.

A 'crush' on someone, which occurs usually in early adulthood, has intense feelings, desires and passions associated with it. If the crush is requited it often creates long lasting memories that are usually positive and can be very intense. In one's young adulthood there are fewer responsibilities and therefore more 'freedom' to explore and entertain such crushes, though of course if you are unfortunate enough to be on the receiving end of an unwelcome and unwanted crush or limerence it is surely not a pleasant experience, whether in early adulthood or at a later life stage. Passions and desires when they are not obsessive serve an important purpose from a mating and reproduction perspective.

But passions and desires when they are unrequited, or when they are obsessive and / or cyclical, can be problematical, both at the time of their occurrence and long after in middle and late adulthood, and can cause future negative memories which are both intense and can potentially affect future dating strategy and relationship interactions. As most folk get older, and establish a successful relationship and have children, and become creators of life's boundaries and infrastructure in which the next generation of young folk can 'play' and consummate their 'passions' as they please, the passions and ardour of youth seem to wane, or at least are more controlled – perhaps with the development of successful adult relationships any 'rough edges' remaining from one's bonding and attachment period of childhood are removed and smoothed. However, it's not clear if passion is still 'felt', in a wistful way, by most folk as they age. The success of films and books (such as Jeannette Winterson's beautifully written books) dealing with unrequited love and lust, or of obsessive desire turned pathological (most folk of my generation will surely still get a 'queasy' feeling when remembering the 'bunny boiler' film Fatal Attraction, where the character portrayed by Glenn Close developed an almost fatal limerence / obsessive compulsion for that of Michael Douglas' character) would indicate that issues related to desires, passions and 'crushes', whether they are unrequited or have a 'happy ending' as happens in most films and books, are still at play / being processed in the psyche of most folk as they go about their daily routines and business.

My wise cousin, Andy Shave, often reflected in our youth on whether love or lust was more important in and for a successful relationship. The answer probably lies in the taming of the wild horses of passion, and the keeping of lust on a tight rein. But in the deep of the night, most folk still probably 'dream' of or at least remember wistfully the passions and high emotions and crushes of their youth, when late at night they sighed and gasped at the thought of their still unrequited love / lust object, and sang along to the Chris Isaak song, 'what a wicked game to play, to make me feel this way, what a wicked thing to do, to let me dream of you'. But at some point in life, these passions need to become and remain as dreams and memories, and one has to forego the passion and lusts of youth in order for those horses of passion to become one's servants, rather than one's chaotic master, even if this is supremely challenging for those who have lived a lot of their lives travelling along the blood vessels of the city of the interior, somewhere between the swamp and the mountains, between fear and sex, between God and the Devil.

Essay 12. The Stanford marshmallow test - Civilization and its discontents

Perhaps an even more challenging situation for a person to contend with than controlling one's emotions, is when their emotions are controlled or stifled by external forces, and they cannot release their 'inner child' in moments of anger, lust, or frustration. In many ways, society does this to humans, in that it creates an environment where folk are expected to not show extreme emotions and are embarrassed when they do in front of others. This constant inhibition can lead to health or psychological negative consequences but being able to control one's emotions in public and societal hallmark is regarded as a necessary requirement to being successful as a valued component of a particular society, for remaining part of teams, or assuming leadership roles managing others. In this Essay we examine one of the most cited and most controversial tests of emotional control, the Stanford marshmallow test, in order to assess whether emotional control does indeed lead to greater societal success, or whether it has a more negative effect on the human psyche.

A great discussion this week during a training session on conflict management and optimising communication by Professor Johan Le Roux, as part of a leadership course for our School of Medicine's Heads of Departments we initiated when I began my current job, got me thinking of Sigmund Freud's ground-breaking book 'Civilization and its Discontents' which I read in my late thirties, and which made a significant impression on me. As a way of making the team think of the need to understand that one's own impulses and needs play their part of any conflict an individual is involved with, Johan described the Stanford Marshmallow experiment to the team. In this study, children under the age of ten were offered a choice of either one reward which could be eaten immediately – a marshmallow (or in some experiments a cookie or a pretzel) – or double the reward – two marshmallows -- if they waited for a period of time (15 minutes) before eating them, during which time the scientist left the children alone and they were filmed. The resulting video was fascinating (and both funny and sweet) to watch, as some of the children who did not immediately eat the single marshmallow tried several tactics to try and last the full 15 minutes, such as putting their hands over their eyes, walking around, and picking up and putting down the marshmallow in a continuous manner. Approximately two thirds of the children ate the single marshmallow immediately or could not last the full 15 minutes, and one third managed to maintain their self-control through the full 15 minutes and received their double reward. The interesting scientific part of the experiment was that the scientists then followed up the children's development and life outcomes over the next few decades and found that those who waited the full fifteen minutes tended to have better exam scores, educational levels, body mass index values and other life measures indicative of 'success'. The study was therefore about the effect of delayed gratification of needs, and the effect on future life success, and there was indeed a correlation between these two parameters.

The one measure that is not well discussed in the literature resulting from the experiment is the children's level of happiness during their lifetime, as compared to the more formal indices of success used and most often described as outcomes of the Stanford Marshmallow test, and it was trying to find these data after Johan's excellent leadership session that got me thinking of Freud's book, in which he examined what he described as the fundamental tension between civilization and the individual. In Freud's viewpoint, an individual at a deep level has an always present desire for instinctive freedom and satisfaction / gratification of their basic needs, and when the individual lives for a prolonged period where their basic needs are met, this would create a feeling of contentment in the individual, which Freud described as the 'pleasure principle'. While there are several basic needs (food, shelter, security for example), to Freud the basic needs were the desire for sex, and the predisposition to violent aggression towards authority figures and sexual competitors, both of which could obstruct or deny the capacity of the individual to gratify their personal sexual needs. Obviously, these basic instincts and desires of an individual described by Freud, if acted out, would be harmful to the well-being of the community in which individual lives, and therefore civilization creates laws that prohibit killing, rape and adultery, for example, and punishes individuals severely for these acts in order to maintain the integrity of the community. Therefore, according to Freud, these laws would restrict the 'pleasure' that would result from satisfying these basic desires, and so he suggested that it is an inherent quality of living in a civilized environment that it creates a feeling of discontent in its citizens. Freud further suggested that such basic drives and the desire for instantaneous gratification of all needs is evident in young children, and during their development these basic needs are over time suppressed by their parents and teachers according to societal expectations. With time, as children develop into adults, they develop consciences, which both regulates their activities and suppresses their basic drives as per the norm of the society in which they live. However, the 'price' of this suppression of desires as part of conscience development are the feeling of remorse developing in response to transgressions of the developed conscience and 'absorbed' societally condoned rules, and the feeling of guilt developing in response to wishful thinking about the basic need's individuals have which are counter to that of society's rules and expectations. In some people these feelings of remorse or guilt become perpetual and damaging and lead to the development of a neurosis.

Of course some folk would say that there is clearly a feeling of contentment that comes from living in a well-regulated society, but most folk if honest would also say that at some point in time in the privacy of their own reflective thoughts they have been aware of this paradox which underpins our daily life, and that at times that they felt a strong desire for some need gratification that they have had to exercise self-control to overcome. As part of my brain related research talks that I give, I often ask the audience if we scientists developed a device which could monitor their internal thoughts continuously and clearly (I remain hopeful from an academic perspective that this will indeed happen), would anyone volunteer for the study where we could record every single thought they have. To date I have not had one volunteer / person who says they would be happy to be involved in such a trial, which is telling related to these concepts of 'basic drives' that folk are embarrassed and guilty about, even if they are part of everyone's personae and mind. There is also the issue of what occurs in civilizations which have rules, or which acts in a way that is damaging rather than protective of individuals that live in them. There are several well documented historical and current examples, where cruel and barbarous acts are committed by states and individuals in positions of authority, or indeed in the mass actions of one community towards other communities in the name of protecting their own community, or against people in their own community who are regarded as 'outsiders'. As William James, another pioneering psychologist pointed out, when commenting on a spate of lynching's which occurred in the community in which he lived, a problem exists when the capacity for 'murderous excitement' in a group of individuals becomes collective, and murder is regarded as punitive or a protective societal duty. It then would paradoxically provide the greatest danger to, rather than future protection of and for, its own community. He used examples from this period of life (the late 1800s / early 1900s) such as 'hereditary vendettas', the custom of duelling, and religious massacres, as being examples of personal homicidal customs, which had become societal and when they are such are very difficult to attenuate or exterminate from the particular society which endorses these hostile acts. In a paradoxical way, these examples would allow an individual to satisfy their own basic desires in a way that is endorsed by a state and create both a personal and societal pleasure principle environment, and it needs brave individuals and other societies or states to involve themselves in changing these types of hostile environments to one that is more / again civilized, given the primal nature and ethos of such aggressive societies and state. History is full of stories and honours those that have sacrificed themselves while acting against aggressive states in the past, though of course history is mostly written by those that 'win' conflicts and thus often underplay their own contribution to the societal or national violence they became involved with.

So how does knowledge of the marshmallow test result, and the philosophies and principles described by psychologists like Sigmund Freud and William James (amongst many others), help us in developing leadership skills, conflict management capacity and indeed enhance one's everyday life. For me I guess it is about being aware of the constant 'conflict' in oneself between the desire for instantaneous gratification of one's needs and the desire to be an accepted member of society / the need to feel protected and safe from the gratification of others' impulses which could be associated with a negative impact on one's own life. Each day we live we are faced by many decisions and choices that this conflict lies at the root of, and each day we probably 'win' some and 'lose' some of these decisions and choices. Of course, making the 'right' decision is in the best post-modern sense dependent on everyone's own personal valence of their need for self-gratification of their urges against that of the need to be a respected member of society. Therefore, perhaps the level of 'happiness' of each person relative to each of these decisions is related to how much they value either of these 'sides' of the eternal conflict between passion and reason which resides in all of us. Each day we face decisions similar to that of the children and the marshmallow test, no matter what our age, and these decisions are made more complex by the current status of the community in which we live and the rules it has that are there to guide us, but which can paradoxically be primeval rather than protective of those that live in or around them. So is it one marshmallow now or two later – the choice is ours to make every day, in every situation we face where we interact with others as part of a community or society, and our level of happiness or discontent related to those choices is surely relative, but surely also important both to ourselves and those around us. Two marshmallows for me, please. Or did I mean one but say two?

Essay 13. The Milgram electric shock experiments - Is evil innate, learnt, or created by group dynamic behaviour?

One of the most concerning facts regarding human existence is the ability of us to be evil, and to do harm to our fellow humans. Of course, humans are part of the animal world, and animals still kill each other for food, while we have sanitised this requirement and animal deaths for our own sustenance happens away from our eyes in abattoirs. But in the history of humankind there has also been mass killings for ideological rather than hunger-based reasons, with obvious examples such as the holocaust in World War Two that is troubling to all of us from the concept of how it could happen. In this Essay we look at the origin of evil, whether it is a purely psychopathic phenomenon, or whether it can be a learned behaviour or developed 'group' mentality and do so by assessing the famous Milgram shock experiments, which assessed whether ordinary folk could be induced to perform evil acts upon their peers.

Perhaps one of the most horrific things I have seen to date in my life are the pictures which circulated recently of a captured pilot in a cage being burned to death in the cage by his captors, while his death was filmed by them and then displayed on public internet viewing sites. I read in the newspapers this week of a teenage boy who died after a long period in hospital after being attacked and beaten by a group of older boys on his way home from school. I read also that a film came out in the cinemas recently about a sniper who was famous for killing several hundred individuals in the ideological group that his country opposed. My emotional response to these images was to hope and pray that similar fates to those described above never came the way of my loved ones and children, and that they manage, like I have to date, to stay out of harm's way or such situations as these horrendous ones described above. My academic response was to wonder what were the underlying causes of such evil acts, and I spent a bit of time this week reading up again on the famous Milgram electric shock experiments, which potentially shed some light on how individuals that live on the same planet as I do, breathe the same air that I do, and see the same sun each day that I do, can have done such things to other individuals probably at the same time as I walked my dogs, spent quality time with my family, and worried about how I was going to solve the latest management issues that need attention at work.

The Milgram electric shock experiments were performed in the 1960s at Yale University by Professor Stanley Milgram. His graduate dissertation work examined conformity in decision-making. Being affected by the violent events of World War Two which still resonated in his (and others') minds at that point in time (and still do), he extended his dissertation work to examine whether evil acts such as torture, murder, and genocide could be related to conformity / obedience to the system that ordered it, or whether it was related to psychopathic tendencies in those that performed them. In his experiments he asked volunteers to give electric shocks of increasing intensity to people sitting in an adjacent room who were trying to learn a task but were making errors in the task, in order to punish them each time they made an error and in this way attempt to enhance their task performance. Of course, the people who were being shocked were actors, and they did not receive shocks, but they did scream each time they were 'shocked' and begged for mercy / not to be shocked, and these screams could be audibly heard by the volunteers who were giving the shocks to the 'actors' under instruction of the laboratory scientists.

The astonishing finding of Milgram's study was that nearly two-thirds of the volunteers did not refuse to give the shocks when hearing the screams of the 'actors', and did not stop participating in the experiment, but continued increasing the voltage on the demand of the laboratory scientists until they had reached what they were told was the maximum voltage output of the shock-giving device. Milgram expected that the maximal number of subjects that would do this if psychopathy was the cause (i.e. individuals with a personality disorder that predisposed them to perform evil acts without any empathy or conscience for the victims), to be around / a maximum of 10 percent of the volunteers as per the putative societal prevalence of psychopathy. The much greater number of volunteers whom he found were happy to continue shocking the actors suggested that 'normal' folk could do something evil like this if they were told to do so and in an environment where they thought they were doing the right thing – in this case presumably given that they were part of a scientific experiment and were told to perform the shocks by the scientists in control of the study, they may have felt it to be 'right' to do so. The study was repeated with the 'actors' in the same room, and again with the volunteers required to actively hold down the 'actors' hands on the shock device, and while the number of volunteers who continued the experiments was reduced in these follow-up trials, still approximately 30 percent of the volunteers continued giving the shocks to maximum levels despite the 'actors' screaming in pain and begging them to stop. Despite several concerns being raised about the study since it was published all those years ago, mostly regarding the conclusions Milgram reached about his findings, it has been repeated several times over the decades since and had the same outcome described for it wherever it has been performed. Milgram concluded that the capacity for evil was innate in all people, and that similar evil actions which caused such anger during World War Two could be performed in a created environment where people were instructed to perform evil acts by any individual from any American town. Sadly, for Stanley Milgram, apparently this conclusion was too controversial to be accepted by his university and the broader American community, and he was denied tenure by Yale, and had to move on to complete what was a successful career at another university, despite producing one of the most robust study findings ever.

So, what does this fascinating study tell us about the terrible acts of evil that I used as examples above? Perhaps there is a higher than the mean incidence of psychopaths in those people who become snipers, or who prey as a group on weaker individuals, or who burn someone to death in a public forum. More likely from Milgram's findings is that the people involved in performing such evil acts believe they are doing 'right' due to the idea, as Milgram suggested, that they are being obedient to the group they belong to, and perceive they are doing 'right' due to an affirmatory belief generated by being part of the group itself. This latter hypothesis is troubling in itself, but does allow one also to believe that if the group dynamics of those committing evil acts are altered, or can be externally influenced to change, there is a hope that such evil behaviour can be attenuated. An example is that of war and killing – during war it is perceived to be 'acceptable' that soldiers kill while performing their duties, and they are protected if doing so by international law. Fortunately, most soldiers when they return to their non-war home environments understand that to continue killing would not be societally or legally acceptable, and most soldiers returning to their non-combat environments change their 'killing paradigm' accordingly. The problem of course is how to change those whose living environment is continuously abnormal, and those who are so brutalized by their environments that such a change to a 'good' rather than evil state cannot occur.

What is not often discussed, associated with the Milgram study, is of course that one-third of the volunteers who participated in the experiment chose to stop giving the shocks, despite the encouragement of the scientists to continue doing so, and understanding that they were part of a bona fide experiment and therefore 'evil' actions were 'acceptable' because these acts were part of the experimental conditions. There is hope for us, therefore, that a reasonable percentage of folk, when confronted by situations where they must make choices, even when in a group environment where the pressure to conform and be obedient to the 'rules' of the group is high, will choose to negate the pressure to perform evil acts, and maintain their moral courage. The lesson to all of us from the Milgram experiments, therefore, is to perhaps be aware that group dynamics may cause us to perform acts of evil and condone them in our minds as being acceptable, given that they are 'group' practice and therefore can or should be done. Each day, while most of us are not confronted with such terrible situations as where folks are burned alive or beaten to death, we come face to face with actions, whether in the workplace or social environments, where such evidence of 'group evil behaviour' occur, such as when fun is made of people that look or talk differently, or when an individual holds a different viewpoint to that of the group one works in or socializes with, amongst numerous other examples. In our own way, we have the choice to submit to and join in the group's evil behaviour, or maintain our own moral courage, and the danger, of course, is that each time one does not maintain one's moral courage, and joins the group's behaviour, eventually there is the potential that an environment will be created where we will consider it acceptable to burn someone alive, and to film it while it is being done. Therefore, we need to be individually aware of the danger of group behaviour, and be brave, always, and understand bravery is not just about saying yes in difficult situations, but often is also about saying no, and turning away from those around one. As much as we want to all be an accepted member of a 'group', at times we need to be an 'outsider' to the group if the group one is attached to chooses to perform acts which are evil, even if it means being ostracized for one's standpoint, for the greater good. Society ultimately perhaps depends on enough folk doing so, though of course the percentages of folk happy to shock other people in Milgram's famous experiments will always be deeply concerning, and make me worry each night whether my loved ones will stay safe as they 'walk through the valley of the shadow of death' / go along their own life's journey, which has the potential to be either enjoyable or terrible, depending on which group one associates with, or bumps into on a random day when walking home from school, or when one's plane crashes in the wrong place.

Essay 14. Courage under fire - Both physical and moral courage are complex phenomena

In order to resist evil, and to be in control of one's emotions when they are often 'bursting out' telling you to run or that danger is ahead, courage is required, and is perhaps the most lauded of all the human 'emotions' or characteristics. While difficult to pin down with an exact definition, everyone remembers the first time they showed courage, when standing up to a school bully, or helping a friend in physical danger, ore rescuing a pet from a fire. Equally, everyone remembers with embarrassment and guilt when they succumbed to their fears and did not 'stand up and be counted' and show courage in situations when it was needed. In this Essay we examine the different forms of courage, notably physical and moral courage, and attempt to understand the mechanisms which create 'courage'. We further examine occasions when courage may be misplaced, with negative consequences both to the courageous individual and those around them from purportedly courageous acts.

The week past at work was a challenging one, with a number of different issues to deal with that were and are complex, and perhaps more political and moral than medical, and all which needed, or do need, some moral courage to resolve. I have also been reading the autobiography of American president and most famous civil war general, Ulysses S. Grant (Personal Memoirs), and watched a video called American Sniper, about the USA's most successful sniper, who showed great physical bravery, albeit in a morally challenging environment. The advertising for the video suggested that it would be a great Father's Day gift, but while being thought-provoking, I was left feeling distinctly 'queasy' after watching it, for a number of moral / ethical reasons (which the film subtly attempted to address). All three 'events' this week got me thinking about courage, how it is defined and what it really is. The dictionary definition of courage is the ability to disregard fear. Clearly, courage is related to fear, or at least resisting the life-preserving emotion which the sensation of fear essentially is. Courage is also defined as the choice and willingness to confront agony, pain, danger uncertainty and / or intimidation, and not 'back away' from any of these challenges. There are also perhaps different types of courage, with two broad categories being physical courage, which is defined as courage in the face of physical pain, hardship, death or threat, and moral courage being defined as the ability to act 'rightly' in the face of popular opposition or the potential for shame, scandal or discouragement to be the consequence of enacting one's moral standpoint. But many acts of heroism and many human actions which have been defined as being courageous may be rooted in behaviour that is self-serving, or may occur in individuals who do not 'feel' fear to the degree that most folk do. In these cases, the concept of courage becomes more complex, and may be underpinned by human impulses not as noble as they would be if 'pure' courage was the ultimate source of the actions.

To understand courage, one also must understand and acknowledge the existence of fear. Fear is defined as an emotion induced by a threat perceived to be a risk to life, status, power, security, wealth or anything perceived to be valuable to the individual who becomes aware of the threat, which causes changes in brain and organ function, and ultimately behavioural changes, such as freezing, hiding, running away from, or confronting, the source of the fear in order to attenuate it by removing the threat. There are physical symptoms of fear, including increased breath rate, heart rate, increased muscle tension, 'goose bumps' and raised hair follicles, sweating, increased blood glucose, sleep disturbances and dyspepsia (nausea and 'butterflies in one's stomach'). All of these changes serve purposive functions, and result from primitive protective functions known as the 'fight or flight response', which make the individual 'ready' to either flee or fight the danger which causes the development of these symptoms, with the sensation of all of these changes as a collective becoming the 'feeling' of the emotion we call fear. Fear is an important life-preserving complex emotion, without which both humans and animals would not last long in either wild or modern environments. It's important to note that not all people 'feel' fear, for example sociopaths and psychopaths do not – while in some folk fear is felt to extreme levels, where it is defined as a phobia. A 2005 Gallup poll of adolescents in the USA between the ages of 13 and 17 suggested that the top 10 fears of the folk interviewed were, in order, terrorist attacks, spiders, death, being a failure, war, criminal or gang violence, being alone, the future, and nuclear war. A further analysis of top ten online searches with the phrase 'fear of...' by Bill Tancer in 2008 described fear of flying, heights, clowns, intimacy, death, rejection, people, snakes, failure, and driving as being the most searched for. It is clear from these that folk have a fear of a wide variety of 'thing's, some personal, some social, some physical and some psychological.

As described above, the ability to 'stand up to' one's own personal fears, whatever these are, is described as courage. Courage appears to be a 'learnt' behavioural trait, with most folk remembering with clarity the first occasion they showed physical courage / stood up to the local bully that was tormenting them and understood what it meant by doing so. For example, in his excellent book on Courage, the previous Prime Minister of the UK, Gordon Brown, could pinpoint / remembered the age / date / time of the situation that required him to be courageous and which made him aware of it as a concept. In the classic book on courage written by Lord Charles Moran (also well known for being Winston Churchill's personal physician during World War Two), titled The Anatomy of Courage, four 'orders' of people were described based on how they showed physical courage, or the lack of, according to his observations of soldiers under fire in World War One. These were, firstly, people who did not feel fear (today these would be called sociopaths/psychopaths); secondly, people who felt fear but did not show it; thirdly, people who felt fear and showed it but did their job; and fourthly, people who felt fear, showed fear, and shirked their responsibilities. He perceived that level of fatigue or length of exposure to situations which induced fear (such as constant shelling during World War One) could 'wear out' any person and could lead to any person changing who were in one of the first three categories to eventually 'fall into' the fourth. He suggested that imaginative / intelligent (sic) folk felt fear more than unimaginative 'bovine' individuals (one could add sociopaths to this latter group, though he did not discuss them), and that it was more challenging for 'imaginative' folk to show courage because of this, and perhaps more exemplary when they did. Finally, he felt courage was all 'in the head', and that moral courage was one step 'higher' than physical courage and needed even greater 'levels' of whatever it was that created courage in someone to occur, and that 'few men had the stuff of leadership (moral courage) in them, they were like rafts to which all the rest of humanity clung for support and for hope'.

Moral courage is usually understood and enacted later in life, often when one is in a leadership position for the first time. For Ulysses S. Grant, it was in 1861, when being confronted by a rival 'rebel' force led by a General whom he knew. Grant felt terrified that if he ordered an attack, it could potentially fail, and he would be both blamed for and responsible for it. He perceived that, as had been the case in his military career to that point in time, if he was one or any rank lower than the General in command, he would have no hesitation on acting on the orders given, but that it was very different when all the responsibility for success or failure rested on him, and for the first time he felt 'moral fear'. In a life changing moment for him, and perhaps the history of the USA, when he finally ordered the attack, his troops found that the rebel General and his troops had deserted their camp and retreated, and Grant realized that his opposite number was as fearful as he was and had acted on this fear before Grant had. In Grant's words, 'From that point on to the close of the war, I never experienced trepidation upon confronting an enemy, though I always felt more or less anxiety. I never forgot that he had as much reason to fear my forces as I had his. The lesson was valuable.' While some historians have pointed out that Grant may have taken this lesson too much to heart, and that he should have respected his enemies' capacities more in later engagements, a lack of which perhaps resulted in high levels of bloodletting in all the future battles Grant led, ultimately it was his moral courage that led to the war being won for the United States Union armies.

It must be noted that to take a stance or way of leading that demands moral courage requires a belief that there are virtues higher than 'natural' ones that needs to be protected, as the philosopher Hobbes pointed out. In the example of Grant, he was fortunate to win the war and be famous because of it, and in his case he was on the side of 'good', from the context that the American civil war, while starting out ostensibly as a conflict about states staying in or withdrawing from the Union, was really about slavery and its abolishment in the rebel states, and there are few folk that would not agree that the Union cause, and therefore that of Grant's, had the moral high ground in the conflict. There are other examples, such as religious or national wars, where the issue of moral courage was more 'cloudy', as when folk take a stand, maintain a conflict or start a war against other folk due to some religious or national belief or doctrine, which could be defined as morally courageous (and indeed physically too) from that person's or nation's perspective, but would be defined by other folk as being that of a zealot or being misguided courage as best. There are also innumerable folk in history who took a morally courageous standpoint and ended up on the 'losing' side or died for their standpoints, or whose morally courageous standpoint was in the context of a greater morally corrupt environment, and for which they received no reward or respect for doing so. An example of this would be the Japanese Kamikaze pilots during World War Two, who sacrificed their own lives by crashing their planes into Allied ships to save the Japanese empire. These folks must have been hugely brave, and believe their stance was morally correct (Japanese dogma during the war was that it was the Allies, rather than Japan, that were the aggressors). But most folk would now say, and said then, that the cause they were dying for was morally bereft. So, for folk like these Kamikaze pilots, doing what was for them both a physically and morally courageous thing had no 'upside' in the long term. While this example is an extreme one, it perhaps does help explain why it is often so difficult to be morally brave in times where those against whom one takes a morally courageous standpoint are much stronger than the individual taking the morally courageous stand, or when the moral standpoint is perceived to be one which other folk believe is actually an immoral one, or later will declare it to be so, either for genuine or political reasons (and history is always written by the winners of any conflict or debate).

So how does this all help with the decisions on a daily basis that one has to make, and surely most folk do, that are complex, have many issues, and require moral courage to take a particular viewpoint or decide to enact a particular change that will not go down well with most folk one works with or interacts with, even if it is perceived by oneself as being the morally correct one. Firstly, one needs to think very carefully about the issue that is requiring a decision or action, to be sure that one is making a difficult decision with the highest level of certainty in the correctness of one's decision as one can possibly be. Secondly, one must be aware of one's own moral 'blind spots', and that one is not doing something for personal gain or one's own benefit when making a tough decision involving others or big groups of people that could be affected by one's decisions. Thirdly, one has to assess the viewpoint, desires or ethical beliefs of a particular group of people, about whom the decision needs to be made or action taken, or are influencing one to decide, to be sure they are not out of kilter with the viewpoints of the greater society in general. Lastly, one must be clear about the consequences of each potential decision, and whether one can live with these, even if it means a change to one's lifestyle and circumstances which may affect not just oneself, but one's family and loved ones, who will suffer if one is fired or even killed for taking a morally courageous standpoint. There are two opposing moral courage perspectives that could occur or be needed in each decision; firstly, to be morally brave from a societal or situational perspective; or secondly, to be morally brave in protecting one's family and loved ones by not taking the morally brave societal or situational perspective. So being morally courageous can often be both complex and paradoxical. Ultimately, one must decide each time one is faced with a challenging situation that produces a fear of consequences, whether to avoid it, or to act. To not act is often prudent. To act requires moral courage, but as above, moral courage is often complex. As Pastor Martin Niemöller's haunting words remind us 'First they came for the Socialists, and I did not speak out – because I was not a Socialist. Then they came for the Trade Unionists, and I did not speak out – because I was not a Trade Unionist. Then they came for the Jews, and I did not speak out – because I was not a Jew. Then they came for me – and there was no one left to speak for me'. Unless one is a sociopath, each of us feels fear the same as everyone else. Each one of us has to learn first physical courage, and later moral courage. Each one of us on a daily basis has decisions to make which require either physical or moral courage. Each decision we make, or do not make, causes ripples that affect both our lives and those around us. In a complex world, full of complex issues, especially where there is no clear wrong and right, or paradoxically particularly when it is obvious what is wrong and right, physical courage, and perhaps even more so moral courage, is often all that stands in the way between societal annihilation and salvation, and perhaps more importantly, underpins us attaining our own state of grace, whatever its level or importance or influence. To be is to do. Or was that to do is to be?

Essay 15. Self-identity, life transitions, and the ageing process - Growing older and wiser is not always a linear experience

When one is young, old age seems to be a million miles away in the future, and old age is often associated when young with one's parents who continuously caution one, or limit one's freedoms, and create rules and boundaries. It comes as quite a surprise to one (at least it did to me) when one wakes up one morning and realises one is a parent of teenage children and are older than one's parents when one thought them old, and one's children are complaining about the same issue regarding oneself as a parent as one did about one's own parents all those years ago. Life feels like a continuous passing of time mostly, but one does realise often quite a while after it happens, that one has 'transitioned' into a new reality or way of thinking — for example as a twenty year old sport may be the most important thing in one's life, but in one's thirties ones job and young family become the most important thing, and one realises often with surprise that one is not so 'caught up' in sport as one used to be. Having said this, one does feel that one is the same 'actor' throughout one's life, even if one does develop new interests and lose physical function as one ages. In this Essay we therefore examine the concept of ageing, and life transitions, and see how these transitions appear to be important for 'successful' ageing, and for 'readying one' for the next stage of life, whichever one is due to live 'in' as the next phase of one's three score and ten years of life on Earth.

Last weekend I attended our twenty-fifth-year medical class reunion at the University of Cape Town, and it was great to see so many old friends and medical student colleagues from my university days. What struck me most was that many of us had aged physically, but most folk's basic personality seemed to have not changed much since the days of our youth, although just about everyone seemed to be more at peace and more comfortable 'in their skins' as they approached their fifties than I remember them (and myself) to be in the halcyon days of our youth in our twenties. What was interesting too was hearing about everyone's lives and the life changes they had gone through – for example, one or several marriages, the birth of children and their growth into young adults, moves overseas or to other cities, and / or a succession of jobs. Most folk were in senior medical clinical or management positions in esteemed institutions across the world, which made us all laugh to remember how fancy-free and footloose we were in our twenties, and it in many ways surprised us that we had all done relatively well compared to how we thought we would all turn out back then. This reunion experience got me thinking about the concept that while us alumni at our reunion last week were all different individually, we all seemed to be pretty much in the same stage of life currently, with the same expectations and concerns for the future phase of our career, and often with the same reflective knowledge as wisdom. The same could have been said for the time period of our lives 25 years ago, when we also then had the same expectations and concerns as a group, albeit very different issues and concerns back then compared to what they were now. This got me thinking about life transitions and the effect of these on the development and maintenance of one's personality and self-identity through the life cycle, and how we all seemed to have managed to negotiate these life transitions, both negative and positive, and have got through to this different life stage in a reasonably similar way and with reasonably similar life expectations and world views, when one would rather have expected folk with different daily experiences over 25 years to have wildly divergent world views and significant changes in their personalities and self-identity 25 years later.

A transition is defined as a passing or change from one place, state or condition to another. It has long been recognized that the process of life requires or involves the individual transitioning or passing through a number of different stages. For example, in William Shakespeare's play, As You Like It, seven stages of 'man' were described, with all men and women being 'merely players' in them, having their 'entrances and exits', and that 'one man in his time plays many parts'. Shakespeare (or whoever wrote the plays attributed to Shakespeare) described seven different stages we go through, from the infant 'mewling and puking in the nurse's arms'; to the whining school-boy 'creeping like a snail unwilling to school'; to the lover 'sighing like a furnace'; to the soldier 'jealous in honour, sudden and quick in quarrel, seeking the bubble reputation'; to the justice 'in fair round belly, with good capon lined, with eyes severe and beard of formal cut, full of wise saws and modern instances'; to the lean and slippered pantaloon 'with spectacles on nose and pouch on his side'; to finally second childishness and 'mere oblivion, sans teeth, sans eyes, sans taste, sans everything'. These wonderful descriptions of the stages we go through by Shakespeare are difficult to match, but of course a number of psychologists, such as Erik Erikson, have more formally described a number of stages we go through during life, particularly during childhood and early adolescence, and suggested further that in order to reach a subsequent stage, one has to successfully negotiate the prior stage as a learning platform on which the following stage develops. For example, in early infancy we learn basic hope and basic trust (and mistrust) from our interactions with our primary parent (usually but not exclusively our mothers). If this trust and hope successfully develops, it forms the basis for positive self-identity, and allows the infant to move on to a phase of learning about will and autonomy (and shame), where again parents or caregivers are required to balance protection and safety with the requirements of the young child to explore the world in a reasonably autonomous way. Doing so will allow development into the next phase of purposive activity, followed by a learning of competence phase, then one of learning fidelity and identity (as an adolescent), then love and intimacy (in the early 20s), then care and generativity as an adult, and finally wisdom and integrity as an old adult. Erikson suggested that failure to develop successfully at any stage will lead to development of such negative self-concepts as mistrust, shame, guilt, feeling of inferiority, role confusion, isolation, stagnation, and despair at different points in a person life as they move through it.

What is interesting is that these stages appear to be crucial to our personal development and self-identity, but often do not occur as smoothly as these above descriptions suggest. In a brilliant scientific article published a few years ago, an old colleague of mine from the University of Northumbria, Dr Linda Allin, suggested that life transitions are not always predictable, and while the formal stage transitions described above could be defined as structured transitions, there are also transitions that occur that are self-initiated in response to intolerable living conditions, or are forced on one due to external events that are dramatic enough to require the self-initiation of a major life-changing response. For example, Linda describes the case of an athlete, whose whole self-concept and identity is that of an athlete, who sustains an injury that is severe enough to lead to the athlete's career being abruptly terminated. The athlete thereafter has to in effect transition to another life stage directly as a result of the injury, and indeed has to successfully negotiate an entire change in self-concept from that of being an athlete to that of being something else, which is obviously tremendously challenging, and can often lead to a period of catastrophic psychological breakdown before a new stage of life is reached and acceptance of a new self-concept and identity is obtained – perhaps as a coach, or teacher, or any other career related to, or not related to, their old athletic career or self-concept. There are a number of such challenging forced transitions to overcome during most folk's life, such as getting retrenched from a job, getting divorced (marriage itself is a transition creating challenge), the death of loved one, or a major illness, which all can create forced transitions and changes in self-concept and identity.

What appears to be strongly / tightly linked to relative success or failure of life stage transitions (and perhaps therefore failure or success of life itself) is an individual's self-concept / self-identity, interchangeable concepts that are defined as the extent to which one's self-knowledge is defined, consistent and applicable to one's attitudes and dispositions. Self-identity is different to, but linked, to the concept of self-esteem, with self-identity being descriptive of oneself, while self-esteem is evaluative of the self. For example, one's self-identity may be that one is a doctor / father / husband, while one's self-esteem would create a personal (and often self-fulfilling) perspective that one is either a good or bad doctor / father / husband. Self-identity is generated during prior / early life stages and is related to self-assessments in childhood and interpretations of others' assessments of oneself during adolescence and early adulthood of one's personality, skills and abilities, occupations and hobbies, and physical characteristics. Paradoxically, not only do prior life stages generate self-identity (and self-esteem), but successful negotiation of life transitions between the different life stages requires positive self-identity and self-esteem (though to what degree is still controversial), so life stages, life transitions and self-identity and self-esteem all appear to be inextricably linked. A failure of development during a life stage or transition, which is associated as above with self-identity issues in a causative or interactive manner, will lead to both an inability to develop in life and an identity crisis in some folk. The psychologist James Marcia suggested there are four 'statuses' of identity 'crises' associated with life stage transitions. Firstly, there is identity foreclosure, where a transition is made without exploring alternatives or, for example, when career or life decisions are made on parental beliefs or ideas that are accepted without question. If no external life-changing events occur, this can lead to a 'successful' transition in life but can also lead to a complete psychological breakdown when challenging external events occur. For example, if someone plans to become a farmer because one's parents own a farm, that may be well and good, but if one's parents subsequently sell their farm, this will obviously create a self-identity crisis and transition issues in the person that puts 'all their eggs in this one career basket'. Marcia's second 'status' was that of identity diffusion, where adolescents and young adults are unable to face or make commitments or career or life decisions due to failure to transition adequately, and 'drift' through life battling to make commitments or identify with other folk and become indecisive and / or do not 'grow' as most folk do through successfully overcoming the challenges related to each formal or forced stage transition. Thirdly, Marcia suggested there is an identity moratorium status, where folk in the middle of a transition-related crisis also remain uncommitted and indecisive but are also actively exploring alternatives and are trying to change. Folk with identity moratorium often describe anxiety and that they have an 'identity crisis', and for them, the 'world is not a predictable place, and they are engaged in a struggle to make it so'. The fourth 'status' is identity achievement, where when stage transitions are successfully worked through, self-identity is enhanced, and folk who achieve this eventually develop an internal, as opposed to an external locus (which most adolescents and young adults have) of self-identity. Folk in any of the three other 'statuses', particularly the identity moratorium status, can eventually reach this pro-active identity achievement stage, and thereafter successfully 'tackle' the next stage of life and its associated challenges.

How do these concepts help us understand how a 'successful' life develops, and how can they be related to the folk I saw at my twenty-fifth-year medical reunion last week? Transitions and self-identity appear to be inextricably linked – to be successful in transitioning through the stages of life one needs to have a well-developed and positive self-identity, and to have a well-developed and positive self-identity one needs to be successful in transitioning through the stages of life. It was fascinating to have this twenty-five-year long gap, and the two 'windows' the passing of time created then and now, which allowed me to 'observe' the changes as a result of life transitions in the folk I interacted with during my medical training all those years ago, and again, albeit for a brief period, last week at our reunion. Clearly, it appeared that most of the folk I saw again had successfully adjusted to and developed from all the transitions and life changes they had undergone, or were forced to undergo due to external challenges, and were 'successful' and had a contentment about them which was not always obvious in them (and me) twenty-five years ago. It must be noted though that one does not have to successfully transition through the stages of life or have a positive self-identity to be successful in one's career – one can be a tormented soul and still be a great surgeon or scientist in the 'doing of it' – even if one is perhaps not happy or at peace when doing so as one would be with a 'healthy' self-identity and life stage transition history. Furthermore, I realized at the reunion when we were all recounting stories from our medical school times, that the folk who interact with one / who one meets at later stages of one's life may be surprised at, or even not believe, stories from previous life stages they are told about which they were not privy to. For example, from a personal perspective, the folk who have only met me now, when I am in the contented 'capon lined' justice phase of life and currently involved with university / clinical management as my career focus after a 20-year period as a clinical and basic researcher, and with a happy family life, would be astonished by the stories folk could tell about my time in the Shakespearean lover / soldier phases of my life 25 years ago. Then my self-identity was very different and perhaps that of a sportsman who did medicine, and later a bouncer / doorman who did science and responded with the 'passion of youth' to each challenge faced then, rather than with the calmness and reflection of the justice phase we are currently in, and which is how now I mostly respond to any challenging situation (like we all do and did). Everyone will have similar stories and likely more intense 'lives' in earlier stages of their life – but if one didn't have those passionate times of our youth, and been able to successfully transition away from them, would one be the person one is now? Each person's life is a rich kaleidoscope of history, experiences, challenges met, and failures accepted. Each person's needs and life history may be very different, and often appears full of daily drama, with countless changes and issues to face, and never 'seems' to travel a linear / straight line from 'A to B'. But ultimately, we all seem to go through the same stages of life and end up most often in the same 'place' in the end / in later life. The life stages and transitions we go through appear to set boundaries and conditions for our lives, yet impact on us in a way that is often unnoticed until we are long past them and reflect and realize we have changed, hopefully for the better. And if we haven't changed, perhaps we are drifting because of issues related to our self-identity and lack of capacity to pass through each life stage successfully and have thus remained in the river of life rather than floating out into the wide blue sea. Eventual awareness / insight about this 'drifting' status may in itself become an external factor allowing eventual growth and change through acknowledgement of one's own stasis and consequent initiation of action to attenuate the stasis and move on to a 'new', different and potentially 'better' stage of life more synchronous with that of one's peers.

At the end of the day, it seems that change and transition is the basis of our life and development, and the capacity to do so is strongly related to our self-identity and self-esteem in a circular way. Sadly, for me and my medical colleagues at the reunion last week, the bad news is that the only stages ahead for us are the baggy pantaloon and second childhood phases with our 'big manly voices turning again toward childish treble, with pipes and whistles in our sounds', and our 'youthful hose, well saved, a world too wide for our shrunk shank'. Hopefully at our 40-year reunion, which is planned to be held 15-years hence, the organizers will take note of this wisdom and natural law, and ensure we have enough balloons, whistles, and cakes to satisfy us all in our second childhood phase which by then will be well upon us. Sans teeth. Sans eyes. Sans taste. Sans everything – except for a life past full of unforgotten and unforgettable memories, and a life lived to the full.

Essay 16. Death and our own dying - Death related anxiety and the understanding of its certainty patterns our daily life

Almost surely the biggest thing that looms ahead in our life is our own death. While most societies have largely sanitized death and banished it from most people's lives until it happens to themselves, everyone is surely aware that no-one gets off this earth alive, and that the grim reaper awaits us at some point in our future life. While most folk accept this as an inevitable fact of life, some folks become obsessed by thoughts of their own death, or 'trapped' into a life of continual anxiety and fear at the thought of their own mortality and how they will die. What happens after death is of course a complete mystery, and folk invent different stories to make sense of what occurs 'after death' such as those of Gods and Heavens, or Eternal Re-birth, or that Nothingness is what awaits us when we 'shuffle off this mortal coil'. In this final Essay of this first section of Essays, we examine death and dying, and how it affects one's life, even at a subconscious level, and acts in many ways as a controlling factor on how we live our life during its various stages.

In the last few weeks our family has had to come to terms with the fact that the health of our wonderful dog, Grauzer the Schnauzer, who's been our faithful companion of 11 years, and has travelled with us from Cape Town in South Africa to Newcastle upon Tyne in the UK, and then back to Bloemfontein in South Africa, is failing, and as much as we don't want it to happen and hope he lives on for a few years more, it is very likely in the next few weeks he will be taking the journey to the next world of unlimited lamp-posts and cats and ferrets that do not move as quickly as they do in this one. My old friend and world leading Sport and Exercise Scientist, Professor Andy Jones, last week retweeted some fascinating data of what folk die from during their lifetimes at different ages, and it was fascinating to see this and understand that one had got 'safely past' some of the childhood and early adult related causes of death, but that equally, now being well into middle-age, a whole host of nasty causes of death could potentially be one's fate at any time from now into the future. My great brother, John, heard the unfortunate news that one of his school classmates had passed away of natural causes at the age of 47, and we soberly reflected over the Christmas period that 'there by the grace of god went we', and we resolved to pay more attention to our health and fitness, in the chance that this would make a difference and prolong for as far as possible into the future the inevitable fate which awaits all of us. All these got me thinking about death and dying, the biggest mystery of life, and perhaps the biggest factor at play in our lives and consideration of our future.

Death is defined as the final cessation of vital functions in an individual or organism which results in the ending of life. One's death can be a result of a number of different phenomena, from senescence (biological ageing, or in more common terms, old age), disease, violence and murder, predation by wild animals, accidents, suicide, and any number of other mechanisms that potentially can cause one to die. While how exactly to define and diagnose the occurrence of death is still debated in medical circles, generally most folk would accept that someone has died when their heart and respiratory organs stop working and cannot be sustained without external artificial assistance, along with evidence of brain death as evidenced by a 'flat-line' EEG (which monitors the presence of rhythmical brain waves) and a lack of cortical function or primitive brain reflexes. When this happens, the body of any person or organism starts decaying and decomposing shortly after the onset of death. Interestingly, not all 'living' organisms die (the definition of what constitutes a 'living' organism is still hotly debated), with exceptions being the hydra and jellyfish species, which appear to be immortal and never die, and can maintain their existence 'forever' unless they are physically torn asunder. Similarly, organisms which reproduce asexually, and unicellular organisms, also appear to 'live' eternally. So, one can postulate that death is a 'by-product' of a complex cellular structure, where somatic (body) cells are created in a complex arrangement by a combination of some 'plan' and some energy form, which allows the occurrence of 'life' as we know it, but decays with time and eventually deteriorates functionally to a degree that 'death' occurs.

What happens to us around the time and 'after' death is of course still a matter of conjecture. A fair bit of research has been done on folk who have had a near-death experience where they have been clinically 'brought back from the dead' after either a heart attack, or a near drowning, or accident-related trauma, all of which lead to hypoxia (shortage of oxygen supply) to and of the brain. Most describe a feeling that they are 'blacking out' for what to them is an unknown and unpredictable period of time, and an awareness that one is dying, until by chance / good medical practice they are 'brought back to life' by resuscitation and other clinical interventions. A lot of these folk also describe a sense of 'being dead', a sense of peace and wellbeing and painlessness, an out-of-body experience as if they were 'floating' above and 'watching' their physical self, a 'tunnel experience' of entering darkness via a tunnel of light, reviewing their life in a manner often described as 'seeing their life history flashing before their eyes', or seeing 'beings of light', all before the absolute darkness / nothingness of unconsciousness ('death') occurs, or they 'return' to their body as they are resuscitated. Of course, all this is first person / qualitative descriptive information, and is impossible scientifically to replicate, but it is interesting that so many folks describe similar experiences as they 'die'. We also do not know at all what then occurs after this phase, as all these folks are 'brought back to life', so we are not aware what happens 'next' as part of the death process. Into this knowledge void folk put their own interpretation of what happens, or will happen to them, when they do die - religious folk would describe and I guess hope for some type of 'heaven' as the 'next phase', or some transcendence or continuation of one's 'spirit' or 'soul' into another body or as an entity which exists and 'drifts' through the ether eternally – while secular folk would either say they are not sure of what happens, or believe that there is nothing 'after' death, and everything just switches off and a blankness / nothingness occurs similar to when one is in a deep sleep. Of course, all of these are pure conjecture, and it is for each of us to experience and understand what is 'ahead' for us after own deaths only when it happens, when all shall be made clear, or we will disappear into the eternity of nothingness, and know nothing about it or anything further of our life, past, current or future.

What is for sure is that for most folk, the thought of one's own imminent or potential mortality causes anxiety (and I have never heard anyone say with any sincerity that they really are totally not scared of death and dying, and in those that do, it is almost always manifestly evident bravado), often to a morbid degree, where it is known as thanatophobia. Thanatophobia, or death anxiety, is defined as a feeling of dread, apprehension or anxiety when one thinks of the process of dying, or the totality of death, and its impact on one's own 'life' which is all that we know and 'have'. Death anxiety can be related to the fear of being harmed and the way one will die, or to existential fear that nothing may exist after we die, or to the fear of leaving behind loved ones and things and processes we believe are reliant on us for their continuation. It has been suggested that folk 'defend' themselves against the anxiety they feel about their own death and dying (or that of loved ones) by 'denial', which results in a lot of transference, acting out, or 'covering up' behaviour either consciously or subconsciously, such as attempting to acquire excessive wealth or power, or committing violence against others, or breaking rules and life boundaries, or celebrating / living life in a manic way, all of which have an emotional cost, and do not usually attenuate the underlying death anxiety. Interestingly, a century and more ago, most folk used to die in a more 'open' way than what currently occurs, usually in the comfort (or discomfort) of their homes, surrounded by their loved ones. In contrast, today a greater proportion of folk die in hospitals or hospices, 'away' from the 'visible' world, and it is usual for most folk never to see someone actually die in their lifetime until their own death is imminent. It has been postulated that this 'hiding' of death from us may have paradoxically created a greater fear of death because of us never 'seeing' or being involved with death, and therefore death is an 'unknown' entity or occurrence which causes an exacerbated fear due to the fear of the unknown nature of death, rather than just a fear of death itself. It has been suggested that folk with more physical problems, more psychological problems or a 'lower ego integrity' (lower self-confidence) suffer from greater death anxiety. Folk like Viktor Frankl have suggested that having some life 'meaning', or a sense of peace from achieving life goals, or paradoxically letting go of life goals, may attenuate the feelings of death anxiety. Supporting this, death anxiety is apparently greatest during the ages of 35-65 (and is felt by children as young as five years old), but after 65, again paradoxically, death anxiety appears to decrease, perhaps because after retirement one 'lets go' of earthly goals and desires or reaches a sense of peace regarding one's life and achievements. Of course, there must be a relationship between goals / desires and death anxiety for this to be true, and it is not clear if such a relationship clearly exists, even if it does seem to be a logical 'link'.

Folk that 'give their life away', whether in combat as part of a perception of national duty, or to save a family member, or in a life-threatening emergency where they react to such a situation and are prepared to die to save others, are challenging to understand in relation to the death anxiety and fear of death issues described above which most folk would admit to having. Clearly having a 'higher cause' must be calculated by these folks to be more important than their own life, or their lives must be perceived to be meaningless enough to 'give it away' in such instances. It is difficult to tell which of these (a perception of a higher cause or a meaningless life) is most germane in these different examples, and indeed whether these folks have a fear of death or anxiety about it but continue with their course of action despite feeling such, or whether some cognitive process or learned way of thinking removes this fear / anxiety before they perform their last act of sacrifice or wilful death. Sigmund Freud suggested that there is a death drive in all folk, which opposes the 'Eros' drive (lust for life / breeding / survival), and that when folk want to die, or risk their life doing, for example, extreme sports like parachuting or mountain climbing where there is a high chance of death occurring, it is part of some primordial desire to 'go back' to some pre-life state, though of course a theory like this is difficult to prove or disprove as we cannot yet measure 'drives' in a direct way.

So how does knowledge of this anxiety related to the awareness of death as the final life process we will go through, and indeed of death itself, both affect and assist us with how we live our life? We do seem to either consciously or unconsciously create a 'scaffold' or pattern of our life plans and life stages related to the relative perceived imminence of death. For example, in our twenties we explore 'life' with mostly a freedom from the fear of death (though paradoxically this exploratory behaviour often can end in accidental death), perhaps because one believes that one has many years of life ahead of one, and death will occur at a time far in the distance ahead. As one enters one's thirties, one is for some reason to a greater degree confronted by an understanding of one's mortality, perhaps due to early signs of physical deterioration such as not being able to compete as well as one used to at sport, or hair loss / developing baldness, or experiencing the death of one's parents which 'brings' awareness of both the reality and finality of death to oneself, amongst many other potential reasons. Because of this one therefore starts 'planning' the life left ahead of one based on average mortality figures (most folk believe and hope they will live to between 70-80 years if things go well for them) – for example buying a house that will be paid off before one 'retires', having children at a young enough age to see them grow up to adulthood, or writing a will for the first time. The concept of retirement is interesting related to death and dying, and is surely based on a 'calculation' of a death age beyond the retirement age, thereby allowing one to have a little 'down time' / a time of peace before shuffling off this mortal coil, even though paradoxically health reasons often do not allow folk as much enjoyment of this time as they would if they rather planned a work 'gap period' in their forties or early fifties where they took time out from work to relax or travel, and subsequently worked on until death occurred, rather than waiting until being 'old' to enjoy retirement with the time left before their death. Thus, a lot of our life appears to be patterned and planned out based on an understanding that a finite number of years are available to us. This is perhaps why when one has a health scare, or a cancer diagnosis, or when a young person goes to war where the chance of death is manifestly increased at this 'incorrect' time of the person's life, fear of death, death anxiety and denial mechanisms come into play, that can be very difficult to attenuate or 'put out' of one's mind.

As much as one would like to, as the main character in the film 'Lawless' concluded after his much-revered brother, whom he thought was immortal, died at the end of the film, no-one leaves this world alive. Understanding this creates a sense of anxiety in us (unless we perhaps have strong religious beliefs), both for what we will lose, and for what we will leave behind. But, paradoxically, the thought of death perhaps also creates a sense of wonder each day we wake up that we are indeed alive for another day, and makes the grass seem greener, the sun shines brighter, and the water seem wetter, given we know that one day we will no longer 'have' all these things around us. Once in my youth I capsized when paddling down a river in my kayak and was pinned under a rock for a period of time and had that 'out of body' feeling described above, and my whole life to that point played out in a fast sequential 'movie' in front of my eyes, and then I felt everything go black and remembered nothing more. Fortunately, I was 'let go' / washed out from under the rock, and when I regained my senses, everything did indeed seem much sweeter, lusher, brighter, and more brilliant, and does still to this day. I am of the age when according to the statistics I should most fear death, and indeed, with a young family, each day I do fear that I will not see my son and daughter grow up if I die suddenly. I held my wonderful dog Grauzer in my arms as I brought him home from the vet this morning with the news that I might not be able to hold him such for much longer, and a feeling of immense sadness and impending loss almost overwhelmed me. But then I thought about the good times we have had together, and understood that the circle of life, which for him is nearly complete, was and is a full and happy one, and I understood also that part of my sadness for him is my fear for my own mortality and the sense of permanence that accompanies his impending death. I took note of the fact that, as described above, at the end of one's life the fear of death is usually paradoxically attenuated and lessens and hoped that dogs get to that similar point of peace at the end of their time too. And yes, his fur does feel softer, his wagging tail and uplifted 'happy' face each time he sees me seems even 'sweeter', given I know that soon he will go forever into the great unknown, and will be with us no more. Death and dying is still the greatest mystery life have for us, and a challenge we all have to go through on our own, and we will only gain the knowledge of what death is 'about' when we go through the dying process ourselves. When eventually facing one's own imminent death, perhaps the best one can do is try and find the courage to meet it 'head on', as suggested in the wonderful words of the Nick Glennie-Smith song, 'Sgt. Mackenzie', written in homage to his grandfather who died in the first Great war – 'Lay me down in the cold, cold ground, where before many men have gone. When they come, I will stand my ground, and not be afraid' - though of course we all hope that the need to do this will occur many years from now, with all our loved ones around us, and with the contentment of a life well lived in our final moments. But we can be sure of one thing, and that is we will never get out of this world alive, unless we are an amoeba or jellyfish. And maybe, just maybe, the world is a better place because of this, or at least it feels such in those moments when we ponder on the glory of life, with the aching awareness that at some future point in time we no longer will be 'in it', and will go off on our own journey, alone, into the great big, wide, unknown.

Section 3. Understanding Human Physical Performance

Section 3.1 Introduction

In the previous section, we examined the poetry of life and activity in the basic 'building blocks' of either function, organ, behaviour or movement that all together 'create' the human body and experience. In these following five essays, we look at the 'whole human' performing at their limits, during exercise or maximal physical tasks. In the unforgettable opening scene of the film Chariots of Fire (with unforgettable-Vangelis created music), it shows a phalanx of athletes training for an Olympic Games in the 1920s running along the beaches of St Andrew's in Scotland, and the scene perfectly captured the perfection and poetry of motion of gifted athletes performing their trade to the best of their ability. While the goals of athletes are lofty, and watching them perform their tasks and feats of strength or endurance wonderful to watch, research in this field made me realise that sadly, underlying this physical perfection, is often psychological dysfunction and a damaging childhood. But this cannot take away from the magic of sport, and the visible poetry of individuals pushing themselves to their utmost, often to places where there are fine balances between not just winning and losing, but also successfully completing the event without collapsing with major physical systems breakdown and potentially death or permanent physical harm the result. On to an examination of and Essays on harder, quicker, and better, life.

Essay 17. The capacity for maximum physical performance in humans - Do we ever really go 'all out'?

One of the most fascinating and awe-inspiring things one can observe is athletes pushing themselves to their 'utmost' to beat their competitors and so win a race or competitive event. Anguished looks on their faces, mouths open trying to draw in the most possible air with each breath, a distant look in their eyes, and bodies bathed in sweat make one feel with some certainty that athletes are trying their utmost to succeed and cannot go faster, particularly in the last few moments of an event. Most research has accepted this as a truism, and attempts to explain how absolute fatigue happens using laboratory techniques which show, usually in animal models, that fuels 'run out', or metabolites 'build up' to such levels that they 'poison' the muscles and thus slows them down — think lactic acid, for example. But recent research has suggested that athletes may never push themselves to the absolute levels of fatigue, and always keep a small percentage of power output in reserve, even when they 'feel' they are going maximally. In this Essay, therefore, we look at the indicators of maximal effort and fatigue, and what the evidence is for folk to suggest that exercise may never be maximal, except in extreme emergency situations, when from visual signals it looks as if the athlete is making supreme efforts to do the best they can.

I read an article in the newspaper this week about a group of pedestrians who lifted a car off a lady who was trapped under it after the car crashed into her as they were walking by the scene of the accident. A few weeks ago, I watched young world class cyclists in the Tour de France push themselves up miles of uphill road in some of the highest mountains in France, and who looked completely exhausted at the end of each stage. I have had some fun Twitter repartee recently with Samuele Marcora, Jeroen Swart, Andy Renfree, Ross Tucker and others – old science collaborators, friends and academic 'sparring partners' – regarding whether folk ever use their maximal physical capacity, and if not, whether their performances are regulated by processes in the body or brain, and if in the brain, whether algorithmic neural processes are involved, or rather more intangible mental motivation related processes are behind our maximal physical performances during races or athletic events. I spent a fair amount of time, particularly when working at the University of Cape Town a decade and more ago, examining these concepts, and developed a theory for them, along with colleagues Tim Noakes and Vicki Lambert, called the Central Governor theory, which caused some controversy then, and still does today, with folk either loving or hating it, as what happens with all theories in science.

For a long time, the concept of maximal performance, and what finally results in folk reaching the absolute limits of what they physically can do, could be described as a 'catastrophic' model of fatigue. In the catastrophic model, the body, when pushed hard during an athletic event, either runs out of key nutrients or energy fuels, or is 'poisoned' because of metabolites that cannot be cleared out of muscles quickly enough, either due to lack of oxygen delivery capacity of the lungs or blood supply which have been 'overwhelmed' by the demand placed on them by the physical activity. The lactic acid theory was the classical example of this – the 'burning' pain one feels in one's muscle during extreme exercise was thought to be related to lactic acid build up, which eventually 'poisoned' the muscles to the point that they simply stopped working.

Most of these theories developed from animal studies, or isolated muscle studies, where muscles were removed from their normal anatomical environment and stimulated with electrical shocks until they stopped contracting completely (developed rigor for the scientists reading this). At this point of absolute fatigue, a variety of parameters such as lactic acid were measured, and given that the levels of these parameters were very high (or very low in the case of fuels), a cause / effect relationship between absolute fatigue in these isolated muscles and lactic acid for example, was suggested to be occurring during these trials. But the action of muscles of human folk performing exercise does not occur in an isolated state or in a petri dish. We therefore did some work in the University of Cape Town labs, building on work by greats in the fatigue field such as Roger Enoka and Simon Gandevia, amongst others, and looked at how much muscle was recruited during real life endurance and sprint athletic activity, using fairly novel techniques (at least at that point in time!) such as electromyography (EMG), which indirectly measures muscle recruitment (though one could write a book on the merits of this technique to measure fatigue, or the lack thereof). In a breakthrough study for us, we found that the muscles of folks in the lab who pushed themselves to the point when they said they were absolutely exhausted still had reserve capacity / had not used their muscles absolutely maximally, which was both astonishing and exciting to us. We did muscle biopsies at the beginning and end of the trial, and also found that the levels of fuels such as muscle glycogen and glucose, essential fuels of the body, were low but not zero, indicating the presence of a fuel reserve capacity too. We repeated this type of study in several different population groups and types of athletic events, and found similar results, and concluded that the brain of an athlete 'stopped' an athlete in an anticipatory way prior to them ever being completely fatigued, even if they did 'feel' absolutely exhausted. Therefore, some process in the brain appears to 'disconnect' the sensation of fatigue from what exactly was happening in the body, likely as a protective mechanism to prevent the occurrence of either muscle damage or general circulatory failure which could (and occasionally does) occur during an athletic event in a very motivated athlete.

Several of other examples of this protective 'central' / brain protective mechanism came to light during our further experiments, or from experiments in other labs around the world. Derek Kay, Jack Cannon and Frank Marino in Australia found that in a lab study using race-like conditions, participants started fast, slowed down in the middle and sped up the last 10 percent (or so) of the trial. The EMG activity in their study tracked these increases and decreases in pace, which indicated that these changes were probably initiated and regulated by the brain.

The increase in pace in the last 10 percent of the trial was described as an 'endspurt' – speeding up at the end of an event or activity – and of course if one's muscles are being 'poisoned' by a continuous build-up of metabolites during a race, or if one did run out of a fuel completely, there would be no way that the trial participants could speed up and show an endspurt at the end of the race. A fascinating study performed in the 1960s, which came to light when we investigated what we were finding, which perhaps would not have passed muster these days from an ethical perspective, showed support for this concept. Trial participants were asked to contract their leg muscles as hard as possible in a leg strength testing device where the movement of the leg was resisted, and the force output of the leg muscles recorded. The subjects were encouraged to keep on going until they claimed they were absolutely exhausted and could not continue for even a few seconds longer, and at this point a second researcher, who unknown to the participants had entered the room behind them, fired off a shotgun blank shell, without the participants seeing them do so. This obviously caused a massive shock to the participants, and the interesting finding from a study perspective was that the subjects put out between 20 and 30 percent more force after hearing the gunshot, despite saying prior to hearing the gunshot that they were absolutely exhausted. Again, this was strong evidence for the presence of the muscle reserve capacity at exhaustion and a 'disconnect' between the sensation of fatigue and the physical changes associated with the fatiguing process.

We, and other scientist folk, have had a long look at how this sensory / perceptual disconnect during the fatigue process and at the point of absolute 'fatigue' occurs. Clearly there is teleology behind this finding, and it is likely that it is a protective mechanism which uses 'trickery' to keep folk safe from their own motivational drives, but it is does 'boggle the mind' to think that one's own brain in effect 'lies' to its own 'self' to protect 'it' from 'itself'. The origin of sensations and the perception of emotional constructs such as fatigue, and how they develop in underlying brain structures (or indeed how they are even related to physical brain structures), is difficult to understand, given how little we unfortunately know about basic brain function, mental states, or indeed sensory awareness of anything. However, using indirect methods, we were able to show that the dissociation of the sensation of fatigue from the underlying physical fatigue processes can be fairly easily elicited. One of the most fun studies I have been involved with (though which has very relevant findings pertaining to this research area), was a study we (Rachel Winchester and others) did during my time at Northumbria University, where when young male participants who were running on a treadmill said they were feeling exhausted, we introduced either an attractive female or an athletic male into the lab who interacted with them while they were running. There were profound changes in the levels of reported sensation of fatigue by the athletes – when the attractive female interacted with them, they reported significant reductions in the level of fatigue they felt, but when an athletic male interacted with them, they reported being significantly more fatigued because of the interaction. So, this was classic (and humour inducing) evidence showing that the sensation of fatigue can be actually fairly easily 'dissociated' from what is happening in the body itself, and that the sensation of fatigue has a psycho-social component, or at least can be 'interfered with' by psycho-social factors.

So, what does all this tell us about the limits to performance and whether athletes, or indeed folk who perform recreational sport, ever really are 'maximally' fatigued, even if they do feel as if they are. The evidence described above would seem to clearly indicate that, at least in these scientific studies, one's brain as a protective mechanism appears to limit one's activity to an always submaximal level, even if one 'feels' that one is pushing oneself to absolute maximum. How the brain (or mind) does this is currently not clear, but there is clearly some interplay or calculation between one's motivations and desires for success, and one's fear of damaging oneself during athletic, or indeed any, physical activity. Interestingly, in the wild, animals being chased by predators do occasionally push themselves so hard to not be eaten as prey, that even if they escape, they die because of their muscles becoming so damaged by overheating or over-exertion that they become necrotic, which results in kidney failure and death from multiple organ failure due to toxin build up from the badly damaged muscles. Clearly us humans are never in a situation in our routine lives that these animals face, and therefore perhaps this 'reserve' capacity is some relic of our ancestry where we were indeed potentially a larger animal's prey, and there was benefit of always maintaining a reserve for this 'death-defying' challenge if it occurred, though of course it will always be nothing more than conjecture when speculating on ancestry or evolution as a cause for modern day behaviour or function, particularly when brain function or mental behaviour is involved. Though some athletes do collapse during and after events (and why they do so is still a mystery), the vast majority, even Tour de France winners, know that they need to leave a small level of physical capacity to allow them to be able to climb off the bike, have a shower, get their medal, or leave something 'in the tank' to race the next day. So, when we think we are completely exhausted, we probably never are. When we see the person with the car on top of them in the middle of the road, we do have the capacity to perform life-saving feats (obviously within reason) and have 'strength' that we are not aware of. Whether it is wise to use this inherent reserve, and risk 'all', even one's life, for that single instance of extreme use of strength or endurance capacity in whatever circumstance, is of course another story. As is persuading my scientific colleagues, who despite all this evidence described above, still think the concepts are baloney and nothing more than a good story.

Essay 18. The sensation of fatigue - A complex emotion which is vital for human survival

The sensation of fatigue acts as a conscious warning signal, telling us to slow down and / or stop doing the activity in which we are currently engaged before we potentially harm ourselves by pushing our physical systems too hard or too long. Despite a large amount of research examining the sensation of fatigue, curiously there still not a lot known about where and how it is generated, and what body, brain, or mind parts are most important for its genesis. In this Essay, therefore, we look at this complex sensation, to try and shed some light on its causes and effects.

After a couple of weeks back at work following a great Christmas season break, I have noticed this week a higher than normal level of fatigue than I normally 'feel' at the end of a routine working week. After one of the hottest December months on record in my current hometown, where temperatures for a while were consistently hovering around 40 degrees Celsius, we have had a wonderful rainy, cool period, and I have noticed that I feel less fatigued in the cooler environment, and routine daily activities seem 'easier' to perform than when it was excessively hot. As part of a New Year's resolution 'action plan' to improve my level of fitness, I have increased my level of endurance exercise, and as always have enjoyed the sensation of fatigue I feel towards the end of each long (though I know that 'long' is relative when compared to younger, fitter folk) bike ride I do as part of this 'fitness' goal. All of these got me thinking of the sensation of fatigue, an emotional construct which I spent a great many years of my research career trying to understand, and which still is very difficult to define, let alone work out its origins and mechanisms of elicitation in our physical body structures and mental brain functions.

As described in these three very different examples from my own life, fatigue is experienced by all folk on a regular basis in a variety of different conditions and activities. Perhaps because of this, there are many different definitions of fatigue. In clinical medicine practice, fatigue is defined as a debilitating consequence of a number of different systemic diseases (or paradoxically the treatment by a variety of different drugs) or nutritional deficits. In exercise physiology, fatigue is defined as an acute impairment of exercise performance, which leads to an eventual inability to produce maximal force output because of metabolite accumulate or substrate depletion. In neurophysiology, fatigue is defined as a reduction of motor command from the brain to the active muscles resulting in a decrease in force or tension as part of a planned homeostatic process to prevent the body from damage which could result from too high a level of activity or too prolonged activity. In psychology, fatigue is defined as an emotional construct – a conscious 'sensation' generated by the cognitive appraisal of changing body or brain physiological activity which is influenced by the social environment in which the activity changes occur, and the mood status, temperament and background of the person 'feeling' these physiological changes. It will be evident from all of these different definitions how complex fatigue is an 'entity' / functional process, and how hard it is for even experts in the field to describe to someone asking about what fatigue is, let alone understand it from a research perspective.

Several different physical factors have been related to the development of the sensation of fatigue we all 'feel' during our daily life. During physical activity, it has been proposed that changes in the body related to the increased requirements of the physical exertion being performed cause the sensation of fatigue to 'arise'. These include increased heart rate, increased respiratory rate, increased acid 'build up' in the muscles, reduced blood glucose or muscle or liver glycogen, or temperature changes in the body, particularly increased heat build-up – though for each study that shows one of these factors is 'causal' of the sensation of fatigue, one can find a study that shows that each of these specific factors is not related to the development of the sensation of fatigue. It has also been proposed that changes in the concentration of substrates in the brain structures associated with physical or mental activity are related to the sensation of fatigue – such as changes in neurotransmitter levels (for example serotonin, acetylcholine, glutamate), or changes in the nutrients supplied to the brain such as glucose, lactate or branched chain amino acids. But, again, for each study whose findings support these hypotheses, there are studies that refute such suggestions. It has also been suggested that a composite 'aggregation' of changes in all these body and brain factors may result in the development of the sensation of fatigue, via some brain process or function that 'valences' each in a fatigue 'algorithm', or via intermediate sensations such as the sensation of breathlessness associated with increased ventilation, the sensation of a 'pounding' heart from cardiac output increases, the sensation of being hot and sticky and sweating which result from temperature increases in the body, and / or the sensation of pain in muscles working hard, all of which are themselves 'aggregated' by brain structures or mental functions to create the complex sensation we know and describe as fatigue.

Which physical brain structures are involved in the creation of the sensation of fatigue is still not known, and given the complexity of the factors involved in its generation, as described above, large areas of the brain and a number of different brain systems are likely to be involved – the motor cortex as muscle activity is often involved, the sensory cortex as signals from changes in activity in numerous body 'parts' and functions are 'picked up' and assimilated by the brain, the frontal cortex as cognitive decision-making on the validity of these changes and the need for potential changes in activity as a result of this 'awareness' of a changed state is required, the hippocampus / amygdala region as the current changes in physiological or mental activity must be compared against prior memories of similar changes in the past in order to make valid 'sense' of them as they currently occur, and the brainstem as this is the area where ventilation, heart function and a variety of other 'basic' life maintaining functions are primarily controlled, for example, amongst many other potential brain areas. We don't know how the function of different brain areas is 'integrated' to give us the conscious 'whole' sensation we 'feel', and until we do so, it is difficult to understand how the physical brain structures 'create' the sensation of fatigue, let alone the 'feeling' of it.

How the mental 'feeling' of fatigue is related to these physical body and brain change 'states' is also challenging for us research folk to understand. Clearly some 'change' in structures, baseline physical values or mental states by whatever induces the fatigue process, be it physical or mental exertion or illness, is required for us to 'sense' these and for our brain and mental functions to 'ascribe' the sensation of fatigue to these changed states. It has previously been shown that the sensation of fatigue which arises during exercise is related to the distance to be covered and increases as one gets closer to the finish line. While this sounds obvious, as one would expect the body to become more 'changed' as one exercises for a longer period, it has been shown that when folk run at the same pace for either five or ten kilometres, despite their pace being identical in both, at the 4-km mark in the 5-km race the rating these folk give for the sensation of fatigue is higher than it is at 4km of the 10-km race, which is 'impossible' to explain physiologically, and suggests that folk 'set' their perceptual apparatus differently for the 5- and 10-km race, based on how far they have to go (what H-V Ulmer described as teleoanticipation), by changing the 'gain' of the relationship between the signals they get from their body depending on how far they plan to go. Two great South African scientists, Professor Ross Tucker of the University of Free State, and Dr Jeroen Swart of the University of Cape Town, have expanded on this by suggesting that there is a perceptual 'template' for the sensation of fatigue in the brain, and the sensation of fatigue is 'created' in an organized, pre-emptive 'way' by mental / cognitive processes in the brain, and the sensation of fatigue is 'controlled' by this template depending on the distance and / or duration of a sporting event. If something unexpected happens during an event, like a sudden drop in temperature, or a competitor that goes faster than expected, this will create an unexpected 'change' in signals from the body and requirements of the race, and the sensation of fatigue will become more pronounced and greater than what is expected at that point in the race, and one will slow down, or change plans accordingly. Ross and Jeroen's fascinating work show how complex the mental component of the sensation of fatigue and its 'creation' by brain structures is.

There are multiple other factors which are involved in the generation of the sensation of fatigue, or of its modulation. I did my medical PhD (an MD) on chronic fatigue syndrome which developed in athletes who pushed themselves too hard until they eventually physically 'broke down' and developed the classical fatigue symptoms associated with chronic fatigue, where they felt fatigue even when not exercising, which was not relieved by prolonged periods of rest. These athletes clearly pushed themselves 'through' their fatigue symptoms on a regular basis until they damaged themselves. As one of the pioneers and world-leading experts in the fatigue field, Professor Sam Marcora, has pointed out, one's ambitions and drives and 'desire for success' are a strong indicator of both the level of the symptom of fatigue folk will 'feel', and how they resist these symptoms. In these chronically fatigued folks we studied, something in their psychological makeup induced them either to constantly continue exercising despite the symptoms of fatigue or made them 'feel' less sensations of fatigue for the same work-rate (assuming their fitness levels and physical capacity was similar) to most folk who do not experience this syndrome (the vast majority of folk). To make the matter even more complex, these folk with chronic fatigue described severe sensations of fatigue at rest, but when we put them on a treadmill, some of them paradoxically felt less, rather than more, sensations of fatigue when running as compared to resting, and their extreme sensations of fatigue returned (to an even greater degree) in the rest period after they completed the running bout. Furthermore, if one gives stimulants to folk when they exercise, such as caffeine, it appears to reduce the 'awareness' of the sensations of fatigue. Sam is doing some interesting work currently looking at the effect of caffeine on attenuating the sensation of fatigue – as did Dr Angus Hunter several years ago – and thereby using it as a 'tool' to get folk to exercise more 'easily' as they appear to 'feel' fatigue less after ingesting caffeine. All this shows again that the sensation of fatigue is both a very complex emotion, and a very 'labile' one at that, and can change, and be changed, by both external factors such as these stimulants, and internal factors such as one's drive or 'desire' to resist the sensation of fatigue as they arise, or even 'block them out' before they are consciously generated. More research, and very advanced research techniques, will be required for us to clearly understand how and such potential 'blockages' of the sensation of fatigue happen, if they indeed occur.

The sensation of fatigue is therefore an immensely complex 'derivative' of several functions, behaviours, and psychological 'filters', and what we finally 'feel' as fatigue is 'more' than a simple one-to-one description of some underlying change in our physical body and brain that requires adjustment or attenuation. The sensation of fatigue is clearly a protective phenomenon designed to slow us down when we are exercising too hard or too long in a manner that may damage our body, or when we are working too hard or too long and need a 'time out', or when the environment one is performing activities of daily living in may be harming one. But there are usually more complex relationships and reasons for the occurrence of the sensation of fatigue than what on the surface may appear to be the case. For example, the increase in work-related fatigue I feel is surely related not just to the fact that it is the end of a busy week – it is perhaps likely to be related to a 'deep' yearning to be back on holiday, or to the fact that my mind is not 'hardened' yet to my routine daily work requirements, or has been 'softened' by the holiday period so that now I feel fatigue 'more' than is usual. In a few weeks' time this will surely be attenuated as the year progresses and my weekly routines, which have been 'honed' over many years of work, are re-established, and I will feel the 'usual' rather than excessive symptoms of fatigue as always on Thursdays and Fridays. The extreme feeling of fatigue I felt during the very hot December month may also be related to some subconscious 'perception' that my current living environment is perhaps not optimal for me lifestyle wise for a long- term living basis, and this 'influenced' how I perceived the environment as one of extreme heat and therefore extreme (and greater than expected) fatigue last month. And that I am 'enjoying' the sensations of fatigue I feel when exercising may mean that I am perhaps not pushing my exercise bouts as hard as I could, and need to go harder, or that my mind and body is setting a pace that feels enjoyable, or both, so I continue doing it, or to protect me from a potential heart attack if I go harder. All of these may be the case, or equally, all of these could be mere speculation – the science folk in the area of fatigue have a big mountain to climb, and many more hours in the lab, before we more fully understand the complex emotion which the sensation of fatigue is, and how and from where it arises and is controlled.

A time may come when Sam Marcora and other excellent research colleagues like him find the 'magic bullet' that will 'banish' the sensation of fatigue, and we will be able to work harder and exercise longer because of it. But then would the cold drink after exercise taste so good, or the feeling of accomplishment one gets at the end of a long exercise bout because of resisting the sensation of fatigue long enough to achieve one's goals for the particular exercise bout one has just completed still occur? This is something to ponder on, when fatigued, as I am now after two hours of writing, as I sip my cup of coffee, and wait for my 'energy' to return so I can begin the next task of a routine Sunday, whether it be cycling with the kids, walking the dog, or any other fatigue-removing activity as I prepare for the next fatiguing cycle that is the work and sport week ahead.

Essay 19. The self as soliloquy - The mind's inner voices make a winner or loser out of you during exercise and competitive sport

Anyone who has watched tennis will be aware of how much the players talk to themselves during matches, sometimes encouraging, sometimes critical. All of you with kids will remember how as babies they burbled and talk about anything, then at a certain pre-teen age this stopped and by teenage years they hardly say a thing. All of you will know that in quiet reflective times one has 'inner dialogues' with oneself, solving daily problems, reminding oneself of things that must be done, or worrying oneself about things in the external world that are currently of a concern to one. Self-talk, or inner dialogue is a fascinating 'viewpoint' into the subconscious, or at least is the 'point of emergence' of subconscious thoughts to our conscious mind, and recently some interesting research and theoretical work has shed more light on this somewhat disregarded component of our daily life and sense of self. In this Essay we examine self-talk, also known as 'inner dialogue', and assess what its function is, and what happens to it under times of stress or change, and whether it always tells us the 'truth' in any given situation.

I was watching the highlights of an Australian Open warm-up tournament a few days ago and noted how players often spoke aloud to themselves during the game, either congratulating themselves, or telling themselves to keep on going, or being critical of themselves when making an error. I have been trying to keep cycling through the Christmas break, even though it has been pretty cold and occasionally icy in the North-East UK, and I have had to have conversations with myself (internally, rather than out loud like the tennis players) both to get on the bike when sitting in front of a warm fire with a good book seemed a better option, and when I was out on the cycle path, and my toes and fingers felt frozen, to not stop, and keep on going. I have always been aware of the inner dialogue that continues incessantly in my mind throughout the day, either thinking of a science puzzle that I can't work out, or how best to sort out a challenge at work, or being reminded by an inner voice to get presents for the family for Christmas, amongst a million other discussions I have with myself, and I am sure each of you reading this is aware of these inner voices similarly. Curiously, there has not been a lot of attention paid to inner dialogue or the inner voices, which is surprising given how central one's inner dialogue is to one's life and are indeed a constant component of one's life of which one is usually very aware of. Even less work has been done on the effect of inner voices, either positive or negative, on athletic performance (or indeed any type of performance, be it sport, work, or any activity which puts stress on one), or indeed if one's inner voices alter during either competitive sport or exercise participation. A few years ago, I worked with one of the absolute legends and mavens in the Sport Science academic community, Professor Carl Foster, from Wisconsin in the USA, in order to try and understand a bit more about this curious yet fascinating subject, and we eventually published a theoretical review article on it a decade ago. All of these recent observations reminded me of this article we published, and the role of inner voices and the inner dialogue they create, and how this inner dialogue affects, and is altered by, competitive sporting activities and challenges.

Inner speech has also been described as self-talk, private speech, inner dialogue, soliloquy, egocentric speech, sub-vocal speech, and self-communicative speech, amongst others. Inner speech is predominantly overt during early childhood, and children up to four years of age believe that a mind of a person sitting quietly is 'not doing anything' and is 'completely empty of all thoughts and ideas'. With increasing age, and associated increasing self-awareness, children reduce the quantity of overt inner speech, particularly when in large groups or around teachers, until overt inner speech only occurs when the child is alone, due to them becoming aware of the social consequences of unchecked overt inner speech. This change of inner speech from overt to covert appears to be related to appropriate physical and cognitive developmental changes, as children with Down's syndrome continue to use overt inner speech, and folk who are Schizophrenic also use overt inner speech, and indeed feel that their inner speech is generated 'outside' of their heads and by an external agent, and often feel tormented by the ongoing dialogue which to them appears to be 'outside' of their minds. In adolescents, increasing negative or self-critical inner speech has been related to psychological disorders such as depression, anxiety and anger.

As described above, the makeup and function of the inner voices during sport have not been extensively researched previously. However, Van Raalte and colleagues examined overt inner speech in tennis players, and found that a large percentage was negative, and that there was a correlation between the quantity of negative inner speech and losing, which was not present between positive inner speech and winning, a somewhat puzzling finding. The laboratory group of father and son academics Lew and James Hardy have done some excellent work in this field. A study by their group, first authored by Kimberley Gammage, where they looked at the nature of inner speech in a variety of sports, found that 95% of athletes reported they used / were aware of inner speech during exercise (why 5% of folk do not is perhaps more curious than those folk that did), and noticed their inner speech to a greater degree when they were fatigued, when they wanted to terminate the exercise bout, and near the end of the exercise bout. Their inner speech was described most often to be phrases (such as 'keep it up' or 'don't stop') rather than single words or sentences, and interestingly, they used the second person tense more frequently than the first-person during exercise. The athletes perceived that they used inner speech for motivational purposes, maintaining drive and effort, maintaining focus and arousal, and to a lesser degree for cognitive functions such as ensuring correct race strategy, or using methods that would enhance their performance, such as breathing regularly. Helgo Schomer and colleagues did a great study where they got folk doing long Sunday runs to take walkie-talkies (the study was done in the 1980's) and he would contact them randomly during the run and ask what they were thinking. While there will always be a degree of self-censorship of personal thoughts and inner discussion, he found that at lower running speeds, most inner speech was described as conversational chatter or problem solving social or work issues, and at higher speeds monitoring their body function, and the environment.

While all this work is excellent in describing what type of inner speech is 'spoken' at rest and during exercise, some of the best 'deep' theoretical work I have ever read in this field was generated by George Mead more than a hundred years ago, where he suggested that inner speech is a 'soliloquy' which occurs between at least two inner voices, rather than a single voice in one's mind / brain. Mead defined these as an 'I' voice, representing the voice describing a current activity, or urging one to act, and a 'Me' voice, which takes the 'perspective of the other' and with which the 'I' voice is assessed. Mead also suggested that previous social interactions with other individuals allowed one to gain a viewpoint of oneself or one's actions or thoughts, and therefore that 'taking the perspective of the other' is the ability to understand that another person's viewpoint may be different to one's own, and to use that opinion to change one's own behaviour or viewpoint. Inner speech thus allows or creates the internalisation of this mechanism for taking another person's perspective, as one can describe to a 'real' person (someone whom one has interacted with in the past that was significant to one), or an imagined person one has never previously interacted with, in one's mind the reasons for behaving in a certain manner in a previous or 'current' situation, or how one is 'feeling' the effects of current activity, and the 'Me' voice takes the opinion of the other (and can be a conglomeration of many others, and be a 'generalised other') to assess the validity of how one says one is feeling. These concepts fit in well with the findings of Gammage and colleagues, who as described above, suggested that inner speech as mostly being reported as occurring in the second person tense ('Me'), but with first person speech also occurring (which would be the 'I' voice), though why the 'Me' voice would be 'heard' more than the 'I' voice during exercise, if the findings of Gammage and colleagues occur in all athletes during all sporting events, is not clear.

A further fascinating hypothesis about inner speech was made by Morin and others, who suggested that inner speech was crucial for self-awareness (and one's sense of self), by creating a time distance or 'wedge' between the 'self' and the mental or physical activities which the 'self' was currently experiencing. This time-wedge would enable retrospective analysis of the activity in which the individual was currently immersed in, thus facilitating the capacity for self-observation and thus both awareness of the 'meaning' of the activity and its effect on the individual, and self-awareness per se. In other words, if an individual was completely immersed in their current experience, they could not understand the meaning of the experience, because a time or perceptual gap is needed to create the time required to get enough 'distance' from the activity and assess and understand the meaning of an experience, and whether it is a threat to the individual if it continues. Inner speech therefore has been suggested to be the action that generates the time-wedge by creating a redundancy of self-information. This redundancy is the result of the difference between the actual physiological changes associated with the experience creating one unit of information about the event, and the descriptive 'I' inner speech creating a second (retrospective) unit of information of the same activity or event, separated from the first unit of information by a time-wedge. This time-wedge and redundancy of the same information allows retrospective comparison and analysis of the two different activities – the one in real time, and the other a retrospective copy, and a judgement is made of what is happening and how best to respond to it, by the 'Me' voice. This theory would suggest that all inner speech is retrospective, even the 'I' voice, and allows the retrospective analysis of an event in an ordered and structured way. Lonnie Athens, one of my all-time best creative thinkers, suggested 10 'rules' that well describe all these complex inner speech processes described above: 1) People talk to themselves as if they are talking to someone else, except they talk in short hand; 2) When people talk to each other, they tell themselves at the same time what they are saying; 3) While people are talking to us, we have to tell ourselves what they are saying; 4) We always talk with an interlocutor when we soliloquise – the 'phantom others' (which is the 'Me' voice as described above); 5) The phantom community is the one and the many. However, we can normally only talk to one phantom at a time during our soliloquies; 6) Soliloquising transforms our raw, bodily sensations into perceived emotions. If it were not for our ability to soliloquise, we would not experience perceived emotions (like fatigue during exercise) in our existence. Instead, we would only experience a steady stream of vague body sensations; 7) Our phantom others (the 'Me' voice) are the hidden sources of our perceived emotions. If we generate emotions by soliloquising about our body sensations, and if our phantom others play a critical role in our soliloquies, then our phantom other must largely shape the perceived emotion we generate; 8) Our phantom community (the 'Me' voice) occupies the centre stage of our life whether we are alone or with others. Talking to the 'phantom others' about an experience we are undergoing is essential to understand its emergent meaning. Only in conversation with our phantom community do we determine its ultimate meaning; 9) Significant social experiences shape our phantom community (which are incorporated into our 'Me' voice); and 10) Given that some soliloquies are necessarily 'multi-party' dialogues, conflicts of opinion are always possible during inner speech soliloquies.

Relating all this fascinating theoretical work to an exercise bout, therefore – as exercise continues, and physiological sensations change, these changes would be picked up by physiological sensors in the body and transferred to the brain, where they would be raised into our conscious mind by the 'I' voice, which already has a time-wedge to make sense of the raw feelings. Therefore, the athlete's 'I' voice would say 'I am tired', and the 'Me' voice would respond to this assessment of the 'I' voice, based on their 'perspective of the other' viewpoint. The 'Me' Voice may be either positive in response (motivational – 'keep going, the rewards will be worth it') or negative (cognitive – 'if you keep on going, you will damage yourself'). As the race or physical activity continued, as described above in the work of Kimberley Gammage and colleagues, athletes become more aware of their inner speech, probably because the symptoms of fatigue and distress described by the 'I' voice become more profound, and more persistent, and the 'Me' voice has to keep on responding to the more urgent and louder voice of the 'I' voice', given that the 'I' voice is describing changes that have greater potential to be damaging to the athlete. It is likely that the relative input of each of the 'I' and 'Me' voices (and of course the subconscious processes that generate them) are either related to, or create, the temperament and personality of the individual, and their perception of success or failure in sport. For example, the 'Me' voice may suggest that it is not a problem to slow down when the 'I' voice indicates that the current speed the athlete is producing is too fast and may damage the athlete, if the familial, genetic or psychological history that created the 'phantom others' / 'Me' voice of the athlete perceived that winning sporting events to not be of particular importance. In contrast, the 'Me' voice may disagree with, and disapprove of, the desire of the 'I' voice to slow down, if the familial, genetic, psychological history of phantom others that make up the 'Me' voice believed that winning was very important and slowing down a sign of personal failure and weakness. These relative viewpoints of the 'Me' voice will therefore likely shape the personality and self-esteem of the athlete (and indeed, all individuals), and whether they regard themselves a success or failure, if they try to keep on going and win, or try to keep on going and slow down due to having reached their physical body limits, which may not be congruent with the athlete's psychological desires and demands. Furthermore, the 'will' of the athlete is probably to a large degree related to the forcefulness of the 'Me' voice in resisting the desire of the 'I' voice, or if the 'I' voice remains relatively silent even under times of duress or hardship and is also likely created by the family history or genetic makeup of the athlete when creating the generalised phantom other / 'Me' voice. The relative input of both the 'I' and 'Me' components of an individual's inner speech and the 'viewpoint' of the 'Me' voice may therefore be the link between the temperament and performance of an athlete or may actually be part of or influence both.

In summary, therefore, those tennis players with their overt inner speech (usually accompanied by fist pumping or smashed rackets depending on its positive or negative nature) open a window for us to understand one of the most potentially crucial and amazingly complex constituents of the perceptual loop of how sensations generated by the body under stress are changed into emotions that we 'feel' and respond to, which both explains to us how our body is feeling, behaving and 'doing' by the vocalisation of an 'I' voice, and at the same time creates our sense of self as a result of how the dialogue responds to this explanation, vocalised as inner speech, through our 'Me' voice, which is both reflective and created by the phantom others which shape us and regulate us. However, the inner voices can be our worst enemies, if they are too strong, or too harsh, or too demanding on us, and if so, they are probably produced by a damaged childhood with over-demanding parents, coaches, or teasing peer children which make us feel like what we are doing is never 'enough', even though of course what 'enough' is will always be a relative thing, and different for every person on earth. Some Sport Psychologists have tried to improve sporting performance of athletes they work with by altering the content and nature of their inner speech, though Lonnie Athens made the relevant point that if one's inner speech was too changeable, one's sense of self would be fluid and not permanent, which in most folk it seems to be, and that only extreme psychological trauma, such as assault, divorce, near death or death of a loved one, where a state of existence is created which the 'Me' voice has no frame of reference, will allow the 'Me' voice to be changed, and of course, it may change from a positive or neutral to a more negative 'commentary state'. Having said that, my own inner voices have changed subtly as I have aged and are (fortunately) more tolerant and forgiving as compared to what they were like in my youth. Often when doing sport, in contrast to when I was young when my 'Me' voice was insistent I keep going or be a failure, my inner voices now I am in my fifties often encourage me to slow down and look after myself, now that my body is old, less efficient, and damaged by the excesses of sport and wilful behaviour of my youth. So clearly there is some capacity to change and maintain one's sense of self. Having said that, my sense of self is also subtly different from what it was in my youth, so this may be related to the changes in the make-up of my inner voices (and their underlying subconscious control mechanisms, perhaps due to the desires of my youth mostly being fulfilled in my life to date), or may not be related to them at all. More research work is needed for us to better understand all these concepts and mental activities that are continuously active in our mind and brain.

At this point in time our inner speech is the only real-time window we have into our subconscious and is both 'ourselves' (as hard a concept this is to understand and accept) and our continuous companion through each minute of each day of our life. Often one wishes to turn off one's inner voices, and interestingly some drugs do seem to reduce the amount of 'heard' inner voices, but this does open up the philosophical challenge of whether if one has no inner speech, whether one will be aware that one is conscious, or aware of one's current state of being. My inner voice has been 'shouting at me' during the last two paragraphs of writing this, telling me I am tired and hungry, and it's time to stop writing for the day and go in from my garden shed home working office to spend time with the family, and get some food and drink to replenish my energy levels. While I resisted their siren tune until completing this piece of writing, now it's done, I will bow to my inner voices incessant request and sign off and head in for some welcome rest and relaxation. Of course, I know that after a short period of relaxing, my inner speech will be chattering at me again, telling me to go back to my garden shed office and check the grammar and spelling of this article, and start preparing for the next. There is no peace for the wicked, particularly from our ever present, and ever demanding, inner voices.

Essay 20. Teleoanticipation - Activity performed during a task or journey is set before starting it

One of the most amazing things about endurance athletic events is that nearly all folk participating in them complete the event in about the time they expect to do it in, and very few collapse during the event or fail to complete it due to extreme exhaustion. Equally, the roads are abuzz with folk taking trips in their cars, and just about all folk make it to their destination without running out of petrol or becoming too exhausted to drive due to a lack of drink or food in their car or with stops planned to take on board food and fuel. Some incredible calculations in the brain are in effect required to enable this successful completion to occur, mostly occurring at a subconscious level so we are not even aware that they are happening, along with anticipatory planning and pacing during the event or activity, in a process which has become known as teleoanticipation. In this Essay we will examine the interesting concept of teleoanticipation, what it is, what parameters are required to work successfully, and what 'signature' events during the event or race occur which allow us to conclude that teleoanticipation is indeed occurring and doing so in all events we plan to do and complete.

Due to some poor time planning on my part this week, and a too full work diary, I nearly ran out of petrol in my car, and for two days drove it with the warning lights saying I was about to run out of fuel. These two days, during which I experienced some anxiety each time I drove it between sequential work engagements, got me thinking of the theory of teleoanticipation. This theory was generated by H-V Ulmer in the early 1990s, and suggested that before beginning any task or journey, our brain considers all the factors that are likely to be involved in the task or could affect the task, including most importantly the expected duration of the planned task, and comes up with a strategy / template for how the task should be performed. This strategy would then define how one managed and performed the task for its entire duration. In other words, one plans everything for tasks and activities prior to performing them in an anticipatory manner, and this planning allows both for their successful completion in the most optimal way, and at the same time ensures that one is not harmed in any way during the completion of the task, which could be the result of either over-extending oneself, or not planning for unexpected events that could impinge on one, while the task is being performed.

The concept of teleoanticipation is underpinned by the twin concepts of homeostasis and pacing. Homeostasis is defined as the tendency towards maintaining a relatively stable equilibrium between interdependent elements and is one of the basic concepts underpinning all life and activities in life. Pacing is defined as the optimal management of resources so as to be able to complete a task in the fastest possible time while maintaining adequate resources in order to finish the task. So teleoanticipation associated regulatory processes set the strategy for a task with the overarching goal of maintaining homeostasis as best possible in those performing the task. Pacing, or how one paces oneself during a task, is the 'operative manager' of how homeostasis is maintained and how the teleoanticipatory planning processes are 'operationalized' during the task. What Ulmer suggested was that the endpoint of the task, whether it be a known time duration or a distance to be travelled or activity to be performed, would be the ultimate controller of the task in its entirety. Using the process of teleoanticipation, the brain would work 'backwards' from the endpoint and plans the activity for each phase of the task from start to beginning with the endpoint / duration / distance in mind, and with the overarching goals of both maintaining homeostasis and completing the task in the most optimal way.

A great example of the teleoanticipatory process is evident in the behaviour of migrating birds, who travel up to 4000 km as part of their annual migratory journey, often overseas and lakes, where incorrect 'planning' of their flight would invariably be fatal to them. Before migration birds calculate the metabolic requirements of their flight and increase the quantity and alter the composition of their fuel stores, embarking on their migration only when they have sufficient body fat stores. They also modulate their flight speed and flying patterns during the migratory flight to accommodate the extra body weight caused by their increased fuel reserves in order to successfully reach their destination. It is interesting that entire flocks of birds migrate as a unit, meaning that their teleoanticipatory planning processes and pacing strategies for their migration are either universal to all of them, or are commonly linked. Another example of teleoanticipation is seen in ants, which can gauge with superb accuracy the distances they have to travel in a range of different environments to go back to a food source during several different / separate journeys. In humans, we seem to be able to accurately predict distances we plan to travel or the duration of tasks we perform. Our plans and the way we pace ourselves during different tasks is usually astonishingly predictable and repetitive, although this appears to be a learned behaviour. Some fascinating work from my academic colleague and friend, Dr Dom Micklewright, has shown that pacing and task planning in children is a learned thing, and up to the age of around six or seven young children have no pacing strategies, and simply start as fast as they can, and either stop before reaching the task finish point, or slow down precipitously before doing so, which would indicate a lack of teleoanticipatory capacity in young children. After the age of eight or nine children start using pacing strategies and become more successful in completing tasks, events and races in a well-regulated manner. Therefore, prior experience, or repeated exposure to tasks, appears to be essential for setting and 'honing' the teleoanticipation associated regulatory control processes.

A key finding in most studies of teleoanticipation and pacing is the presence of an 'endspurt', where folk speed up as they reach the last 10 percent of completion time or duration for any goal. Apart from this endspurt activity occurring almost always around 10 percent from the end of a task showing that folk have extremely accurate timing mechanisms, it also indicates that we keep a 'reserve' capacity in all tasks we perform, as if we did not, we would not be able to accelerate in the completion of any task towards its end. Why we keep this reserve capacity right up to the end of a task is probably also a protective response, to ensure we have redundancy of choice / the ability to alter out chosen teleoanticipatory strategy in the case of a life-threatening event, even if from a control systems perspective, this would not be the most 'efficient' way of completing a task or event. Teleoanticipation as a regulatory process appears to exist in just about every task or activity we perform or are involved in, from setting our work schedules for daily, weekly, monthly and yearly durations, to how we drive cars and run or cycle races, to how stock market trading activity occurs on a daily basis, to even how folk order beers during an evening out period and as the pub's closing bell time approaches – everything we do that has a finite goal, duration or distance appears to be regulated by these teleoanticipatory processes in our brains, which mostly seem to occur at a subconscious level, unless unexpected factors we did not account for impinge on our task performance.

So, coming back to my incident this week of nearly running out of petrol, understanding the concept of teleoanticipation, and its 'twin' concepts of pacing and homeostasis, allows one to make a few deductions from what happened to me and how I reacted to the incident from a control perspective. My diary management for the week may have been optimal from the concept of performing my work tasks optimally, but clearly it impacted negatively on my usual teleoanticipatory strategy for ensuring I as normal had enough petrol in my car so that I did not run out, which usually operates at a 'subconscious level', and is very conservative, as normally, like most folk do, I fill my car up with petrol long before I reach the 'reserve warning light' level. My response was to be alarmed when I realized that I was operating out of the boundaries of the normal 'plan' for my car fuel level strategy, and I worried about this during my daily activity, even though with my diarized work commitments I could not do anything about it, which means that clearly our brain's teleoanticipatory centres put up conscious alarm signals when the normal 'pacing' strategy, in this case for car travel, was 'messed up'. Finally, given that I did not run out of petrol, but made it to the start of the weekend without running out, and then went as my first task to fill the car up with petrol after judging I would just make it to the weekend before running out, even if I was driving the last two days very much 'in the red', indicates that in effect my 'teleoanticipatory' strategy in the end did ultimately 'work' and 'petrol level homeostasis' was maintained – even if by doing so (filling up the car at the start of the weekend) impinged on and 'messed up' my routine weekend home activities. This example shows how robust the control processes underpinning teleoanticipation in our lives are, and how essential they are to our survival and optimal functioning. So next time one goes on a trip or performs a task, one can do so with assurance given the knowledge that one's subconscious brain has probably performed myriad calculations prior to starting it to ensure its successful completion. How much one worries about planning for tasks is perhaps associated with how novel an environment is, and how many factors which one has little control over could be associated with impacting on it, such as my poor diary management. This is perhaps one reason why airplane travel is so stressful for so many folk, given that most of the planning for and control of the trip is taken completely out of one's own hands, and one has to rely completely for one's 'homeostasis' / life on the teleoanticipatory planning of another person (the pilot), who like the migratory birds has very complex factors to plan for, and one is very aware of the potential consequences of any error in these teleoanticipatory calculations while having no control over them. What happens with, or how, task activity without goals or duration or distance is regulated is another question, but of course do we ever really perform any activities which are such, as much as we wish that we could – even holidays are not endless and have an endpoint.

Essay 21. Elite athlete performance and super-achievers in sport - Is the essential ingredient for success an inner mongrel or unrequited child rather than purely physical capacity?

To be an elite athlete, one needs to have some 'x-factor' which makes you faster, stronger, more agile, or fitter than one's competitors. Most research and talent identification programmes looking for the next generation of elite athletes have traditionally perceived that the physical capacity of folks who win races are what sets them apart from their competitors, but in the last few years, with so many athletes shown to have similar physical characteristics necessary to do well in their specific events, the focus has shifted to the mental strength, and great 'drive to succeed' in elite athletes. Surprisingly, and perhaps somewhat sadly, it has been found that 'mongrels' — those from broken homes, or who have been abused in childhood, or were sent off to a hated boarding school — may have a greater 'desire to achieve' than 'thoroughbreds' who come from impeccable homes and backgrounds where their every need was met when growing up. In this Essay we examine the concept of elite athletes, including what makes them such, and why they have the capacity to go that bit further, or that bit faster, than their less successful competitors.

Above my desk at home is a picture of my great university friend, Philip Lloyd, and I in our paddling days many years ago completing a race, shortly before he switched to mountain climbing, a sport where he achieved great success and pioneered several astonishingly difficult routes in a very short space of time before tragically falling to his death when a safety rope failed on a high mountain in Patagonia. Each year I enjoy watching the Tour de France and I am awed by the cyclists' capacity to sustain pain for so long in the high mountain stages, and their capacity to train for huge amounts of time daily to ensure they get to the race in peak condition. This week I read about the extent of doping in sport and wondered not only how they appeared to have gotten away with it for so long, but how so many athletes could have and do take drugs when there is so much evidence how potentially harmful performance enhancing drugs can be to the body of those that take them. All of these got me thinking about why people push themselves to such limits to win races, and what 'separates' these race winners and super-achievers in sport, including those that in order to win become dope takers, not only from their less successful peers, but the vast majority of the human population to whom cycling a few kilometres would be regarded as a big effort and achievement, and who would probably prefer to have a cup of coffee while reading a newspaper as their activity of preference.

It is clearly necessary for folk who are successful in sport to have the 'right' physical characteristics to be able to compete at the highest level, be it the right body shape for their chosen sport, or a big lung capacity, or great muscular strength, or good balance or agility. But you can have all of these, and yet if one doesn't have the required amount of 'will' to push one's body, no matter how specially 'designed' it is, to train for hours daily or to push oneself to near collapse during a race itself, one will never be a 'winner' during athletic events. Where this 'will' be generated from, and how it is stimulated to be maintained in the face of extreme hardship, is still not clearly understood or determined. One of the biggest 'wow' moments of my science career was when after doing competitive sport for many years and studying as an academic how sport was regulated for many years after that, I realized after spending thousands of hours reading about drive and motivation theories that performing sport is an essentially abnormal activity / thing to do. That might sound strange, but this 'wow' moment was underpinned by the knowledge that our bodies and brain have very well-defined protective mechanisms, both physically and psychologically, that protect us from damage and resist any effort to get out of our 'comfort zones'. In the physical sciences these processes are called homeostatic mechanisms, and in psychology they are described as being part of the 'constancy principle'. Homeostasis was defined by Claude Bernard in the 1860s as the tendency to maintain the body in a state of relative equilibrium well away from the limits of the body's absolute capacity using protective physiological mechanisms. The constancy principle was developed by Sigmund Freud in the early 1900s as an offshoot of his 'pleasure principle' theory and central to the principle is the concept that the human being is a biological organism which strives to maintain its level of 'excitation' at an always 'comfortable' level. To achieve this goal, Freud suggested that humans avoid or seek to diminish any external stimuli which are likely to prove excessive or which will threaten our internal state of equilibrium, using mechanisms in either the conscious or subconscious mind. So, when we get up and exercise, which increases our body's metabolic rate tremendously, and mentally requires effort, we are doing something that is essentially 'anti-homeostatic', and which would naturally initiate a number of mechanisms designed to make us resist the desire to continue exercising, or even stop completely. The symptom of fatigue would be an obvious example of one such protective mechanism which would be an overt part of or result of either physical homeostatic or psychological constancy mechanisms.

So why do folk do sport then if there are all these protective mechanisms. A possible reason may be 'higher order' homeostatic / constancy mechanisms, such as material or social rewards that may result from participating in sport, which are beneficial for the long-term future of the individual and are 'chosen as being more 'important' than the short-term risk of being out of one's safety 'zone' when doing sport. For example, being fitter would perhaps be thought to make one more desirable for a potential mate from a biological offspring choice perspective, or if one won a race this would lead to financial gain which would again make one more socially desirable, and thereby enhance the reproductive capacity of the individual participating in sport because of the perceived increased 'esteem' associated with being a winner. This is a very biological theory for sport and race participation, and suggests that doing sport, racing and winning are beneficial from a Darwinian perspective, and involving oneself in such events would be part of some deep-rooted 'propagation of species' biological drive or motive.

The problem with this biological theory is that it does not explain why people push themselves to the level of collapse in sport or why folk continue competing either with warning signs of impending physical catastrophe such as angina (chest pain associated with heart disease), or take drugs in order to improve their chances of success, or become dependent on / addicted to sport (there are numerous examples of this and it is an increasing psychopathological problem), all of which would potentially damage rather than enhance one's future life prospects and therefore also one's reproductive capacity, so perhaps something 'deeper' is involved. Albert Adler, around the time that Freud proposed the constancy theory, put forward his theory of the inferiority complex, which suggested that performing great feats were related to a sense of inferiority related to prior issues, and that one competes or performs events as a mechanism of 'hiding' internal perceived inadequacies or short-comings of the self after previous negative experiences (being bullied in one's youth, or teased about physical weakness in adolescence, for example). Freud suggested that damaging events in one's youth led to a state of 'ego-fragility', where in order to 'block out' painful experiences from one's past, one 'represses' these damaging memories or experiences and one 'projects' or externalises these internal conflicts into external drives or desires which are 'transferred' onto something or some action that can 'compensate' for these early formative related issues. Therefore, for example, if one feels one is the cause of one's parent's divorce, to compensate one spends the rest of one's life winning races or doing well at work in order to try and 'make up' for the 'damage' one perceives one has caused at some deep subconscious level, even if one is not the cause of it, and one does not even consciously realize that one is doing something for this 'deep' reason. Symptoms and signs of projection and transference include fanatical attachment to projects and goals, envy and dislike for other folk who are successful or receive awards and falling apart when failing to complete a challenge successfully – all of which are endemic and part of the 'make-up' of the sporting world.

If this sounds 'odd', or far-fetched, there are some interesting data and information that can be gleaned from athlete autobiographies and academic studies that would suggest that this theory may have a degree of veracity. Dave Collins and Aine Macnamara wrote a very interesting review a few years ago, in which they suggested that 'talent needs trauma' and described data that would support this concept. For example, academy football players who eventually made it to become elite football players apparently have a greater number of siblings (more competition for parents' attention) and a three times higher parental divorce rate than peers who did not reach elite level activity. They also suggested that successful footballers come from backgrounds with a higher incidence of single parent families, while rowers commonly reported an increased level of early childhood departure to boarding school (which Collins and Macnamara, rightly in my mind, suggested would be a 'natural source of early trauma'). Looking at successful cyclists' information gleaned from their autobiographies or articles written about them describe that, for example, Lance Armstrong's parents split up not long after he was born and he grew up with a stepfather he didn't like; Bradley Wiggins's parents similarly split up when he was young, as did Mark Cavendish's, and Chris Froome's parents also separated when he was young. If all this described family history for these cycling champions, footballers and rowers is indeed true, it would be supportive of Collin's and Macnamara's suggestion, and that perhaps some of these athletes' drive to succeed (and in Armstrong's case to the level where he was willing to take drugs to do so) is related to some inner drive created by their challenging conditions in their youth (though of course it can be said that growing up in a divorced family environment may often be more easier than doing so in a marriage where there is continuous conflict between parents, or stifling living conditions), or is a compensation for it.

As I said earlier, us scientist folk are still not completely sure what makes an elite athlete, or why some folk push themselves to extreme levels of physical activity. My friend Phil Lloyd was interesting to me as he had such potential in all aspects of his life (and was such a great person and friend), yet he seemed to have some inner 'edge' that made him always restless and always want to go 'higher' or 'do more' and never seemed completely satisfied with what he had achieved – like a lot of us when we were young, there was always a more dangerous river to paddle down than the one we had just got out of, or a higher mountain that needed to be climbed. While I surely had my own demons in my youth, I remember asking Phil why he climbed these very and increasingly dangerous routes he was doing before he died. He gave several reasons, but one which always stuck with me was that when he was solo climbing 'up there' miles away from help and people, it felt a bit like when he was young and at boarding school as a child, and it helped him work through these memories. I did not understand his answer then, and thought he was perhaps joking with this answer, but after a career in science and reading basic psychology texts for many years, his answer eventually made sense to me (and perhaps was the 'seed' that led me to write this specific article). There are incredible rewards for those who achieve great success in sport. Those who do well / attain the pinnacle of success in any sport deserve our utmost admiration for what they put themselves through during races and daily when training. But perhaps there is an element that all this effort, which takes them (and me in my youth) far out of their own 'constancy' / homeostatic zones, is in effect in part potentially a compensation for trauma of times past that creates an 'inner mongrel' which refuses to give up until the 'prize' is won that will 'make up' for that past loss or trauma. In a way by doing so, perhaps (and hopefully) all these folk by winning enough will gradually attenuate the 'unrequited child' which may still reside in them, and reach psychological 'peace', and wake up one morning and choose to go and have a cup of coffee in a warm shop rather than ride a bike or kick a football for six hours in the pouring rain, and be happy and be able to feel relaxed when doing so. There is a huge energy cost and price involved over many years if indeed winning anything is related to an inner mongrel that won't 'keep quiet' – and in the case of my great friend Phil, his drive to succeed in his chosen sport perhaps in part led to his death, and we never got the chance to see him reach his full potential, which he possessed in such abundance in all aspects of his work, social and sporting life, and each day I work at home I see the picture of us paddling together and feel a sadness for this lack. Equally though, if there was no inner mongrel and / or unrequited child, would there ever be winners, and would the high mountains of the world ever have been climbed? I'll ponder that question more later today when I head off with the family to the coffee shop for our weekly Sunday coffee and newspaper routine.

Section 4. Understanding Human System Breakdown and Medical Issues

4.1. Introduction

In the previous section, we looked at the poetry of life in its fullest action and activities, and the body functioning at its maximal capacity as part of exercise performance. In the following section, which consists of 12 Essays, we examine the other end of the threshold, namely when the body systems fail, or when activity become pathological rather than health or superior performance inducing. While the list of things that damage the body and mind, and ultimate robs the individual of their life essence if it overwhelms the life force or will to live, is very long and exhaustive, we have chosen a small number of different physical pathologies or psychopathologies that I have personally studied and is representative of the number of ways the body and mind can be harmed or harms itself. What was one of the most interesting things that I began to understand while researching these illnesses and disorders, is that when one becomes ill, or the body breaks down, a number of redundant protective pathways and activities are activated to try and either attenuate the effects of the pathology, or to correct the organ imbalances which have occurred as the result of injury or damage to organs, and when one sees visual changes in activity in either whole body activity or in specific organ function when pathology occurs to the same or other organ, one may be viewing a response that is attempting to 'fix' the problem, rather than the problem itself. Even in a state of illness or failure, life shows its exquisite poetry, and the marvellous complexity of its function, which includes sometimes never used healing or system replacement capacity.

Essay 22. Anxiety, stress, and the highly sensitive person - Too much of something always becomes a bad thing that damages one in the end

Anxiety is defined as worry about future events before they occur and is felt by all folk to varying degrees unless they are sociopaths / psychopaths. There is good reason on many occasions to feel anxious about events one is worried about such as job interviews, difficult conversations, visits to the doctor and suchlike, but one can get oneself into a pickle by either worrying too much about things, worry about too many things, or worrying for too long about the same things. Too much anxiety can lead to physical pathology such as high blood pressure, and chronic anxiety can be psychologically debilitating, and the incidence and prevalence of folk being medically treated for anxiety disorders is increasing rapidly. In this Essay, therefore, we examine anxiety and assess its negatives and positives, and whether 'too much of a necessary thing becomes a bad thing'.

I am one of those people that worries all the time. If there is an issue at work or at home that is of concern, I will up at 2.00 am in the morning wondering how best to solve it and worrying about it until I am sure it is solved. When all is as well as it can be I will still find something to worry about – my plans for the future, pension funds (or lack of them), my kids' health, anything and everything. In many ways this has been a good thing, as it has helped me always plan ahead, find solutions to problems and be aware of challenging situations as they develop, or even before they do. In many ways this has been a bad thing, as it means I get irritable and stressed when things are not working out well, and I am at the age when this continued mental 'strain' has the potential after many years of being the 'status quo' to cause cumulative physical damage to my body resulting potentially in such clinical conditions as migraines, high blood pressure, heart attacks, and strokes amongst others. There is clearly a genetic or physical environment component to this 'worry' state, as my father was very similar, and always seem to be worried when he was not almost overly exuberant and happy (there never was a middle ground with him, which made life as a child both fun and challenging), and for most of his adult life until he suffered a series of heart attacks in his early fifties, he smoked 90 cigarettes a day (and was in his early years 'proud' of this fact and his capacity to smoke prodigiously, given that in his era it was the 'done thing' to smoke) and was never to be seen without a cigarette in his hand, surely as an antidote for and a mechanism to assist him to cope with the stress he felt on a daily basis and which he surely worried about continuously. I have noticed since the advent of the mobile phone, during meetings I sit in at work, or when I go out for a social evening, folk around me check their phone for text messages or emails on a regular basis, with some folk doing so seemingly every few minutes, which is also surely a pathological sign of something 'worrying' these folk, or of a 'worry' type of personality in these folk who seem to need to check on information coming to them on an almost continuous basis. All these got me thinking about 'worry' – known clinically as anxiety – and what causes it to occur, and why some folks appear to feel it more than others and seem to be 'highly sensitive' to stressful situations.

Anxiety is defined as a worry about future events before they occur, and is different, though related, to the concept of fear, which is defined as a psychological reaction to current events. Related to both concepts are those of stress, homeostasis and allostasis. The theory of homeostasis suggests that our natural preferred state of existence is one where we are in 'equilibrium' with the environment in which we live, and our body and mind are in a 'steady state', free of requirements, needs and challenges. When this steady state we exist in is challenged, for example by low energy levels in the body, we notice this as a stressor to our steady state existence ('hunger' is the mechanism by which we 'notice' this particular stress factor), and this stress induces us to respond to it, by in this example generating actions and plans that will allow us to source and eat food, thereby increasing our body's energy 'levels' back to the state in which we are comfortable and 'happy' with. Similarly, if we become hot, we move to a place where cooler conditions exist. In more complex examples, if our social or community life changes in a way we feel uncomfortable with, we make plans and enact changes that will attenuate this social stress by either moving to a new place or environment, or taking steps to remove whatever or whoever is causing us discomfort if it is in our power to do so. The process of achieving stability, or homeostasis, using behavioural and psychological changes, has recently been described as allostasis (though some of us believe this is an unnecessary definition as the definition of homeostasis incorporates what is now described as allostasis). These allostatic responses attenuate stressful changes, or changes which are at least perceived as stressful by us, by means of releasing stress hormones in the body (for example cortisol) via the hypothalamic-pituitary-adrenal gland pathway in the body, or by activating the autonomic nervous system (for example the sympathetic nerves which are responsible for initiating 'fight or flight' responses in the body), or by releasing cytokines (which are humoral blood-borne 'signallers' which also induce a number of physical body responses to stress), or other systems which are generally adaptive in the short term. These pathways all induce a number of 'general alarm' or 'specific response' changes in the physiological systems and different organs in the body, such as increasing the concentration of glucose in the blood and re-distributing it to areas of the body that need it most as a result of the induced stress, increasing cardiac output, blood pressure and blood flow to specific organs in the body such as the muscles while reducing blood flow to the digestive and reproductive system, and altering the immune system response, amongst others – which all in turn lead to symptoms one 'feels' such as dry mouth, rapidly beating heart, increased breathing rate, shaking muscles, nausea, diarrhoea, and even dizziness and confusion in extreme conditions. Like all things, some stress and occasional activation of this stress response 'allostatic' system is beneficial to one both for reducing the targeted stress and for making the response systems more efficient by 'practice'. But, like all things, if the stressor is not removed, or if multiple different stressors occur at once, and these responsive systems remain 'wide open', this can result in a status of 'chronic response fatigue' in these systems, and ultimately cause damage to the body by the very mechanisms that are designed to protect (for example a raised blood pressure allows blood to be pumped quickly to targeted organs requiring increased blood flow for their optimal function, but chronically raised blood pressure causes 'backflow' problems to the heart which leads to heart failure eventually, or 'forward flow' problems to other organs such as the kidneys, which are eventually damaged by continuously increased blood pressure over a period of time). What is defined as the 'allostatic load' is the 'wear and tear' of the body (and mind) which increases over time when someone is exposed to repeated or chronic stress and represents the physiological consequences of chronic exposure to the hormonal and neural responses described above, which are ultimately damaging to the person who is 'feeling' the stress and whose body is continuously trying to react to it.

These allostatic responses described above are reactive to an already occurring, or perceived to be occurring, stressful situation or environment, and the sensation of fear would be the psychological accompanying emotion associated with perceiving such already occurring situations. But as described above, anxiety is somewhat different, in that it is a worry about future, rather than already occurring events. When one is anxious, one is thinking about all the potential, rather than actual, implications of possible scenarios that could occur based on one's 'reading' of current situations or events occurring around one that may, rather than will, occur and potentially impinge on one and possibly cause stressful situations at some time point in the future. Interestingly, anxiety 'uses', or is at least associated with, several of the physical allostatic 'response' systems described above, such as the hypothalamic-pituitary-adrenal system, autonomic and interleukin systems, and a number of the symptoms of anxiety are associated with activity of these 'fight or flight' response systems and the physiological perturbations they induce. In episodes of acute anxiety (also known as panic attacks), symptoms including trembling, shaking, confusion, dizziness, nausea and difficulty breathing occur, all of which are induced by the allostatic stress-related pathways described above. While some anticipation of the future and resultant planning for it can only be good for one from a long term safety and security perspective, and therefore occasional anxiety can also be beneficial in 'encouraging' the planning of and 'making ready' future reactive plans for potential stressors one is concerned about after 'reading the runes' of one's current life, generalized anxiety disorder is a clinical condition that is characterized by excessive, uncontrollable and often irrational worry about future events that occurs in between three and five percent of the population worldwide, where folk have a high level of anxiety about everyday problems such as health issues, finances, death, family / social / work problems, or anticipated catastrophic situations which are not commensurate with their actual level of probability of occurring. Individuals with chronic anxiety disorder have a wide variety of 'psychosomatic' (body and mind) symptoms, including fatigue, headaches, nausea, muscle aches and tension, numbness in their hands and feet, fast breathing, stomach pain, vomiting, diarrhoea, sweating, irritability, agitation, restlessness, sleep disorders and an inability to either control the anxiety and / or its physical symptoms. If not adequately controlled, generalized anxiety disorder can result in a number of what are known as chronic 'lifestyle' disorders, such as high blood pressure, diabetes, migraines, heart attacks and strokes, as well as depression or irritable bowel syndrome, as well as a host of what are defined as 'psychosomatic' disorders'. What causes an individual to develop a generalized anxiety disorder is currently not well understood (it occurs more often in folk who have a family history of it), but it most often begins to manifest itself between the ages of 30-35, but can also occur in childhood or late adulthood, and appears to 'tap in' and chronically activate the allostatic physiological response mechanisms described above.

Another interesting 'relative' of anxiety disorders is what has become known as the Highly Sensitive Person (HSP) 'disorder'. Folk who are highly sensitive people have a high degree of what is known as sensory processing sensitivity, or in other words they appear to respond to, or be aware of physical body symptoms of stress and anxiety, or to social or environmental situations to a greater degree than folk who do not 'suffer' from this disorder. Folks who have HSP 'feel' all these body allostatic responses in an extremely sensitive way, via mechanisms that are still currently not well understood. Because of this, they are also 'hyper-aware' of social situations or environments that may trigger the 'release' of these physiological anxiety / stress-related response pathways in their bodies (or vice versa and they may be hyper-aware of these social situations because of their natural 'up-regulated' physical sensory state). This HSP state is either a curse or a blessing (or both), as it makes folk who 'suffer' from it prefer low stimulation environments and try to construct their lives to avoid over-stimulation, and predisposes them potentially to higher risk of chronic stress / anxiety related disorders, but it also make them 'feel' life more, have more insight into and early awareness of developing social situations that others may not even be aware of, and make them more 'intuitive' to what is going on around them. Whether HSP folk have higher levels of anxiety or greater incidence of a generalized anxiety disorder is currently not well known, but given both 'tap into' the same allostatic physical body systems and mechanisms make it more likely that this is indeed so. It must be noted that the concept of a highly sensitive person has been differentiated from that of a hypersensitive person, who are defined as folk who over-react to any stimuli or slight. Folk with HSP may simply be quiet, appear introverted or 'shy', or are able to 'hide' their HSP 'condition', while hypersensitive folk are typically very challenging to deal with socially, but they also may have underlying anxiety as a cause of their over-reactions, 'temper-tantrums' and rages. The treatment of all of these different anxiety-related disorders is challenging, and requires lifestyle change, psychological intervention (such as cognitive behavioural therapy) and / or medication, but there is always a relatively poor cure rate and a high degree of recidivism, and folk with anxiety and stress related disorders need to themselves understand, acknowledge and work on their underlying condition, though the problem for doing so is that a hyper-sensitivity responsive 'state' or condition is very difficult to understand, let alone treat. Several folk use smoking, alcohol consumption, or avoidance behaviour, as methods of 'dealing' with their anxiety or high level of sensitivity, but these short term 'emollients' create their own specific problems and may themselves paradoxically increase anxiety and stress in those that use them as a stress / anxiety reducing mechanism.

Worry, therefore, can be a useful thing to prepare one to enact future potential responses to what one is 'picking up' in one's current circumstances that causes one to worry, if it continues for a short period of time only and if it is about a specific issue. Worry, if chronic or if it is a clinical disorder, through the allostatic pathways and circuits it uses to initiate and mediate 'fight or flight' body changes, can cause a wide array of unpleasant symptoms and diminish one's quality of life, and can ultimately cause major physical damage to one's body if one does not manage it carefully, or treat it as something that needs to be 'cured'. The 'trappings' of modern society such as mobile phones and increased work and social connectivity and immediate communication capacity have many benefits, but these can also 'tap into' and reinforce these anxiety-related allostatic pathways and create continuous stress of their own making – it is likely that those folk who compulsively reach for their phones to check their messages every few minutes almost certainly have an anxiety disorder, or are prone to developing one, and future research is surely needed to ascertain the veracity of this possibility. I personally am a 'worrier', and almost certainly am a highly sensitive person, as was my father before me. This has created blessings and challenges both for us and those around us – life can be beautiful, but life can also be challenging, on a daily basis, with most of it 'raging' around in our own minds rather than in the 'real' life around us per se. At age 25, I would have said the benefits of being and living such as a highly sensitive person and 'worrier' surely outweighed the challenges – the rose surely smelt better, the rain surely felt softer, the love was deeper, the anger stronger, the passion for life greater too, and for us compared to how most folk around us probably experienced their less 'perceived' life. However, now I am about to reach the age of 50, and am reaching the 'tiger territory' period of life for high blood pressure, heart attacks and other 'diseases of a lived life', I am not so sure, and the thought of a calm life, without worry, without stress, lived in soft colour and tranquil shades and hues, seems to be perhaps the better one, and one that should have been chosen as the preferential way of living all those years ago, or at least changed to now I am more aware both of my own highly sensitive 'condition' and the potential negative effects such a life can have on one's physical response mechanisms and body organs and physiological systems. But, at the end of the day, can one ever really 'choose' one's own 'sensitivity to stimuli' levels? Perhaps our own anxiety and stress levels, or at least our own perception of them, were set in our ancestors' bodies thousands of years ago and passed down to us, even if they are redundant as a 'need' in our modern life and are therefore almost impossible to materially change despite our wishes and best efforts to do so. More research is needed to better understand if sensitivity to stimuli levels, and indeed those of anxiety itself, can ever be permanently attenuated, or rather if they stay permanently 'as is', and one merely learns rather how to cope and 'deal with' them better with the passing of time or with enhanced understanding, treatment or therapy.

One's life will surely happen to oneself, as it does for each of us as we move through life and its challenges, whether one worries about it or not, or whether one 'feels it' more or less, I guess, but in many ways it surely 'feels' more like it is 'happening to one' when one worries about it than when one does not – though doing so appears to damage one's physical survival mechanisms by over-use as part of the process. It must be wonderful to live a life in the always warm, always comfortable environment which is the one in which has no worries. But, equally, one can never maintain a hot fire without some internal combustion occurring which creates the heat, or even more so, put out a fire once it has been burning for a long time and has created the 'heat' which is manifestly evident in the life lived with maximal sensitivity to stimuli and responsivity to all around it. Would one choose to put this 'fire' out and reduce the 'heat' in oneself if one could do so? How one answers that question will perhaps ascertain for oneself where on the spectrum of anxiety and sensitivity to stimuli scale one is, or at least where one would like to be (without the need to reach for one's mobile phone to get the answer to it as we do these days, or lighting up a cigarette in order to help one reflect on it like they did in my old man's days). I'll ponder this question myself as I listen with delight to the sound of the birds chirping in the garden outside that 'feels' as if they 'pierce' my ears, as I sip my coffee and go through what I have written this morning, wondering if it has been a good or bad writing session, as I bang the table in frustration when I discover that my printer has run out of ink and I can't print it out for my records, and as at the same time I worry if I have all my 'ducks in a row' ahead of those important meetings I have at work on Tuesday after the public holiday Monday. Reflect, reflect, reflect. Worry, worry, worry. For some there is no peace, even on the quietest of days.

Essay 23. Chronic fatigue syndrome - Is this contemporary neurasthenia an organic neurological or psychiatric disorder associated with childhood trauma related chronic anxiety and resultant ego depletion?

Chronic fatigue syndrome is one of the strangest and challenging disorders to treat and manage, due to those suffering it describing an array of fatigue symptoms and physical and mental performance related deficits, but when being tested against age and activity matched controls they do not show significant differences to 'healthy' folk, and even more puzzling, any number of a battery of medical and clinical tests are found to be normal in those suffering from chronic fatigue syndrome. Epstein-Barr virus has been found in most folk suffering from the syndrome, but equally, it is also found in many 'healthy' folks. Even more difficult to get one's head around is that folks suffering from the syndrome want it to be called a Neurologic, and therefore organic disorder, whereas Neurologists who treat them want it to be called a Psychiatric, or Psychological, and therefore a mental disorder. In this Essay, therefore, we look at chronic fatigue syndrome as an entity, including what is thought to cause it and who it affects, what other illnesses it is related to, and how it is managed by clinicians treating it.

I was watching the Two Oceans running marathon in Cape Town yesterday on the square box, and marvelled not only at the aesthetic beauty of Cape Town, but also at how many folk of all ages ran the iconic race, and at their visible efforts to resist the sensations of fatigue they were clearly all feeling as the race reached its endpoint and as they laboured valiantly to reach the finish line in the fastest time possible for each of their abilities. Some recently published top-notch research articles on the mechanisms of fatigue by Roger Enoka, Romain

Mueusen and Markus Amman, amongst others (surely with Simon Gandevia the scientists who have shaped our contemporary view of fatigue more than anyone else), have been doing the 'rounds' amongst us science folk on research discussion groups the last while and has 'reignited' an interest in the field in me. A large period of my research life was involved in trying to understand the mechanism behind the symptoms of fatigue, mainly in athletes, but also in those suffering from the clinical disorder known as chronic fatigue syndrome. As I come up quickly to the big age of 50 later this year, I notice that the daily physical and mental activity which I used to do with ease in my youth fatigue me more easily now. Because of this I have to 'pace' myself more carefully in all aspects of life to 'preserve' energy to 'fight the good fight' another day, in order to not run the risk of collapsing completely in the manner I witnessed in those folks with chronic fatigue syndrome I tried to assist both as a clinician and scientist during my earlier career, who pushed too hard and subsequently became moribund because of it. These recent observations have got me thinking of chronic fatigue syndrome (CFS), also known as myalgic encephalomyelitis (ME), what causes it, and why it manifests in some folk and not others.

Fatigue is a complex emotion which is felt by all folk on a daily basis, but paradoxically is very difficult to define. It has mental and physical symptoms and signs and is often increased by and related to exertion of any kind. Fatigue can be either acute, where there is a direct correlation of the symptoms of fatigue to a specific task or activity and the symptoms attenuate when the activity ends, or can be chronic, when the symptoms of fatigue remain for a prolonged period and are not attenuated by a period of rest, and the reasons for these chronic symptoms remaining are very difficult to understand. In the sporting world, chronic fatigue is caused by pushing oneself too long and too hard in training and racing, and is known as over-training syndrome, and has a symptom complex which includes apart from the symptom of extreme fatigue also those of 'heavy legs', increased waking pulse rate, sleep disorders, weight loss (or weight gain), lack of motivation, depression and decreased libido, which do not improve unless there is a prolonged period of rest with no physical training.

Working at the University of Cape Town with great scientists **Mike Lambert, Liesl Grobler, Malcolm Collins, Karen Sharwood, Wayne Derman,** and others, for my medical doctorate in the late 1990s we examined athletes who were moribund from over-training, and found that a number of them had pushed themselves so hard and so long that they had developed skeletal muscle pathology (damaged mitochondria in particular) to go with all these chronic fatigue symptoms, and we called this symptom complex the fatigued athlete myopathic syndrome, and later acquired training intolerance. The words the athletes we examined used to describe their symptoms were classic and perhaps 'explained' the issues better than scientific or medical terms – with one sufferer declaring that they had 'no spring in the legs', another that 'one kilometre now feels what equalled 100 km previously', and another that 'at its peak, the fatigue left me halfway between sleeping and waking most of the time'. Although there was perhaps a degree of hubris in these self-reported symptoms of fatigue, all these folks felt that the symptoms profoundly affected their exercise performance and lifestyle. Significantly, the majority of folk had evidence of suffering from depression, and also did not want to stop training and racing, and indeed found it almost impossible to stop training and racing despite these profound symptoms of chronic fatigue.

I carried on my interest in this field when moving to Northumbria University in the UK in 2006, and assisted Paula Robson Ansley and her PhD student Chris Toms, who did some great work examining causation, clinical testing of and exercise prescription for folk with classical chronic fatigue syndrome, as opposed to those with acquired training intolerance (though there is surely a relationship between these syndromes). Folk with CFS have symptoms of both chronic and extreme fatigue which is persistent or relapsing, present for six months or longer, not resulting from ongoing exertion, not attenuated substantially by rest and causing impairment of activities that were previously easy to perform. They also have four or more 'other' diagnostic criteria, including impaired memory or concentration, sore throat, tender cervical / axillary lymph nodes, muscle pain, multi-joint pain, headaches, unrefreshing sleep, or post-exercise malaise. It is importantly a diagnosis of exclusion of other medical causes of fatigue such as cancer, TB, endocrine or hormonal imbalances, or psychiatric or neurological disorders, and a clinician must always be careful to exclude these specific organic medical causes before diagnosing someone with CFS. The cause of CFS is unknown and hotly debated – it is usually precipitated by a viral infection such as Epstein-Barr Virus infection (glandular fever), and viral or infective causes, immune function issues, toxic pathogens or chemicals have all been suggested to be the cause of CFS, but not all folk who have CFS have any or all of these potential triggers or causal agents as part of their presenting history. It is notoriously difficult to treat, and some folks are left moribund and with significantly impaired lives for decades, although in some folk the syndrome seems to 'burn out' and they improve with time or learn to live with their symptoms by managing them carefully. Unfortunately, there is a high level of suicide in folk suffering from CFS, though it is not clear if this is related to the underlying causation of the disorder or due to its long-term effect on lifestyle and physical capacity.

What is interesting (and of concern) for those folk studying CFS and trying to understand its aetiology and how to treat it, is the controversy and level of emotion attached to its diagnosis and treatment. Chronic fatigue syndrome used to be more well known as myalgic-encephalomyelitis (ME), first diagnosed in the 1950s after a group of doctors and nurses in a specific hospital developed post-viral syndrome with symptoms including chronic fatigue and with some neurological muscle and central nervous system related symptoms (hence the name ME) and it was first thought to be a neurological disorder. But with time, and as it was found that more folk who were diagnosed with ME did not have classic 'organic' neurological signs, it became thought of more as a psychiatric disorder and became more often described as CFS, due to the predominant symptomatology of fatigue as being the major 'descriptor' of the disorder. What is astonishing is that, as well described in a fascinating article by Wotjek Wojcic and colleagues at King's College, London, in a survey of neurologist specialist members of the British Neurologist Association, 84% of respondents did not view CFS as a neurological disorder but rather as a psychiatric disorder. But, paradoxically, a number of patients with CFS would prefer it to be described as a neurological rather than a psychiatric disorder (and would prefer it to still be called ME), because of the social stigma of the label of having a psychiatric disorder. Somewhat astonishingly, as described by Michal Sharpe of the University of Edinburgh, there was even a negative response to a study of his which found that cognitive behavioural therapy and graded exercise therapy (the PACE trial) helped improve the symptoms of sufferers of CFS/ME, with several major patient organizations apparently dismissing the trial findings and being critical of them, because the findings could suggest that the syndrome was psychiatric in origin if cognitive behavioural therapy worked, rather than what would be the case if it was an organic neurological disorder, in which case such therapy should not work. As Sharpe concluded, in his own words it is a 'funny old world' when a study shows that a therapy works, but patients are angry because they didn't want it to work, because of the stigma it would potentially create by it working.

Wojcic and colleagues also made the point that the majority of symptoms of CFS are almost identical to that of neurasthenia, a psychiatric disorder which was prominent in the 1800s and early 1900s but has become almost unheard of as a diagnosis in contemporary times. Neurasthenia was described as a 'weakness of nerves' by George Beard in 1869, and as having symptoms of fatigue, anxiety, headache, heart palpitations, high blood pressure, neuralgia (pain along the course of a specific nerve) and depressed mood associated with it. The ICD-10 definition of neurasthenia is that of having fatigue or body weakness and exhaustion after minimal effort, which is persistent and distressing, along with depressive symptoms and two of the symptoms of either muscle aches and pains, dizziness, tension headaches, sleep disturbances, inability to relax, irritability and dyspepsia (indigestion). William James referred to neurasthenia as 'Americanitis' (he suffered from neurasthenia himself) as so many Americans in the 1800s were diagnosed with it, particularly women, and it was a 'popular' diagnosis whose treatment was either a rest cure or electrotherapy. In World War One neurasthenia was a common diagnosis for and of 'shell shock', and folk with shell shock related neurasthenia were treated with prolonged rest. In the 20th century neurasthenia was increasingly thought of as a behavioural rather than a physical condition, and eventually it 'fell out of favour' and was 'abandoned' as a medical diagnosis. As Wojcic and colleagues suggest, not just the symptoms, but the 'trajectory' of the classification of the disorder have and follow a strikingly similar pattern to that of CFS/ME, which also started off as being diagnosed as an organic / neurological disorder and is now thought of a psychiatric disorder, which is (sadly) increasingly stigmatized by lay folk and indeed even some clinicians.

Neurasthenia was thought by Beard to be caused by 'exhaustion' of the central nervous system's energy reserves, which he attributed to the (even in those days) stresses of urbanization, increasingly competitive business environment and social requirements – it was thought that neurasthenia was mostly associated with 'upper-class' folk and with professionals working in stressful environments. Sigmund Freud thought there was a strong relationship to anxiety and to the basic 'drives', and as he almost always did, related neurasthenia to 'insufficient libidinal discharge (i.e. not enough sex) that had a poisonous effect on the organism'. Both Freud and Carl Jung believed that drives were the result of the 'ego' state, and that disorders such as neurasthenia were a result of imbalances in this ego state. In their model, the 'id' was the basic component of the subconscious psyche which encompassed all our primitive needs and desires. The 'ego' was the portion of the psyche which maintains the sense of self and recognizes and tests reality. A well-functioning ego perceives reality and differentiates the outer world from inner images and desires generated by the id, and 'controls' these. The ego develops in the first part of life and is associated with a history of object cathexes. Cathexes are attachments of mental or emotional energy upon an idea or object. Object cathexes are generated by the id, which 'feels' erotic and other 'trends' as needs. The ego, which to begin with is feeble, becomes aware of these object cathexes, and either acquiesces or understands these needs and manages them (and thus becomes 'strong') or is disturbed by them and 'fends' them off by the process of repression (and becomes weak and 'conflicted'). If weak, the ego deals with its inadequacy by either repressing unwanted thoughts (thrusting back by the ego from the conscious to the unconscious any ideas of a disagreeable nature) or developing a complex (a group of associated, partially, or wholly represented ideas that can evoke emotional forces which influences an individual's behaviour, usually 'outside' of their awareness). As a result of these complex developments, folk either use projection, which is a mental mechanism by which a repressed complex is disguised by being thought to be belonging to the external world or to someone else, or transference, which is the 'shifting' of an affect from one person to another or from one idea to another, either affection or hostility, based on unconscious identification, to deal with them at a subconscious level. Albert Adler described the inferiority complex as such – that a combination of emotionally charged feelings of inferiority operates in the unconscious to produce either timidity, or as a compensation, exaggerated aggression, or paradoxical perception of superiority, and one's drives were a result of, or compensation for, feelings of inferiority derived from previous unpleasant experiences. For example, competing in extreme sport would be a compensation for being bullied in the past, or being abused as a child, or being ignored by a parent when young. Signs of such complexes included for Freud and Jung disturbing dreams and 'slips of the tongue', nervous tics and involuntary tremors, fanatical attachment to projects and goals, envy and dislike of individuals who are successful, falling apart when failing to successfully complete a challenge, desire for public acknowledgement and seeking of title and awards, compulsive exercising, and the development of neuroses and psychoses, all of which can be used to diagnosed the presence of 'unsolved' complexes, projections and transferences. Importantly for the development of neurasthenia (and chronic fatigue), Jung and Freud thought that there was an 'energy cost' to maintaining repressions and their associated complexes – Freud defined drives as the 'psychical representative of the stimuli originating within the organism and reaching the mind, as a measure of the demand made for work in consequence of its connection to the body' – and this energy cost eventually leads to the 'breaking down of the will' by the constant 'fighting' to maintain what was 'hidden' that was painful and not wanting to 'come out', and this breakdown of the will / 'mental exhaustion' leads to the signs and symptoms described above, which could in a circular way be used to diagnosed the presence of the underlying disorders. In a positive final observation, both Jung and Adler thought that the psyche was self-regulating, and that the development of these symptoms was purposive, and an attempt to 'self-cure' by compensation, and by bringing the destructive repressions, which exist at a subconscious level so are not directly perceived by the folk who have them, to their attention, or at least to that of their clinician or therapist, it would eventually lead to cure or at least 'individuation' and acknowledgement of the underlying issues, which to therapists of that era was the start of the cure.

Therefore, in this 'id and ego' model developed by Freud, Jung and their colleagues all those years ago, symptoms of chronic fatigue and burnout may be the psyche's way of creating knowledge of and thereby attempting to cure latent psychic drives which lead to obsessive work or sporting goals and activity, created by past psychological trauma and a resultant 'weak ego', which results in chronic fatigue when the psyche cannot 'cope' with 'fighting' these often unperceived issues for a long period of time / for the life period up to the point when they collapse. Interestingly, while these theories have been mostly long forgotten or have fallen into disfavour, there has recently been an increase again in interest in the concept that mental and physical 'energy' is a finite commodity, with psychologist Roy Baumeister's theory of 'ego depletion' gaining much traction recently, which suggests that a number of disorders of 'self-regulation', such as alcohol addiction, eating disorders and obesity, lack of exercise or excessive exercise, gambling problems and inability to save money and personal debt, may be related to one using up one's 'store of energy' resisting the 'deep' urges which lead to these life imbalances, and eventually willpower decreases to a level where one cannot resist 'doing' them, or cannot raise the effort to continue resisting the desire to act out one's wishes. In Baumeister's own words, a tempting impulse may have some degree of strength, and so, to overcome it, the self must have a greater amount of strength, which can eventually be worn out or overcome, leading to adverse lifestyle choices in this 'impaired mental energy state'. All lifestyle diseases and disorders may in his model therefore be related to an insufficiency of self-regulatory capacity, and there is an energy cost to resisting the 'urges' that lead to poor lifestyle choices, that may with time lead to either acute mental or physical fatigue, or in extreme cases to the development of chronic fatigue. Like with most contemporary psychology, the underlying reasons for such potential eventual failure of self-regulation were not deeply examined by Baumeister to the level that it was by Freud, Jung and colleagues, perhaps because so much of Freud, Jung and Adler's theories are difficult to prove or disprove and therefore psychology and psychiatry have in the last few decades 'turned against' their theories and embraced neuroscience as having the best chance of understanding how the mechanisms underpinning self-regulation or the lack of it 'work', but neuroscience is currently far too 'weak' a discipline methodologically wise to be able to do such. Having said this, it is surely important that folks like Roy Baumeister are re-breaking such ground, and our understanding of such complex disorders such as CFS, and others such as fibromyalgia, which are also complex diagnostic dilemmas, is enhanced by the insight that mental energy 'ego' depletion may play a part in them. Sadly, there is evidence (described by Tracie Afifie and colleagues at Manitoba and McMaster Universities) that folks who suffered physical or sexual abuse in childhood, or were exposed to between-parent physical violence at a young age, have an increased association with a number of chronic physical conditions (including arthritis, back problems, high blood pressure, migraine headaches, cancer, stroke, bowel disease, and significantly also CFS), and also a reduced self-perceived general health in adulthood, all of which would support the 'ego and id' psychopathology development theories of Freud and Jung to a degree, though of course surely not all folk who develop CFS have such childhood trauma issues.

Like the definition of neurasthenia and CFS, perhaps our understanding of their 'deep causes' is also moving in a 'full circle', and our knowledge of the underlying causes of CFS, if it does not have a specific organic or viral / toxic cause, needs to reconsider these basic concepts proposed by Jung, Freud and Adler more than one hundred years ago, and currently appears to be potentially re-occurring in a 'repackaged' version as suggested by Baumeister and his contemporaries' theories in recent times. Perhaps the drive to keep on exercising that we found in all those athletes we examined in our studies at the University of Cape Town all those years ago was the key factor in the cause of their chronic fatigue and was an 'external' manifestation of issues that they were not even aware of. We did not know enough about the subject back then to even ask them about it when we were trying to understand the causation of their symptoms. Perhaps a major component of CFS is mental exhaustion associated with continuously 'fighting' underlying past psychological trauma that the folks suffering from it are not even aware of, or at least this is part of the cause of the symptom complex along with other more organic or infective causes. Of course, describing a disorder as either neurological or psychiatric is reductive, and indeed dualistic, and surely similar physical brain neural mechanisms underpin both 'neurologic' and 'psychological' disorders which we just cannot currently comprehend with the research techniques currently available. One has to try to understand the reasons why one is 'driven' to do anything, particularly as one gets older and one's physical (and perhaps mental) resources diminish and need to be 'husbanded' more carefully, though paradoxically CFS is a disorder which afflicts folk most often initially in their early twenties, and often 'burns out' / attenuates with increasing age, perhaps because part of growing older is often about understanding one's issues to a greater degree, dealing with them, and living more 'within one's means' all of materially, socially, physically, mentally and spiritually (although for some folk such learning never occurs). Ageing may therefore be curative or protective from a CFS perspective (or one may die of 'corollary damage' such as heart attacks rather than developing CFS as a result of chronic stress related to unfulfilled drives).

Fatigue as a symptom is surely the body and mind 'telling us' that something is not 'right' and we need to rest – either acutely when we are doing sport, or chronically when we are 'fighting' something we do not understand or are aware of. The challenge is for us not just to rest, but to try and understand why we so often resist resting (well, those of us with complexes rather than those of us who are completely self-actuated and do not have stress or drives), and why life balance is so hard for many folks to find. The need (or unwanted requirement) for a prolonged rest / period of avoidance of one's routine life / a 'long sleep' is often perhaps the last resort of those who are chronically fatigued and is nature's way of 'telling' folk that they have 'run out' of responsive resources, and healing will not happen without it, though the healing may paradoxically be not of the fatigue itself, but of its underlying 'deep' causes. Now I am finished this it's time to rest, and ponder what caused the need to write it in the first place, and why I have spent my Easter holiday period preparing for its writing, and 'stoking the creative demon' which never rests and which surely eventually damages one even as it creates, rather than just sitting in a coffee shop watching the world go by and thinking of nothing but how nice the next sip of coffee is sure to be. Demons of the past, away with you, before you lead to permanent mental and even physical damage, and tire folk out in the process.

Essay 24. Athlete collapses - Paying the price for a rampant Id or an incomplete Ego

Anyone who has watched an endurance athletic event has probably seen the 'splendidly awful' sight of an athlete collapsing during the race, usually close to or within sight of the finish line, and the athlete does not quit, but attempts to get up to finish the event, and if this is impossible for them to do, they crawl to the end and collapse over the finish line, or are helped to the finish line in a state of semi-consciousness by fellow athletes. Some athletes sadly also collapse and die during athletic events, usually at any stage of the event, but again, often in the latter part of it. In this Essay we look at firstly why athletes collapse during events, and secondly, and perhaps more interestingly, once collapsing why they try their utmost to complete the event, no matter how unwell they are or in whatever conscious state they are in. Clearly some primordial instinct is pushing them to complete the challenge they have set, even if it may kill them, and even if they do so for a race which they have no chance of winning.

A few days ago, I read of a veteran athlete who collapsed and died during an endurance event. Last weekend I watched the highlights of an epic six-day off-road cycle event around the beautiful Cape Town countryside and noted that a number of competitors were 'veteran' folk whose best athletic days were perhaps past, but were still pushing their physical limits to their utmost as part of the event. These got me thinking of why athletes push themselves to the point of collapse, and occasionally past it to the point where they die during the sporting event which they are participating in. I was reminded of some theoretical and research work I did a while ago with some great work collaborators – Professors Kevin Thompson, Carl Foster, Jos De Koning, Jack Raglin, Dom Micklewright and Bill Roberts, with whom we developed an 'alternate' theory of the reasons why athletes collapse, during a wonderful 'brainstorming' session where we all got together at Vrije University in Amsterdam to work on the theory as a team a few years ago.

Our bodies and minds have some exquisite protective mechanisms that usually prevent us from pushing ourselves too fast and collapsing / damaging ourselves when playing sport – an obvious example being the inner voices we hear when 'pushing it hard' urging us to slow down and warning us that there may be negative consequences of continuing performing the exercise bout too long or too hard. But athletes and folk exercising, particularly during competitive events, often 'resist' these cautionary 'voices' and processes, and usually push themselves as hard as they possibly can in order to perform the best they can during their chosen competitive event. So, there is a competition between homeostatic protective mechanisms and psychological drives to achieve success that are in a continuous 'negotiation' during any exercise bout or competitive event.

There are a number of reasons why folks competing in an event collapse, often related to heart dysfunction, such as heart attacks, arrhythmias (faulty electric rhythms in the heart), and cardiomyopathies (an enlarged heart), but also potentially due to a host of other non-cardiac reasons, such as exercise-induced bronchospasm (asthma), low blood sugar, exertional heat illness (when one's body becomes too hot), hypothermia (when one's body becomes too cold), and exercise induced postural hypotension (low blood pressure) amongst other causes. It's interesting that most folk who collapse do so close to the finish line or just afterwards, or close to the cut-off times for medals or race closure times, which clearly indicate that athletes collapse and die usually when trying to complete or reach a particular set 'target' for the competitive event they are performing. An athlete that collapses during an exercise bout without feeling any symptoms of any of these disorders is understandable and unfortunate – they just collapse without knowing they have anything wrong with themselves, and there is not much that can or could be done for folk like this. There is perhaps an element of 'bad luck' in folk who collapse in such circumstances – while numerous studies of performing exercise on a regular basis indicate that it is healthy to do so, and enhances longevity, numerous studies have also shown that during an exercise bout itself, the risk of sudden death increases significantly, so there is a 'play off' always between the long term benefits of habitual exercise and the increased risk of dying each time one does exercise. Therefore, in folks who collapse without symptoms, in effect the risk ratio / chance has simply worked against them, from a statistical and 'luck' perspective.

A more 'interesting' group of folks who collapse during performing exercise, from an academic and research perspective, are those who feel warning symptoms of impending collapse or medical catastrophe, such as chest pains from a heart disorder, or dizziness due to either heart disorder or decreasing blood sugar for example, and yet still continue exercising. There is clearly an issue in these folks, who must feel that completing the event and achieving their set goal is more important than the chance of collapsing and dying, and who try and do so with obvious 'warning signs' such as these physical symptoms that disaster for them is impending. With my colleagues I mentioned above, we had a long think about this, and came to the conclusion that social factors must be associated with either winning or completing an event to the individual that does this, that are important to a greater degree than they would be to most 'normal folk' who don't feel the need to compete in athletic events, or who stop when they feel the development of such symptoms and go to their doctors to be assessed as a matter of urgency. These 'needs' may include the need to appear fit and healthy and perhaps therefore more desirable to prospective sexual partners, or to increase one's perceived esteem in one's social circle, or to simply 'prove' to oneself' that one can complete a challenging event, for example. They also may be indicative of overt psychopathology, such as an addiction to the sport being performed. Several studies have shown that habitual exercisers get depressed when they cannot perform their routine exercise or are unable to challenge themselves by competing routinely, due to illness or other reasons. A neat study performed by some excellent graduate students and colleagues of mine examined this concept of social need in the sporting context, in a study on male runners who ran three times on a treadmill at the same speed.

The first time they ran alone, in the second an attractive female 'actor' came into the room halfway into the trial and spoke to them while they were running, and in the third, a muscular male 'actor' did likewise. They were asked to rate how tired they felt, and with the introduction of the attractive female, the male runners told the experimenter, who was present at the room at the same time, that they felt significantly less tired when in the presence of the attractive female as compared to when running alone (though they did not realize they had rated it differently at the time). In contrast, when a muscular male spoke to them, they reported feeling significantly more tired after the male actor interacted with them, despite the pace being the same in all three trials. This study shows that there are social factors at work during any exercise bout, and a large 'ego' involvement occurring during exercise performance, and this study perhaps gives us some clues on why folk push themselves during competitive activity, even in the presence of warning symptoms of impending physical catastrophe – the psychological need to do so is greater even than the need to keep oneself alive, and in these folk, who continue exercising even in the presence of warning physical symptoms, is surely evidence of some psychological issues that have not been resolved, and are in need of attention.

Therefore, coming back to the point raised above on the number of veterans competing in testing endurance athletic events, which seems to be increasing, one must consider what is 'at play' in the minds of these folk. I must be honest and say in my youth I exercised and competed to extremes on a regular basis, and collapsed twice during competitive athletic events, once from hypoglycaemia and once I think from hyponatremia (low blood sodium) and had to be revived in the medical tents on both occasions, so I know myself the 'feeling' of pushing oneself beyond one's limits to a state of unconscious. But after a decade or so of doing competitive sport, I came to realize that I was doing it to 'prove' something to myself. Somehow, perhaps by doing so for a long period of time, and / or perhaps eventually understanding after some self-reflection that a 'need' underpinned this extreme level of activity I was performing in my early twenties, made it no longer a 'need', and sport took its 'rightful' place in my life since then of being something to do for enjoyment and to keep as fit as best possible within the constraints of a busy career and family life, but not as a key factor of my daily activity (psychology folk like Jung would perhaps say my 'ego' had been requited and I had achieved 'wholeness' eventually – at least in this sporting realm). So, when watching the older folk competing in such epic events such as the multi-day cycle race, one admires them for being 'up for' such challenges, and part of one wished that one could still be doing such events that look to be such fun. But one also wonders if there is some unfulfilled need in such folk / an ego not yet complete / a midlife crisis being acted out – and a dangerous one at that, given that the risk of heart dysfunction increases significantly with increasing age. And if some of these veteran (and indeed all) competitors are feeling such symptoms and keep on going, we need to understand why such individuals feel the need to complete such competitive athletic events, that in the 'grand scheme of things' are almost completely unimportant, in the face of impending physical catastrophe, which may be life threatening. As Freud suggested more than a hundred years ago, one's 'muscles are the conduit through which the ego imposes its will upon the world', and folk who feel the need to compete against others, or perhaps more importantly with oneself, particularly at an older age, need to think carefully what their issues are, and the causes of such 'needs' that induce one to do so. There's a lot to be said for a relaxing cycle on a Sunday morning with one's mates and / or family. But there is also a lot to be said for sitting quietly with a cup of tea admiring the roses – particularly as we move closer to the end stages of our allotted 'three score years and ten', if we are to perhaps give ourselves the best chance of seeing out our allotted time on Earth.

Essay 25. Athlete pre-screening for cardiac and other clinical disorders - Is it beneficial or a classic example of screening and diagnostic creep?

There can be few things more awful than watching a young person, in apparently healthy state, who while playing soccer or any other sport collapses and dies on the field of play, despite the collective efforts of his peers and first aid folks to revive them. It has been suggested that universal screening of young folk should occur, to prevent the chance of anyone who is asymptomatic but who screening picks up as having a heart anomaly or other organ pathology from either participating in sporting activity or, if doing so, from collapsing and dying without their pathology being treated beforehand. However, mass screening is very expensive, and there are many both false positive and false negatives associated with screening young athletes in a specific sport or specific country. Athletes fear screening in case they do have something abnormal picked up in them, which would preclude them playing the sport they love, even if continuing doing so may kill them. In this Essay therefore we look at the incidence and prevalence of sudden death in sports, and the effect of screening programmes which have been initiated in the past on attenuating the incidence and prevalence of sudden death in the populations screened for organ deficits or anomalies which are not asymptomatic.

Last week the cycling world was rocked by the death of an elite cyclist, who died competing in a professional race of an apparent heart attack. A few years ago, when living in the UK, the case of a professional football player who collapsed in the middle of a game because of having a heart attack, and only survived thanks to the prompt intervention of pitch-side Sports Medicine Physicians and other First Aid folk received a lot of media attention, and there were calls for increased vigilance and screening of athletes for heart disorders. Many years ago, one of my good friends from my kayaking days, Daniel Conradie, who apart from being a fantastic person won several paddling races, collapsed while paddling in the sea and died doing what he loved best of an apparent heart attack. Remembering all of these incidents got me thinking of young folk who die during sporting events, and if we clinical folk can prevent these or at least pick up potential risk factors in them before they do sport, which is known as athlete screening, or pre-screening of athlete populations, and which is still a controversial concept and is not uniformly practised across countries and sports for a variety of reasons.

Screening as a general concept is defined as a strategy used in populations to identify the possible presence of an 'as-yet-undiagnosed' disorder in individuals who up to the point of screening have not presented or reported either symptoms (what one 'feels' when one is ill) or signs (what one physically 'presents with' / what the clinician can physically see, feel or hear when one is ill). Most medicine is about managing patients who present with a certain disorder or symptom complex who want to be cured or at least treated to retain an optimal state of functioning. Screening for potential disorders is as described a strategic method of pre-emptively diagnosing a potential illness or disorder, to treat it before it manifests in an overt manner, in the hope of reducing later morbidity (suffering because of an illness) and mortality (dying as a result of the illness) in those folks being screened. It is also enacted to reduce the cost and burden of clinical care which would be the result of the illnesses not being picked up until it is too late to treat them conservatively with lifestyle related or occupational changes, and costly medical interventions are needed which put a drain on the resources of the state or organizing body which consider the need for screening in the first place. Universal screening involves screening all folk in a certain selected category (such as general athlete screening), while case finding screening involves screening a smaller group of folks based on the presence of identified risk factors in them, such as if a sibling is diagnosed with cancer or a hereditary disorder.

For a screening programme to be deemed necessary and effective, it has to fulfil what are known as Wilson's screening criteria – the condition should be an important health problem, the natural history of the condition should be understood, there should be a recognisable latent or early symptomatic stage, there should be a test which is easy to perform and interpret and is reliable and sensitive (not have too many false positive or false negative results), the resultant treatment of a condition diagnosed by the condition should be more effective if started early as a result of screening-related diagnosis, there should be a policy on who should be treated if they are picked up by the screening programme, and diagnosis and treatment should be cost-effective, amongst other criteria. Unfortunately, there are some 'side-effects' of screening programmes. Over-screening is when screening occurs as a resultant of 'defensive' medicine (when clinicians screen patients simply to prevent themselves being sued in the future if they miss a diagnosis) or physician financial bias, where physicians who stand to make financial gain because of performing screening tests (sadly) advocate large population screening protocols in order to make a personal profit from them. Screening creep is when over time recommendations for screening are made for populations with less risk than in the past, until eventually the cost/benefit ratio of doing them becomes less than marginal, but they are continued for the same reasons as for over-screening. Diagnostic creep occurs when over time, the requirements for making a diagnosis are lowered with fewer symptoms and signs needed to classify someone as having either an overt disease, or when folk are diagnosed as having a 'pre-clinical' or 'subclinical' disease. Patient demand is when patients push for screening of a disease or disorder themselves after hearing about them and being concerned about their own or their family's welfare. All of these contribute to making the implementation of a particular screening programme to be almost always a controversial process which requires careful consideration and an understanding of one's own personal (often subconscious) biases when making decisions related to screening or not screening populations either as a clinician, health manager or member of the public.

With respect to specifically athlete screening, there is still a lot of controversy regarding who should be screened, what they should be screened for, how they should be screened, and who should manage the screening process. Currently, to my knowledge, Italy is the only country in the world where there is a legal requirement for pre-screening of athlete populations and children before they start playing sport at school (including not just physical examination but also ECG-level heart function analysis). In the USA, American Heart Association guidelines (history, examination, blood pressure and auscultation – listening to the heart with a stethoscope – of heart sounds) are recommended but practice differs between states. In the UK, athlete screening is not mandatory, and the choice is left up to different sporting bodies. In the Nordic countries, screening of elite athletes is mandated at the government level, but not all athlete populations as per what happens in Italy. There is ongoing debate about who should manage athlete screening in most countries, with some folk feeling it should be controlled at government level and legislated accordingly, other folk suggesting it should be controlled by professional medical bodies such as the American Heart Association in the USA or the European Society of Cardiology in Europe, while other folk believe it should be controlled by the individual sporting bodies which manage each different sporting discipline or even separately by the individual teams or schools that want to protect both the athletes and themselves by doing so. Obviously, who pays for the screening factor is a large factor in these debates, and perhaps there is no unanimity in policy across countries, clinical associations and sporting bodies as described above, because of this.

The fact that there is no clear world-wide policy on athlete screening is on the one hand surprising, given the often emotional calls to enact it each time a young athlete dies, and also because the data from Italian studies has shown that the implementation of their all-population screening programmes has reduced the incidence of sudden death in athletes from around 3.5/100 000 to around 0.4/100 000 (for those interested these data are described in a great study by Domenico Corrado and colleagues in the journal JAMA). However, the data described also suggests that there is a relatively low mortality rate to start with – from the above figures of 100 000 folk playing sport, only 3.5 of these died when playing sport before the implementation of screening, and a far higher number of folks die each day from a variety of other clinical disorders. The number of folk 'saved' is also very small in relation to the cost – a study by Amir Halkin and colleagues calculated that based on cost-projections of the Italian study, a 20-year programme similar to that conducted by the Italians over 20 years of ECG testing of young competitive athletes would cost between 51 and 69 billion dollars and would save around 4800 lives, and the cost therefore per life saved was likely to range between 10 and 14 million dollars. While each life lost is an absolute tragedy both for that person and their family and friends, most lawmakers and government / governing bodies would surely think very carefully before enacting such expensive screening trials, with such low cost/benefit ratios, again with high burdens of other diseases that require their attention and funds on a continuous basis to be managed in parallel with athlete deaths. So, from this 'pickup' rate and cost/benefit ratio perspective one can see there is already reason for concern regarding the implementation of broad screening trials for athlete populations.

Of equal concern is that of the level of both false negative and false positive tests associated with athlete screening. False negatives occur when tests do not pick up underlying abnormalities or problems, and in the case of heart screening, if one does not include ECG evaluation in the testing 'battery', there is often a high rate of false negative results described for athlete testing. Even using ECGs are not 'fail-proof', and some folk advocate that heart-specific testing should include even more advanced testing than ECG can offer, including ultrasound and MRI based heart examination techniques, but these are very expensive and even less cost effective than those described above. False positives occur when tests diagnose a disorder or disease in athletes that is not clinically relevant or indeed does not exist. In athletes this is a particular problem when screening for heart disorders, as doing exercise routinely is known to often increase heart size to cope with the increased blood flow requirements which are part of any athletic endeavour, and this is called 'athlete's heart'. One of the major causes of sudden death is a heart disorder known as hypertrophic cardiomyopathy, where the heart pathologically enlarges or dilates, and it is very difficult to tell the difference on most screening tests between an athletes' heart and hypertrophic cardiomyopathy, with several folk diagnosed as having the latter and prevented from doing sport, when their heart is 'normally' enlarged rather than pathologically as a result of their sport participation. A relevant study of elite athletes in Australia by Maria Brosnan and colleagues found that when testing them using ECG level heart test, of 1197 athletes tested, 186 of these were found to have concerning ECG results (in their studies using updated ECG pathology criteria this number dropped to 48), but after more technically advanced testing of these concerning cases, only three athletes were found to have heart pathology that required them to stop their sport participation, which are astonishing figures from a potential false positive perspective. Such false-positive tests can result in potential loss of future sport related earnings or other sport participation related benefits.

Beyond false-negative and false-positive tests, there are several other factors which ensure that mass athlete screening remains controversial. For example, Erik Solberg and colleagues reported that while most athletes were happy to undergo ECG and other screening, 16% of football players were scared that the pre-screening would have consequences to their own health, while 13% of them were afraid of losing their licence to play football, and 3% experienced overt distress during pre-screening itself because of undergoing the tests per se. The issue of civil liberties versus state control therefore needs to come into consideration in debates such as screening of athletes as a 'blanket' requirement if it is enacted. While most athlete screening programmes and debate focusses on heart problems, there are a number of other non-cardiac causes of sudden death in athletes, such as exercise-induced anaphylaxis (an acute allergic response exacerbated by exercise participation), exercise-associated hyponatremia, exertional heat illness, intracranial aneurysms and a whole lot of other clinical disorders, and the debate is further complicated by whether these 'other' disorders should be included in the screening process. Furthermore, most screening programmes focus on young athletes, while many older folks begin doing sport at a later age, often after a long period of sedentary behaviour, and these older 'new' or returning sport enthusiasts are surely at an even higher risk of heart-related morbidity or mortality during exercise, and therefore one needs to think of whether screening should incorporate such folk too. However, whether there should be older age specific screening for a variety of clinical disorders is as hotly debated and controversial as it is young athlete screening and adding screening of them for exercise specific potential issues surely complicates the matter to an even greater degree, even if an argument can be made that it is surely needed.

In summary, therefore, screening of athletes for clinical disorders that may harm or even kill them during their participation in the sport they perform is still a very controversial area of both legislation and practice. There is an emotional pain deep in the 'gut' each time one hears of someone dying in a race, and a feeling that as a clinician or person that one should do more, or more should be done to 'protect them from themselves' using screening as the tool to do so. But given the low cost/benefit ratio from both a financial and 'pickup' perspective, it is not clear if making a country-wide decision to conduct athlete screening is not an example of both screening and diagnostic creep, or if athlete screening satisfies Wilson's criteria to any sufficient degree. If I was a government official, my answer to whether I would advocate country-wide screening would be no, based on the low cost/benefit ratio. If I was a member of a medical health association, to this same question I would answer yes, both from an ethical and a regulatory perspective, if my association did not have to foot the bill for it. If I was head of a sport governing body, I would say yes to protect the governing body's integrity and to protect the athletes I governed, if I did not have to foot the bill for it. If I was a clinical researcher, I would say no, as we do not know enough about the efficacy of athlete screening and because there is a too high level of false-positive and false-negative results. If I was a sports medicine doctor I would say yes, as this would be my daily job, and I would benefit financially from it. If I was an athlete, I would be ambivalent, saying yes from a self-protection perspective, but saying no from a job and income protection perspective. If I was the father of a young athlete, I would say yes, to be sure my child is safe and would not be harmed by playing sport, but I would also worry about the psychological and social aspects if he or she was prohibited from playing sport because of a positive heart or other clinical screening test. It is in these conflicting answers I myself give when casting myself in these different roles, to which I am sure if each of you reading this article answered yourself would also similarly give a wide array of different responses, is perhaps where the controversy in athlete screening originates and what will make it always contentious. I do think that if as a newly qualified clinician back then in our paddling days, if I had tested my great friend Daniel Conradie's heart function and found something that was worrying and suggested he stop paddling because of it, he would probably have told me to 'take a hike' and continued paddling even with such knowledge. I am sure as a young athlete I would have done similar if someone had told me they were worried about something in my health profile back then but were not one hundred percent sure of it having a negative future consequence on my sporting activity and future life prospects. Athlete screening tests and decisions related to them will almost always be about chance and risk, rather than certainty and conclusive determination of outcomes. To race or not race, based on a chance of perhaps being damaged by racing, or even dying, given the outcome of a test that warns you, but may be either false-positive or false-negative, that is the question. What would you do in such a situation, as an athlete, as a governing body official, or as a legislator? That's something to ponder that doesn't seem to have an easy answer, no matter how tragic it is to see someone young dying while doing what they love doing best.

Essay 26. Anterior cruciate knee ligament injuries - The end of the affair for most sports careers despite the injury unlocking exquisite redundant neuromuscular protective mechanisms

For my PhD dissertation, I studied the Anterior Cruciate Ligament (ACL) in the knee, what happens to the surrounding muscles in the knee joint, and the firing of the nerve pathways to and from the brain and the knee after the ACL is injured, and it is a truly fascinating subject. Many Orthopaedic Surgeons, Physiotherapists and Rehabilitation Therapists would reassure folks who suffered from an ACL injury that after the reparative operation and post-operative strengthening exercises that function would return to normal / pre-damage levels, but sadly, most studies have shown that the quadriceps function never returns to more than 80-90 percent of previous function, and the knee is never 'perfect' again, with increased risk of re-injury either in the same knee, or somewhat surprisingly, in the other knee joint too. In this Essay, therefore, we examine what happens after an ACL rupture, how the brain and body tries to adjust to the illness by adjusting firing patterns to the muscles surrounding the knee to ostensibly protect it from further damage, and what happens to these firing pattern changes after operative repair.

I was watching a rugby game recently and saw a player land wrongly in a tackle and immediately collapse to the ground clutching his knee joint, and heard later that he had suffered a ruptured anterior cruciate ligament injury that would require nine months post-injury before he would be able to return to his chosen sport. Many years ago, in my student days, after a few too many beers at a party, I jumped off a low wall, landed wrongly, and tore the meniscus in my left knee. The next day it had swollen up, but I did not think much of it and tried to drive to university, and always remember the horror I felt when getting to the bottom of the road and I tried to push in the clutch with my left leg to allow use of the brake at the stop street, and my leg would not react at all, and I only avoided an accident by turning off the car while working the brake pedal with my right foot. It always puzzled me afterwards why my leg would not respond at all despite my 'command' for it to do so, as even with the injury, I expected, while perhaps it might be painful to do so, that I would still have reasonable control over my leg movements, which appeared okay when walking slowly to the car and taking my weight on my uninjured leg. Perhaps this triggered a 'deep' interest in what controlled our muscles and other body functions, and when I started a PhD degree with Professors Tim Noakes, Kathy Myburgh and Mike Lambert as my supervisors at the University of Cape Town in the early 1990s, I chose to look at neural reflexes and brain control mechanisms regulating lower limb function after anterior cruciate ligament knee injury. So, what happens when the knee joint suffers a major injury, and can one ever 'come back' from it?

The knee joint is one of the most precarious joints in the body, and as compared to the hip and shoulder joints, which have quite a degree of stability generated by their 'ball and socket' design, it is simply made up of three individual bones (the femur, tibia and patella) moving 'over' each other while being attached to each other with a number of ligaments and muscles, which are pretty much all that creates stability in and around the knee joint. The knee mostly moves in a backwards / forwards (in medical terms flexion and extension) plane and has a small degree of rotation inwards and outwards but is basically a 'hinge' type joint that moves in one plane only. The major ligaments of the knee joint preventing too much flexion and extension are the anterior cruciate ligament (ACL), which prevents hyper-extension (the lower limb calf region moving too far 'forwards' relative to the upper thigh) and the posterior cruciate ligament (PCL), which prevents hyper-flexion of the knee joint. There are also relatively strong ligaments on each side of the knee joint (the medial and lateral collateral ligaments), as well as several ligaments and tendons securing the patella in place in the front of the knee. Two large pieces of cartilage, the medial and lateral menisci, 'sit' on the tibia and allow smooth movement to occur across the entire range of movement between the two big bones (femur and tibia) of the knee joint and protect each of these from damage which would occur if they 'rammed' into each other each time the bone moved without the protection of the two menisci.

While these ligaments (and there are several others in the knee joint beyond those I have described above), tendons and menisci provide the majority of support to maintain the fidelity of the knee joint, the surrounding muscles – particularly the quadriceps and hamstrings muscles – also provide important secondary support to the knee joint during active movement such as walking or running, when a greater degree of dynamic stability beyond the static stability the ligaments and tendons supply, is needed. Therefore, muscles are not just creators of movement, they are also important stabilisers of the body's joints, and there needs to be a high degree of dynamic control of them by the central nervous system during movement to ensure things work 'just right' with not too much and not too little force being applied to the joint at any one time during any movement. The hamstring muscles have been shown to be agonists (assistants) of the ACL, and when they fire they 'pull back' the lower part of the knee joint so as to reduce pressure on the ACL when the knee extends to its limits, while the quadriceps muscles similarly assist the PCL from having too much pressure on it associated with too much flexion of the knee joint (though only at certain angles of the knee joint and not through its entire range of movement). Interestingly, the quadriceps muscles are not just agonists of the PCL, but also are 'antagonists' of the ACL, and their activation can also increase hyper-extension pressure on the knee joint (and therefore on the ACL) when the quadriceps contracts, particularly when the knee is in an extended position. So, the quadriceps muscles can be the 'friend' of the ACL and knee joint, but can also be its 'foe'.

What is fascinating in this process is the structure and function of the nerve pathways both from and to all of the knee joint, ACL and muscles around them, and how these nerve pathways act differently in an intact ACL as compared to the damaged ACL state. In the intact

ACL are mechanoreceptors (receptors which pick up mechanical pressure) which fire when the ACL is put under pressure / moves, and they send information back via nerves to the spinal cord, and cause increased firing of the hamstring muscles, in order to protect both the ACL and integrity of the entire knee joint. When the ACL is ruptured, receptors called free nerve endings in the surrounding capsule of the knee joint fire in response to movement of the entire knee joint, which would happen to a greater degree in the absence of the ACL after it ruptures, and importantly, these injury associated capsular free nerve ending reflexes don't just increase the firing to the hamstrings muscles, they at the same time reduce firing to the quadriceps muscle, in order to protect the knee from further damage which could occur if the quadriceps were active maximally in the absence of the ACL. This free nerve ending pathway is known as a redundant pathway, as it only 'fires' when the ACL is damaged but does not do so normally. Interestingly, the redundant free nerve ending related pathway does not seem to stop working even if the ACL is repaired or replaced, which means that even if one fixes the ligament materially, one cannot ever completely repair the sensitive neuronal control pathways as part of the operation.

While these redundant neural firing pathways are protective and are designed to help the knee from incurring further damage, they are unfortunately not helpful in allowing athletes who suffer ACL injuries from getting back to their full strength and a return to sport with the one hundred percent function they had prior to suffering the injury. The quadriceps muscles inhibitory firing pathway is particularly a problem from a return to sport perspective, as it means that the quadriceps muscles will always be weaker than before the ACL injury, and this is borne out from most studies of quadriceps strength after injury, which show a continued deficit of at least 5-10 percent injured limb compared to the unaffected limb, and that is when rehabilitation of the injured limb is done post-injury or operation, and is even higher when it is not. Furthermore, the altered firing synergies, even those of the increased hamstring firing, appear to be sub-optimal from a functional pattern of movement perspective, even if they are protective, and there even appears to be whole body / both limb firing pattern changes, with athletes favouring the injured leg and taking more weight on the uninjured limb even if they are unaware of themselves doing this (though some folk speculate that using crutches for a prolonged period of time after ACL injury may be in part a cause of these whole limb and gait changes). These changes surely are at least to a degree responsible for the high rate of re-injury of the damaged ACL observed in those athletes who return to competitive sport after ACL injury, and potentially the high rate of ACL or other knee joint injury in the unaffected limb which some folks suggest occurs with return to sport after ACL injury.

So therefore, sadly for those who suffer ACL (and other) knee injuries and want to return to competitive sport, or to their pre-injury level of sport, redundant neural mechanisms between the knee joint and the surrounding muscles, while functionally being designed to give a measure of protection to the knee joint in the case where the ACL is damaged or absent, paradoxically ensures by its very activity that the function of the surrounding muscles is attenuated, particularly in the quadriceps muscle, and they will never have 'full' functional activity of the knee joint after the injury, despite them having a brilliant surgeon who performs a perfect mechanical replacement of the ACL surgically, and despite the best rehabilitative efforts of either the athlete or those assisting them with their rehabilitation. An athlete has two choices after suffering an ACL injury (and other associated ligament injuries which worsen the prognosis even more). Firstly, they can attempt to return to their sport as they did it before their injury but with changing how they perform it by 'compensating' for their injury – if in team sports by improving other aspects of their game so that their reduced capacity for agility and speed after injury is not 'noticed', and in individual sports by altering pacing strategy or style of performing their sport (though particularly in individual sports this is not really an option and the loss of competitive capacity is 'painfully obvious'), and with the awareness that they have a good chance of re-injuring themselves. Secondly, they can downgrade their expectations and level of sport, either retiring from their sport if competitive or changing the level of intensity they routinely perform their sport to a lower level, as hard as it is for athletes to come to terms with having to do this. But there is no 'going back' to what life was like before the injury, and this creates a potential ethical dilemma for those involved in rehabilitating athletes after ACL injury - if one works on increasing, for example, their quadriceps strength, one is 'going against' a natural protective mechanism 'unlocked' by the ACL injury, and one may be paradoxically increasing the chances of future damage to the athlete by the very rehabilitation one is trying to help them by doing so, and one should perhaps rather be 'rehabilitating' them by working on their psychological mindset so that they are able to come to terms with the concept of permanent loss of some function of their injured knee and the need to potentially look for alternative sporting outlets or methods of earning their salaries.

The wonderful period of my life as a PhD student back in the early 1990s, learning about these exquisite neuromuscular protective mechanisms surrounding the knee joint that are 'activated' after knee ligament injury (and potentially meniscal injury too), started a lifelong work 'love affair' with the brain and the regulatory mechanisms controlling the different and varied functions of the body, that has lasted to this day, and 'unlocked' a magical world for me of neural pathways and complex control processes that has ensured for me a lifetime without boredom and never a moment when I don't have something to ponder on, apart from initiating an amazing 'journey' trying to understand how 'it all works'. But this scientific exploration has not helped me fix my knee joint after the injury all those years ago – my left leg has never been the same again after that injury, which required a full meniscectomy eventually as treatment, and still swells up if I run at all and even if my cycle rides are too long, and the muscles around the affected knee have never been as strong as they were no matter how much gym I do for them. So, by understanding more about the nature of the mechanisms of response to something as major as anterior cruciate ligament knee injury, I have also come to understand more about the concepts of fate and acceptance of things, and that a single bad landing (or indeed having one beer too many leading to that bad landing) can create consequences that there are no 'going back' from, and that will change one's life forever. After a bad knee injury, nature has given us the capacity for a 'second chance' by having these redundant protective mechanisms, but that second chance is designed to work at a slower and more relaxed pace, and with the caution of experience and the conservatism the injury engenders, rather than with the freedom of expression that comes with youth and the feeling of invincibility associated with it. Rivers do not flow upstream, and we don't get any younger as each day passes, and our knee joints sadly will never be the same again after major injury, despite the best surgery and rehabilitation that one gets and does for them. Nature ensures this 'reduction in capacity' happens paradoxically for our own 'good', and the biggest challenge for clinicians is to understand this and convey that message to the athletes they treat, and for athletes it is to accept this potential 'truism' too, and let go of their sporting ambitions and find a quieter, more sedate life sitting on the bank of the river they used to ride the flow of prior to suffering their knee injury. But please, left knee, let me have a few more good bike rides in the cool morning air far from the madding crowd, before you pack up completely.

Essay 27. Low carb high fat Banting diets and appetite regulation - A research area of complex causation appears to have brought out a veritable Mad Hatter's tea party ensemble

---

Every decade or two a new diet fad becomes 'vogue' and faithful adherents to it preach its efficacy to all and sundry, as if it is the new miracle cure for all ills combined with the ultimate elixir for youth, health and happiness. In the last few years, the low carbohydrate, high fat diet (LCHF), also known as the Banting diet, has been the diet which has captured the world's attention, and its followers have become almost like adherents to a religious sect, and follow LCHF 'gurus' slavishly, and suggest anyone that disagrees with the diet are 'shills', in the pay of 'big pharma' or 'big sugar' companies. In this Essay we examine the LCHF diet, and assess in which populations it works, in which populations the jury is still out about its efficacy, and finally what statements and suggestions of the LCHF 'fraternity' are frankly absurd.

Perhaps one of the astonishing things I have read in my career to date was a recent Tweet apparently written by my own previous lab boss of University of Cape Town days, now many years ago, Professor Tim Noakes. The text of this tweet included 'Hitler was vegetarian, Wellington (Beef), Napoleon insulin resistant – Did LCHF determine future of Europe'. Tim has, in the last few years, endorsed the Low Carb / High Fat (LCHF) 'Banting' Diet as the salvation and 'holy grail' of healthy living and longevity, and appears to have recommended that everyone from athletes to children should follow the diet. As part of this diet, if I have heard / read him correctly, sugar (carbohydrate) is the 'great evil' and has an addictive capacity, our ancestors lived on a diet high in fat and low in carbohydrates and were, as a result, according to Tim, more healthy than us contemporary folk, and our current diabetes and obesity epidemics are linked to an increase intake of sugar (but not fats, proteins or simply an absolute increase in caloric intake / portion size) in the last few decades, related to a variety of factors. All this has been astonishing to me, given that for many years when I worked in Tim's lab, he was a strong proponent of carbohydrates / sugars as the 'ultimate fuel source' and wrote extensively on this, and we did a number of trials examining the potential benefits of carbohydrates which were funded by sugar / carbohydrate producing companies. While anyone can have a paradigm shift, this is one of great proportions, and given that I worked closely with Tim for a number of years (we have co-authored more than 50 research papers together, mostly in the field of activity regulation mechanisms), I have found this one, and some of the statements like in the Tweet above, to be, put conservatively, astonishing. So perhaps it would be interesting to look at some of the points raised by the folk that champion the LCHF diet and whether they have any veracity.

Firstly, one of the basic tenets of the diet is that our ancestors in pre-historic times used to follow a LCHF diet and were as a result healthier because of it. Of course, it is almost impossible to say with any clarity what folks ate beyond a few generations back, given that we have to rely in the period since writing started on folks' written observations of what they ate, and before that, on absolutely no empirical evidence at all, apart from sociological speculation. The obvious counterargument is that the life span has increased dramatically in the last few centuries, so while mortality rates are always multifactorial, to say that a diet used in the ancient past was beneficial is clearly difficult to accept when folk died so much younger than they did today, or that they were healthier or leaner in pre-historic days. As pointed out by Professor Johan Koeslag in my medical training days, based on the figurine the Venus of Willendorf, created in 24,000-22,000 BC, which depicted a female who was obese, it is as likely that folk back then were obese as it could be that they were thin. But the point is that to make any argument based on hypotheses of what was done in ancient times is specious, as we just cannot tell with any certainty what folk ate then, and it is likely that folk in ancient times ate whatever they could find, whether it was animal or plant based, in order to survive.

Based on this 'caveman' ideal, as nebulous as it is, the LCHF proponents have suggested that it is more 'natural' for the body to 'run' on a low carbohydrate diet, and Tim has suggested that athletes will perform better on a LCHF diet. But perhaps one of the best studies that would negate this concept was performed by my old friend and colleague, Dr Julia Goedecke, of which both Tim and I were co-authors. Julia looked at what fuels folk's metabolism naturally 'burnt' as part of their metabolic profile, and found that there were some folk who were preferential 'fat burners' (and would perhaps do well on a high fat diet), some who were preferential 'carbohydrate burners' (and would perhaps do best on a high carbohydrate diet), but the large majority of folks were 'in between', and burnt both carbohydrates and fats as their selected fuel. If you are a 'fat burner' and ate carbohydrates, you may run into 'trouble', as equally if you are a 'carbohydrate burner' and ate fats you may run into trouble similarly, but again, most folk 'burn' a combination of both, and the obvious inference would be that most folk would do best on a balanced diet (and of course without huge lifelong cohort studies one cannot say what 'trouble' either group will run into health-wise without such data).

It has also been suggested by Tim and the LCHF proponents that sugars / carbohydrates are highly addictive, and it is specifically the ingestion of this food source that has led to increased levels of obesity and health disorders such as type 2 diabetes in the last few decades. But absolute caloric intake has increased over the last few decades, so a simple increase in portion sizes and overall food ingestion should surely be a prime suspect in the increased levels of obesity described. It's likely also that high fat foods are also potentially as 'addictive' as sugars / carbohydrates are, if they are indeed such, and folk may also be as likely to be addicted to eating per se, rather than specifically addicted to one food type of the food they eat. The causes of an increase in appetite and the sensation of hunger is an incredibly complex field – a hundred years ago it was apparently suggested that when the walls of an empty stomach rub against each other, it causes the sensation of hunger to be stimulated. But we have more understanding now of these processes (though still a lot to learn), and the signals controlling hunger are incredibly complex, including hormone signallers arising from the gut (such as leptin and ghrelin) that go up to the brain (principally the hypothalamus) and which induce eating focussed behaviour and activity, and these are responsive to a wide variety of food types ingested. But even suggesting that one type of food and addiction to it is the cause of obesity is manifestly absurd, given how many other reasons could be suggested to be involved in eating patterns and food choices – for example the social aspect to eating food, the community habits of different populations of folk associated with eating patterns, and the psychological needs and issues associated with eating that go beyond simple fuel requirements and fuel dynamics, let alone genetics and innate predisposition to obesity and an obese somatotype some folk inherit from their parents. To note also that weight gain is not just related to single episodes of food ingestion, and some fantastic work from old colleagues from my time at Northumbria University, Dr Penny Rumbold, Dr Caroline Reynolds and Professor Emma Stevenson, amongst others, has shown that eating habits and weight gain are monitored and adjusted over long time periods in an incredibly complex way, by mechanisms that are not well understood, and it is in understanding these long term regulatory mechanisms that the changes in weight gain we see both in individuals and societies over time will surely be best understood, rather than 'blaming' one type of specific food group and its marketing to the public as a food type. As has been pointed out to me by my old (and much respected) academic 'sparring partner', Dr Samuele Marcora, both low carbohydrate and low-fat diets can be successful in initiating weight loss – but equally, both types of diets are shown to be very difficult to maintain (as are all diets) – one so often 'falls off' diets because these inherent, complex food intake regulatory mechanisms are pretty 'strong' and perhaps difficult to change.

One of the most controversial issues is the effect of LCHF / Banting diets on either optimising or damaging health, and the jury is still very much out on this, and will be until we have big cohort long term morbidity and mortality statistics of folk on the LCHF diets for prolonged periods of time. There are a lot of studies that show that eating too many carbohydrates increases morbidity and has a negative effect on health. But there are also a lot of studies that show a high fat intake also has a negative effect on one's health. Similarly, for high caloric diets, and yet also similarly increases in morbidity in diets deficient in one type of food type, or indeed, very low caloric diets. So, it is also difficult to get a clear picture from scientific studies exactly what diet works or is optimal – my 'gut feel', to excuse the pun, would be that a prudent, balanced diet will surely offer the best alternative, though with the rider as evident from Julia's study, that some folk will do better on a higher carbohydrate percentage diet, and some with a higher fat percentage diet. There are some other interesting confounding issues, such as what is known as the survival paradox, where folks with moderate levels of obesity do 'better' than their thinner counterparts in some age-related disease mortality rates – particularly apparently in folks once they get over 70 years of age, when obesity may paradoxically become protective rather than pathological. A point has also been raised that there are increasing levels of people with appetite disorders and body image disorders in the last few decades too (such as anorexia nervosa, bulimia and muscle dysmorphia, amongst others), and while the genesis of these appetite related disorders is also incredibly complex, diets such as LCHF, like many other very rigidly defined diets with specific eating requirements, may be propagating the capacity for such disorders to flourish, and indeed, a number of the 'zealots' who 'convert' to such diets and stick to them 'through thick and thin', may have appetite related disorders and are able to 'use' the camouflage of sticking to a LCHF diet to 'mask' a latent eating disorder. I can't comment on the veracity of this suggestion, without seeing more research on it, but my 'gut feel' again is that there may be something like this.

Eating patterns and dietary choices, and their relationship to health, are surely some of the most complex and multifactorial areas of research that there can ever be in science. Because of this it is so hard to find and do good science that can give a clear indication of the 'best' diet or eating pattern for any one person, and most science in the field concentrates on one food type or one outcome of specific food type ingestion, and makes conclusions based on their results that are well intentioned, but always succumb to the problem of the complexity of the human and social dynamics associated with what and how much folk eat, that is perhaps impossible ever to reduce to a single laboratory or even field based experimental protocols. Because of this (and the fact that people need to eat on a daily basis to survive, so in effect everyone is a 'captive audience' for and to information), it is a field which is susceptible to anyone 'getting up on a soap-box' and putting their 'five cents' into the debate, and with modern communication methods available to us like blogs and the social media channels currently available, these opinions can spread rapidly and be taken as 'gospel' in a very short period of time. When someone whom I respected so much as Tim Noakes, and with whom I have published so prodigiously together as a co-author in the past (though not in the field of LCHF / Banting diets), starts 'banging off' with tweets such as the above about the future of Europe potentially being determined by folk eating a LCHF diet or not (part of me is sure that Tim, if he did write this, perhaps did so in jest, or it was written as a 'spoof', as it is such a 'left field' post), I do wonder whether the field of nutrition, and those interested in it, has become something of a 'mad hatters tea party' (though of course I have great respect for the large majority of my nutritionist colleagues). Surely like all diets, the LCHF / Banting diet will fade away as people find it hard to stick to it, as a new diet fad is announced and takes its place, and as science 'chips' away at some of the astonishing claims for its veracity made by its proponents. Surely in the end, a balanced diet, like a balanced anything, will ultimately prevail as the diet 'champion'. Until then, March Hare or Mad Hatter, whoever of you is pouring the tea, can I please have two spoons of sugar in my tea? If having such prevents me from ruling Europe, or dominating the world, so be it.

Essay 28. Doping and drugs in sport - A complex causation perhaps more societal rather than just sport based

While not being a great cyclist myself at any stage of my life, like many other folks in the early 2000's I was fascinated by the Tour de France cycling successes of Lance Armstrong and watched each race avidly as he went on to be race winner in seven consecutive years and be thus the greatest bike racer of all time. He seemed to have it all — great cycling skill, a succession of beautiful women at his side and a growing family along with a fast-growing bank balance, a clean 'All-American' look, and various Presidents and significant world leaders on speed dial. And all this after he had survived a significant cancer scare, and his return to top-level cycling seemed almost a miracle. Well, it was too much of a miracle — it eventually came out that he was doped up with performance enhancing drugs in each of his Tour de France wins, and he personally admitted this in an interview with Oprah Winfrey a few years after the allegations first arose. What makes folk take drugs to perform better in sport, even if they may damage the athlete in the long term, is still not well understood. Thus, in this Essay, we look at doping and drugs in sport, and try to understand why folks decide to take them, and what factors make it feel worthwhile for them to do so.

It is the time of year which is most enjoyable for me as an armchair sports fan - the Tour de France cycle race is on and for three weeks we are privileged to view an incredible sporting and human drama spectacle, where young folk push themselves to the absolute limit daily across the cobblestones of Holland and Belgium and across the mountains of France. Like many others, I became interested in watching the Tour during the Lance Armstrong era (and like many others, I am an ardent forty-something occasional cyclist who gets on his bike as often as work constraints allows), and I remember being enthralled by all of his seemingly effortless individual performances when winning seven consecutive Tours, the strength of his team, and his larger than life personality which seemed during the late 1990s to be everything a top athletic achiever should be. Sadly, like most folk I guess, while being aware of the doping allegations at the time, I wanted to believe in him and his performances, and was deeply disappointed when these doping allegations were confirmed in later years / more recently, along with revelations about a murkier / darker side to his personality and behaviour. My first scientific article, published in 1994 when I was busy with my PhD laboratory work, was a philosophical piece on doping in sport, and how it should be managed and viewed by medical doctors, in which I advocated a fairly liberal approach to both managing doping practices and athletes who use drugs during sport. I have to be honest and say while I am proud of each and every one of the scientific articles I have written or been involved with to date, this is perhaps the only one I would have written differently with the wisdom of hindsight and the changing viewpoint inculcated by increasing age and life experience. Doping and drug taking in sport is a problem that goes beyond sport and, given the impact of sport on our daily life and sport heroes on our young developing athletes, it is a problem which needs strong management and well thought out regulation.

Doping in sport (and indeed all aspects of competitive life) is not a new concept and has been occurring for a long period of time. The reason folk take drugs is to gain an advantage over their rivals and optimise their chances of winning whatever event they are competing in or have rivals for. Drugs are used to either increase strength or enhance endurance capacity. Historically, in Scandinavian mythology, their ancient warlike folk many centuries ago – the Beserkers – drank a potion, potentially incorporating mushrooms, which was thought to greatly increase their strength and power, at the risk of increasing their chances of insanity during and after a battle. In both World Wars, pilots were given amphetamine-like tablets (also known on the street as 'uppers' or 'speed') to keep them awake and theoretically increase their task attention and vigilance during aerial combat. Anabolic steroids were developed in the early part of the last century, and in the 1950s and 1960s came to the attention of athletes as an easy way to increase their strength and power output, and their use become commonplace in even Olympic events until they were banned in the 1970s. In cycling, there is anecdotal evidence from even a century ago of competitors using a variety of doping products to enhance their physical capacity, from fairly innocuous sherry and other alcohol ingestion to the use of both stimulants and later anabolic steroid use. Currently, a variety of drugs are used as doping agents, including stimulants and steroids, but also products like erythropoietin, a drug which increases red blood cell capacity and therefore enhances oxygen delivery to the cells and thus performance, and a variety of other doping products, from cortisone (which enhances tissue recovery) to growth hormone (which enhances muscle growth) to asthma-related drugs such as clenbuterol, which enhances oxygen uptake in the lungs, and may also increase lean body mass.

The authorities who regulate the Tour and other sporting events responded to the use of all these doping agents by banning the drugs and working with academic laboratories to develop testing procedures that detect these drugs, and if athletes are caught with any of these products in their body, they are banned for a period of time before being allowed to compete again. But these dope testing methods are never one hundred percent reliable, and what has developed has been something of a 'cat and mouse game' between the testers / authorities and athletes, who when a test is developed for a particular doping product that has good sensitivity and detection capacity, change what they use, either to new products, or ways of taking performance enhancing drugs. For example, when testing for erythropoietin became successful, cyclists started to remove their own blood before the Tour and re-infused it back during the rest days of the Tour, to circumvent the laboratory tests. When a laboratory test that could prove that such re-use of own blood had occurred was developed, cyclists changed to using erythropoietin again but in micro-doses on a daily rather than weekly big dose basis, and once again it proved difficult to prove they were using the drug, given that levels were marginally higher than normal only, and it could not be proven that the results were not merely the result of statistical variability. The issue of testing is further made more complex by the need for and use (and abuse) of therapeutic use exemptions (TUE), where athletes theoretically with valid medical conditions who could not compete without taking medication are allowed to take their medication as long as they declare their use prior to competition time. This has become a 'grey area' for drug control, as a large percentage of cyclists now have at least one TUE and some many. For example, a high percentage of Tour riders say they have asthma and therefore must use asthma drug inhalers, but of course, it is not possible to prove if they definitively have asthma or are using the asthma drug inhalers as a doping product to increase their competitive advantage (from a scientific / medical point of view, it is very 'odd' that so many top cyclists profess to have asthma or allergies that need similar medication, given that it would be perceived that suffering from such medical conditions would attenuate one's capacity to perform sport at a social level, let alone allow the development of elite athlete competitors who win / do well in the Tour de France). So as much as the race organizers and authorities try and combat doping in sport, the cyclists and athletes appear to always be trying to stay 'one step ahead' of whatever is put in place to detect their use.

So, what, therefore, can be done to attenuate doping in sport, and be sure that we are watching a 'fair' contest (though of course sport will always be absolutely an unfair environment, from the context that those who are fortunate enough to have inherited the most favourable genes and home and social environments will always have a greater chance of success than those who are less fortunate from either a gene or meme perspective)? One way, which has been tried in all drug related enforcement work, is to increase the level of law enforcement involved in its 'policing', and to have custodial sentences for those who are either caught using or supplying doping products during and for sporting events, rather than just leaving its supervision to race organizers and sporting federations (who are notoriously lenient on their athletes who are caught using performance enhancing drugs, and whose athletes often are exonerated due to often bizarre legal technicalities and arguments). Indeed, cyclists became far more cautious (but sadly one would argue their drug use just became more technically smart) when French police became more involved and started arresting cyclists or team officials suspected of drug use in the early 2000s, and it was the involvement of the FBI, and the threat of criminal charges, in the investigation of Lance Armstrong's potential drug use over a few years that finally led to admissions by him and his team members of culpability of performance enhancing drug use, despite him and his team-mates passing a large number of drug tests during their career. But like all 'stick' approaches, while this will work to a point, unless we understand why athletes take drugs in the first place, and try and remove the reason for doing so, it is likely that this approach will never completely work, and will rather just take the quest of athletes to find the 'ultimate drug' – one that works and which cannot be detected so they cannot be caught for its use – to a more technically efficient and / or more 'underworld' way of trying to find their doping products.

Perhaps also we need, as armchair spectators and as members of the greater society, to understand that we are as big a part of the doping problem as the athletes themselves. Since the 1800's, when sport was popularized as entertainment for working and middle-class populations, sport has become increasingly important in our daily lifestyle. Sport has been used by country leaders to both engender and manipulate national pride, as a method of disciplining and preparing young adults for military activity, and as a way of providing mental and physical 'toughness' for the challenges in life. As societies became industrialized, the occupations of an increasing number of folks became sedentary and non-physical. It was perhaps because of this that sport in the last century became a means to maintain physical fitness, and sport was, and is, used today, to maintain physical 'fitness' and / or aesthetic desirability. This trend was perhaps exacerbated by the media and advertising, which propagated the notion (based on our desire for it to be so) that athleticism in both men and women was and is a sign of social success and positive self-discipline. In the last few decades, the financial turnover in sport has decreased dramatically. As it became obvious that watching sport had become a form of relaxation and leisure activity for several different countries and societies, the economic sector realized that sport had the potential to be a source of revenue. With the advent of pay-channel television, sport has become a multi-billion-dollar industry, and as a result of this, athletes are able to become professionals and as a result devote their entire working day / life to their sport related training and activities (of course only if they were serial winners / successful in their chosen sport). Sport, and in particular success in sport, therefore, has become the source of income for many athletes today, and this was almost certainly related to the increased incidence of the use of performance enhancing drugs in the last 50 years. As the financial and social rewards of success have increased, so has the pressure on athletes whose livelihood and way of life is related to success in their chosen sport, to use performance enhancing drugs to do so, despite the potential negative clinical side effects of their use, and the potential damage that will be caused to their lifestyles and social status if they are caught using them, as described above. Thus, each athlete must and surely does asses the risk / benefit of using performance enhancing drugs, and if the benefits to their current and future lifestyle are perceived to outweigh the potential negative side effects of either suffering physical harm from drug use, or being caught and branded a cheat, and having their lifestyle dramatically altered if being caught, then they will continue to use performance enhancing drugs, and always will do so.

Therefore, perhaps we need to understand that by paying for the TV channel that allows us to watch the wonderful spectacle of human drama which is the Tour de France, it creates a wealth generation chain that ultimately allows the successful athletes that compete in the Tour de France to be paid the huge salaries they currently are, and consequently we are to a degree part of the problem of doping in sport, and are contributing to its continuation. In my first philosophical academic piece described above, I suggested that because of this, we would never really ever completely 'win' the 'fight' against doping in sport, and that we needed to think either of introducing a salary cap and paying all cyclists the same wage irrespective of their results / performance outcome (though obviously in the current free market world this is an impossibility, or at least highly unlikely to happen in the visible future), or legalize the use of drugs in sport to at least allow the use of the performance enhancing drugs to be clinically monitored to ensure the health of those that use them to be maintained. But of course this is, and was when I wrote it, a far too simple way of looking at what is an extremely complex phenomenon, and the obvious criticism of this viewpoint would be (and was by a number of folk who criticized my article then, and with whom I now agree) that it would mean then that those who did not want to use performance enhancing drugs would be forced to do so, even if monitored, to be sure they were 'playing on a level playing field', even if it was a drug-fuelled one. I now perceive that increasing the societal awareness of the problem and education of athletes about the use of drugs, coupled with the threat of receiving a custodial sentence for their use – i.e. the classical 'carrot and stick' approach – is perhaps the best way forward and method of dealing with the issue. Interestingly, a study in Australia, where a big anti-drug education programme is active, showed that positive results seem to be occurring because of it. A few years ago, when athletes there were asked if they took a performance enhancing drug that would ensure success in their chosen sport, but also ensure they died because of its use within five years (known as Goldman's dilemma / test), up to 50 percent of athletes said they would do so. But, after the education programmes (or whatever well Australia is doing in this field of sport doping prevention), the numbers of respondents who answered this question positively was far lower, and not much different to the results found for the general population of Australia.

However we do it, we need to keep on working at trying to attenuate what is a very difficult problem, and perhaps assist younger folk embarking on their athletic careers to understand the cost-benefit ratio of using performance enhancing drugs, and hopefully this will help reduce the culture of drug use, which was seemingly endemic to cycling (and probably a lot of other sports) a few years ago, even if no intervention is likely to completely eradicate performance drug use in sports as long as big salaries are paid to the athletes who participate in them, and as long as we keep on watching them. And us armchair sport fanatics perhaps need to understand that we are potentially a causal part of the problem simply by enjoying watching the great spectacle of young folk pushing themselves to levels of pain and stress which would be intolerable to most, and the vicarious pleasure we get from watching them doing so, which may be related to our psychological requirements to have champions, winners and losers in society in order to satisfy our own interests and perhaps unsolved psychological needs (though this is of course another complex / different discussion for the future), which take pleasure in seeing others either suffer or be successful. Long live the passion and endeavour that makes young folk on a yearly basis nearly destroy themselves to be successful on one of the most gruelling sporting stages, though hopefully their efforts are carefully considered cost-benefit ratio wise. Long live us older folk whose best athletic days are long past, sipping a cup of tea and watching them doing so from the safety of our armchairs, but hopefully with an understanding of why these young folks have the potential to turn to performance enhancing drugs, and why we are in some way complicit in them doing so. Long live the Tour de France and the vicarious pleasure we get from viewing it. Vive La France! Allez Allez Allez.

Essay 29. Anorexia nervosa and the eating disorders - A tragedy of faulty mirrors, control or the lack of it, and a walk back to the abyss

One of the most challenging psychological disorders to treat and manage is anorexia nervosa. Unlike alcohol and drug dependency, where addiction is to substances which are not needed to survive as a human being, we all need to eat to survive, and therefore a person who develops a resistance to eating, for whatever cause, is faced with a cruel dilemma every day and usually three times a day, when their peers or family sit down to eat meals and expect them to do likewise. It is also sadly one of the most dangerous psychological disorders, with more folk dying of anorexia nervosa than any other psychological problem or dependency, and the recidivism rate of those 'cured' is very high. Paradoxically, usually the causes of anorexia nervosa are not food or weight related but appear to have deeper and darker causation related to prior abuse and / or control issues. In this Essay we examine anorexia disorder from all angles, to assess in whom and how it develops, what are its root causes, and why it is so difficult to treat.

I was in a gym last week and noticed an emaciated woman running on a treadmill, who was so thin that individual muscles and bones were visible in her exposed flesh around her gym clothes. I wondered if, wearing my clinical hat, I should speak with the gym staff about her, given it was clear she either had a chronic disease that caused profound secondary weight loss, or she had an eating disorder, most likely anorexia nervosa. I have noted with concern when watching cycling races how thin elite professional cyclists are during long stage races and was interested when reading the autobiography of one of the world's best cyclists that they believed that both themselves and several of their cycling colleagues would probably satisfy the criteria for a full-blown eating disorder diagnosis, and that they had battled with food ingestion both during their career, and even after they had stopped being competitive. As a teenager I was sent to boarding school and didn't settle well into the strong routine and rules-based environment that boarding schools require so that they can function optimally, and I stopped eating as a 'silent protest' to get attention to my dislike for my environment. I eventually cut my weight to almost zero body fat, and folk wondered if I had a bone fide eating disorder, though fortunately when my parents accepted that I could not continue at the boarding school in my state of refusing to eat and resultant massive weight loss, they took me out and put me into a day school, and almost immediately I started eating again, my weight normalized, and the problem was pretty much resolved for me. Seeing the lady on the treadmill, reading the book on the eating travails of the elite cyclist, and reflecting on my own weight reduction story of my youth, got me thinking about anorexia nervosa, what causes it, and why some folk both start to refuse to eat food, and continue to do so, even if it causes them to literally starve themselves to death in an environment of plenty, and with so many of their loved ones around them willing them to eat normally, put on weight, and live a 'normal' life as they apparently used to do.

The symptoms and signs of anorexia nervosa were first described in medical texts as early as in the 1600's, and was termed anorexia nervosa in the late 1800's. The term is Greek in origin, with 'an' describing negation and 'orexis' describing appetite – so literally a psychological negation of appetite. Its classical symptom is obviously food restriction resulting in rapid weight loss, and it can be accompanied by compulsive behaviour such as excessive exercise (in order to use up calories and thereby lose weight), a paradoxical preoccupation with food, recipes, or cooking food for others which is not consumed by themselves, food rituals such as cutting food into small pieces and not eating it, refusing to eat around others or hiding and discarding food, and purging themselves with laxatives, diet pills, or self-induced vomiting in order to attenuate the effect of eating any food whatsoever, no matter how small the portion (to note these purging actions also occur in its 'cousin' disorder, bulimia nervosa, but there is usually not the marked food restriction in bulimia nervosa, and weight loss may not be evident in folk suffering from bulimia nervosa). There are several other signs which are diagnostic of anorexia nervosa, including low body mass index for one's height or weight, amenorrhea in females, the development of lanugo (fine, soft hair growing over the face and body), intolerance to cold, halitosis (bad breath), orthostatic hypotension (low blood pressure when lying down), chronic fatigue, and changes in heart rate (either slowing down or speeding up). However, most of these may be related to the chronic and extreme weight loss, rather than to anorexia nervosa per se. Clinicians generally have to be very cautious before diagnosing anorexia nervosa to be sure to exclude a wide variety of clinical disorders that can lead to profound weight loss, including cancer, type 1 diabetes, thyroid hormone disorders, and a host of other clinical conditions. Anorexia nervosa is thought to occur in approximately 1-4 percent of females, and 0.5 percent of males, and often begins during the teenage or young adulthood years.

There is much debate still about what causes anorexia nervosa. There has been an increased incidence of the diagnosis of anorexia nervosa in the last 50 or so years, and this increase has been correlated with an increase in social pressures, particularly on females, but more recently on males too, for the 'ultimate body', with most cultures increasingly favouring a slender shape and the 'size zero' model, where clothes and fashion are displayed on waif-like models. This is theorized to put pressure on most folk to be thinner than what is possible for most people. But correlation is not causation, and the counterargument to this social theory would be that 96% of women and 99.5% of men see similar fashion images and models and do not develop anorexia nervosa. There is a strong familial link to it, with twins and first-degree relatives of someone diagnosed with anorexia nervosa having a significantly higher chance of developing the disorder. It has also been suggested that the prevalence of anorexia nervosa is higher in athletes doing sports that require weight control, such as gymnasts, runners and cyclists, and in those folks whose careers similarly require weight regulation, such as ballet dancers and jockeys. It has also been suggested that folk with gastrointestinal disorders such as inflammatory bowel disorder and coeliac disease may have a higher prevalence of anorexia nervosa, due to the increased requirement to be 'aware' of what food types are ingested if suffering from other of these challenging gastro-intestinal disorders, and indeed eating any food whatsoever may initiate their symptoms. There has been an increase in interest in 'extreme' diets such as the keto, carnivore, and vegan diets, amongst others, and it has been suggested that engaging with such diets may precipitate the development of anorexia nervosa, or indeed be a 'mask' for those with eating disorders to 'hide' behind as a label that would allow them to explain their weight loss and extreme thinness in a way that was more socially acceptable than telling those around them that they have anorexia nervosa, or allows folk suffering from the disorder to feel part of a group of similar food conscious folk.

Anorexia nervosa would be easy to diagnose, treat and manage if the disorder was as simple as that described in the paragraphs above. But a major confounding issue is that a high percentage of folk who suffer from it deny having anything wrong with themselves, deny having an eating disorder, and some resist being treated to the point of requiring to be restrained and force-fed to keep them alive. It sounds terrible that folk must be force fed against their wishes (and some doctors have an ethical problem doing so), but unfortunately anorexia nervosa has the highest mortality rate of any psychiatric or psychological disorder, around 10-12 times that of the general population, with the risk of committing suicide being 50 times higher. Anorexia nervosa sufferers literally starve themselves to death, or commit suicide while doing so, and there is a high recidivism rate, with only half of the folk who have it 'recovering' (if they ever do), with the rest relapsing or becoming chronic and a permanent 'way of life' until death intervenes. Therefore, something is clearly desperately 'wrong' in these folks, who either know about it and acknowledge it, know about it and don't acknowledge it, or not know that they have the disorder and perceive themselves to be well – clearly the latter group being the most challenging to treat, though all three groups require major psychological assistance and intervention. Anorexia nervosa is classified under Feeding and Eating Disorders in the 'bible' / official manual of psychological disorders (known as the Diagnostic and Statistical Manual of Mental Disorders –

DSM5), but there is a high prevalence of other associated psychological disorders, including obsessive-compulsive disorder and obsessive-compulsive personality disorder, anxiety disorder, and depression. An array of other psychological disorders has also been linked to anorexia nervosa, including borderline personality disorder, attention deficit hyperactivity disorder, autism spectrum disorders, and body dysmorphic disorders, and while some of these linked disorders require further research to understand their prevalence and linkage to anorexia disorder, it is thought that having these comorbidities worsens the prognosis for folk suffering with florid anorexia nervosa.

With all these challenging psychopathology and comorbidity factors, three key issues appear to be fundamental to anorexia nervosa. The first is precipitating factors, the second, loss of interoceptive (body state) awareness, and the third perception of loss of control in folk with the disorder. It is thought that a stressful incident in one's past life, or a change in circumstances for an individual already predisposed to develop the disorder, or by being in a sport which requires weight regulation, can precipitate the development of anorexia nervosa in a susceptible individual. Sadly, a number of folks who develop anorexia nervosa have a history of childhood trauma, including abuse, parental divorce, or a conflict-filled environment, and a study published last year found there was a 25 percent incidence of sexual abuse during childhood reported as occurring before the onset of anorexia nervosa. Equally, a change of environment that is challenging, such as moving geographically, or going to boarding school, or the death of a parent or sibling or loved one, or being teased about one's body shape in childhood or adolescence, may also be precipitating factors. While difficult to prove direct linkage as a response to these psychologically 'shattering' events, what appears to happen as a result of these traumatic challenges is that a process of 'disembodiment' occurs (also described as 'interoceptive loss') where one's body image is altered, or one does no longer 'recognize' one's current body image, perhaps as a way of 'denying' the trauma that was done to it as would have occurred as a result of being sexually abused, for instance. It has also been suggested that someone with anorexia nervosa undergoes a 'loss of emotional self', where one no longer recognizes one's own emotions and feelings, in a similar way, and for similar reasons described above, as why one no longer recognizes one's physical body. Lonnie Athens, one of my most admired Psychology researchers, has suggested that one cannot have too weak a sense of self, as one would not be able to have a stable sense of self-identity if so. However, he suggested that with a profound change, such as being the victim of a violent episode, divorce, loss of a job, or some other profound experience, for which the individual has no prior frames of reference or experience of, and which their current self-identity system (whatever this is) cannot provide interpretation of or make sense of, resulting in changes to the sense of self similar to that found in folk with anorexia nervosa. In his model, the factors which set the sense of self in the brain become confused in a crisis for which there are no previous precedents to benchmark the current experience against. Because of this, the sense of self becomes fragmented, and replaced by a different sense of self, if the individual can make sense of what happened to them and 'move on' from what happened, but if not, remains permanently fragmented, and folk develop into a permanent state of sense of self 'flux', in which the individual is to a degree unrecognizable to themselves in a manner which becomes habituated.

The underpinning issue of all these factors, and the 'unfinished' response to them, is a sense of loss of control. The individual who has suffered life trauma, and the resultant 'shattering' of their sense of self, no longer feels in control of their life and situation. One thing that can be controlled is their food intake, and in the case of folk who develop anorexia nervosa, they stop eating due to the desire either to control one factor in their existence which they can have complete control over, or actually do want to starve themselves to death, as a compensation or 'way out' of their current psychological 'fragmentation', and they stop eating as a way of enacting a prolonged suicide. For this reason (amongst several other reasons), folk with anorexia nervosa do not believe that they have an eating disorder, as by limiting their food intake, they feel that they are, for the first time since whatever precipitated the development of the condition of anorexia nervosa, 'controlling' something in their own body, and it would be too psychologically draining for them to 'lose' what becomes in effect a control 'mechanism' that they feel completely 'in control of'. At the same time, the individual may deny or 'forget' that they ever had any abuse or traumatic episode happen to them, as it is too threatening to their already damaged psyche to admit such, and as a mechanism of psychological denial, they 'remove' it from the conscious self to the nether world of their subconscious, where it continues to 'trip them up' and damage their lives until they confront it. So, paradoxically, folk with anorexia nervosa can be all of completely out of control (from the context that they have been 'ripped up' psychologically by prior damaging events), in control (from the context of what they choose not to eat), and in some folk not aware of (due to protective psychological denial processes) their current physical state, sense of self, or underlying psychopathology. The distortions of body image, and dread of adding on even a pound of weight, are a result of these three 'issues' (amongst others) at play in their deep psyche and if this 'lack of awareness' is not addressed, the person with anorexia nervosa will literally starve themselves to death, as a method of maintaining control, or of negating the damage caused to them of whatever led to the development of their condition. Therefore, in many cases, folk forget that anorexia nervosa can be a symptom of some deeper psychopathology, which may or not be 'hidden' from view, apart from it being a psychopathology in itself.

All of these 'entangled issues' make anorexia nervosa extremely difficult to treat. If folk deny that they are sick, it becomes very difficult to treat them, as whatever one does, they will not 'stick with' the treatment offered. Admitting that they are sick, or that they have a mental illness, requires them to acknowledge the psychological damage underpinning their anorexia nervosa (with anorexia nervosa being a symptom itself), and that they have no control over their life, and indeed that their own 'treatment' they have chosen to 'cure' their underlying psychopathology such as sexual abuse or other issue, namely not eating, or controlling their eating patterns to an extreme degree, has been wrong. A large number of folk with anorexia nervosa want to be left alone, and find it difficult to cope with being diagnosed as having anorexia nervosa due to the requirement this would make on them to confront their underlying psychopathology, and indeed, sadly, being diagnosed as suffering with anorexia nervosa creates a stigma of its own, and may 'label' and define them for life as such, and this is yet another psychological challenge to accept in their challenged state (that they have both an eating disorder and also underlying psychopathology) for the folk suffering from it. Treatment of the disorder involves trying to restore the person to a functional weight, treating the underlying psychological disorders that led to the development of anorexia nervosa, and reducing behaviours and activities that result from the disorder becoming habituated (such as not eating in front of other folk, hiding food, as well as of course not eating at all most of the time). Psychotherapy, cognitive behavioural therapy, and family-based therapy have all been used with varying degrees of success to treat folk with the disorder. However, given that eating is a basic requirement of life, each day is an ordeal from the context that eating is required to happen so that life can continue, and at each meal there is thus a conflict and habitual cycle of negation that is very difficult to alter or attenuate. Force feeding has been used in extreme conditions, but there are of course ethical issues associated with this, such as the individual's rights, though of course the debate is whether folks with anorexia nervosa are in a 'right' state of mind and / or can make decisions that are good for themselves, rather than being damaging for themselves (similar issues of treatment occur in folk with alcoholism or who self-harm, amongst others). In the end, as described above, it is a disorder that is extremely challenging to manage, with a high level of chronic morbidity and mortality, very much as if the folk with the disorder 'want to die', as challenging as it is to describe it as such, or as a clinician to understand it as such.

Anorexia nervosa, for the reasons described above, is one of the most challenging disorders clinicians, friends and families of people that have the disorder have to manage and live with. To all of us watching the lady in the gym last week it was clearly obvious that she had a severe case of anorexia nervosa, yet she appeared oblivious to this, and was indeed working hard in the gym to 'maintain fitness' (thought of course in this case the exercise may be both a symptom and vehicle of psychopathology itself). In many ways, society advocates restrictive eating and thinness, and from this perspective, the lady in this example would be congratulated for doing this to such extremes. Yet, paradoxically, someone like this who appears to be so in control, is in reality completely out of control, and even more strangely, in many cases is not aware of it. The 'mirror' / self-image assessment function in their brains, however it works in both health and disease, appears to warp and become convex, and to the anorexic, their body image is usually so 'fragmented' that they see big where they are indeed thin. Even more sadly, as a clinician seeing folk like this makes one wonder what traumatic event the individual has gone through to trigger their anorexia nervosa, and whether they hopefully are in counselling to try and help them get to terms with whatever issue is causing their ongoing self-harm. Sadly though, this is so difficult to do, as control mechanisms are involved which have become extreme, and make them unable to 'move on' from a life spent in the shadows to one in the light. Sigmund Freud suggested that folk have both a life instinct (Eros) and a death instinct (Thanatos), and one's Thanatos instinct compels us humans to engage in risky and destructive behaviours that can lead to our own personal death. Clearly, in folk suffering from anorexia nervosa, a trigger has changed their 'behavioural setting' from Eros to Thanatos, and once changed, the God of Death appears to be somewhat resistant to change. Much research is needed in the field to help us understand the psychopathology underlying anorexia nervosa better, and how to treat, or at least manage the condition. Mirror, mirror, on the wall, am I the thinnest person of them all may be the mantra of this disorder, but sadly the mirror is telling a lie. Each time I put in the two spoons of sugar which I enjoy in my tea, I thank my parents for removing me from boarding school, before a fast of defiance became overwhelmed by Thanatos, the God of Death, and before I too went down to the place where everything which seems real is not, and where once one is over the edge of the abyss, there is very little chance of ever coming back. Dying by starving oneself to death may paradoxically represent a victory to the individual that pushes themselves to their own death, but the fight between Eros and Thanatos in a loved one, when Thanatos wins, is surely one of the most tragic things a clinician, family member or loved one can ever watch from a distance and understand, or even begin to comprehend, without wanting to smash the distorted mirror, and by doing so rebuild the fragmented spirit underneath it, no matter how impossible in **real life** this is.

Essay 30. Muscle dysmorphia and the Adonis complex - Mirror, mirror on the wall, why am I not the biggest of them all

While for a long period of time, abnormal body perception was thought to be a predominantly women's disorder, with most folks suffering anorexia nervosa and bulimia being women. However, in the last few decades, an increasing number of men have been diagnosed as suffering with anorexia nervosa, and a 'new' disorder, predominantly of men who strength train, named muscle dysmorphia has been identified, where men who are very well muscled believe they are thin and weak, and have poorly developed muscles. No matter how huge they become, they become physical recluses as they fear folks commenting on their 'weak' builds, will not take their clothes off in public, and spend more and more time in the gym and more money on supplements and anabolic steroids to help them 'grow' even bigger. In this Essay, we examine the causes and issues related to the development of muscle dysmorphia, and what societal pressures are involved, if they are, in men even thinking that they will be more attractive if they put on more muscle mass.

I have noticed recently that my wonderful son Luke, who is in the pre-teenage years, has become more 'aware' of his body and discusses things like 'six-pack abs' and the need to be strong and have big muscles, probably like most boys of his age. I remember an old colleague at the University of Free State mention to me that her son, who was starting his last year at school, and who was a naturally good sportsperson, had started supplementing his sport with gym work as he perceived that 'all boys his age are interested in having big muscles', as my colleague described it. A few decades ago, my old colleague and friend Mike Lambert, exercise physiologist and scientist without peer, and I did some work researching the effect of anabolic steroid use on bodybuilders and noted that there were not just physical but also psychological changes in some of the trial participants. I did a fair amount of time in the gym in my university days, and always wondered why some of the biggest folk in the gym seemed to do their workouts with long pants and tracksuit tops, sometimes with hoods up, even on hot days, and how in conversation with them I was often told that despite them being enormous (muscular rather than obese-wise), they felt that they were small compared to their fellow bodybuilders and weightlifters, and that they needed to work harder and longer in the gym than they were currently doing to get results. All of these got me thinking of the fascinating syndrome known as muscle dysmorphia, also known as the Adonis complex, 'bigorexia', or 'reverse anorexia' and what causes the syndrome / disorder in the folk that develop it.

Muscle dysmorphia is a disorder mostly affecting males (though females can also be affected) where there is a belief or delusion that one's body is too small, thin, insufficiently muscular, or lean, despite it often being normal or exceptionally large and muscular, and related to obsessional efforts to increase muscularity and muscle mass by weightlifting exercise routines, dietary regimens and supplements, and often anabolic steroid use. This perception of being not muscular enough becomes severely distressing for the folk suffering from the syndrome, and the desire to enhance their muscularity eventually impacts negatively on the sufferer's daily life, work, and social interactions. The symptoms usually begin in early adulthood, and are most prevalent in bodybuilders, weightlifters, and strength-based sports participants (up to 50 percent in some bodybuilder population studies, for example). Worryingly, muscle dysmorphia is increasingly being diagnosed in younger / adolescent folks, and across the spectrum of sports participants, and even in young folk who begin lifting weights for aesthetic rather than sport-specific purposes, and who from the start perceive they need to go to the gym to improve their 'body beautiful'. Two old academic friends of mine, Dave Tod and David Lavallee, published an excellent article on muscle dysmorphia a few years ago, where they suggested that the diagnostic criteria for the disorder are that the sufferer needs to be pre-occupied with the notion that their bodies are insufficiently lean and muscular, and that the preoccupation needs to cause distress or impairment in social or occupational function, including at least two of the four following criteria: 1) they give up / excuse themselves from social, occupational or recreational activities because of the need to maintain workout and diet schedules; 2) they avoid situations where their bodies may be exposed to others, or 'endure' such situations with distress or anxiety; 3) their concerns about their body cause distress or impairment in social, occupational or other areas of their daily functioning; and 4) they continue to exercise and monitor their diet excessively, or use physique-enhancing supplements or drugs such as anabolic steroids, despite knowledge of potential adverse physical or psychological consequences of these activities. Folk with muscle dysmorphia spend a lot of their time agonizing over their 'situation', even if it is in their mind rather than reality, look at their physiques in the mirror often, and are always of the feeling that they are smaller or weaker than what they really are, so there is clearly some cognitive dissonance / body image problem occurring in them.

What causes muscle dysmorphia is still not completely known, but what is telling is that it was first observed as a disorder in the late 1980s and early 1990s, and was first defined as such by Harrison Pope, Katharine Phillips, Roberto Olivardia and colleagues in a seminal publication of their work on it in 1997. There are no known reports of this disorder from earlier times, and as suggested by these academics, its increasing development appears to be related a growing social obsession with 'maleness' and muscularity, that is evident in the media and marketing adverts of and for the 'ideal' male in the last few decades. While women have had relentless pressure on them from the concept of increasing 'thinness' as the 'ideal body' perspective for perhaps a century or longer from a social media perspective, with for example the body size of female models and advertised clothes sizes decreasing over the years (and it has been suggested that in part this is responsible for the increase in the prevalence in anorexia nervosa in females), it appears that males are now under the same marketing / media 'spotlight', but more from a muscularity rather than a 'thinness' perspective, with magazines, newspapers and social media often 'punting' this muscular 'body ideal' for males when selling male-targeted health and beauty products. Some interesting changes have occurred which appear to support this concept, for example the physique of GI-Joe toys for young boys changing completely in the last few decades, apparently being much more muscular in the last decade or two compared to their 1970 prototypes. Matching this change, in 1972 only 15-20 percent of young men disliked their body image, while in 2000 approximately 50 percent of young men disliked their body image. Contemporary young men (though older men may also be becoming increasingly 'caught up' in similar desire for muscularity as contemporary culture puts a price on the 'body beautiful' right through the life cycle) perceive that they would like to have 13 kg more muscle mass on average, and believe that women would prefer them to have 14 kg more muscle mass to be most desirable, though interestingly when women were asked about this, women were happy with the current mass of their partners, and many were indeed not attracted to heavily-muscled males. Therefore, it appears that social pressure may play a large part in creating an environment where men perceive their bodies in a negative light, and this may in turn lead to the development of a 'full blown' muscle dysmorphia syndrome in some folk.

While the concept that social pressure plays a big role in the development of muscle dysmorphia, other factors have also been suggested to play a part. Muscle dysmorphia is suggested to be associated with, or indeed a sub-type of, the more general body dysmorphic disorder (and anorexia nervosa, though of course anorexia nervosa is about weight loss, rather than weight gain), where folk develop a pathological dislike of one or several body parts or components of their appearance, and develop a preoccupation with hiding or attempting to fix their perceived body flaw, often with cosmetic surgery (and this apparently affects up to three percent of the population). It has been suggested that both muscle dysmorphia and body dysmorphic disorder may be caused by a problem of 'somatoperception' (knowing one's own body), which may be related to organic lesions or processing issues in the right parietal lobe of the brain, which is suggested to be the important area of the brain for own-body perception and the sense of self. In folk that have lesions of the right parietal cortex, they perceive themselves to be 'outside' of their body (autoscopy), or that body parts are missing / there is a lack of awareness of the existence of parts of the body (asomatognosia). Non-organic / psychological factors have also been associated with muscle dysmorphia, apart from media and socio-cultural influences, including being a victim of childhood bullying, being teased about levels of muscularity when young, or being exposed to violence in their family environment. It has also been suggested that it is associated with appearance-based rejection sensitivity, which is defined as anxiety-causing expectations of social rejection based on physical appearance – in other words, for some reason, folks with muscle dysmorphia are anxious that they will be socially rejected due to their perceived lack of muscularity and associated appearance deficits. Whether this rejection sensitivity is due to prior negative social interactions, or episodes of childhood teasing or body shaming, has not been well elicited. Interestingly, while studies have reported inconclusive correlations with body mass index, body fat, height, weight, and pubertal development age, there have been strong correlations reported with mood disorders, anxiety disorders, perfectionism, substance abuse, and eating and exercise-dependence / addiction disorders, as well as with the clinical depression, anxiety, and obsessive-compulsive disorders. There does not appear to be a strong relationship to narcissism, which perhaps is surprising. Whether these are co-morbidities, or they have a common pathophysiology at either a psychological or organic level is yet to be determined. It has been suggested that a combination of cognitive behavioural therapy and selective serotonin reuptake inhibitor prescription (a type of antidepressant) may improve the symptoms of muscle dysmorphia. While these treatment modalities would support a link between muscle dysmorphia and the psychological disorders described above, the efficacy of these treatment choices is still controversial, and there is unfortunately a high relapse rate. It is unfortunately a difficult disorder to 'cure', given that all folk need to eat regularly in order to live, and most folk incorporate exercise into their daily routines, which make managing 'enough' but not 'excessive' amounts of weightlifting and dietary regulation difficult to regulate in folk who have a disordered body image.

Muscle dysmorphia appears, therefore, to be a growing issue in contemporary society, which is increasing in tandem with the increased media-related marketing drive for the male 'body beautiful', which now appears to be operating at a similar level to the 'drive for thinness' media marketing that has blighted the female perception of body image for a long time, and has potentially led to an increased incidence of body image disorders such as anorexia nervosa and body dysmorphic syndrome. However, none of these are gender specific, and it is not clear how much of a relationship these body image disorders have with either organic brain or clinical psychological disorders, as described above. It appears to be a problem mostly in young folk, with older folk being more accepting of their body abnormalities and imperfections, whether these are perceived or real, though sadly it appears that there is a growing incidence of muscle dysmorphia and other body image disorder in older age, as society's relationship and expectations of 'old age' changes. As I see my son become more 'interested' in his own physique and physical development, which must have obviously been caused by either discussions with his friends, or due to what he reads, or what the 'actors' in his computer games look like which he so enjoys playing, like all his friends, I hope he (and likewise my daughter) will always enjoy his sport but have a healthy self-image through the testing teenage and early adult period of time. I remember those bodybuilders my colleague Mike and I worked with all those years ago, and how some of them were comfortable with their large physiques, while with some it was clearly an ordeal to take off their shirts to be tested in the lab as part of the trials we did back then. The mind is very sensitive to suggestion, and it is fascinating to see that males now are being 'barraged' with advertising suggesting they are not good enough, and if they buy a certain product, it will make them stronger, fitter, better, and thus more attractive, to perhaps the same level females have been subjected to for a long period of time. The mind is also sensitive to bullying, teasing and body shaming, as well as a host of other social issues which impinge on it particularly in its childhood and early adolescent development phases. It's difficult to know where this issue will 'end', and whether governmental organizations will 'crack down' on such marketing and media hype which surely 'target' folks' (usually perceived) physical inadequacies or desires, or if it is too late to do so and such media activity has become innate and part of the intrinsic fabric of our daily life and social experience. Perhaps education programmes are the way to go at school level, though these are unfortunately often not successful.

There are so many daily challenges one has to deal with, it may seem almost bizarre that folk can spend time worrying about issues that are not even potentially 'real', but for the folk staring obsessively at themselves in the mirror or struggling to stop the intrusive thoughts about their perceived physical shortcomings, these challenges are surely very real, and surely all-consuming and often overwhelming. In Greek mythology Adonis was a well-muscled half man, half god, who was the ultimate in masculine beauty, and according to mythology his masculine beauty was so great that he won the love of Aphrodite, the queen of all the gods, because of it. Sadly, for the folk with muscle dysmorphia, while they may be chasing this ideal, they are likely to be too busy working on creating their own perfect physique to have time to 'woo' their own Aphrodite, and indeed, contemporary Aphrodites don't appear to even appreciate the level of muscularity they eventually obtain. The mirror on the wall, as it usually is, is a false siren, beckoning those weak enough to fall into its thrall – no matter how big, never to appear as the biggest or most beautiful of all.

Essay 31. Narcissistic personality disorders and sociopathy - One bad apple can the whole barrel ruin

Surely one of the worst possible things that can happen to anyone is to find out they are working with a sociopath (also known as a psychopath) or narcissistic personality disorder, or even worse has a one of these psychologically flawed types as a family member or life partner. These folk lack empathy or remorse and feel entitled to 'use' everyone around them for their own gain. What makes them challenging to diagnose and why they cast 'spells' over folk is because they can be very charming and 'cosy up' to folk they feel they can get something out of or use for their own gains. Once challenged, sociopaths and narcissistic personality disordered folks can become very aggressive and do their best to 'destroy' the career or life of the challenger, rather than 'come clean' and admit their shortcomings and try and improve as people. In this Essay, we examine the underlying causes and distinguishing characteristics of sociopaths and narcissistic personally disordered folk, and how best to 'manage them', if this is possible, once one has become aware that they have entered your life or circle of friends or work environment and is or has been manipulating you for their own gains. In the words of the Sheryl Crow song, surely the best thing one can do in such cases, is to 'Run baby, run', to survive them and their spider-like webs they try to entangle you in.

We have been dealing with some workplace issues which like nearly all management concerns, come down to challenging personalities and how to deal with them. I also recently had a discussion with an old colleague about a former acquaintance of ours who for a long part of a very successful career continuously worked hard to always be in the media or spotlight of attention, was always trying to claim personal responsibility for any innovative idea or concept developed by the team, and was always pretty nasty in undermining or aggressively rebutting anyone who disagreed with him, either on public stages or in the press, and we wondered if the individual had some of the symptoms of a narcissistic personality disorder or sociopathy. In management circles, a common way of describing routine daily life is that 95 percent of one's working day is spent dealing with five percent of the staff in one's team who are challenging and create difficulties for all that work around them. There is a growing perception in the scientific community that a number of these folk may not just be difficult folk in the work environment, but may have one of a number of different personality disorders that affects all aspects of their life, and all folk around them in a negative way, in both the work and home environment. The challenge is how to recognize them, as the signs of personality disorders are often subtle, and their presence may lead to overt success in the work environment from an output metrics perspective, although at the expense of a harmonious workplace. How to manage them is an even more difficult challenge, as is treating them for clinicians. So, what are personality disorders, and how can we recognize them?

Personality disorders are defined as a class of mental disorders that are characterized by enduring maladaptive patterns of behaviour, cognition, and inner experiences, exhibited across many contexts and deviating markedly from those accepted by the individual's culture, and are not due to use of any substance or another medical condition. There are several different personality disorders, which are described in the Diagnostic and Statistical Manual of Mental Disorders (DSM) of the American Psychiatric Association, which is the psychiatrist's 'bible' for classification of psychiatric disorders. These include obsessive-compulsive, antisocial, histrionic, borderline, schizoid, and paranoid personality disorders, amongst others, and while they all have some symptom overlap, they also each have unique characteristics and features. The personality disorder most associated with workplace dysfunction is narcissistic personality disorder, in which an individual is defined as being excessively preoccupied with personal adequacy, power, prestige, and vanity, is mentally unstable, but is unable to see the damage they are causing to other people. The term narcissism originated from the mythological Greek youth Narcissus who became infatuated with his own reflection in a lake, and did not recognize it as his own reflection. When he did, he died of grief for having fallen in love with someone that did not exist outside of himself – and therefore the term is used to describe excessive vanity and self-centredness. In the DSM, signs of narcissistic personality disorder include 1) having a grandiose sense of self-importance with exaggeration of achievements and talents and an expectation to be recognized as superior; 2) having a sense of entitlement and expectation of favourable treatment and requires excessive admiration; 3) is inter-personally exploitative and takes advantage of others for their own end; 4) lacks empathy and is unwilling to recognize or identify with the feelings and needs of others; 5) is often envious of others or believes that others are envious of them; and 6) believes that they are 'special' and unique and can only be understood by other special or high status people. The causes are multi-factorial and are speculated to include either an 'overs-sensitive temperament at birth', over-indulgence or over-evaluation by parents, family members or peers, or paradoxically emotional abuse in childhood, amongst other causes. It is thought to affect between one and five percent of people in society, and there is potentially, perhaps somewhat paradoxically given it is defined as a psychopathology, a greater percentage of narcissistic personality disorders found in folk who are high achievers as compared to the general population.

A second personality disorder, which is perhaps even more toxic to the work environment, is the sociopathic personality disorder, commonly described as sociopathy, and is also known as psychopathy. Sociopathy is defined as a personality disorder characterized by enduring antisocial behaviour, diminished empathy and remorse, and disinhibited or bold behaviour. There is some overlap of the symptoms of a sociopath with that of narcissistic personality disorder, though sociopaths are more 'dangerous' and are prone to delinquency and overt criminal behaviour. Common symptoms include glibness and superficial charm, grandiose sense of self-worth, pathological lying, need for stimulation and prone to boredom, parasitic lifestyle, impulsivity, a lack of remorse or guilt, callous and lacking in empathy, failure to accept responsibility for their actions, and poor behavioural control and delinquency. Sociopaths have been divided into 'unsuccessful' sociopaths, who are involved with regular crime, including violence, sexual offence, conduct disorder and other antisocial behaviour. In contrast, 'successful' sociopaths are corporate 'high climbers' who are successful in the work environment due to their anti-social symptoms and behaviour, which allow them to 'climb over' colleagues and show boldness for new challenges without any feelings of remorse or guilt that may prevent them doing so. It is not clear what the underlying causes of sociopathy are, or how they develop, and it has been speculated that either genetic or early social abuse in childhood could be at the root of its development. Sociopathy is thought to occur in around one percent of the population, and like narcissistic personality disorder, is found in a high percentage of 'high achievers' in the work environment.

Both these personality disorders can cause significant problems in the workplace environment, and if present in an individual in a position of authority, can cause damage to an entire work-force team, and increase the levels of bullying, conflict, stress, staff turnover and absenteeism in the work environment. Folk with either narcissistic personality disorder or sociopathy can often be charming and friendly to staff at a higher level in the work environment, but abusive to staff below their level. They can 'put on a mask' as required in social situations, and this makes them very difficult to 'diagnose' when first meeting them, and one is often taken in by their positive presence (which would only be on display if they could gain something from the person they are interacting with). They assess what people want to hear and will interact with an individual in a way that will gain trust, but if interacting with someone from who there will be no gain, or challenges them, they will publicly humiliate colleagues or team members, spread malicious lies, rapidly shift between emotions and use a specific emotion to gain advantage over their 'rivals', take credit for other people's accomplishments, blame others for their mistakes or incomplete work, encourage co-workers to harass or humiliate their 'rivals', and threaten 'rivals' with job loss, disciplinary procedures or harassment charges if this will be to their benefit. Sociopaths can bully folk in a purposeful way if they will gain from it or if it will help them achieve their goals, but can also bully in a predatory way, just for the simple pleasure they feel in tormenting people who are either vulnerable or susceptible to being bullied by nature of their workplace status. The problem is that because they are charming in required situations, they do well in job interviews, and manipulate situations to their own gain once entering an organization, and are therefore well ensconced in a workplace environment, or even have been promoted to a high leadership position, before folk working around them become aware of their true personality, and the damage they are causing to those around them and the environment they work in.

So, what can one do if one is a manager, or indeed a co-worker or team member, of someone with a sociopathic or narcissistic personality disorder? Sadly, these personality disorders are notoriously difficult to manage, with sociopathy in particular being regarded almost as an untreatable disorder, and narcissistic personality disorder being similarly problematical as folk who have the disorder respond badly to / refuse to accept criticism, or acknowledge that they have any problem, and frequently 'point the finger back' and say the manager has the problem, and will often respond quickly with a harassment charge on a manager who dares to challenge them such with the fact and potential diagnosis of their disorder. In a great book on management theory, James McGrath and Bob Bates suggested what to me are the best ways of dealing with these challenging disorders in the workplace, including 1) using the boxing maxim, defend yourself at all times; 2) if you think someone is a sociopath or has a narcissistic personality disorder raise your concerns with human resources as soon as possible and get them recorded; 3) maintain meticulous records of your dealings with these folk, as they are compulsive liars and will distort past events and conversations; 4) protect your staff by monitoring their dealings with the person and the consequences of these interactions; 5) develop your own good relationships with other staff and managers, so when they charge you with harassment or make malicious allegations against one, there is character reference 'backup'; 6) when dealing with the person, follow the organization's policies and procedures to the utmost, as they will use any deviation from this to attack you back; and 7) attempt to isolate or corral the person's work activity away from other staff members in order to protect them. Sadly, they also suggested that if your boss or manager is a sociopath, perhaps the best solution is to simply look for another job, or hope they move on or away from your work environment, as it is almost impossible to reason with folk with either of these personality disorders, and once they detect you are resistant to them, they will do all they can to make your life difficult or remove you from the work environment yourself.

Probably everyone has had some experience dealing with a work colleague, friend, or (heavens above) a life partner who has a narcissistic personality disorder or is a sociopath and has scars from the interaction. The problem is again that these personality deficits paradoxically often make these folk successful in their work, sport or social environment, even if they leave a trail of damage and discontent behind them. It's always interesting to look back at folk who society would assess as having been successful and one has interacted with when young, before experience teaches one to lookout for such folk and avoid them, and when assessing their personalities and modus operandi in the work-place, realize that their success was and is not based on their individual skills or efforts, but are potentially related to a personality disorder which allowed them to use people such as oneself, and others around them for their own gain, often with one knowing at the time. These folks in essence are 'successful' and go through life being successful as a result of gain from, or manipulation of, others. More often though, one is caught in a disastrous and damaging environment before one recognizes that one is working in the presence of, or interacting with, someone who has a narcissistic personality disorder, and one is 'locked in a battle for survival' with them, and as described above. Strong management is needed, or brave decisions, if such a person is involved within one's personal life, to either eject the individual from the environment or leave the environment oneself – ultimately unfortunately there is very little chance of successfully managing such individuals if they maintain their presence in the environment in which one works or lives. One rotten apple really can the whole barrel ruin, but unfortunately, locating and removing that rotten apple from the barrel is not easy, and many a barrel has indeed

253

been ruined by one rotten apple ultimately affecting the rest. It's a brave and resilient manager that tries, and eventually succeeds.

Essay 32. Rites of passage ceremonies, initiation, and hazing - How and why did something so traditional become so often criminal and psychologically damaging acts

Many folks feel a deep 'need' to belong to groups of similar humans, perhaps for safety, or for socialization, or due to some societal structural 'meme'. This need to form groups or 'tribes' must be deeply embedded, given that animals too tend to form into herds, or packs, or flocks. Often part of an 'outsider' joining a group is the requirement that they go through a ritual of initiation, that helps bond them with the other folk by showing they are willing to go through whatever challenges or rituals initiation throws at them. Sadly, with initiation rites, particularly at universities and in sporting and military groups in particular, most of the initiation involves 'hazing' new folk, which basically is physically and mentally brutalizing them, to the extent that each year young folk die due to severe forced alcohol intoxication or physical harm, and to me it is astonishing that such initiations are allowed to continue when this happens with sadly regular frequency. In this Essay therefore, we look at initiation and rites of passage ceremonies, and assess what is at their root, and why such terrible behaviour is 'accepted' and encouraged by the folks who do such to initiates, and the institutions which tolerate, or even encourage these deeply troubling activities.

At a recent rural medicine conference which I attended a few weeks ago, there was an interesting session on initiation practices in rural communities, and how doctors can optimally assist with attenuating the possibility of clinical consequences associated with them. I have been in discussion with the (great) senior management team of my current university regarding concerns I have about initiation ceremonies in the hostels and how they impact on the medical students we train, and how we can prevent them. I waved goodbye to my ten-year-old son last week when he went off on his first night away from home on an official trip with his school class to a campsite and felt a huge feeling of fear and concern for him that there would be the possibility of hazing occurring during it and was relieved to hear afterwards that it was all great fun and well organized by the top-notch school he attends. All of these got me thinking about rites of passage, initiation ceremonies, and the horrific practice of hazing, which is astonishingly still ubiquitous whenever social groups form in any community, be they sports teams, gangs, military units, university residences, or school, amongst many others.

Initiation ceremonies have been present in societies since time immemorial and are defined as a rite of passage marking entry into and acceptance into a group or society, or as a formal method of marking a transition into adulthood. Initiation ceremonies can be somewhat informal – for example at the university I graduated from as a medical doctor, a bagpiper traditionally 'piped' in the results that we had passed our exams, and a celebratory party occurred afterwards. When sailors or passengers on boats pass over the equator for their first time, they are given an initiation ceremony that welcomes them into the naval / sailing 'community' by doing so. They can also be very formal, such as occurs with the Christian Baptism, Jewish Bar Mitzvah or Tribal Manhood ceremonies.

Hazing, in contrast, is the contemporary definition of 'organized bullying' associated with initiation practices and is defined as the practice of rituals and other activities involving harassment, abuse or humiliation used as a way of initiating a person into a group. Hazing practices include: i) relatively (though to me awful anyway) 'benign' activities such as forcing initiates to march in line, perform long road trips, participate in physical activity, perform periods of silence or personal servitude to senior group members; ii) relatively 'malignant' activities such as the forced consumption of food or drink (including alcohol) or other noxious substances, acts of humiliation and degradation such as streaking or wearing humiliating apparel, or restrictions on eating and bathing, amongst others; and iii) frankly criminal activities such as branding, paddling, beating, or whipping – i.e. physical abuse – or forced sexual activity and abuse. Despite hazing being almost completely banned across the world, it is interesting to note that it is still extremely prevalent, with for example approximately one quarter of students in the USA acknowledging that they had been the victims of hazing, and several deaths reported each year are caused specifically by hazing practices.

The reasons why folk agree to, or submit to, hazing practices when joining a university residence, or starting military training, or joining a sports team, are complex and still not well understood, as is indeed why ritual initiation practices are required in any shape or form. The classical reason for their occurrence is the team building one, and that initiation practices, particularly those associated with hazing, create team identity and group cohesion by uniting folk undergoing hazing by the adversity associated with the process, and by successfully completing the ordeal imposed on them. In this theory, hazing causes firstly a separation phase, which removes the initiate from their previous social group due to the trials they go through, challenging their old identity enough in order for them to 'open up' to change; then a transition phase, in which the initiate goes through the challenges and psychologically 'fragments' during the process; and finally the incorporation phase, when after completing the tasks, the initiate has a new identity which is synchronous / part of the group controlling the initiation process. But, a recent great study by Liesbeth Mann and colleagues has shown that the use of hazing, particularly when it targets individuals as compared to groups of initiates at one time, has a negative effect both on team function and identity, with most folk who go through such humiliating hazing practices feeling less, rather than more, affiliation both to fellow initiates and the group that imposes them, even if they do not overtly 'show' this negative perception to the group. Even the military, which has long used hazing practices as team-building practice, has realized that hazing does not increase 'esprit du corps', and is working on alternative, less abusive methods of doing so.

So why do folk who join a new residence at a university, or sports team, submit to the process of hazing, rather than refusing to participate and reporting such practice immediately it happens? Perhaps most importantly, most young adults and adolescents feel the need to 'belong', and if hazing is the price to 'pay' to belong to a particular group, they will go through it – even if, for example when signing up for a residence at a university, hazing would not be expected to be an organized part of induction. Most folk of all ages have a strong drive for connection and self-preservation, and these 'drives' may contribute to an acceptance of hazing by those undergoing it. Conformity and obedience to authority may also be part of the reason – most folk submit to authority and perceive that if senior / older folk are telling them to do something, it must be associated with acceptable authority. There is also thought to be a fear of retribution and alienation associated with refusing to participate in such rituals, and the concept of the 'silence', where those folks who do complain are not supported with their complaint by other group victims of hazing, or by anyone in the group doing the hazing. Indeed, from a fraternity or sport team perspective, it may be the case that those whom the complaints are taken to, such as residence heads or coaches, were previously part of the same fraternity or sports team, and turn a 'blind eye' or actively encourage such hazing behaviour, and 'fob off' those that complain, which is obviously devastating to those that do so. There is also the concept of cognitive dissonance that is posited as a reason why folks allow themselves to submit to hazing – they are aware that such behaviour is abusive and degrading, but in order to cope, 'downplay' the negative aspects of the hazing process they are undergoing by rationalizing that it is 'not too bad' or 'good for team-building', and thereby cope with something that is perceived to be unacceptable to them.

If it is hard to understand why folk accept the process of hazing happening to them, it is even harder to understand why folk involve themselves in organizing hazing or are part of groups that haze younger initiates. Some individuals who haze initiates surely have personality disorders such as sociopathy and take pleasure from humiliating and / or abusing others. There is also the concept of abuse 'cycles', where folk who have been hazed in the past themselves, are at a greater risk of hazing others because of a misplaced desire for revenge – if the 'system' where the hazing takes place is perceived to be 'too big' to challenge, then some folk will 'take it out' on future initiates to 'make up' for what they suffered. There is also the concept of 'groupthink', which is defined as a process in groups where faulty decision making occurs as a result of the group dynamics, including pressure for unanimity and conformity, suppression of moral objections, and degradation of 'outsiders', which is what initiates would be perceived as being until they have gone through the rite of passage defined as being required by the group as necessary in order to be part of the group. So 'groupthink' would result in the condoning of hazing practice, though it is not clear if each person individually feels like the 'group' when alone as compared to when in the group environment. It is also suggested that those in groups involved in hazing initiates may do so due to fear of reprisal for not doing so, or a perceived lack of alternatives available to the hazing process for incorporating new folk into their 'group', whatever their group is.

The question arises why something so barbaric still is so ubiquitous, and what can be done to 'stamp it out'. There is clearly something seemingly innate in most folk that leads them to believe that some 'rite of passage' is needed as part of the transition periods of life, particularly adolescence into adulthood, and is needed to 'cement' one's place in a group, and indeed potentially create group dynamics. But clearly hazing is more than a 'step too far' and needs more active management than what appears to be the case up to this point in time to eradicate it. Researchers, law officials and leaders are beginning to realize that there needs to be a three-pronged approach to dealing with the problem of hazing. The first is that it needs to be absolutely spelt out that not only is hazing 'not nice' and not appropriate, but it is categorically illegal / criminal activity, and folk who organize hazing practice should be punished to levels commensurate with what type of hazing is performed, even if this is a custodial sentence. In other words, universities, and sports teams (and indeed any group activity where hazing is a problem) need to work with law enforcement folk to be sure their codes of conduct and disciplinary procedures are not just 'in house' but carry the full weight of the law behind them – and those in positions of authority in any environment who support hazing need to be 'rooted out' by senior management / law enforcement folk. Second, there needs to be credible alternatives created to hazing, that are positive rather than damaging, and that allow a rite of passage to occur in new initiates that is pleasant rather than damaging, and these alternatives need to be articulated and encouraged by senior management of whatever institution is afflicted by hazing practices. Thirdly, there needs to be a strong marketing and external communication campaign that clearly states that hazing is unacceptable, and people can speak up about their concerns regarding hazing and can refuse to participate in any ritual initiation ceremony, whether it includes hazing or not, without fear of prejudice or retribution. Until these actions are taken, hazing will continue unabated as routine, history and tradition work to keep on taking it forward. We need mentors rather than thugs inducting our youth, encouragement rather than humiliation, and welcome rather than aggression masquerading as 'play'.

I have got to the age in my life when I try and see the 'middle path' in most debates and issues, and try and always be pragmatic in controversial debate, but there is no doubt that the issue of hazing fills me with a feeling of horror and a sensation of nausea when thinking about it (and indeed writing about it now) which is visceral and extreme (for the record I don't have any memory of any hazing episodes in my past that would induce such feelings directly), and probably most folk reading this would think and feel similarly. I simply cannot understand how anyone can force someone else to engage in practices that are humiliating to them for any reason whatsoever, let alone as part of some group initiation practice. What is in the mind of someone who forces someone else (usually younger or 'weaker') to drink urine, or eat faeces, or who as a group whips people as they run past, or worse – it is something that to me almost defies belief, despite writing about the potential causes of hazing in a rational manner above. Who benefits from forcing first year students to wear strange uniforms on campus in their first year? Who benefits from hitting a new sports team member on their backside with a bat? Who benefits from making someone grovel in front of them or be their 'servant' for a year, and at a place of higher learning as it so often does, of all places? I didn't sign up for such things when I went to School or University, or played competitive sport in my youth, and I don't think many folks do. Hazing really has no place in modern, or any society, and I fervently hope my children are not exposed to it in their lifetimes when they go through their own 'rite of passage' from adolescence to young adults. As much as there is a sociopathic 'groupthink' that perhaps lies behind the causation of hazing, perhaps those of us who feel nausea at the thought of it can create a more positive 'groupthink' of our own, and work to get it eradicated, or replaced by something which perhaps better incorporates the 'old' virtues associated with rite of passage ceremonies, such as mentorship, welcome, and celebration – if they indeed ever existed in the initiation practices of times and traditions past.

Essay 33. The Kübler-Ross five emotional stages of grief - Dealing with bad news is a complex business

Everyone at some point will likely go through a severe period of grief and loss, sometimes so severe that it can affect their self-identity, world view and / or mental health. This may be the death of a loved one or pet, the destruction of one's life work in a fire or external disaster or finding out a life partner has been cheating on you for many years without you knowing, amongst many other psychologically damaging events and occurrences. Eventually, the greatest challenge for most folks is hearing they have a tumour that is inoperable, or an organ is failing that cannot be cured, and one must come to terms with the horror of one's own death and permanent removal from all life that one knows and lives. Elisabeth Kübler-Ross described five stages of emotional grief that occur when one gets very bad news, which have stood the test of time, and appear in many ways to be the mind 'working through' what it faces, in an attempt to make sense of what is happening and make peace with the fact that life for them will never be the same again or will be ending soon. In this Essay we look at the Kübler-Ross stages of grief, and assess their capacity to attenuate the symptoms of grief, and 'move' the suffering person to a place of understanding and acceptance, and hopefully finally peace, while living in the eye of their final storm.

I have been reading the fascinating Oliver Sacks autobiography 'On the Move', and was touched by his descriptions of his early neurology days interacting with patients whom he had to give bad news to about their diagnosis, and was reminded of the early days of my medical career when I had to do similar. This week a career project I have been working on for a while turned out not as I wanted it, and I noted my own response to the news when I got it. I have also been part of an interesting Twitter discussion on doping in sport, involving the response of those accused of doping to the accusations levelled against them. All of these got me thinking of the Kübler-Ross model of the emotional stages of dealing with bad news, and how important they are in understanding one's own reactions, and those one is interacting with or observing, and struggling to understand their actions and responses to receiving news or a diagnosis of something that is neither welcome nor positive.

The Kübler-Ross Model was generated by Elisabeth Kübler-Ross, a Swiss-American psychiatrist, who worked with terminally ill patients, and was horrified by how they were treated and managed, and by how death and dying in modern culture (in her case in the mid-twentieth century) were 'hidden' by society and not talked about or acknowledged. She encouraged the medical students she taught to both confront death and dying, and work with their patients to optimally do so. As a result of her work, she published a book about her experiences – 'On Death and Dying' – and proposed a theory called the Five Stages of Grief Model, outlining how people faced with death both respond to and cope with firstly the news of, then the process of, their own death. The five stages included denial, anger, bargaining, depression and finally acceptance. While her work was controversial, with some scientists and clinicians believing the model to be too simplistic, it has in many ways 'stood the test of time' and is now being used to explore other areas of grief and responses by individuals to bad news, and not just in the specific context of death and dying.

The first reaction to bad news in the Kübler-Ross model is denial. In this stage the individual receiving bad news believes that the diagnosis, information, or news is mistaken and refuses to accept it, and 'clings to a false, preferable reality'. There are several defined types of denial, including: i) simple denial, where the reality of the unpleasant news or facts is denied altogether; ii) minimisation, where the bad news is acknowledged, but its seriousness is denied (this is in effect a combination of both denial and rationalization); and iii) projection, where both the bad news and its seriousness is acknowledged, but responsibility for the bad news is denied by blaming somebody or something else. The denial phase is followed by a phase of anger, where the individual recognizes eventually that the denial cannot continue, either due to progression of symptoms if faced with a terminal or life-threatening illness, or when evidence or facts supporting the bad news becomes overwhelming, and they become frustrated and lash out at those around them, or at the bearer of the bad news. The third phase is bargaining, which implies a sense of hope that the individual can in some way 'overcome' the bad news by making some bargain or compromise, such as a reformed lifestyle, with or without the comprehension that such bargaining is futile and will not change the situation in any way materially. The fourth phase is depression, where the individual becomes aware that the mathematical probability of their impending death is overwhelming, or that the bad news is surely true, and becomes depressed and goes into their own 'shell', refusing visitors or communication about anything, let alone their illness or bad news. The fifth, and final, stage is acceptance of what has happened or what is coming, and in this important last stage individuals accept whatever fate has befallen them, and either prepare for their impending death or accept the bad news as real, but with stable emotions and a feeling of calmness and acceptance.

All these stages are clearly part of a complex pattern of coping behaviour which allows the individual to not completely collapse and become catatonic in the face of bad news, and which allows them to eventually 'move on' to a state of acceptance of an altered state of being that is imperfect or not what was the ideal state of the individual either at the time before they received the bad news, or for their future life plans. Why folk need to go through all these stages, and not jump immediately to the phase of acceptance, is not completely clear, but it is suggested that the process is needed to integrate new, unexpected information that dramatically conflicts with previous beliefs or plans, and which threatens one's personal identity, life plans or way of life in a potentially permanent and negative way. Kübler-Ross suggested that not all individuals go through all five phases sequentially always, that some individuals could cycle through some of the stages in a repetitive rather than linear way, and that an individual's personal surrounding environment could be a factor in influencing the use of a specific cycle. But, in her opinion, all folk do go through at least two of the stages after receiving bad news or a terminal clinical prognosis. Her work led her to believe that if one did not go through such stages, one would remain in denial, and continue to 'fight' death (or the bad news, whatever it is) or be paralysingly afraid of it, and therefore endure a more difficult and less 'dignified' death or an ongoing maladapted life situation or way of life (although it has been pointed out that not confronting death or bad news is for some individuals an adaptive process in itself). Interestingly, she believed that the stages were a form of communication, either externally or with oneself, and a way of someone being able to review and compare both their past life and their current state and process this information in an ordered way that would be helpful to both the individual and those assisting them, once they realized and understood that their emotions were part of an ordered / structured process. Because of this, Kübler-Ross supported the concept of hospice care movements which supported folk with terminal illnesses during their last days and as they went through the psychological cycle described above, rather than the concept of euthanasia, which to her prevented people from 'completing their unfinished business' before they died, or accepting whatever loss of pride, prestige, or lifestyle loss the bad news signified or entailed.

Both Kübler-Ross and others became aware that the model could be used in a variety of setting and situations when bad news was involved – be it children grieving during a parents' divorce, grieving for a lost relationship, or problems with substance abuse. As in the examples above, it can also potentially be used when some work which one has invested a large amount of emotional energy in is irretrievably 'lost' or rejected with no prospect of a 'comeback', or when an athlete fails a drug test, that if shown to be true, has enormous impact not just on the fidelity of their past achievements and successes, but also on their current social status and perhaps even future financial wellbeing. It has also been noted that particularly during the denial and anger phases, folk can cause a lot of harm to those around them, either by projecting blame for their actions as part of the denial process on to those informing them of the bad news or discussing such news personally in the media. Denial can take the form of: i) denial of impact, when it is related to continuing behaviour which is harmful both to the person themselves or those around them; ii) denial of cycle, when related to repetitive patterns of behaviour that are ongoing, unchanging, and negative; iii) denial of awareness, where mitigating factors are used to 'lessen' the severity of the bad news; and iv) most difficult to manage, denial of denial, which is an extreme form of self-delusion where the person convinces themselves that the bad news or evidence of bad actions in themselves is not true. All these forms of denial are major impediments to both changing behaviour and allowing the five grief stages to progress to the stage of acceptance and psychological peace. Folk who are in denial can clearly potentially provide great challenges and negative consequences to both themselves and to those around them who are attempting to assist them to come to terms with their current life status or condition.

Whether the Kübler-Ross five stages are 'real' or not, or occur in sequential fashion as outlined by Elisabeth Kübler-Ross, they are important in helping us understand the behaviour, often initially negative, in those facing terminal illness, or the effect of bad news either in one's family, social, or work environment. In our modern (western) society, death and dying is 'swept under the carpet' and not talked about or acknowledged almost at all. This in many ways perhaps makes it more difficult to come to terms with our own mortality when it is challenged, or when we get our own terminal 'death sentence' from a doctor we go to for a worrying symptom that will not go away. Furthermore, in modern society (actually, probably since the time of the first origin of any 'society'), most folk have developed a need to project an 'aura' of success and vitality and have a belief that to be successful in society they need to do such. Because of this, when we get bad news or negative outcomes that could materially or socially affect our life and lifestyle, this becomes difficult to accept because of the perceived loss of status, or future wellbeing, or acceptance in the broader society which folk perceive will be the case if the bad news, or evidence of prior non-optimal behaviour, becomes 'public' knowledge. But people do accept and admire someone that says 'sorry' unreservedly. People do accept failure when it is acknowledged and learnt from. People do not just want to accept, but also want to help those that they love who are ill or dying. Therefore, when one is confronted with someone behaving 'badly' after they have received news that is not to their liking, perhaps we need to understand that they are going through some part of the Kübler-Ross cycle (though we must be careful not to exclude the possibility of overt sociopathy or personality disorders in those behaving as such). We also have to understand that when we hear the bad news of others, particularly those whom we are close to, be it one's child, spouse, parent, friend, or work colleague, this may trigger a similar Kübler-Ross grief cycle in oneself, at the same time as the other person is going through similarly, and this can become mutually challenging and co-morbid. Each one of us faces bad news of varying degree on an almost daily basis, and unless one dies suddenly of an unexpected heart attack, each one of us is destined to eventually hear a definitive diagnosis and prognosis from a well-meaning clinician that we have a terminal illness and that our days are numbered. The challenge for us is to try and accept these setbacks and bad news with the best grace possible, and be aware that sometimes our own responses, whether denial, anger, or depression, are part of a cycle of psychological 'healing'. Rather than 'fight' these emotions, we need to attempt to 'work with them' to get as quickly as possible to a state of acceptance and peace about wherever our journey is due to take us because of that fateful discussion that brings us the bad news, that at first is so difficult to accept.

As the great saying goes, 'of time you would make a stream upon whose bank you would sit and watch its flowing, yet the timeless in you is aware of life's timelessness and knows that yesterday is but today's memory and tomorrow is but today's dream'. Perhaps an overt awareness of the inevitability of one's death, and that one surely will receive bad news and have failures despite all one's best efforts as part of the natural process of life and time passing, makes us appreciate more each day that ends well, and allows us to wake up at the start of each new day hopeful for its outcome, yet aware each day could bring some life changing negative event to us. All we can do is deal with the bad news when it comes, and eventually, with time and the Kübler-Ross cycles, accept it, even if we wish the river of life to pause or flow back, something which it surely can never do. The last words of General Stonewall Jackson, the superb Confederate military leader in the American Civil war, who died of pneumonia after being shot by his own men by mistake and losing his arm, were 'Let us cross the river and rest in the shade of the trees', words said apparently to his wife who had come to be by his side with a smile on his face. The prior life until we get that really bad news is surely like a flowing river or stream, which after the bad news arrives, becomes a raging sea. But this raging sea may be part of a planned accumulation of underlying currents, which enables one to get as quickly as possible, and eventually safely and calmly, to the other shore, wherever and whatever that far shore is or will be.

Section 5. Understanding human research and science issues

Section 5.1. Introduction

In the previous sections, we looked at the beautiful poetry and complexity of the building blocks of life and being a human as we know it, as well as what happens when we push our bodies to extreme efforts, and what changes in us when we get sick. In the next nine Essays, we look at how and where all these wonderful facts and deep knowledge of the human existence and body function are elucidated, generated, and recorded, namely universities, research centres and academic environments via research processes and laboratory technology. While there have been examples of single folk working outside of academia making big breakthroughs in a field, such as Albert Einstein working as a clerk when he wrote his breakthrough scientific papers in the early 1900's, most of the information described and discussed in these Essays occurred in academic environments. As we have become more aware of how complex the mysteries of life we still have to unlock and understand are, the bigger the teams of academics and researchers have become trying to 'tackle' the problem of solving them, and it will be surprising if a single individual will be able to make major breakthroughs on things like how the brain works, or where and how thoughts are maintained discretely and permanently as memories, or what happens beyond our current galaxy, as several complex problems we still have almost zero understanding of. There is an absolute poetry and beauty to the workings of academic life – the yearly routines and traditions of robes and hierarchy, of days in the laboratory, of generating data that allow one to 'see' some new fact or finding, the intellectual discussions over mid-morning coffee breaks and 'corridor conversations' that lead to new ideas and new breakthroughs, and it has been my privilege to work in the academic environment for most of my life to date. Statistical group data are important, but so too are individual data and experiences, and at the bottom of all breakthroughs, are firstly the creative ideas that lead to 'doable' experiments and having the equipment to be able to do the actual experiments themselves. Hearing a neuron fire through an amplifier of single nerve recording electrodes or seeing hands twitch after firing electromagnetic waves through a study participants skull into the motor cortex, are truly magical events to witness, and are poetical both from an observational perspective, and for the actual events which they underscore. In many ways research has come so far in knowledge generation. In many ways more, though, research still has a long, long way to go to understand the full depth and breadth of the poetry which is life.

Essay 34. Research and public engagement - Generating new knowledge, but often confusing the public

Research and the academic endeavour will always be the 'pole-star' for the generation of new findings, for explaining social and health problems and finding cures for them, and for deepening our understanding of the world around us, and our body and brain function within us. But, it is a complex area of life to be involved in, with often different folk coming to different conclusions from the same data, with some data not being able to be replicated due to too small testing groups or the wrong use of statistics, and sadly, a small number of researchers are charlatans who will 'cheat' the due process of science, either altering data to make it fit the 'paradigm' or answer they want, or simply making up data without doing the studies that are needed to produce them, usually because big breakthroughs result in big academic reputations, financial rewards, and a quick path to the 'top' of the academic discipline they work in. In this Essay we look at the process of research, how it can be a force for good, but also sadly, how it can be used by some folk for their own gain, rather than for the betterment of the world and humankind.

A vigorous debate erupted this week in the Sports Medicine and Health worlds after my old colleague and laboratory head during my long past University of Cape Town days, Tim Noakes, published some ideas of his (and his collaborators) that exercise did not work to reduce weight if one did not improve one's diet concurrently. This idea of Tim's followed up other controversial ideas he has put forward during the last few years, that carbohydrates are bad, and that one should eat a high fat diet and reduce carbohydrates to almost zero to optimize health. He has gone even further and suggested recently that one's exercise capacity is optimized by a high fat diet as compared to a high carbohydrate diet, and furthermore that children should be 'weaned' onto a high fat diet from an early age, if I heard his message right. The problem for a lot of folks is that for more than 20 years before this, Tim strenuously advocated a high carbohydrate diet, and that carbohydrates were 'king', before having his epiphany and change of heart on diet, due apparently to himself being diagnosed as suffering from Type 2 diabetes a while ago and trying to alter his own diet as a result of this. Whether Tim is right or wrong with either his 'old' or 'new' messages, if all this is confusing for us scientists, I can imagine how difficult it must be for the general public to understand what is 'right' in the nutrition field, and why most folk often view the messages scientists propose with a high index of suspicion. So why does research and science often seem to confuse any issue rather than clarify it?

Research is defined as an endeavour to discover new, or collate old facts, by the scientific study of a subject or by a course of critical investigations. Research is not a new endeavour, and indeed most of any civilization's progress must have been based on the testing of a hypothesis, or a change in lifestyle, and then accepting that change as custom / habit if it improved living conditions or quality of life. However, although research and science developed into a distinct entity with its own rules and way of doing things over hundreds of years, until the 20th century no detailed statistical testing was applied to any findings, and researchers and scientists merely reported individual case studies, or pooled data from several different case studies, with no attempt to control any variable, and made deductions from them. In the early part of the 20th century, with the advent of inferential statistics, researchers and clinical scientists began to believe that these case report studies were too simplistic, and possibly biased or prejudiced by external influences which were not reported or controlled for. From the 1930s to the 1960s, research methodology was technically improved, and studies were required to be well controlled before they were accepted for publication in scientific journals, which is and always has been the principal 'vehicle' of how research findings are made available to the scientific community and general public. Participants were required to be chosen randomly, variables well-controlled, and prospective replaced retrospective studies as the 'gold standard' for scientific / clinical research trials. Journals are now rated on the quality of research they publish, and studies that randomly select subjects, are 'double-blind' (meaning that neither the research subjects nor scientists know about the contents of a particular intervention or drug being tested during the trial), and examined participants in a controlled environment, have a greater chance of being published in a 'quality' journal than do studies that do not have these characteristics.

Unfortunately, this rigidity, while commendable, has led to problems of inference to the general public of the findings of such 'gold-standard', well controlled studies. In such trials, an individual is taken from their normal environment and turned into a laboratory 'rat' for the duration of the study / clinical experiment, and every possible variable is kept the same for each person in the trial, and any transgression of the 'order' of the trial leads to the expulsion of the participant from the trial. But human beings are not laboratory rats (and rats I am sure would say that not all laboratory rats are similar!). For example, during the 'best' drug or nutrition trials, participants are sometimes required to stay in a hospital or laboratory for the duration of the trial, and must all eat the same food and follow the same daily routine. The results assimilated from these artificially constructed environments are then published, and for example, a new drug or diet, based on the success of the trial, is approved and marketed to the general public. However, all individuals in their normal life will be following their own routines, probably with alcohol and perhaps tobacco consumption and unique diet, and to apply the average results derived from the original trial to this general public may be misrepresentative. All one can say with certainty after a well-controlled 'gold standard' trial is that in the specific group studied, in the specific environment where the test occurred, the drug or diet tested produced changes that were different from those produced by the placebo or other drug or diet it was tested against.

A further problem with extrapolating research results to the general public is that researchers generally produce average values (means) to describe the outcomes for the group of individuals involved in a specific trial, and then suggest to the general public that their data averages / the results of their trials are applicable to the general public from which they were originally selected. But human beings are individuals and not averages, and it is therefore problematic to extrapolate averages from clinical or nutritional (or indeed any) trials to larger population groups. For example, to tell a patient or person who follows a particular diet that research has shown that they have a 30% chance of dying younger than those following another type of diet is fraught with potential error – each individual's date with death could be anywhere along the bell-shaped mortality curve, independent of whatever diet they choose to eat in their daily life. Indeed, they may live to be 90 or 100 whatever they eat if that is what their genetic and physical programme entails (and a good degree of 'luck' / chance is also perhaps involved given how many things can kill one en-route to one's programmed life end time), despite there being a difference in average age of death between those who eat the diet being tested and those eating another diet. The problem of inference / extrapolation is made even more complex because of the fact that most research relies on the current research techniques / tests available to test a diet or drug at the time the trial occurs, and these tests available may be too simplistic to pick up potentially significant signs of toxic changes occurring in the individuals being tested. For example, 70 years ago, anabolic steroids were routinely used in large doses to cure 'melancholia' and depression. A few decades later scientists and clinicians started realizing, as their assessment techniques improved with time, that anabolic steroid drugs in large does could cause liver, heart and lipid profile disorders, and might even lead to dependency and psychological dysfunction. Therefore, the clinicians and researchers who initially recommended the therapeutic use of anabolic steroids were unwittingly placing their patients at risk, because of a lack of adjunctive knowledge and simplistic research techniques available to inform their decision at the earlier historical time points.

Therefore, for all the reasons above, even the best researcher has to be cautious about extrapolating their findings to the general public, due to the inherent weaknesses of even the 'best' science, and a good scientist would always be cautious when announcing their findings, and when availing themselves to the press to discuss them. The problem of course is that a scientist's ego often gets in the way, and they often rush to announce their findings, or perspectives on a finding of another scientist, to get their name in the press, and get themselves 'in the spotlight' as much as possible. A lot of science, as nicely put by Ad Lagendijk in an article in Nature a few years, involves aggressive men (this gender focus was specifically used in the article) 'fighting for their scientific claims to, at best, miniscule advances' in scientific knowledge, with 'territorial behaviour' underpinning their claims, and with 'successful scientists incessantly travelling round the world performing their routine (speeches about their findings and theories) like circus clowns – forcefully backing up their assertions over what their contributions are to the latest scientific priorities and findings' (sic). While this is a somewhat gloomy / negative assessment of the behaviour of a lot of (male) scientific folk, there is potentially a grain of truth in this, and unfortunately some scientists are perhaps too quick to engage with the public about their own findings, in order to assuage a huge / weak ego, and this can only complicate a research 'message' even more than just the methodological issues described above. The chance for a scientist's ego to be more involved than it should is made even easier in modern times with the advent of the internet and publication vehicles beyond that of the routine scientific peer-review process (though the peer-review process is not without its faults either) where any work published is peer-reviewed and too extreme conclusions are required to be 'toned down' before publication, such as Blogs, Twitter, Facebook, and other methods where scientists now can very easily speak directly to the public, and in some ways can cause more 'harm' than good potentially by doing so.

So going back to the initial discussion of my old colleague Tim's 'flip flop' on his diet message from high carbohydrates to high fat as being the best diet, and now that exercise may not be of benefit for weight loss (if I have read his latest message right, though it is very opaque what exactly is being said), folk should understand that scientists do have their own opinions and biases, do enjoy being in the limelight and press, and even if they have generated their conclusions on the basis of their own lab data, this data itself may be 'flawed' due to the reasons described above to no fault of the researcher themselves beyond not being cautious enough about their data. Therefore, all scientific information received by the public from scientists, particularly those scientists and clinicians that 'shout the loudest', should be taken with a strong 'pinch of salt' and heard with caution. For scientists themselves, we have to keep on remembering when venturing out of our labs to engage with the public that every word we say is 'fraught with danger' / has the potential to be incorrect or proved wrong in the future, and that the goal of every scientist and clinical researcher should perhaps not be to make a big new finding, but to be always dispassionate and cautious, no matter what one finds or concludes from one's time in the laboratory. As a friend and colleague of mine (and great scientist), Dr Angus Hunter once advised me, those that are the most passionate in science are the worst, and those that are most cautious in their message 'the best' (or words to that effect!). There is perhaps some truth in these words, at least when engaging with the public as a scientist, or conversely, when the public is trying to work out the validity of what a scientist / science is saying. Eat fat? Eat carbs? As the old wise words always suggest, moderation and balance are surely always best, and this goes not just for eating choices, but also for when scientists and clinicians engage with the public about their research work and findings.

Essay 35. Universities - Providing a function to society similar to what mitochondria do for the cell

I have spent most of my life, apart from my clinical years, studying and working in University and Research Centre environments, and can attest that they are truly extraordinary places, and not just in a positive way, being often poorly led, confused as to whether they are places of learning, businesses, or research drivers, filled with staff some of whom are incredibly creative, but some of whom don't publish or do anything innovative from not long after they get tenure. But they are also truly brilliant entities, as if they are worth their salt, they maintain an absolute independence from any state, governmental or business entities, they produce research that changes the world we live in and how we think of it, they teach folk who have been spoon-fed learning at school how to think independently, and try to maintain moral imperatives, which means that when governments become imperious or fascist, they tend to become the breeding ground of civil rights movements and revolutionary activity. In this Essay, therefore, we look at universities as entities, how they developed, and what their functions are in the contemporary internet connected and social media dominated world.

I was reading up on basic cell physiological function, specifically that of cellular mitochondria, last week, around the time that at my university alma mater, the students there currently were protesting vigorously for the removal of statues of historical figures they did not appreciate which were on the campus. The student protests got me thinking of what the teleological function of universities is, beyond just places of learning, and it struck me that they serve a function for states and societies similar to those which mitochondria serve for a cell. A university is broadly defined as an educational institution designed for instruction, examination (or both) of students in many branches of advanced learning, for conferring degrees in various faculties, and often embodying colleges and similar institutions. The original Latin word for a university is 'Universitas', which describes a number of persons associated into one body, a society, or an institution, which is self-governing, independent and determines the qualifications of its members. To this day universities have traditionally strongly protected their autonomy and independence from state institutions, even if paradoxically they are usually dependent on the state in which they operate for their existence in the form of funding and financial grants from the state for their running costs. Universities as we know them are thought to have developed from church teaching structures, starting in around the 6th Century AD in Europe and developing into the structures they still exist as in the 10th and 11th Century AD – for example the University of Bologna was established in 1088, the University of Paris in 1150 and the University of Oxford in 1167. Universities were set up initially as teaching institutions and developed over the following centuries to incorporate research / knowledge generation as another important component of their business. In the early years, universities generally taught general or 'preparatory' subjects such as arithmetic, geometry, music, politics, astronomy and languages, but with time developed increasing subject specialization in subjects like medicine, law, engineering and accounting amongst others. Modern universities offer a huge, diverse array of courses, from sport science to clothing and building design, and even more specific postgraduate courses have been added to the university business offering / portfolio, along with Doctoral degrees which are traditionally research focussed, and associated with developing novel knowledge via the research endeavour in the field in which they are awarded. While these additions have strengthened and added to the rich tapestry of most university environments, and universities are now ubiquitous through all countries in the world, what is interesting is that the basic concepts of the university which were present from their start all those years ago, of autonomy from the state and self-governorship, along with the same campus and faculty based working environment, and of course all the peculiar traditions such as gowns, caps, and professorial academic ranking, which are treasured by those working and attending universities, still exist, even if they often appear asynchronous with modern garb and work environments.

Universities fulfil other functions in society beyond the formal teaching of specific subjects. Apart from being a place for developing an individual's specific creative talents beyond that which could occur in the required uniformity of the school environment, Universities also are, or should be, an environment where the 'human' dynamic is nurtured and developed, as my current charismatic Rector, Professor Jonathan Jansen, well describes it. The 'human' virtues are those intangible ones, related to the quest for knowledge, the quest for truth, the quest for virtue, and the capacity in a protected environment, which universities usually are, to challenge current thinking, challenge dogmas, and challenge any status quo. It is not for nothing that even today general degrees such as those of the humanities are still highly prized, given that they train future students to be leaders and managers, and not just skilled artisans in their particular area of training, who are able to see the 'big picture', are able to debate in a skilled way, and are able to understand that most of life is about influencing any activity one is involved in a nuanced and 'politically' astute and 'humane' way, rather than by brute force or 'might is right' way.

Perhaps because of both this autonomy from surrounding state and other structures, and due to the inherent encouragement of universities to challenge dogma, and to resist external change if it is deemed unethical or if it could potentially undermine the autonomy of the university itself, university folk, in particular the student body, are often 'at odds' with external individuals and organizations in society who have authority, and are often early agents for change in society. An example of this is evident in the 1950's Hungarian student uprising against Russian control of Hungary, which led to a nation-wide revolt, which while ultimately being unsuccessful and leading to a brutal suppression by Russia, weakened the 'Iron Curtain' which 'hung' over Eastern Europe for most of the second half of the 20th century. Another is that of the Kent State University demonstrations in the USA in the 1960s against American involvement in the Vietnam war.

The demonstrations turned violent after several protestors were shot by Ohio state guardsmen and spread from Kent State University across university campuses throughout the USA, and eventually into the broader American society, and therefore surely played a part in the USA eventually withdrawing from the Vietnam conflict. So, in effect, universities can be a major agent for social change, and its academics and students are often at the forefront of societal debates. Because of such protest action and civic demonstrations (and other forms of more benign methods of protest such as writing and debate), universities often, as in the examples above, play the part of a societal moral conscience, or a 'barometer' of a society's needs or perceived shortcomings, to which the society's rulers potentially have a 'blind spot', or in societies whose leaders have brutal / repressive policies against their own citizens or a segment of them.

It must be noted though that universities, because of the fact that they treasure their autonomy so highly, can also become 'out of sync' with their society in a conservative way too, and are not always progressive 'vehicles' for change. They may, in a changing social environment, retain practices which are deemed unacceptable, unethical, or unhealthy by the society in which they exist. These include, for example, the practice of 'hazing' new students in university residences – initiation practices which are regarded as 'right of practice' and being part of university tradition by those who perform them, but in any contemporary environment would be regarded as overt bullying behaviour. In South Africa, a particularly challenging problem is transforming the ethnic demographics of university academics. As a relic of the Apartheid era, a number of universities still have a predominantly white academic body, which is incongruous in relation to the ethnic demographics of South African society. Yet, when such universities are challenged to transform, they often use university autonomy principles as a method of opposing any such changes, in either an overt or covert manner. It will long be a debate in such instances of how and when both the state and indeed society needs to intervene in such university environments – they have a powerful tool to do so in their capacity to 'turn off' the funding 'tap' – and whether the state, society, or indeed the universities own students should physically intervene, as the students did at my alma mater a few weeks ago by demonstrating against their own university and its management in order to change the status quo which was perceived (rightfully in my opinion) to require change. So as much as universities can be a vehicle for positive societal change, paradoxically due to their requirement for autonomy they can also be a vehicle for resisting positive change, and thus become out of kilter themselves morally and ethically with the society in which they exist. When this happens, strong moral leadership is required by both university and state leaders and managers to get things 'right' while equally maintaining the universities conventional level of autonomy.

Coming back therefore to the example of the mitochondria in the cell and its relevance to the teleology of the university as an entity and its relationship to the State, the mitochondria occur in every cell in the body, and are essential for life, as they are responsible for breaking down most of the food and fuels we ingest into energy which is used by all the processes and activities in the cell. Yet, mitochondria are completely self-sufficient and autonomous and even have their own DNA and replicate independently of the cell's DNA and routine cell replication. Some scientists believe mitochondria were incorporated into cells millions of years ago, before which they were unique and separate entities, and only when mitochondria did become part of the cell did 'life' as we know it begin (of course while being a great theory, the question one naturally asks is how the cell existed then before the mitochondria were incorporated!) in each cell, and then combinations of cells, and then the life forms which we currently know and exist as. In folk who have non-functioning or poorly functioning mitochondria, often due to genetic abnormalities or to toxins damaging them, individuals can live and function, but cannot 'get out of first gear' – exercise is difficult or impossible, and all affected cells and body systems function sub-optimally. Universities are therefore in some ways analogous to the mitochondria in the function they serve to the state and society. Without them, society and states would continue to exist, but would perhaps lose their capacity for invention, for new energy (in the form of the new leaders and thinkers they generate), and for new ways of doing things. Paradoxically, with all their centuries old habits and traditions, their funny gowns and academic hats, like mitochondria for cells, universities are the 'energy generators' of states and societies and ensure that there is constant renewal, replacement, and regeneration of all of the state and society's functions, activities and ways of thinking. Long may Universities exist, and indeed be allowed to exist, by the society in which they continue to ply their trade in an autonomous yet surely essential way, so that societies and states can keep on developing, innovating, understanding, and moderating their own behaviour and way of doing things.

Essay 36. The Harvard psilocybin, marsh chapel and concord prison experiments - Tuning in, turning on, dropping out both metaphorically and scientifically

Most scientific experiments are conducted in University or Research Institute environments, where they are tightly controlled and monitored by Research Ethics Committees, which must agree that the specific research being undertaken is ethically sound and there is no chance of harm either to the study participants or the ethical integrity of the University or Research Institute. Sometimes though, sadly, maverick researchers, who are generally self-absorbed and doing it for their own fame and glory, cut corners, or become involved in the study themselves, or fake data either of outcomes or potential harmful side-effects of what is being tested on the study participants. In this Essay we look at some of the most famous cases of this happening — the Harvard psilocybin, Marsh Chapel and Concord Prison experiments, all which occurred in the 1960s — and assess the harm these studies and their Chief Investigators caused to the general scientific community, and what lessons were learnt from them.

A few weeks ago, I attended and spoke at a great Neuroscience Conference at the University of Pretoria, and one of the talks that was excellent and held everyone's attention was by Dr Michael Knott from the University of Namibia, who gave a tour-de-force synopsis on mind-altering compounds and their capacity for social engineering. At the same time, I finished reading for the second time a fascinating book, Rational Mysticism, by science writer John Horgan (author of The End of Science), in which he examined the work and theories of both scientists and new-age gurus attempting to explain the meaning of life, and the limits of our conscious understanding of it, by using mind-altering / psychedelic substances. Both of these got me thinking again about the controversial drug experiments known as the Harvard Psilocybin, Marsh Chapel and Concord Prison experiments, which took place at Harvard University in the early 1960s, led by psychologists Timothy Leary and Richard Alpert, and which had dramatic effects on both American society and culture at the time, and on how we conduct research experiments from a process and ethical perspective.

While mind-altering / hallucinogenic / psychedelic substances such as psilocybin (a naturally occurring psychedelic compound found in more than 200 species of mushrooms), mescaline, peyote and ayahuasca have been ingested by folk for hundreds, if not thousands, of years as part of tribal practice and personal desire to 'get high', in the 1930s psychedelic substances such as LSD (lysergic acid diethylamide) were artificially created for the first time under laboratory conditions, which produced similar psychological effects as these 'natural' psychedelic compounds. These included altered thinking processes, closed and open eye visual hallucinations, synaesthesia (the production of a sensation relating to one sensory organ by the stimulation of another), an altered sense of time, and spiritual experiences. These substances were mostly legal up until the 1960s, and interest in them was heightened in the 1950s by writers such as Aldous Huxley, whose book The Doors of Perception described what were to him life-changing effects (in his case positive reported changes) of ingesting psychedelics, and was a bestseller. It stimulated interest in researchers in the late 1950's and early 1960's (and still does today) because of the potential capacity of psychedelic drugs to enhance our understanding of the pathophysiology of mental disorders such as schizophrenia, and for their potential capacity for therapeutic social engineering such as reducing recidivism rate in habitual criminal offenders.

Between 1960 and 1962, two Harvard University academics, Dr Timothy Leary and Dr Richard Alpert, performed a number of experiments that were to become famous (or infamous) both for their findings and for their effect on society and research methodology. In the Harvard Psilocybin experiment, students at the University were asked to volunteer for the trial and were given LSD and psilocybin, and the psychological effects of ingesting these drugs were monitored by Leary and Alpert and their co-workers. Similarly, in the Concord Prison experiment psilocybin was given to prisoners at the Concord State prison, and the acute effects of the psychedelic drug on the prisoners, and the long-term effects of ingesting the drug on recidivism rate, were monitored. In the Marsh Chapel experiment (also known as the Good Friday experiment), divinity students were given psilocybin prior to the Good Friday church service, and its effect on the level of the student's religious / spiritual experience were monitored during and after the church service. It was reported by the researchers that the outcome of all these experiments was overwhelmingly positive, with the students describing increased clarity of mind and a life-changing expansion of their conscious perception of life, the prisoners being more repentant for their crimes and less likely to repeat their offences, and the religious students describing profoundly intense spiritual experiences during and after the service.

Unfortunately (or perhaps fortunately), while these experiments generated enormous public interest, and made Leary and Alpert famous, the consequences of them were ultimately negative, and as the scientific spotlight fell on the methodology of each trial, questions about their scientific rigour were raised. The researchers used the same drugs as the volunteers during all the trials – the researchers suggested that this was to enable to them to qualitatively understand what the volunteers were feeling – but the obvious point raised was how they could have adequately recorded what the volunteers were experiencing if the scientists were intoxicated themselves. They also chose not to report on the negative hallucinations experienced by some of the volunteers, with some of the subjects apparently experiencing psychological deterioration because of the trial which required therapeutic intervention, and further studies showed that the recidivist rate of the prisoners was no different, or may have even been higher, after participating in the trial. They also did not store the drugs 'under lock and key', and some of the researchers kept some of the trial drugs for their own recreational use, and actively encouraged the use of the psychedelic drugs to their students in routine classes and in after-hours social events. When word of the positive experiences of the trials spread across the Harvard campus, the number of students wanting to volunteer for the trial increased dramatically, and a thriving psychedelic drug culture developed on the university campus that spread into the neighbouring community, and eventually across other University campuses and American culture as part of the 1960's growing anti-establishment and anti-war culture which was occurring at the time.

Being concerned about these research methodology issues and developing drug culture, the Harvard University senior management folk requested that these studies be halted, and that Leary and Alpert stop using the clinical trial drugs for their own personal gratification. When they refused, they were fired by the University. This did not deter them though, as both became more interested in being 'salesmen' for the drug and its positive psychological effects rather than researching its putative psychophysiological effects in controlled laboratory conditions. Leary started up a number of communes in both Mexico and the USA after leaving the employment of Harvard University, where LSD and other psychedelic drug taking was encouraged, and in 1966 developed the 'League for Spiritual Discovery' to represent his interest and ideas. When the USA government and law enforcement officials realized the danger of what was occurring and that psychedelic drug use was spreading across the country, they banned the use, sale, and scientific testing of all psychedelic agents. Unfortunately, this appeared to increase Leary's fame rather than decrease it, and he became popular as a TV and radio talk-show guest, where he espoused the use of psychedelic drugs in these public forums (Alpert eventually moved to a commune in India and renamed himself as Ram Dass), which resulted in interest in the drugs similarly increasing rather than decreasing. The Beatles song 'Come Together' was apparently written as a tribute to Leary and his 'work', and President Richard Nixon described him as the 'most dangerous man in America', due to the impact his 'marketing' was having on drug use and counter-culture development across the USA. Leary was increasingly investigated by the FBI, until eventually he was jailed for several years for using and selling psychedelic drugs. By the time he was released in the 1970s, the 1960s anti-establishment drug era was over, and while he wrote prolifically and still 'sold' his psychedelic message after his release from prison, his influence waned, and as LSD and other psychedelic drugs were eventually banned throughout the world for both recreational use and scientific investigation purposes, their use and popularity became attenuated over time.

So, what lessons can be learned from this astonishing period of scientific research and its impact on social culture? Firstly, that all universities need to be very rigorous in their control and management of scientific studies in a pre-emptive manner. Currently research in most respectable universities and countries throughout the world (as Harvard University is and always has been) needs to go through ethical clearances before they are allowed to begin, and if such processes had been in place at the time of these experiments and / or been stringently adhered to, the trials would probably not have been allowed to go ahead, and if they had done so, would have occurred under far more rigidly controlled laboratory conditions. Secondly, there is always the danger of loss of objectivity when 'maverick' researchers with their own agenda initiate and control experiments which have a large degree of self-interest involved in their development. While Leary and Alpert may have started their studies with the idea of using the psychedelic drugs to help understand psychological disorders and as a positive social reinforcement therapeutic tool, they appeared thereafter to become too interested in the benefits of psychedelic drugs to themselves as individuals rather than to their work as scientists, and therefore lost the required detachment from the trials, and dispassionate analysis of the trial results, which is how all scientists need to operate and perform trials they are involved in or manage. Thirdly, it showed the danger also of maverick scientists using social media – in those days the radio and television, now a huge variety of external media and self-marketing tools which are available to do so – to promote their own specific message, particularly to a susceptible audience. We are currently 'awash' with scientists marketing their own agenda and perspectives via the social media outlets, with no 'peer review' of what they say or how they describe their research findings or subjective beliefs. Finally, it was a salutary lesson in how poorly performed and marketed science can actively damage the scientific endeavour from the context that these psychedelic drugs may have had the capacity to enable us scientists to better understand psychological disorders and perhaps even to examine their capacity for therapeutic social engineering, as Michael Knott suggested in his great talk at the conference I attended, although of course (as a perspicacious neuroscience student attending pointed out), the concept of social engineering capacity is fraught with moral and ethical issues beyond just that of drug use.

John Horgan, in his book Rational Mysticism, pointed out that there will always be an interest in most folk to understand better the limits of their conscious perception of life and the reality of the life they live in, and potentially in some folk to escape from their reality (it was suggested in Horgan's book that that the desire for intoxication is the 'fourth' basic drive after hunger, thirst and sex), hence the massive public interest the research work of Leary and Alpert generated in the 1960's. Unfortunately, however, while Leary's catch-phrase for describing (in his mind) the positive effects of psychedelic drugs – 'Tune in, turn on, drop out' – was meant ostensibly to describe the effect of using the drug on expanding one's understanding of life and one's part in it, the ultimate result of his studies and the marketing of them to the general public was that the thing that most 'dropped out' was the capacity of scientists to be able to study the effect of these drugs on basic brain function for the last 50 years, which may potentially have hindered our understanding of basic brain function and psychological and psychiatric disorder pathophysiology. There is therefore also an important lesson for all scientists who attempt to 'market' their own research findings 'too hard and too fast', using the increased capacity of modern social networks and other external media sites, from this astonishing epoch of scientific and social / behavioural experimentation, which is still impacting us as a society, and how we scientists 'do business' today.

Essay 37. Technology and the university environment

One of the most interesting outcomes of the Covid pandemic era was that us folk learned that most business, commercial and university life could continue to exist and survive, if not thrive, in an environment conducted totally in virtual worlds, with meeting and lectures performed on 'Zoom', 'Teams' or 'Skype' computer platform generated meeting spaces, and food and supplies ordered by 'Amazon' and other internet product delivery companies. The question in the post-pandemic era is whether face-to-face teaching (and perhaps general life!) is worth it when so much virtual technology has developed. In this Essay we examine the effect technology has on the university environment, and whether there is still place and 'space' for human 'contact' hours for teaching and research, or whether these old-school modes of teaching methods have become outdated and redundant and need to be retired permanently.

Seeing our medical students graduate earlier this week and reading a Tweet later that evening from a university advertising a one-year online Masters, got me thinking again of something which has been a lot on my mind lately, namely what the role and benefits of technology are in the university environment. Mirroring the changes to our daily life caused by the advent and astonishing growth and proliferation of first computers and then personal electronic devices, along with the associated internet and electronically interactive features they carry, these computer-related and technology led developments have in many ways enhanced the way we do business in the university environment. Beyond most of our daily communication being performed using email and other means of internet, there is now a proliferation of purely online courses available at most universities, and discussion of the benefits and need to embrace potential current and future developments such as flipped classrooms and massive open online courses (MOOCs) occupies a significant portion of our daily debate in university education management discussions.

There are obvious benefits to all of these developments, for example university learning can be extended to a greater number of students, a paperless environment is both cost-effective and more environmental friendly, and there is enhanced capacity to have uniformity and quality assurance of teaching material – these 'online' educational developments would 'banish' the day of the eccentric Professor giving a rambling lecture on a topic no-one in the lecture theatre could understand, and on a topic that was not completely relevant to the core learning requirements of the course that the lecture was being given for.

But in this concept and example of 'banishing' the rambling eccentric Professor lies the paradox and inherent concern raised from this future utopian electronic, online environment for universities in the future, that forcibly struck me when I was watching the students at their graduation ceremony, and in particular the smiles on the faces of each of them, as they got their degrees and diplomas, and the vocal jubilation of the parents when their children were walking across the stage – that what university environments are also for is developing the human dynamic in both students and in those privileged to work with them as lecturers and teachers. I don't believe the memories of those students walking across the stage on Thursday in a few years' time will be of the time spent in their rooms staring at their lecture notes or electronic lectures on their laptop. Surely these times were crucially important for them to develop their technical knowledge as required by the course they registered for. But, what they will remember, and perhaps as important for their own personal development, will be the memories of the physical time spent on the campus of the university they went to – sitting around on the grass in summer commiserating with each other on how hard it was to understand that eccentric Professor in the lecture that just happened, the time their student group sat together and went through their notes together to pass exams, the role model clinical doctor who inspired them with his or her bedside lecture on the causes of lung cancer, and perhaps more importantly, the effect of the cancer on the patient and how this also needed to be thought of and managed (such great teachers would surely become future positive role models for them), and all the fun and social times one has as a student during ones years physically on campus – jumping into the campus fountain during Freshers Week, cheering on the medical student rugby team on inter-varsity sports day, or heck, maybe even that first cup of coffee in the medical school cafeteria with the person that would eventually become their life partner.

So perhaps like in every component of life and society, balance is everything, and while as universities we need to embrace and use technological development to enhance our teaching and learning practice, we also need to perhaps remember the human development side which has the potential to occur on campus in our students, and make sure we maintain a university environment where not only students develop the technical skills which will be vital for their future success in their chosen career, but also an environment where personal and social skills are developed either formally or informally, with memories created of a unique period of their life that will serve them well in the challenges they face in their future workplace and social milieu, which will almost certainly not be only technically related.

Essay 38. Scientific conferences - Redundant or still relevant?

One of the most exciting things for me as a neophyte researcher in the 1990s was going to scientific conferences around the world to present my latest experimental data and laboratory findings. Later, as I grew in experience and knowledge of my subject, I increasingly went to academic conference, or was invited to present at them, work which was more theoretical and 'conceptual' and presented a novel way of thinking about key concepts in the scientific world I worked in. Going to concepts was great as in the pre-Zoom and 'Teams' era, there was no other way one could present 'fresh data' to one's peers and competitors, and at the same time one could meet up with one's academic 'heroes', or at least see them giving presentations and thus put names to faces of good papers one had read, and of course, one got to see new places in the world, and meet new people. However, conference travel is expensive, and in the new Zoom era, and with new publications mostly being available online as they are accepted for publication, the cost/benefit ratio of conferences has been queried. In this Essay, therefore, we examine the benefits of conferences, and whether there is still a place for them occurring in real time as opposed to virtual 'Zoom' reality in contemporary society.

Having just completed both helping organize and being part of a successful conference – the International Sport and Exercise Nutrition Conference at Northumbria University, Newcastle upon Tyne, it made me wonder what the function of conferences are in the electronic age. A few decades ago, before the Internet, PubMed and now Online journal publication, they were the place where one would first present one's 'hot off the press' data to researchers in one's field of scientific interest. Now, it is almost certain that data will be in press or published before it is presented at a conference, and indeed with the speed potential 'rivals' are able to publish data now, it becomes almost a risk to describe novel data or findings at a conference before it is in press at best. Conferences also used to be a place to network and meet up with old or potential collaborators. But, with the advent of email and even perhaps Twitter and Facebook, one can network possibly even more effectively electronically when planning new collaborative ventures or to keep contact once project is ended. So, what is the point of either presenting at a conference or attending a conference? My answers would be that it is still great to see other scientists face-to-face, even if it is from a purely social perspective, it allows younger scientists to 'put a name to a face' of academics whose work they have read and appreciate, or have followed their comments and thoughts in blogs and forums like Twitter, and in my own experience preparing a talk for a conference is always the first step in getting the first draft of either the data paper or theoretical paper together in a coherent way. Apart from that, I guess it is a great way to get away from one's daily work routines, whether they are in the lab or in front of the computer, and get out there and see the world, see your old friends, or even people you have 'sparred with' academically, and enjoy the 'feeling' that science is an alive and dynamic process. Part of me wonders if they will become redundant in the future if the electronic era continues in the way it has in the last few decades, but then I attend a conference and think, 'wow, this is why I do science', even if it is difficult to pin down why I get this positive 'feeling' both during and after a good conference I have attended. Maybe there's a study for someone to do in that.

Essay 39. Contemporary medical training and societal medical requirements - How does one balance the manifest need for general practitioners with modern super-specialist trends?

I have spent most of my life in the medical and health world — I trained as a medical doctor, I worked in clinical medicine, I taught medical and allied health students for most of my career, performed research on many clinical and basic physiology problems, and in my leadership career been head of a large and well established medical school, as well as helping developing plans for a new medical school, and assisting research development in a medical and health faculty as my latest role. What has been fascinating is how the curriculum and way medicine and allied health is taught has changed. In my era, we did years of 'preliminary' non-medical subjects such as physics and chemistry, before only being 'unleashed' on patients in our third and fourth years of study. Now medical students work on clinical patient-based problems from the day they start their medical training, train at solving clinical problems as part of a team with allied health and nursing practitioners, train in the community setting, and there is an increasing push to develop general practitioner focussed training. In this Essay we look at the changes in the medical curriculum of the last few decades, how they have enhanced clinician skill sets and career development, and what conundrums have resulted because of the change in medical training focus.

For all my career, since starting as a medical student at the University of Cape Town as an 18-year-old fresh out of school many years ago, I have been involved in the medical and health provision and training world and have had a wonderful career, first as a clinician, then as a research scientist, then in the last number of years managing and leading health science and medical school research and training. Because of this background and career, I have always pondered long and hard about what makes a good clinician, what is the best training to make a good clinician, how we define what a 'good' clinician is, and how we best align the skills of the clinicians we train with the needs and requirements of the country's social and health environments in which they trained. A few weeks ago, I had a health scare which was treated rapidly and successfully by a super-specialist cardiologist, and I was home the next day after the intervention, and 'hale and hearty' a few days after the procedure. If I had lived 50 years ago, and it had happened then, in the absence of modern high-tech equipment and the super-specialist skills, I would probably have died a slow and uncomfortable death treated with drugs of doubtful efficacy that would not have much benefited me much, let alone treat the condition I was suffering from. Conversely, despite my great respect for these super-specialist skills which helped me so successfully a few weeks ago, it has become increasingly obvious that this great success in clinical specialist training has come at the cost of reduced emphasis on general practitioner-focused training, and a reduction in the number of medical students choosing general practitioner work as a career after they qualify, which has caused problems both to clinical service delivery in a number of countries, particularly in rural areas of countries, and paradoxically put greater strain on specialist services despite their pre-eminence in contemporary clinical practice in most countries around the world. My own experience with grappling with this problem of how to increase general practitioners as an outcome of our training programmes, as a Head of School of Medicine previously, and this recent health scare which was treated so successfully by super-specialist intervention, got me thinking of how best we can manage the contradictory requirements of the need for both general practitioners and specialists in contemporary society, and whether this conundrum should be best managed by medical schools, health and hospital management boards, or government-led strategic development planning initiatives.

It is perhaps not surprising, given the exponential development of technological innovations that originated in the industrial revolution, and which changed how we live, that medical work also changed and became more technologically focused, which in turn required both increased time and increased specialization of clinical training to utilize these developing technologies, such as surgical, radiology investigative and laboratory-based diagnostic techniques. The hospital (Groote Schuur) and medical school (University of Cape Town) where I was trained was famous for the achievements of Professor Chris Barnard and his team's work performing the first heart transplant there, using a host of advanced surgical techniques, heart-lung machines to keep the patients alive without a heart for a brief period of time, and state-of-the-art immunotherapy techniques to resist heart rejection, all specialist techniques he and his team took many years to master in some great medical schools and hospitals in the USA. Perhaps in part because of this, our training was very 'high-tech', consisting of early years spent learning basic anatomy, physiology and pathology-based science, and then later years spent in surgical, medical, and other clinical specialty wards, mostly watching and learning from observation of clinical specialists going about their business treating patients. If I remember it correctly, there were only a few weeks of community-based clinical educational learning, very little integrative 'holistic' patient-based learning, and almost no 'soft-skill' training, such as optimal communication with patients, working as part of a team with other health care workers such as nurses and physiotherapists, or learning to help patients in their daily home environment and social infrastructure. There was also almost no training whatsoever in the benefits of 'exercise as medicine', or of the concept of wellness (where one focuses on keeping folk healthy before they get ill, rather than dealing with the consequences of illness). This type of 'specialist-focused' training was common, particularly in Western countries, for most of the last 50 or so years, and as a typical product of this specialist training system, for example, I chose first clinical research and then basic research rather than more patient-focused work as my career choice, and a number of my colleagues from my University of Cape Town medical training class of 1990 have had superb careers as super-specialists in top clinical institutions and hospitals all around the world.

This increasing specialization of clinical training and practice, such as the example of my own medical training described above, has unfortunately had a negative impact both on general practitioner numbers and primary care capacity. A general practitioner (GP) is defined as a medical doctor who treats acute and chronic illnesses and provides preventative care and health education to patients, and who has a holistic approach to clinical practice that takes all of biological, social and psychological factors into consideration when treating patients. Primary care is defined as the day-to-day healthcare of patients and communities, with the primary care providers (GPs, nurses, health associates or social workers, amongst others) usually being the first contact point for patients, referring patients on to specialist care (in secondary or tertiary care hospitals), and coordinating and managing the long-term treatment of patient health after discharge from either secondary or tertiary care if it is needed. In the 'old days', GPs used to work in their community often where they were born and raised, worked 24 hours a day as needed, and maintained their relationship with their patients through most or all of their lives. Unfortunately, for a variety of reasons, GP work has changed, and they now often work set hours, patients are rotated through different GPs in a practice, and the number of graduating doctors choosing to be GPs is diminishing, and there is an increasing shortage of GP's in communities and particularly rural areas of most countries as a result. Sadly, GP work is often regarded as being of lower prestige than specialist work, the pay for GPs has often been lower than that of specialists, and with the decreased absolute number of GPs, the work burden on many GPs has increased (and paradoxically with computers and electronic facilities the note and recording taking requirements of GPs appears to have increased rather than decreased) leading to increased level of burnout and GPs choosing to turn to other clinical roles or to leave the medical profession completely, which exacerbates the GP shortage problem in a circular manner. Training of GPs has also evolved into specialty-type training, with doctors having to spend 3-5 years 'specializing' as a GP (often today called Family Practitioners or Community Health Doctors), and this also has paradoxically potentially put folk off a GP career, and lengthens the time required before folk intent on becoming GPs can do so and become board certified / capable of entering or starting a clinical GP practice. As the number of GPs decrease, it means more folk go directly to hospital casualties as their first 'port of call' when ill, and this puts a greater burden on hospitals, which somewhat ironically also creates an increased burden on specialists, who mostly work in such hospitals, and who end up seeing more of these folks who could often be treated very capably by GPs. This paradoxically allows specialists less time to do the specialist and super-specialist roles they spent so many years training for, with the result that waiting list and times for 'cold' (non-emergency) cases increases, and hospital patient care suffers due to patient volume overload.

At several levels of strategic management of medical training and physician supply planning, there have been moves to counter this super-specialist focus of training and to encourage folk to consider GP training as an appealing career option. The Royal College of Physicians and Surgeons of Canada produced a strategic clinical training document (known as the 'CanMeds' training charter) which emphasizes that rather than just training pure clinical skills, contemporary training of clinical doctors should aim to create graduates who are all of medical experts, communicators, collaborators, managers, health advocates, scholars and professionals – in other words a far more 'gestalt' and 'holistically' trained medical graduate. This CanMeds document has created 'waves' in the medical training community and is now used by many medical schools around the world as their training 'template'. Timothy Smith, senior staff writer for the American Medical Association, published an interesting article recently where he suggested that similar changes were occurring in the top medical schools in the USA, with clinical training including earlier exposure to patient care, more focus on health systems and sciences (including wellness and 'exercise is medicine' programmes), shorter time to training completion and increased emphasis on using new communication technologies more effectively as part of training. In my last role as Head of the School of Medicine at the University of the Free State, working with Faculty Dean Professor Gert Van Zyl, Medical Program Director Dr Lynette Van Der Merwe, Head of Family Medicine Professor Nathanial Mofolo, Professor Hanneke

Brits, Dr Dirk Hagemeister, and a host of other great clinicians and administrators working at the University or the Free State Department of Health, the focus on the training programme was shifted to try to include a greater degree of community based education as a 'spine' of training rather than as a two week block in isolation, along with a greater degree of inter-professional education (working with nurses, physiotherapists, and other allied health workers in teams as part of training to learn to treat a patient in their 'entirety' rather than as just a single clinical 'problem'), and an increased training of 'soft skills' that would assist medical graduates not only with optimal long term patient care, but also with skills such as financial and business management capacity so that they would be able to run practices optimally, or at least know when to call in experts to assist them with non-clinical work requirements, amongst a host of other innovative changes. We, like many other universities, also realized that it was important to try and recruit medical students from the local communities around the medical school in which they grew up, and to encourage as many of these locally based students as possible to apply for medical training, though of course selection of medical students is always a 'hornets' nest', and it is very challenging to get it right, balancing marks, essential skills and community needs of the many thousands of aspirant clinicians who wish to do medicine when so few places are available to offer them.

All these medical training initiatives to try and initiate changes of what has become a potentially 'skewed' training system, as described above, are of course 'straw in the wind' without government backing and good strategic planning and communication by country-wide health boards, medical professional councils, and hospital administrators who manage staffing appointments and recruitment. As much as one needs to change the 'focus' and skills of medical graduates, the health structures of a country need to be similarly changed to be 'focused' on community needs and requirements, and aligned with the medical training programme initiatives, for the changes to be beneficial and to succeed. Such training programme changes, and community-based intervention initiatives, have substantial associated costs which need to be funded, and therefore there is a large political component to both clinical training and health provision. To strategically improve the status quo, governments can choose to either encourage existing medical schools to increase student numbers and encourage statutory clinical training bodies to enact changes to the required medical curriculum to make it more GP focused or build more medical schools to generate a greater number of potential GPs. They can also pay GPs higher salaries, particularly if they work in rural communities, or ensure better conditions of service and increased numbers of allied health practitioners and health assistants to lighten the stress placed on GPs, to ensure that optimal community clinical facilities and health care provision is provided for. But how this is enacted is always challenging, given that different political parties usually have different visions and strategies for health, and changes occur each time a new political party is elected, which often 'hinders' rather than 'enacts' required health-related legislation, or as in the case of contemporary USA politics, attempts to rescind previous change related healthcare acts if they were enacted by an opposition political party. There is also competition between universities which have medical schools for increases in medical places in their programmes (which result in more funding flowing in to the universities if they take more students) and of course any university that wishes to open a new medical school (as my current employers, the University of Waikato wish to, and who have developed an exciting new community focused medical school strategic plan that fulfils all the criteria of what a contemporary focused GP training programme should be, that will surely become an exemplary new medical school if their plan is approved by the government) is regarded as a competition for resources by those universities who already run medical training programmes and medical schools. Because of these competition-related and political issues, many major health-related change initiatives for both medical training programmes and the related community and state structural training requirements are extremely challenging to enact and are why so many planned changes become 'bogged down' by factional lobbying either before they start or when they are being enacted. This is often disastrous for health provision and training, as chaos ensues when a 'half-changed' system becomes 'stuck' or a new political regime or health authority attempts to impose further, often 'half-baked' changes on the already 'half-changed' system, which results in an almost unmanageable 'mess' which is sadly often the state of many countries' medical training, physician supply, and health facilities, to the detriment both of patients and communities which they are meant to serve and support.

The way forward for clinical medical training and physician supply is therefore complex and fraught with challenges. But, having said this, it is clear that changes are needed, and brave folk with visionary thinking and strategic planning capacity are required to both create sound plans that integrate all the required changes across multiple sectors that are needed for the medical training changes to be able to occur, and to enact them in the presence of opposition and resistance, which is always the case in the highly politicized world of health and medical training. Two good examples of success stories in this field were the changes to the USA health and medical training system which occurred as a result of the Flexner report of 1910, which set out guidelines for medical training throughout the USA, which were actually enacted and came to fruition, and the development of the NHS system in the UK in the late 1940s, which occurred as a result of the Beveridge report of 1942, which laid out how and why comprehensive, universal and free medical services were required in the UK, and how these were to be created and managed, and these recommendations were enacted by Clement Attlee, Aneurin Bevin and other members of the Labour government of that time. Both systems worked for a time, but sadly both in the USA and UK, due to multiple reasons and perhaps natural system entropy, both of these countries' health services are currently in a state of relative 'disrepair', and it is obvious that major changes to them are again needed, and perhaps an entire fresh approach to healthcare provision and training similar to that initiated by the Flexner and Beveridge reports are required. However, it is challenging to see this happening in contemporary times with the polarized political status currently occurring in both countries, and strong and brave health leadership is surely required at this point in time in these countries, as always, in order to initiate the substantial strategic requirements which are required to either 'fix' each system or create an entirely new model of health provision and training.

Each country in the world has different health provision models and medical training systems, which work with varying degrees of success. Cuba is an example of one country that has enacted wholesale GP training and community medicine as the centrepiece of both their training and health provision, though some folk would argue that they have gone too far in this regard in their training, as specialist provision and access is almost non-existent there. Therein lies an important 'rub' – clearly there is a need for more GP and community focused medical training. But equally, it is surely important that there is still a strong 'flow' of specialists and super-specialists to both train the GPs in the specific skills of each different discipline of medicine, and to treat those diseases and disorders which require specialist-level technical skills. My own recent health scare exemplifies the 'yin and yang' of these conflicting but mutually beneficial / synergistic requirements. If it were not for the presence of a super-specialist with exceptional technical skills, I might not be alive today. Equally the first person I phoned when I noted concerning symptoms was not a super-specialist, but rather was my old friend and highly skilled GP colleague from my medical training days, Dr Chris Douie, who lives close by to us and who responded to my request for assistance immediately. Chris got the diagnosis spot on, recommended the exact appropriate intervention, and sent me on to the required super-specialist, and was there for me not just to give me a clinical diagnosis but also to provide pastoral care – in other words 'hold my hand' and show me the empathy that is so needed by any person when they have an unexpected medical crisis. In short, Chris was brilliant in everything he did as first 'port of call', and while I eventually required super-specialist treatment of the actual condition, in his role as GP (and friend) he provided that vital first phase support and diagnosis, and non-clinical empathic support, which is so needed by folk when they are ill (indeed historically the local GP was not just everyone's doctor but also often their friend). My own example therefore emphasizes this dual requirement for both GP and specialist health provision and capacity.

Like most things, medical training and health care provision has, like a pendulum, 'swung' between specialist and generalist requirements and pressures in the last century. The contemporary perception, in an almost 'back to the future' way, is that we have perhaps become too focused on high technology clinical skills and training (though as above there will always be a place and need for these), and we need more of our doctors to be trained to be like their predecessors of many years ago, working out in the community, caring for their patients and creating an enduring life-long relationship with them, and dealing with their problems early and effectively before they become life-threatening and costly to treat and requiring the intervention of expensive specialist care. It's an exciting period of potential world-wide changes in medical training and the clinical health provision to communities, and a great time to be involved in either developing the strategy for medical training and health provision and / or enacting it – if the folk involved in doing so are left in peace by the lobby groups, politicians and folk who want to maintain the current unbalanced status quo due to their own self-serving interests. Who knows, maybe even clinicians, like in the old days, will be paid again by their patients with a chicken, or a loaf of freshly baked bread, and goodwill will again be the bond between the community, the folk who live in them, and the doctors and healthcare workers that treat them. And for my old GP friend Chris Douie, who is surely the absolute positive example and role model of the type of doctor we need to be training, a chicken will be heading his way soon from me, in lieu of payment for potentially saving my life, and for doing so in such a kind and empathetic way, as surely any GP worth his or her 'salt' would and should do.

Essay 40. A career in medicine - The Sisyphus paradox

The teacher in my medical training years whom I most respected, Professor Johan Koeslag, taught us the interesting concept of the Sisyphus paradox in relation to medicine. Sisyphus, due to at various times irritating the Gods, was sentenced to forever roll a heavy ball up a hill, and each time he reached the top, the ball slipped from his grasp and slipped to the bottom of the hill, from whence he had to start the whole, ultimately futile cycle again and again. In this Essay, we examine the Sisyphus paradox as it is related to medical work and assess whether medical doctors ever 'win' in their efforts to save their patients and 'outwit' their always looming mortality.

Our new first year Medicine students attended their welcome ceremony at our university yesterday, and it was wonderful to witness and experience their excitement at starting to study the career of their dreams. Watching them and being involved in the ceremony got me thinking about medicine as a career, and I was reminded of an excellent piece of philosophical writing published at the time I was training to be a medical doctor myself, by Professor Johan Koeslag, a Physiology Professor at the University of Cape Town whose teaching had a profound positive effect on me. In this article he compared a career in medicine to the Myth of Sisyphus, with the role of clinician being likened to that of Sisyphus in the myth.

In Greek Mythology, Sisyphus, who was King of Ephyra (modern day Corinth), attempted to cheat death, and for this and other roguish behaviour he exhibited during his reign as king, Zeus punished him by forcing him to roll a heavy boulder up to the top of a hill. Each time he reached the top of the hill, the boulder rolled down again, and the task had to be repeated continuously for eternity. Therefore, Zeus by this punishment had consigned Sisyphus to performing what was an inherently useless action for eternity, the goal of which was to create an eternity of frustration for the miscreant Sisyphus. With time the Myth of Sisyphus became representative of any activity that is inherently pointless, repetitive, and interminable. An analogy was drawn by Johan from this to the daily work of a medical doctor, namely that no matter what a clinician does, they can never 'cheat death' / permanently cure anyone, as even if they cure a patient of one disease, they will eventually die of something else. From this perspective, if saving life is the job description of a clinician, then medicine must represent the ultimate failure as a profession, with a one hundred percent long term mortality and therefore failure rate. As in the Myth of Sisyphus, clinicians are thus caught in an absurdist paradigm, as they are 'saving' people to face certain death. In his article Johan described this as the Sisyphus Paradox of Medicine, namely that because they wage a losing battle against death in all those that they treat, all clinicians resemble Sisyphus, eternally condemned to perform an impossible task in a repetitive manner until their own point of eternity, or to be more moderate, their retirement day.

This may sound a somewhat depressing view of medicine, but Johan did not stop there. He (and others who have taken forward these ideas) then went on to clarify what clinicians should do to maintain 'faith' while having awareness of this Sisyphus paradox in their daily working life. He suggested that clinicians need to accept this perspective and understand that their 'lot in life' is to maintain commitment to their work, and to their patients, even with this awareness of its ultimate futility, and by doing so they would make themselves as clinicians more balanced and closer to their own state of perfect grace. Secondly, the clinician would need to focus more on creating a pain or illness free environment for their patients, to the best of the clinician's ability. While there may be a teleological reason for pain and suffering, possibly in the context of learning some perspective or self-understanding that would not occur in pain-free routine existence, there would clearly be comfort produced in a clinician's patients by reduction of their pain and suffering, even if at some point in the future the patient's death is inevitable. Thirdly, there would perhaps be benefit in clinicians incorporating scientific analysis into their work life, in order to try and understand better (if possible) such difficult concepts as 'life' or 'death'. Science, as opposed to medicine, philosophy or theology, is likely to be the only method we have which can potentially explain such complex issues as life and death in a 'material' manner, or at least the physiological and anatomical mechanisms related to these 'big' concepts. Fourthly, and finally, clinicians perhaps need to concern themselves more with educating their patients on the certainty of death, in order to better prepare them for this inevitability. In modern times death and dying are almost 'taboo' subjects, and death occurs usually 'behind closed doors', which may in effect be creating an increased fear of death and dying either due to ignorance or avoidance of the issue. if clinicians educated patients (and healthy individuals) about their own inevitable mortality, and that dying is the culmination of life, however paradoxical this observation may be, they may potentially remove their patients' fear of death, or at least make them be more comfortable with their own dying, when their time eventually comes, as it does for all of us.

So watching those folk yesterday at the start of their medical careers, with my own awareness of the Sisyphus paradox inculcated in me by Johan's thought-provoking work, that would likely be an absolute contradiction to the inherent reason most of them probably chose medicine as their preferred career choice, I wished them luck on their own clinical journey, and hoped that by working daily rolling their own 'boulder up the hill' in a never-ending way, that they would all eventually understand the Sisyphus nature of their work, and by doing so attain their own state of perfect grace, and become the best doctor they can be, doing medicine for the right reasons in the best possible way.

Essay 41. Psychology - A discipline struggling to find its identity, direction and technical development focus

While I started my medical career many years ago, I thought I would do something surgical Over the years my interests turned very much into those of the brain and mind. While neuroscience has traditionally physically tried to work out how the brain works, the mental side of the brain and our life — one's thoughts, behaviour, and personality — falls into the realms of Psychology. Psychology had a brilliant start at the beginning of the 20th century, with stars such as Jung, Freud, Adler, Rank, Ferenczi and others setting fire to the discipline (and world, given that their theories became 'popular' and read by lay folk worldwide), but since that great start has languished somewhat, given that without neuroscience it cannot 'prove' its key theories, yet neuroscience has not developed the techniques that would be able to prove its theories. When reading the basic texts of these early pioneers, it all appears so 'right' to me, yet one hundred years later still cannot be proved, and are thus no longer believed by most scientists and academics, let alone lay folk. In this Essay we therefore examine the core tenets of Psychology, how the discipline developed, how it faltered, and how it may be re-energised in the time ahead.

I finished an excellent biography of the Harvard Psychology Professor, William James, this week, and had a great email interaction with my old Dean at Northumbria University, Professor Pam Briggs, who is a quintessential Psychology researcher and was a charismatic and creative Dean, and both these got me thinking of Psychology, a discipline I have increasingly become immersed in both from my own research and from a human-interest perspective. Psychology is broadly defined as the study of mind and behaviour, and psychology practitioners and researchers examine a broad array of concepts associated with the function of the mind and the behaviour which results from the mind's activity, including perception, cognition, attention, emotion, intelligence, motivation, personality, interpersonal and social relations, resilience, brain functioning, and states of consciousness, including the activity and nature of the unconscious. The word psychology derives from Greek origins, where it meant the study of the psyche or soul, though of course attempts to understand these 'big' concepts stretches back to scholars in ancient cultures in Egypt, Greece, China, India and Persia, amongst other places. I am sure most folk in their daily lives at some point in time have wondered why they do certain things, why they thought about something in a certain way, or why they responded to different external stimuli in the way that they do, and these thoughts probably occurred in most folk all the way back to antiquity and the beginning of the capacity for self-reflective thought, whenever that was and however it happened.

Psychology as a discipline has been pretty good at answering the questions relating to 'why' we do specific things or react in a certain way, and the discipline has flourished in many unexpected ways because of this. For example, its principles are used by advertising and marketing companies, with products being created and marketed based on the industry's understanding and uptake of psychology-based research of human behaviour and function such as the need for comfort, pleasure, and / or excitement. Many of us will have had an experience previously related to the visceral feeling one gets when watching an advert that appeals to one (and which makes us go out and buy the advertised product), but equally of course will associate with feelings one gets when watching or listening to adverts that are annoying and 'hit the wrong spot', and which make us not want to associate with or buy a particular product. Psychology has also helped us understand things like why we identify with different social groups, and why we need affiliation and belonging to both create and enhance our sense of self and social identity. For example, some excellent work from old colleagues of mine, Dr Matt Lewis, Dr Melissa Anderson and Professor Sandy Wolfson, has shed light on 'fandom', and why so many folks become so fervently attached to their sport team of choice, and subject themselves to the highs and lows associated when their chosen teams win or lose. These type of emotions, related to the outcome of events which essentially have no direct bearing on one's personal life, have always puzzled me (and I feel them often myself), but the work of these quality researchers have shown it comes down to psychological requirements and needs of the folk that feel them, and is an example of how psychology has helped academia, society, and folk like myself understand emotions and reactions which are puzzling and appear to be 'wasteful' of one's emotional energy (at least to me).

Where Psychology as a discipline has perhaps not done as well is in explaining 'how' things happen in the brain which produces 'behaviour', and where and how the mind works. After several years reading basic psychology texts, in my opinion the 'golden years' for Psychology were in the late 1800s and early 1900s, where astonishing hypotheses on mental and human functioning were developed by groups of clinicians and researchers around the world, which changed both Psychology and indeed how we view the world and understand ourselves. Think names like Freud, Jung, Adler, Hall, James, Janet, amongst a host of others, who brought into popular culture concepts like the unconscious, the ego (and id, though it has not been as well assimilated as an 'entity' as has the ego concept), and the inferiority complex – all concepts we now use in our routine language as 'fact', yet were pretty much unknown before that golden epoch. Incredibly, most of these concepts have still not been completely 'proven' or been clearly associated with any specific brain function or activity, and unfortunately, in many ways it appears that Psychology has 'regressed' as a discipline, moving from these very 'deep' / 'basic' theories to current day theories. For example, the more recently developed self-determination theory explains human behaviour as either caused by 'intrinsic' or 'extrinsic' motives, which to me appear as a theory to be somewhat 'trite' in contrast to what came 100 years before (though all credit to the researchers who developed them). While most Biology-based disciplines each decade seem to go to 'deeper' levels of understanding, Psychology appears to have regressed, and often astonishingly seems these days to ignore the rich work produced in that 'golden era' of psychology research alluded to above.

The reasons for what happened to Psychology is perhaps principally related to the way Psychology developed after this 'golden era', and to the unfortunate dearth of investigative laboratory techniques available to Psychology researchers attempting to understand 'how' the brain 'creates' psychology, and how and where the 'mind' exists in the brain. In the 1900's, after the 'golden era', Psychology research subsequently focussed on behaviourism (think stimulus-response work and Pavlov's dog experiments), then developed areas of research such as 'cognitive' psychology, and produced theories of brain function with wonderful, but completely speculative and currently unproveable, models such as Baddeley's 'visuo-spatial sketchpad' model of working memory. Most theories that were developed generally always were, and are, accompanied by line diagrams of how different parts of the brain would work and be involved with the particular 'theory' that was being developed, which look good as figures, but tell us very little of 'how' things really would work in the brain as related to the theory. A further problem for Psychology also is that it has increasingly relied on its 'twin-sister' discipline, Neuroscience, to provide the equipment and techniques which Psychologists believe would be able to answer the 'how' questions Psychology as a discipline has generated. Unfortunately, from an understanding of how the brain works perspective, Neuroscience has itself proved to be an almost complete failure in its attempts to understand basic brain function. I can say this with some certainty myself after being a Professor of Integrative Neuroscience for many years – before each lecture I give on brain function, I start by saying us neuroscientists are dismal failures, given that we have so little understanding of basic brain function, mostly because of the lack of sensitivity of our currently available laboratory research techniques and equipment, and the difficulty of performing invasive investigations, both ethically and technically, on the brains of alive humans. These thoughts have been echoed / predated by such luminary scientists as Francis Crick, who was awarded a Nobel Prize in the 1950s for his work on how genes replicate, then moved into Neuroscience as a researcher. After a few years Crick came to the same conclusion that the lack of any brain laboratory techniques available to Neuroscience researchers then, which were suitable to understand basic brain function, was blocking his and any others attempts to understand how most of basic brain function occurs that are still a mystery to us, such as consciousness, perception, and memory formation, amongst other processes and functions. Unfortunately, in the last few decades any Psychology paper to be perceived to be 'worth' anything needs to be associated with MRI scanning or other similar current brain techniques available in Neuroscience-related brain research, which generate images that are really no more than 'pretty pictures' showing huge brain areas that 'light up' when a task is performed, and which tell us almost nothing about how the brain operates dynamically, let alone how the 'big' concepts such as consciousness and memory 'work'. Therefore, Psychology as a discipline has perhaps 'gone wrong' by 'hitching itself' to the wrong partner, by allying itself to Neuroscience, which has so little to offer currently to assist it with understanding and explaining the basic concepts and theories generated more than a century ago. It does not help either that some of the 'big questions' Psychology examines, described above, perhaps belong to a large degree in the realm of Philosophy, and would be difficult to answer even perhaps with any technological development whatsoever, such as what and where is the 'soul' and 'mind', which are difficult to define conceptually, let alone explain with any reductive laboratory technique that has been, or will be developed in the future.

So for me, after finishing the biography of William James this week, and having read over the last few years (occasionally labouring through) just about all of Freud's and Jung's basic writing from all those years ago, I do perceive (and perhaps being an 'outsider' to the discipline, or at best a 'late disciple' allows me to do so), that Psychology needs to perhaps have a bit of 'navel gazing' itself as a discipline about where it is, why it may be going in the 'wrong' direction from the 'how' perspective, and that perhaps it has currently 'allied' itself with a discipline (Neurosciences) that is currently in absolute disarray / still very much in the 'dark ages' laboratory wise, and is struggling itself with its own identity, and I can say this with some knowledge perhaps (though always with caution) after working for more than 20 years as an Integrative Neuroscientist. How to do this as a generic discipline is obviously difficult, and I am fairly sure that the problems both Psychology and Neuroscience currently face will be solved by an engineer / physicist, rather than by a Psychologist or Neuroscientist, who does not work in either field, and who develops technology that will allow a 'thought-ometer' to be developed, or something similar, which will be able to 'tap into' the unconscious / psyche and will thus help clarify whether Freud, Jung et al from the 'golden era' were wrong or right in an absolute way, and will thus help Psychology as a discipline find its 'way forward' again from a 'how' perspective.

I do know though, if I could go back in time and attend one conference as my absolute first choice from an academic interest perspective, it would have been the Psychology conference organised by Stanley Hall at Clarke University in Worcester, Massachusetts in the USA in 1909, which was attended by and at which talks were given by all of Sigmund Freud, Carl Jung, William James, Ernest Jones and a host of others who changed our way of thinking about life and our behaviour, whether their ideas were right or wrong. I also know that in 2006, after 15 years of doing lab based physiology and neuroscience related research, and after I had got into reading all the basic texts of these golden era Psychology folk, that before a talk I was due to give back then, I wrote in my 'ideas' diary which I always carry around with me: "Strange paradoxical thought when preparing for this talk on the role of biological sciences in the control of exercise and activity, that so much of the neuroscience that I have worked on, read and discussed seems to be completely nonsensical, although it is based on experimental facts, whereas the psychology theories of Freud and Jung appear to make almost complete sense, and 'feels' right, even though it is at this stage almost completely unverifiable." I hope that before I retire, or indeed 'shuffle off this mortal coil' I will see the development of that 'thought-ometer', that I will see Psychology rediscover it's 'mojo', and that I will observe some of my wonderful Psychology colleagues and friends go on and get Nobel prizes for discovering where memories are and how they are stored, where consciousness resides and how it works, and perhaps more importantly, why I wake up in the wee hours of the morning worrying about things that I don't even realize before I go to sleep are an issue to me. And hopefully also, as in the football fandom example above, why I get grumpy when my beloved football

/ rugby team loses on a Saturday afternoon, why this has the potential to ruin the rest of the weekend, and where in the brain these 'crazy' attachments and emotions are stored.

Essay 42. History and historical revisionism - Is what we read of the past ever a true reflection of how it really happened?

My second work 'love' after my own life's work focus, science, is history, and I often say if I wasn't doing my current work, I would like to be a historian. History is very important in that it tells you where you and the world 'came' from, and why we ended up in our current life environment — due to wars, politics, geographical and climate changes, and of course, in my own field, how science and academia developed and different disciplines of science 'waxed and waned' over the years. But one needs to be careful about putting too much faith into history as being all true, as much is written by the 'winners' of any historic event, and each history writer has their own biases and complex reasons for writing the historical works they do. In this Essay we assess the positive and challenging sides of history as a discipline and as an education tool for us to broaden our own knowledge of the past, and indeed whether history can ever instruct us about the future, or if it never repeats itself.

This week I was alerted to a wonderful quote about books and reading – 'the miracle of literature is that it can get you to understand, even a tiny bit, what it is like to be another human being'. My all-time favourite quote on reading before finding this one, goes 'I read to realize I am not alone'. I have always been a 'bookworm' throughout just about all my life. My mother often used to laugh in my pre-teen years, as whenever she called me, I would never hear her, as my head was always ensconced in a new book, and my mind always enthralled by tales created by great writers of the past to a level that the fiction of what I was reading often claimed more of my attention than that of the reality around me. As I grew older and became an academic, my taste for reading changed completely away from fiction to non-fiction, and I am sure whatever intelligence, viewpoints, perceptions, and way of reasoning I have developed is mostly down to what I have read and absorbed from reading (obviously social interactions, particularly with significant role models, either negative or positive, played their part in my development too). A significant discussion with a highly respected old family friend, Simon Pearce, in my early thirties, when he said to me I should read history to best understand life, had a profound impact on me, and while always being interested in history, perhaps because of this advice from someone whose intellect I greatly admire, the last decade I have read a lot of history, and have indeed benefited I think from doing so in many ways. But history, and the description of it, can be a 'treacherous' teacher, given that it is by nature reflective, dependent on the world-view and background of the historian who writes it, and a product of the contemporary zeitgeist of the current period of time in which it was or is written, and one therefore has to be very careful of how much one 'believes' of what one reads of history as being truly representative of the events as they happened in the times they describe.

History is defined as the study of past events, especially of human affairs. The word history is thought to have come from the Ancient Greek word 'historia', meaning 'inquiry' or 'judge'. Historians are folk who write about history, and it is still controversial if a historian should be merely a chronicler or compiler of past events, or a critical analyst of them. Generally, it is perceived that written documentation or transcripts of past events are necessary for historical accounts to be both assimilated and described, and events occurring prior to the presence of written records are described as 'pre-historic' and fall into the realm of archaeological based academic work. We therefore have a relatively short period of historical 'knowledge', given that the first texts written have only survived from a few thousand years in the past, and the great period of human life and 'history' prior to these is virtually unknown, save what can be gleaned from archaeological digs and speculation from what is found in them. History is divided up into several fields of study, from a generic perspective which includes comparative history (historical assessment of social and culture entities that are not confined to national boundaries) and counterfactual history (the study of history as it might have happened had different circumstances arisen), and from a specific perspective includes the history of epochs of time or the history of specific human activities (such as military or economic history).

Academic researchers studying the field of history occupy themselves with identifying and solving the philosophical conundrums related to studying history such as what the correct 'unit' of study of the past is (for example is it the individual human condition, or the prevalent culture of the time, or the activities of the nation or state and how it impacted on the individual and other nations or states around them), and whether from history patterns or cycles of behaviour at either the individual or nation level can be determined. As described above, a 'problem' of history is that it is always written at a certain contemporary time, which will have a dominant social thinking and view of the past, and it is surely difficult for a historian not to be affected by this when writing their own account of whatever component of history, they are involved with writing about. An even more post-modern view which has been suggested is that history as a concept is irrelevant from a generic perspective, as the study of history is always reliant on a personal interpretation of sources, and thus 'history' as a general concept is a redundant one. History writing itself often moves in 'patterns' of its own, with some epochs focussing more on 'glorifying' the successes of nations or 'great' individuals in history (and clearly many nations create 'official' historical publications as a way of glorifying their past or justifying / 'cleansing' the more sordid components of their past) with subsequent epochs of history writing challenging these 'glorious' interpretations of history in a more dispassionate and reasoned way.

A good example of all the interest of history as a subject, how it can be revised and manipulated for national or individual 'gain', and how with reflection a more balanced interpretation of the true nature of history is derived became evident to me after 'studying' from a reading of history perspective the role of Winston Churchill in World War Two. Churchill was, and perhaps still is, surely one of the most well-known figures in history in the Western world, and if you polled folk for their knowledge and opinion of him, they would say he was the person who saved Britain during the war, and / or led the country to ultimate triumph during the war in a heroic and masterful way (though even the knowledge of Churchill is becoming 'dimmed' with the passing of time as it does with all people). My own interest in him, and the World War Two period, stemmed from growing up in the 60's and 70's with a father who had an interest in military history and was for a short period of time in the civilian force military, and with the knowledge that a grandfather had fought in World War Two and was interned for a long period of it. On our bookshelf in the home of my youth were all Churchill's volumes he himself wrote on the history of World War Two in the decade after it ended, and I remember with fondness many discussions with my dad, or between him and his friends that I listened to way back then, describing or arguing about Churchill's leadership during the war, and the merits of his place in the pantheon of successful military and political war leaders in general historical terms.

I had a mostly positive viewpoint regarding Winston Churchill and his part in 'winning the war' because of these early experiences of 'history according to Dad' for most of my life, until I started reading more carefully other accounts of the events during the war and Churchill's part of them. The most startling of these accounts which very much changed my perspective on Churchill were the war diaries of General (later Field Marshal) Alan Brooke, who was the Chief of the Imperial General Staff (CIGS) and military leader of all Britain's ground forces and worked in tandem with Churchill who was the political leader. Diaries are fascinating, given that as long as they are not altered at a later point in time, they tell things 'how they are' on a daily basis, albeit with the particular viewpoint of the person writing them, and I have read and re-read Brooke's diaries between 10 and 20 times to date (and they are about 1000 pages in length, so each doing so was surely a 'labour of love') given how astonishing the information described in them is. For what became clear to me when reading them, is that Churchill, in writing his own version of the 'history of World War Two' after it was complete, essentially wrote an autobiography giving his own interpretation of his own role during the war, and as such (like so many autobiographies) glorified his own role, attenuated or ignored his own responsibilities for the more sordid or disastrous events Britain suffered or was part of during the war, and perhaps most shamefully, was not generous in acknowledging the role of people around him in 'winning the war' (and I am talking person wise, rather than country wise – surely Russia can take almost 90 percent of the credit for 'winning' that war). Some of the most disastrous campaigns of the war - Norway and Greece for example – were shaped and driven by Churchill himself, yet from reading his books one would assume that the British and Allied Force Generals were almost solely to blame for these disasters, and that he was almost completely uninvolved in the strategic or tactical decisions that led to them. Throughout the war he constantly tried to push forward strategically appalling choices for campaigns – one example being his constant 'push' for an expedition against the 'northern tip' of Sumatra – which his military staff had to work daily to resist him initiating, and which would have dispersed the forces available in a disastrous 'minor campaign', similar to the Gallipoli and Antwerp campaigns in World War One, of which Churchill was similarly the architect. It is astonishing to read Brooke's diary (and the diaries or personal war accounts of a number of other military and political staff of that time, most of which validate Brooke's diary account of the war) to see how many times his advisors and folk like Brooke had to spend most of their day 'heading off' or convincing Churchill not to continue with his wild schemes, rather than what appeared to be the case when reading Churchill's own written accounts of World War Two, when it appeared as if Churchill was the architect of all successes, and his military staff merely carried out his great ideas. And this is to say nothing of Churchill's role in the area bombing of Germany, or his astonishing 'imperial' (a nice word for racially biased) views on India, or his personal habits, or injudicious views on most subjects freely imparted to all and sundry on an almost continuous basis. If he was a politician in modern times, with the current daily media scrutiny they face, he would surely not have lasted more than a few days before having to resign in disgrace and shame because of his utterances and behaviour as a Prime Minister as he did in those times back then.

All of the fascinating and enjoyable times I have spent reading about this topic, apart from being a relaxation 'tool' in itself, did indeed, as our great old family friend Simon Pearce said it would, teach me a whole lot of lessons about not just history, but life itself. Firstly, it taught me that the character of any 'great' person, or indeed any person, is surely complex, and while someone like Winston Churchill surely had many attractive and positive traits, he also had a lot of negative and extremely selfish traits that unless carefully 'looked for' would not 'reach the light of day' when reading most historical accounts either of his life or that of World War Two. Secondly, it taught me that one needs to be cautious in believing only one account of anything, least of all the person who is the one telling the story / giving the account of how things happen. Thirdly, it taught me that history is often created by those involved in it who write about it afterwards in a way that will benefit that person themselves in an unduly positive way (as they say, history is mostly written by the 'winners' of any event being written about). Fourthly, it taught me not to put anyone on a pedestal from reading about past events that they were involved in – as my great current work mentor, Professor Nicky Morgan, often reminds me, even the greatest leaders have 'feet of clay'. Fifthly, it taught me never to have a fixed paradigm about anything from the past – my own interpretation of and 'feeling for' this period of history was very different in the time of hearing about the events then as told by my father, or reading Winston Churchill's own books about World War Two as a teenager, compared to the more complex, less positive perspective I have of Winston Churchill and the events occurring during World War Two today, thanks to a reasonably extensive reading of different sources of information of events occurring at that time in the last few years. Finally, it made me think about the importance of diaries – a long lost 'art' that perhaps needs to be revived – there is much to be gained from keeping a daily diary about events. If Alan Brooke had not spent a few minutes before bed each night writing up a description of his daily life working near Winston Churchill in his diary, we would be the poorer for not having it, and our understanding of events way back then would remain simplistic and perhaps unbalanced.

There are surely, therefore, a lot of lessons one can learn not just about history and historical revisionism (as Churchill's own post-war writings of events surely were), but also in understanding contemporary life and how in describing it some folk who want to personally gain from the telling of it, may be able to do so by how they subjectively describe events of which they were part. There is surely a positive gain from keeping a daily or weekly diary, so that one can be to a greater degree sure of one's own history, or at least of the events happening during a particular period of time from one's past if one wishes to review it, than if one did not have a recorded history of it. Equally, one surely needs to be aware when reading the 'official' history of any person, organization, community or nation state, that it may be written with potentially (some would say surely) an either subconscious or conscious / overt or covert bias (as much as it should also be remembered that each time one personally reflects on or writes about an experience one has been part of, it will surely also have one's own particular bias and perspective), and should therefore always be read with caution. Reading, and for me particularly reading about history, is both one of the most enjoyable activities that I can ever do, and the activity that I learn most from, but I know that a lot of what I read, particularly biographies, and certainly autobiographies, need to be read with a large 'pinch of salt'. So, when I am done with writing this, I will surely look forward to later today taking up again the current historical tome I am enjoying reading. But surely, I will read it with our saltshaker very close to me.

Essay 43. What is normal - Can normative data ever exist in a world of individual differences and qualia?

Most of health and clinical related science relies on us having a clear definition of what 'normal' is, or when someone is 'healthy'. If we don't have a good definition of normality, it becomes difficult for us to assess what abnormality is, who is ill, and what and when we should treat patients based on how different they are from the 'normal' baseline. But it is not easy to define normal, and for what one person is normal, is another person's abnormality. Further, we are not even sure that different folks smell, feel, see and hear the same things as the other, even if they define a noise similarly. In this Essay, therefore, we examine the concepts of normality and abnormality, and whether there can ever be a real 'divide' between the two state descriptors.

In the last few days, I attended a wonderful conference in Dullstroom near the Kruger National Park in South Africa on rural doctors training, and the point was made that what was 'normal' training in the medical school environment would not work when planning to set up training sites for doctors in rural areas. I read a recent Twitter debate which once again discussed whether it was normal for humans to eat carbohydrates or fats, and whether our predecessors had done so in ancient / prehistoric times. Most importantly, I was reminded by Professor Mike Lambert of the University of Cape Town, my old PhD supervisor, mentor, and good friend (and scientist whom I most admire) of one of the most brilliant philosophy of science articles, written by Johan Koeslag in the early 1990s, where he examined the question of 'what is normal' and how we define normality. All these got me thinking of how science and medicine differentiates normality from abnormality, and how we as a society often 'brand' folk as abnormal based on our own worldview and social or clinical

321

paradigms, and by doing so potentially stigmatize those that we label as abnormal.

Johan was a Physiology Professor at the University of Cape Town in the 1980s and1990s who had a profound effect on my way of thinking (and surely a lot of other folks) during my medical and PhD training, by always making us question dogma and routine thinking in science, medicine, and society, in a firm but uncondescending way. He published several incredibly thought-provoking philosophical articles throughout his career, and while all were great, to me perhaps his best was his article on normality and how it is defined. The definition of 'normal' is to conform to a standard, to be usual or typical. Johan suggested that the categorisation of biological phenomena as normal or abnormal was the absolute basis of medical practice, and that without defining individuals such there could be no medical or health services. He perceived that medicine and science used the concept of normality to define at least five independent, and potentially mutually contradictory, states, namely i) not ill; ii) the best; iii) operating as intended; iv) conforming to a cultural norm; or v) the usual. But, as he described, each of these definitions or 'states' of normality is problematic and each has caveats which diminish their acceptability. For example, the concept of 'not ill' as a concept of normality is challenging when one looks at a variety of symptoms that would constitute illness. Johan made the point that while a symptom could indeed often be manifestation of illness, it could also be part of 'normal' activities of daily life. For example, the symptoms of incapacitation, pain, swelling, bleeding, and infection are all used to define illness. But related to incapacitation, is sleep then abnormal, as while we sleep, we are incapacitated. Similarly, childbirth is associated with pain, an erection would be a type of swelling, menstruation is a type of bleeding, and colonic fermentation a type of infection, but none of these are pathological and would be regarding as normal activities of daily living.

Regarding the concept of normality as the 'best' he made the point that weather that is best for agriculture is not the best for tourism. Clinically, he used the example of atherosclerosis, and the perception that reduction of the incidence of atherosclerosis would be the 'best' way of prolonging lifespan and creating 'normal' life conditions for a longer period. Johan pointed out the ideal way of reducing the incidence of atherosclerosis was either chronic under-nutrition or an early death, both of which would mean a less than optimal capacity for productivity during the life span, and therefore prolonging the lifespan by reducing atherosclerosis would not be the 'best' from the perspective of a 'useful' lifespan. Similarly, if one increased the lifespan by attenuating the incidence of atherosclerosis, one would in effect increase the levels of degenerative diseases associated with old age as a cause of death. So, Johan was making the point that what is 'best' is clearly relative, and 'normal' related to 'best' similarly relative to the specific condition being examined, rather than life in its totality.

Johan was also critical of using 'operating as intended' as a state of normality and used examples such as if the purpose of sex is procreation, then homosexuality and masturbation would be abnormal, as would bottle-feeding babies, or indeed using the tongue to lick stamps, the eyelid to wink at a friend, or the legs to kick a soccer ball rather than walking. He felt that in particular the fields of nutrition and exercise science (and one would include sociology in many ways too) were 'guilty' of this 'over-simplification' of 'operational intent' as normality, firstly as scientists in this field often use teleology to explain reasons why things happen in the body or what people do or eat, and / or secondly for suggesting that this purposive behaviour comes from early evolutionary processes that caused it to be so, or that illness is related to modern folk operating differently to what humans used to do. For example, some folk believe that the 'Banting' high fat diet was what our evolutionary ancestors must have eaten, therefore it must be 'right' and should be the 'normal' modern diet. But Johan made the point that we cannot assume the designer's intentions are known when it comes to life processes, nor presume that there was a static nature to how things were either initially when created if a creator was involved, or when natural selection created a certain state. Rather than things being 'at rest' since the time they were created or selected, life processes are continually evolving, and there is therefore no immutable process or function, and normality can only really be described as its current usage, rather than as 'operating as intended', as we can never be really sure why or what things ultimately were intended for. Johan similarly gave short thrift to the idea that normality is related to conforming to a 'cultural norm', given that this definition succumbs to its own logic, given that if a definition is associated with a relative framework, it can never be absolute. While some cultures love rich, salty food, others do not, as much as some cultures find it normal for men to cry, or to watch boxing or bullfighting, while other cultures would find these to be anathema. So, while we often judge behaviours as normal based on cultural norms, these can never be objective.

Johan did perceive that the 'usual' would perhaps be the 'best' definition of normality, given that it allows some latitude to what normality is or is not, and allows a 'spread' rather than a singularity for and of normality. But again, there are the issues of specificity when describing the 'usual'. For examples, as Johan described, it is normal for bears to sleep continuously during winter but not humans. It is normal for babies to sleep for twenty hours per day but not adults to do so similarly. It is normal for female spiders to eat the males that mate with them, but luckily for human males this is not the case in the human species. In science, we use 95% probabilities to define the 'usual', but this means that some 'normal' folk' will always have the chance of being defined as 'abnormal' based on mathematical probability rather than 'real' illness or abnormality. But, Johan did feel that the concept 'of usual' was the one that was closest to being able to define 'normality' (if I read this correctly in his article), particularly when one took a constellation of symptoms or actions or functions together and examined them in a gestalt manner, where they would thus be able to create a general likeness to what is the 'normal' human state or behaviour. He used the example of shortness of breath – it is 'normal' to feel short of breath when walking up a flight of stairs, but not after brushing one's teeth. It is normal to feel short of breath when exercising, but if one feels short of breath when at rest, and it is associated with chest pain, dizziness, and sweating, it would be more likely that all these symptoms combined are indicative of an abnormal / ill state.

So how does all this help us with understanding normality or defining what is normal? Perhaps from all the above, and what Johan's article points out, it is very difficult to say with any clarity what is normal and what is not, and one should perhaps be careful when trying to do so or when defining someone's behaviour, actions or eating behaviour as normal or not. Science often looks at one variable and based on a study makes a conclusion on whether that variable is within a normal range or not. Scientists often use 'operating as intended' arguments to 'prove' the veracity of such statements, but as Johan so well points out, whenever one uses a teleological rather than a mechanistic argument, one is moving into the realms of conjecture rather than fact. Even worse or more concerning is using 'cultural norms' to explain 'normality'. While there is a place for understanding cultural differences in both health and disease, there is a very short 'slippery slope' from observation to prejudice when using cultural differences to label someone or some action as 'not normal'. We are all individuals. We all have a lot of similarities. But defining normality from similarities is always going to be problematic. While our 'gut feeling' often correctly tells us what normal or abnormal behaviours or actions are, as Johan so well describes, the minute one tries to objectively define normality, abnormality, illness, wellness or health, one runs into problems of relativity and subjectivity. Life is always a qualitative rather than a quantitative endeavour, and our own 'quale' (property of life) we perceive as the life we know, is always going to be a little different, a little personal, a little subjective and never identical to anyone else's. That makes life the wonderfully rich tapestry which it is, but of course, it makes it hard for scientists and clinicians to define normality or abnormality, and if need be, treat illness. What is normal? The question is perhaps as impossible to answer as is where we originated from, how the Earth and life on it will end, or how long is a piece of string.

Section 6. Understanding human and general unitary control processes

6.1. Introduction

In previous sections, we have examined the physical activities and behaviours which make up the human and result in the human condition and life as we know it, along with a look at academic life and how academics and the scientific endeavour works in order to help deconstruct the poetry of life into sizeable chunks which can be easily understood and explained than would be possible if trying to look at and explain 'the whole'. In this section, in 14 Essays we examine general unitary control theory and the processes they describe, which do attempt in some ways to explain the 'whole' picture of human life, or at least are part of the requirements or control functions of all systems and life processes. For example, homeostasis is an absolute requirement for all living structures, where temperature, blood glucose and other fuels and metabolic activities are kept within a narrow band of functional capacity, yet homeostasis is a non-physical 'entity' or 'activity limiter' which requires complex interactions between different variables, negative feedback loop activity, setpoint values, and a whole host of other mind-bogglingly complex behaviours and activities. The poetry in these unitary control process behaviours and activities is some of the most magical and profound, is still not well understood, but are essential for sustaining life as we know it.

Essay 44. Entropy - The forgotten universal principle

Entropy is one of the strangest and most challenging to understand universal rules, and suggests that every entity decays as time passes, and in order not to decay, either energy has to be used to counter the force of entropy, or what is damaged by entropy needs to be repaired or replaced as a constant cycle. In this Essay, therefore, we briefly examine the concept of entropy, and assess what it is about, and how its actions underlies not only physical, but also social systems.

A part of our roof becoming detached in a storm last week, and the crashing to the ground of concrete supporting the roof structures, reminded me of the principal of entropy which has been in my mind recently for different reasons. There are several definitions of entropy, but the one I am referring to is that entropy is the measure or description of the inevitable and steady deterioration of a system or society. Several tangible examples of entropy occur in our daily life, for example a house that is not lived in gradually disintegrates, our bodies if not exercised regularly function increasingly less optimally, and indeed an arm immobilised in plaster cast for a too long period withers and the immobilised muscle and other body tissues eventually dies. It can also be found in social systems, for example political parties which stay in power too long become inefficient and corrupt, businesses if maintained too long with a certain way of doing their core work eventually become outdated and redundant, social networks break down without maintenance and injected individual energy, and personal relationships wither and die if an individual does not pay them enough attention.

The reason or reasons why entropy exists or what its teleological purpose is, is not immediately clear, but what is self-evident is that all systems or societies need injected energy and planned attention to be not only enhanced, but even maintained, in order to resist the underlying 'force' of entropy breaking it down. For those in any sphere of life who are resistant to change, or don't make regular, if not constant effort to change their current life environment, should perhaps take note of this basic, often forgotten principle. The evidence of its actions is all around us, and the only mystery is why it is so unacknowledged, in contrast to its partner universal principles, evolution and homeostasis, in so many folks who it acts on and has the potential to damage in a continual way.

Essay 45. Homeostasis and the constancy principle - We are all creatures of comfort even when we go out of our comfort zone

---

Despite the significant differences in temperature and other environmental parameters that occur over the earths surface during summer and winter, humans, and indeed all mammals, do not cope at all well if their body temperature changes by more than a few degrees either up or down from the baseline temperature which is maintained in our body (around 36.5 degrees Celsius). How the body maintains its temperature within these well defined 'liveable' limits is known as homeostasis and involves several socio-biological actions and activities, as well as physiological control mechanisms, which work to prevent too great a 'swing' in body temperature and bring the temperature as quickly as possible to the baseline level if it is above or below it. In this Essay we therefore examine the concept of homeostasis, a non-physical control concept in which several physical activities are regulated by the body and brain in order to maintain homeostasis as best possible and allow humans to live and function as they do in a wide variety of different environmental temperatures and metabolically activating activities, which are heat-generating and require exquisite moderative control.

It is autumn in our part of the world, and the first chills are in the air in the late evening and early morning, and the family discussed last night the need to get out our warm clothes from storage in readiness for the approaching winter, to be well prepared for its arrival. After sharing in the fun of Easter Sunday yesterday and eating some chocolate eggs with the children, a persistent voice in my head this morning instructed me to eat less than normal today to 'make up' for this out of the normal chocolate eating yesterday. It is a beautiful sunny day outside as I write this, and I feel a strong 'urge' to stop writing and go out on a long cycle ride because of it and have to 'will' these thoughts away and continue writing, which is my routine activity at this time of morning. After a recent health scare I have been checking on my own physical parameters with more care than normal, and found it interesting when checking what 'normal' values for healthy folk are, that most healthy folk have fairly similar values for things like blood glucose, blood pressure, cholesterol concentrations and other such parameters, and that there are fairly tight ranges of values of each of these which are considered normal and a sign of 'health', and if one's values are outside of these, it is a sign of something wrong in the working of your body that needs to be treated and brought back into the normal range either by lifestyle changes, medication, or surgical procedures. All of these got me thinking about the regulatory processes that ensure that the body maintains its working 'parts' in a similar range in all folk, and the concept of homeostasis, which as a regulatory principle explains and underpins the maintenance of this 'safe zone' for our body's multiple activities, including the sensing of any external or internal changes which could be associated with the potential for one of the variables to go out of the 'safe zone', and initiates changes either behaviourally or physiologically which attempt to bring the variable at risk back into the 'safe zone' either pre-emptively or reactively.

Homeostasis is defined scientifically as the tendency towards a relatively stable equilibrium between inter-dependent elements. The word was generated from the Greek concepts of 'homiois' (similar) and 'stasis' (standing still), creating the concept of 'staying the same'. Put simply, homeostasis is the property of a system whereby it attempts to maintain itself in a stable, constant condition, and resists any changes or actions on the system which may change or destabilize the stable state. Its origins as a concept were from the Ancient Greeks, with Empedocles in around 400 BC suggesting that all matter consisted of elements which were in 'dynamic opposition' or 'alliance' with each other, and that balance or 'harmony' of all these elements was necessary for the survival of the individual or organism. Around the same time, Hippocrates suggested that health was a result of the 'harmonious' balance of the body's elements, and illness due to 'disharmony' of the elements which it was made up of. Modern development of this concept was initiated by Claude Bernard in the 1870s, who suggested that the stability of the body's internal environment was 'necessary for a free and independent life' and that 'external variations are at every instant compensated for and brought into balance', and Walter Cannon in the 1920s first formally called this concept of 'staying the same' homeostasis. Claude Bernard actually initially used the word 'constancy' rather than homeostasis to describe the concept, and interestingly, a lot of Sigmund Freud's basic work on human psychology was based on the need for 'constancy' (though he did not cross-reference this more physiological / physical work and concepts), and that everyone's basic needs were for psychological constancy or 'peace', and when one had an 'itch to scratch' one would do anything possible to remove the 'itch' (whether it be a new partner, a better house, an improved social status, or greater social dominance, amongst other potentially unrequited desires), and further that one's 'muscles are the conduit through which the ego imposes its will upon the world'. He and other psychologists of his era suggested that if an 'itch', urge or desire was not assuaged (and what causes these urges, whether a feeling of inadequacy, or previous trauma, or a desire for 'wholeness', is still controversial and still not clearly elicited even today), the individual would remain out of their required 'zone of constancy', and would feel negative emotions such as anxiety, irritation or anger until the urge or desire was relieved. If it was not relieved for a prolonged period this unrequited 'itch' could lead to the development of a complex, projection, or psychological breakdown (such as depression, mania, anxiety, personality disorder or frank psychosis). Therefore, as much as there are physical homeostasis related requirements, there are potentially also similarly psychological homeostasis related requirements which are being reacted to by the brain and body on a continuous basis.

Any system operating using homeostatic principles (and all our body systems do so) has setpoint levels for whatever substance or process is being regulated in the system, and boundary conditions for the substance or process which are rigidly maintained and cannot be exceeded without a response occurring which would attempt to bring the activity or changes to the substance or process back to the predetermined setpoint levels or within the boundary conditions for them. The reasons for having these set boundary conditions are protective, in that if they were exceeded, the expectation would be the system would be damaged if the substance or process being regulated (for example, oxygen, glucose, sodium, temperature, cholesterol, or blood pressure, amongst a whole host of others) was used up too quickly or worked too hard, or was allowed to build up to toxic / extremely high levels or not used enough to produce life-supporting substrates or useable fuels, which would endanger the life and potential for continued activity of the system being monitored. For example, oxygen shortage results in death quickly, as would glucose shortage, while glucose excess (known as diabetes) can also result in cellular and organ damage, and ultimately death if it is not controlled properly. For any system to maintain the substance or process within homeostasis-related acceptable limits, three regulatory factors (which are all components of what is known as a negative feedback loop) are required to be components of the system. The first is the presence of a sensory apparatus that can detect either changes in whatever substance or process is being monitored, or changes in the internal or external environment or other systems which interact with or impact on the substance or process being monitored. The second is a control structure or process which would be sent the information from the sensory apparatus and would be able to decide regarding whether to respond to the information or to ignore it as not relevant. The third is an 'effector' mechanism or process which would receive commands from the control structure after it had decided to initiate a response in response to the sensed perturbation potentially affecting the system it controls and make the changes to the system decided upon by the control structure to maintain or return the perturbed system to its setpoint value range.

The example of temperature regulation demonstrates both the complexity and beauty of homeostasis in regulating activity and protecting us on a continuous basis from harm. Physiological systems in most species of animals are particularly sensitive to changes in temperature and operate best in a relatively narrow range of temperature, although in some species a wider range of temperatures is tolerated. There are two broad mechanisms used by different organisms to control their internal temperature, namely ectothermic and endothermic regulation. Ectothermic temperature regulators (also known as 'cold-blooded' species), such as the frog, snake, and lizard, do not use many internal body processes to maintain temperature in the range, which is acceptable for their survival, but rather use external, environmental heat sources to regulate their body temperature. If the temperature is colder, they will use the sun to heat themselves up, and if warm, they will look for shadier conditions. Ectotherms therefore have energy efficient mechanisms of maintaining temperature homeostasis, but are more susceptible to vagaries in environmental conditions compared to endotherms. In contrast, endotherms (also known as 'warm-blooded' species), into which classification humans fall, use internal body activity and functions to either generate heat in cold environments or reduce heat in warm conditions. In endotherms, if the external environment is too cold, and if the cold environment impacts on body temperature, temperature receptors measuring either surface skin temperature or core body temperature will send signals to the brain, which subsequently initiates a shiver response in the muscles, which increases metabolic rate and provides greater body warmth as a by-product of fuel / energy breakdown and use. If environmental temperature is too warm, of if skin or core temperature is too high, receptors will send signals to brain areas which initiates a chain of events involving different nerve and blood-related control processes which result in increased blood flow to the skin by vasodilatation, thereby increasing blood cooling capacity and sweat rate from the skin, thus producing cooling by water evaporation. All these endotherm-associated heating and cooling processes utilize a large amount of energy, so from an energy perspective are not as efficient as that of ectotherms, but they do allow a greater independence from environmental fluctuations in temperature. It must be noted that endotherms also use similar behavioural techniques to ectotherms, such as moving into shady or cool environments if excessively hot, but as described above, can tolerate a greater range of environmental temperatures and conditions. Furthermore, humans are capable of 'high level' behavioural changes such as putting on or taking off clothes, in either a reactive or anticipatory way. It is evident, therefore, that for each variable being homeostatically monitored and managed (on a continuous basis) there are a complex array of responsive (and 'higher-level' pre-emptive) options available with which to counteract the potential or actual 'movement' of the variable beyond its 'allowed' metabolic setpoints and ranges.

There are several questions still to be answered regarding how homeostasis 'works' and how 'decisions' related to homeostasis occur. It is not clear how the regulatory mechanisms know which variable they 'choose' to defend as a priority. Brain oxygen would surely be the most important variable to 'defend', as would perhaps blood glucose levels, but how decisions are made and responses initiated for these variables preferentially, which may impact negatively on other systems with their own homeostatic requirements, is not clear. Furthermore, there is the capacity for 'conflict' between physical and psychological homeostatic mechanisms when homeostatic-related decisions are required to be made. For example, one's ego may require one to run a marathon to fulfil a need to 'show' one's peers that one is 'tough' by completing such a challenging goal, but doing so (running the marathon) creates major physical stress for and on the physical body. Indeed, some folk push themselves so hard during marathons that they collapse, even if they 'feel' warning signs of impending collapse, or of an impending heart attack, and choose to keep running despite these symptoms. To these folks, the psychological need to complete the event must be greater than the physical need to protect themselves from harm, and their regulatory decision-making processes clearly valences psychological homeostasis to be of greater importance than physiological homeostasis when deciding to continue exercising in the presence of such warning symptoms. However, running a marathon, while increasing physical risk of catastrophic physical events during the running of it, if done on a repetitive basis, has positive physical benefits, such as weight loss and increased metabolic efficiency of the heart, lungs, muscles, and other organ structures, along with enhanced psychological well-being which would be derived from achieving the set athletic performance-related goals. Therefore, 'decision-making' on an issue such as running a marathon is complex from a homeostasis perspective, with both short- and long-term potential benefits and harmful consequences. How these contradictory requirements and factors are 'decided upon' by the brain when attempting to maintain both psychological and physical homeostasis is still not clear.

A further challenge to homeostatic regulation is evident in the examples of when one has a fever, where a high temperature may paradoxically be beneficial, and after a heart attack, where an altered heart rate and blood pressure setpoint may be part of compensatory mechanisms to ensure the optimal function of a failing heart. While these altered values are potentially 'outside' of the 'healthy' setpoint level range, they may have utilitarian value and would be metabolically appropriate in relation to either a fever or failing heart. How the regulatory homeostatic control mechanisms 'know' that these altered metabolic setpoints are beneficial rather than harmful, and 'accepts' them as temporary or permanent new setpoints, or whether these altered values are associated with routine homeostatic corrective responses which are part of the body's ongoing attempt to induce healing in the presence of fever or heart failure (amongst other homeostatically paradoxical examples), is still not clear. Whether homeostasis as a principle extends beyond merely controlling our body's activity and behaviour, to more general societal or environmental control, is also still controversial. For example, James Lovelock, with his Gaia hypothesis, has suggested that the world in its entirety is regulated by homeostatic principles, and global temperature increases result in compensatory changes on the earth and in the atmosphere that lead to eventual cooling of the earth, and this warming and cooling continues in a cyclical manner – and most folk who believe in global warming as a contemporary unique catastrophic event don't like this theory, even if it is difficult to support or refute without measuring temperature changes accurately over millennia.

Homeostatic control mechanisms can fail, and indeed our deaths are sometimes suggested to be the result of a failure of homeostasis. For example, cancer cells overwhelm cellular homeostatic protective mechanisms, or develop rapidly due to uncontrolled cellular proliferation of abnormal cells which are not inhibited by the regular cellular homeostatic negative feedback control mechanisms, which lead to physical damage to the body and ultimately our death, for these or other reasons that we are still not aware of. In contrast, Sigmund Freud, in his always contrary view of life, suggested as part of his Thanatos theory that death is the ultimate form of 'rest' and is our 'baseline' constancy-related resting state which we 'go back to' when dying (with suicide being a direct 'mechanism' of reaching this state in those whose psyche are operating too far away from their psychological setpoints, whatever these are), although again this is a difficult theory to either prove or disprove. Finally, what is challenging to a lot of folk about homeostasis from a control / regulatory perspective is that it is a conceptual 'entity' rather than a physical process that one can 'show' to be 'real', much like Plato's Universals (to Plato, the physical cow itself was less relevant than the 'concept' of a cow, and he suggested that one can only have 'mere opinions' of the former, while one has absolute knowledge of the latter, given the physical cow changes as it grows, ages, and dies, while the 'concept' of a cow is immutable and eternal). It is always difficult scientifically to provide categorical evidence which either refutes or supports concepts such as universals and non-physical general control theories, even if they are concepts which appear to underpin all life as we know it, and without which function we could not exist in our current physical form and living environment.

As I look out the window at the falling autumn leaves and wonder whether we will have a very cold winter this year and whether we have prepared adequately for it clothes-wise (pre-emptive long-term homeostatic planning at its best, even if perhaps a bit 'over-the-top'), while taking off my jersey as I write this given that the temperature has increased as the day has changed from morning to afternoon (surely a reactive homeostatic response), and as I ponder my health-related parameters, and work out how I am going to get those that need improvement as close to 'normal' as possible (surely as part of behavioural homeostatic / health-optimization planning), I look forward to that bike ride now I have managed to delay gratification of doing so until I have completed writing this (and feel a sense of well-being both from doing so and by realizing I am now 'free' to go on the ride and by doing so can remove the psychological 'itch' that makes me want to do it and therefore return to a state of psychological 'constancy' / homeostasis). Contemplating all of these, it is astonishing to think that all of what I, and pretty much all folk, do is underpinned by a desire to be, and maintain life, in a 'comfort zone' which feels right for me, and which is best for my bodily functions and psychological state. Given that all folk in the world have similar physical parameters when we measure them clinically, it is likely that our 'comfort zones' both physically and psychologically are not that different in the end. Perhaps the relative weighting which each of us assigns to our psychological or physical 'needs' create minor differences between us (and occasionally major differences such as in folk with psychopathology or with those who have significant lifestyle related physical disorders), though at the 'heart of it all', both psychologically and physically, is surely the over-arching principle of homeostasis. While on the bike this afternoon, I'll ponder on the big questions related to homeostasis which still need to be answered, such as how homeostasis-related decisions are made, how the same principle can regulate not just our body, but also our behaviour, and perhaps that of societal and even planetary function, and how 'universals' originated and which came first, the physical entity or the universal. Sadly I think it will need a very long ride to solve these unanswered questions, and remove the 'itch that needs scratching' which arises from thinking of these concepts as a scientist who wants to solve them – and I don't like to spend too long out of my comfort zone, which is multi-factorial and not purely bike-focused, but rather is part bike, part desk, part comfy chair, the latter of which will surely become more attractive after a few hours of cycling, and will 'call me home' to my next 'comfort zone', probably long before I can solve any of these complex issues while out on the ride watching the autumn leaves fall under a beautiful warm blue sky, with my winter cycling jacket unused but packed in my bike's carrier bag in case of a change in the weather.

Essay 46. The negative feedback loop - The absolute fundamental principle governing all life processes

To maintain the body within the homeostatic limits described in the previous Essay, the body and brain uses a general engineering principle known as the negative feedback loop to maintain control of the function of all cells, organs, and physiological and anatomical function in the body. The negative feedback loop works by feeding information about the amount of product or waste created by a metabolic activity or fuel utilized to perform a task to a prior stage of the process, where it inhibits further activity of the process which creates the product or metabolite, hence slowing down the function and thus controlling its own levels. In this Essay we examine the negative feedback control loop, the basic 'unit' of control in the human body, and indeed all living objects or 'things', how the mechanism works, and what happens when the system of negative feedback breaks down and become dysfunctional.

I was asked this week in my current work role to give a welcoming address to the Society for Endocrinology, Metabolism and Diabetes of South Africa later this year as the University of the Free State is hosting their annual conference this year. This got me thinking of diabetes as a disorder, which occurs because of the failure of regulation of blood sugar concentrations due to several different reasons and causes. Understanding generic regulatory processes and system control mechanisms and activity has been the major focus and interest of my research career to date, and I have spent a lot of my life trying to understand and make sense of what are life's underlying governing principles. Perhaps the most basic control mechanism (and an astonishingly simple one), without which life could not exist in any shape or form, is the negative feedback loop, which can be described as either a governing principle or regulatory process.

Negative feedback is defined as occurring when some function or product, which is the output of a system, process, or mechanism, is fed back into the same system in a manner that tends to reduce the output being generated by the system in response to an external input to the system or a perturbation of the system by an external agent. Negative feedback can be thought of as planned corrective behaviour of any system which brings it back to baseline whenever it moves away from the baseline. It is also important in purposive behaviour, as negative feedback mechanisms allow corrective behaviour to occur if activity is performed which is not in the direction of the intended goal of the purposive behaviour. A nice example describing how negative feedback works was put forward by my long-time polymath collaborator and friend at the University of Cape Town, Professor Vicky Lambert. When one plans to leave a house, one forecasts what clothes one will wear by looking outside and seeing if it looks cold or warm from visual cues one picks up looking through the window at the external environment which one shortly plans to enter, or from checking the local weather forecasts. Whether one has put on too many or too few clothes will only be apparent when one goes outside and one's skin temperature receptors are exposed to the outside air, and this initiates feedback regulation – either taking off clothing, or putting more on, or going back inside if it the temperature is different to what one predicted it would be and is either too cold or hot when outside. These different corrective responses to the stimulus would result in the correct body temperature occurring to allow survival, no matter what the elements outside, and this temperature regulation by addition or removal of clothing is a nice example of how a negative feedback loop control mechanism occurs in our daily life.

As per this example, a negative feedback control system therefore requires three components to work. The first component is the presence of a sensory apparatus that can detect either changes in whatever substance or process is being monitored, or changes in the internal environment or other systems which interacts with or impacts on the substance or process being monitored. The second component would be a control structure or process which would be sent the information from the sensory apparatus, would have stored information about the baseline / routine levels of the system which need to be maintained to allow continued successful function of the system, and would make a decision based on comparing the changes detected to what these baseline 'setpoint' values are, and 'decide' whether to make changes as a result of the information received, or to maintain the current level of activity of the system if deciding that the changes detected do not have the capacity to harm the system. The third component would be an effector mechanism or process which would enact or make the changes to the system decided upon by the decision-making control structures. These basic negative feedback loop components are found in all life processes and structures, and are fundamental to life, as if they were not present, activity that is potentially harmful would continue or accelerate until the system is overwhelmed to the point of being damaged and eventually destroyed. An example is in cancer cells, where for some unknown reason the normal inhibitory feedback mechanisms regulating cell division become dysfunctional, and normal body structures are overwhelmed by aggressively proliferating cells that cannot be 'turned off' by negative feedback processes.

Negative feedback loops are not just found and control the human body but occur also in and regulate all structures and systems that we use in daily life, such as engines, aeroplanes, air-conditioners, speaker amplifiers, for example. All activities we do, such as turning a boat's rudder when seeing an iceberg, or moving a baby away from a hot kettle, or to changing our behaviour or environment after a non-optimal social interaction, are examples of negative feedback control loop mechanisms 'at work' in our daily lives. Indeed, philosophers often suggest that the capacity for negative feedback is the essential factor necessary for determining whether a system, process or structure is 'alive' – though these debates are often surely didactic rather than pragmatic, such as in philosophical discussions of whether thermostats can be considered to be 'alive' as they respond automatically to stimuli, something which sounds easy to answer, but in essence when one thinks about it becomes difficult to take a firm opinion about from a defining 'life' perspective, even if one is aware that such a debate is fundamentally absurd.

Diabetes and the regulation of blood sugar levels is a classic example of the negative feedback loop and how important it is to us for our survival. In healthy folk, after one has a meal, one's blood sugar concentrations start to increase as the meal is ingested, and this would be picked up by sugar level sensors in different parts of the body. These sensors quickly send signals to regulatory control centres in the brain and body, which then directs the pancreas to release insulin, which quickly converts the blood sugar into other forms of stored energy in the different cells of the body (such as fat), and by doing so the blood sugar levels are maintained between fairly tightly 'allowed' boundaries. In diabetes, after food is ingested, for a variety of reasons, when 'instructed' to do so, the pancreas does not respond appropriately, or cannot do so, and insulin is not secreted in some types of diabetes, while in others, no matter how much insulin is secreted, the cells do not respond to it. So, the negative feedback loop mechanism starts failing, and this causes the blood sugar levels to drift either above or below the normally 'acceptable' boundaries allowed by the body, and the elevated blood sugar can cause direct damage to tissues and cells in the body if it stays high for too long a time period. Interestingly, when the fast-acting blood sugar controlling feedback loop starts failing, as it does in diabetes, a number of longer / more complex negative feedback loops are initiated, some involving other hormones being secreted that are not normally utilized to the extent they are in diabetes, in an attempt by the body's regulatory control centre to return the blood sugar levels to tolerable levels, and others being behavioural in response to the symptoms induced by too high blood sugar (such as increased tiredness, weight loss, and increased passing of urine), such as decreasing ingestion of food with high sugar content, exercising more, or seeing the doctor and being given pills and medications to counter the effect of the non-functioning insulin pathways. All these changes would be in themselves examples of longer time-duration negative feedback control loop mechanisms, which are brought into action when the basic negative feedback loop fails, in an attempt to restore the blood sugar levels to the most optimal level possible, in order to ensure life continues as optimally as possible, for as long as possible, even in the impaired state from a system regulation perspective which the diabetes condition creates for those suffering from it.

So, from my own research interest perspective, I am looking forward to hopefully hearing a lot about the latest developments in diabetes management and how metabolic regulation is better understood when the conference comes to town in a few months' time. I am pretty sure though that whatever new information has been found and will be described at the conference, the principle of negative feedback control will remain sacrosanct as the accepted mechanism by which all metabolic activity is controlled in the body. Beyond diabetes though, it creates quite a paradigm shift in how one views life when one understands that just about all activity one does throughout one's daily life (actually, all activity, period) is associated with some particular negative feedback loop cycle – whether it is getting food to maintain our fuel supplies, doing exercise to maintain one's health, visiting friends to maintain one's wellbeing, going to work each day to ensure one has enough funds to allow basic shelter and survival requirements to be ensured, everything we do is related to some negative feedback loop being active and occurring to ensure our ongoing survival and future wellbeing. How such a relatively simple principle came to underpin all our activity and be so fundamental to life and existence, and how such a 'principle' came to be the one that controls and regulates all life at some point in our past, is of course another story, and provides 'grist for the mill' for many more years future study, research and thought.

Essay 47. Metabolic activity setpoint regulation in the body - Conundrum of how we all are so similar deep inside

One of the most curious and interesting mechanisms in the human body and brain is how metabolic 'setpoints' — the values which are the homeostatic 'normal' values to which they are returned if they are raised or lowered in response to external environmental changes and body activity responses, and which are used by negative feedback loops as their 'setpoint' values — are created and maintained. To me it is astonishing that despite all of us having such different body shapes and structures, and doing such different amounts of activity per day, our blood glucose concentrations are all maintained in a very similar band of values in all folks all around the world. In this Essay, therefore, we examine the concept of metabolic setpoints, how they are created and maintained, and what happens if the body functions for a period away from the metabolic setpoint values.

This week I have had a bad bout of flu, along with the rest of the family, and apart from feeling somewhat miserable, everything in my body feels disjointed and not functioning well because of the illness. I have been researching how the brain and body works for more than 25 years, and while the old adage that the more one learns about something, the less one knows about it is certainly true in my case, each journal article I read, or data I examine on how the body and the brain 'work' and are regulated, I marvel still at what a brilliant piece of work the human body is, and 'feeling' my own body not working well this week reinforced this perception for me. One of the most fascinating things about the body is how all the different organs, systems and metabolic activity are regulated to ensure that all its activity functions in a synchronous way and successfully from an integrative perspective. Even at rest, vast numbers of anatomical and physiological functions are operative and interacting with each other continuously to sustain life as we know and 'feel' it, whatever life really is. When one moves or performs activity, all these variables and interactions change in both quantitative and temporal domains, with metabolic activity increasing and the interactions between different organs and physiological systems occurring at a faster rate. Given the large number of physiological processes and activities occurring at any one time in the body, one would expect large variability between different individuals for the value of any single substrate, metabolite or regulatory factor operating at the cellular, tissue, organ, or system level in the body. Furthermore, one would expect that this potential inter-individual variability in physiological function would alter continuously with time. But, astonishingly, the range of values for any metabolic variable or its activity, and baseline levels of activity for most physiological variables, is relatively similar in different folk who are healthy. For example, blood glucose concentrations are usually maintained between 4 and 6 mmol/l in all healthy individuals and breathing rate between 12 and 16 breaths per minute. Therefore, a similar metabolic regulator appears to occur in all individuals, although what sets these similar metabolic ranges in all folks is still currently not well understood.

The first potential regulator of all our metabolic and physiological system setpoints is a control mechanism in the brain or central nervous system. If this is the case, the values of each metabolic setpoint level, and the requirement for every single physiological system at every level in the body, as well as mechanical restraints and cellular architecture are present in the brain. The hypothalamus, a small area of brain tissue at the base of the brain, which has been shown to regulate hormonal function and has signalling connections with the body, has been suggested to be the key area of the brain where metabolic regulation occurs, along with a host of other brain and brainstem regions. These potential areas in the brain have been suggested to have a collection of neural networks that contain a register of the set values for each metabolic and physiological constituent of the body which is 'stored' somewhere and somehow in these brain neural networks. Two innovative researchers, Joseph Parvizi and Antonio Damasio, in the early 2000s suggested that a 'proto-self' exists, as a collection of neural networks that 'map' the physical and physiological state of the body. In their theory, the proto-self is a first-order map describing the state of every physiological variable in the body, and when a change to the internal physiological milieu occurs, such as when one moves or performs exercise, these changes become a further first-order map in other neural networks. When the proto-self values in the one neural network is compared to this 'change map', the difference between the two become a second-order map, which is used by some regulatory process in the brain to initiate changes at either the psychological, physiological system or cellular level by either sending out efferent neural commands (brain signals flowing out to the muscles or organs of the body) or humoral (blood borne) hormonal changes, both of which would attempt to restore the altered metabolic variables to their proto-self values by reducing pace during physical activity or terminating the physical activity, or ingesting fuel or fluid as required to replace the increase in its use, or changing cardiac output or fuel utilization composition to as near what is routine / 'normal' as possible.

This is an attractive idea, but like all things related to the brain, there has been no real development in identifying the mechanisms or components of the brain that would be responsible for the storage of the metabolic proto-self maps and register of all the physiological and metabolic setpoint variables. Two distinct shortcomings of these proto-self and brain storage concepts are, firstly, the level of requirement for 'storage space' given the huge number of variables that would have to be stored, and the intellectual brain activity required to occur continuously to integrate and manage all the different variables at the same time. Secondly, if the values were 'stored' in the neural circuits, one would have expected over the generations there would be slow but substantial changes to these values as part of normal genetic variation that occurs over time, which would create an increasingly diverse array of anatomical brain neural network variations and an associated diverse array of setpoint values with time. Therefore, it is likely that some other mechanism is responsible for the similarity between the metabolic setpoint variables of different folk.

An external agent or force, rather than an internal brain mechanism, may be responsible for establishing metabolic setpoints, either directly or by maintaining similar function in the brains of different individuals by preventing changes which would be produced by the evolutionary pressure of passing time. Everyone would need to respond to the external agent or energy force in the same way, and this similar response would set a similar internal physiological and metabolic state in all individuals. For this type of external regulation to occur, the external energy force would need to be consistently present to allow the physiological response to occur continuously in all individuals. A putative energy force which would fulfil these criteria is the force of gravity. Gravity occurs over the entire surface of the earth, and energy is continuously required by all humans to counteract the effect of gravity on body structures. For example, merely standing upright requires constant force and hence muscle activity, which requires as a result a certain continuous level of metabolic activity. Experiments performed in zero gravity environments show that physiological activity levels are profoundly altered by lack of gravitational force. Therefore, there is a strong possibility that gravity, or other electromagnetic forces around the earth such as the Coriolis force, are, at least partly, responsible for maintaining the similar homeostatic setpoints found in all healthy individuals.

There are, of course, times and conditions when metabolic setpoint variables alter and can be altered. After long term physical training, several setpoint levels are altered associated with increased 'fitness' induced by training. For example, resting heart rate is reduced, blood lipid and cholesterol profiles are reduced, and muscle enzymatic and mitochondrial setpoint functions are altered. These changes are probably due to adaptations in protein regulatory function at the genetic and molecular level, which alters the physical and neural structures associated with physiological activity by changing their size, number, and efficiency of function. But these alterations are maintained only as long as the training bouts are continued. Once the training stimulus is removed, the metabolic setpoint levels in the different physiological systems return to their original values associated with the 'untrained' state, and these reversions occur at a faster rate than do the changes associated with training, indicating that it is easier to return metabolic setpoint values to their untrained values, than it is to alter the setpoint values away from their untrained state.

Chronic disease can also alter resting metabolic values, and in a permanent manner, if the disease is permanent and related to some cellular death. For example, when an individual suffers a big heart attack, there is permanent loss of heart tissue in the affected area, which results in the contractile state of the heart changing, which leads to several other changes occurring, such as increased (or decreased) heart rate or stroke volume, blood pressure changes, and alterations in the flow of blood and fluids between organs. If the body can tolerate these changes, the individuals will survive in this damaged state for a substantial period, with altered resting metabolic variables and setpoint values, until death occurs from some other pathology / disease process. One could describe this as being a functionally different setpoint state, and in complex system research terminology / parlance this is known as a functional bifurcation from the resting state, but it is an artificial state related to illness, and the individual is in effect not functioning in an optimal state, but rather in a state of chronic systemic compensation. In diseases such as diabetes mellitus, there appears to be marked changes in the concentrations of blood glucose, with levels measured at different times of the day either being higher or lower than the concentrations present in healthy individuals. However, these changes appear to be caused by the increased variation in blood glucose concentration associated with changes in the gain (the capacity of the system to return to baseline), and time constant of the gain, of the blood glucose control system in individuals with diabetes, rather than by changes in the metabolic setpoint values themselves.

The metabolic setpoints can also alter in response to acute infection, as happened to my body this week, with increased baseline temperature levels, heart rate and cardiac output. Interestingly, in what has been called the 'setpoint controversy', during a bout of fever such as I have had, changes occur which are not immediately corrective and which return the core temperature to previous homeostatic setpoint levels, but rather create conditions which would lead to further increases in temperature, or maintenance of the raised temperature away from the routine setpoint levels. These include seeking a warm environment, increased vasoconstriction, and shivering, all of which increase metabolic rate and increase generation of heat, despite the individual already having an increased core temperature. The usual response to an increased core temperature when one is in a hot environment, or when the body's core temperature increases due to exercise or physical exertion (hyperthermia), would be to seek out a cold environment, reduce locomotion, increase vasodilation, and reduce metabolic rate. Therefore, the responses to hyperthermia and fever, which similarly cause core temperature to increase above baseline setpoint levels, induce directly opposite effects, which in the case of hyperthermia lead to a reduction in core temperature, and in fever, maintains the increase in core temperature, and these different responses are the nub of the setpoint controversy. The teleological value of the responses to fever would be to allow optimal function of the inflammatory and immune response to remove the threat caused by the organism or process (in my case a flu virus) which induced the fever. The teleological value of the responses to hypothermia would be to prevent catastrophic overheating of physiological systems. How the 'decision' is made by the brain and body to initiate either of these different metabolic setpoint related strategies in response to an increase in core temperature is not currently known.

In summary, therefore, one of the most fascinating aspects of our hugely complex bodies, is that despite this complexity, the setpoint values for each metabolic or physiological function appears to be very similar across all individuals, unless there are differences in fitness or health levels. While these setpoint values may be determined in brain structures and circuits, it is more likely that they are set in response to an external system force, likely to be gravity or other such forces that operate in a chronic and continuous manner similarly in all of us. In a world where our perceived external individual differences are often used politically and socially to differentiate and define us, it is a surety that deep inside we are all very much the same, and all are responding to the same challenges and forces we face and are all so similar in all aspects of our body's makeup and physical function because of this.

So apart from being fabulously complex and mechanistically brilliant, perhaps the deep workings of our bodies, in all their brilliance, can teach us also something socially from how they are made, and how they operate, reacting to external stimuli in the same way, responding internally in a host of different physiological systems in the same way, and returning to the same baseline values in the same way. No matter how different we or others think we are, deep inside, we are all very much the same, and this similarity is perhaps the fundamental tenet which allows the ongoing existence of life as we know it. Who would ever have believed that gravity would perhaps be the ultimate force potentially underpinning all of our body's functions, and ensuring the physiological similarity of all of us residing on this planet of ours, as we rotate daily around the sun and go about our daily business, if indeed this is the case. Sadly though, it couldn't prevent me developing an illness because of a nasty flu virus, which appears to have knocked everything out of kilter this week, including most of my metabolic setpoints, to say nothing of my psychic harmony.

Essay 48. Teleology and determinism - Concepts banishing randomness and chance from our daily lives

Teleology is the philosophy / concept of describing an object by the purpose it serves, rather than just as a description of the entity in an observational way as it lies in front of one. For example, a house is described as purposive, and that purpose being to keep us humans warm, out of the cold, and away from harm's way from wild animals or aggressive humans due to the walls and doors of the house which protect us. As my great university physiology lecturer Johan Koeslag pointed out to us many years ago, the 'danger' of taking a teleological stance to all things in life is that implicit in it is the concept of determinism, that there is 'purpose' to all things and actions. But what if life is purposeless, and things outside of man-made objects are purposeless too? Indeed, existentialism tells us that all life is purposeless, which puts it in direct opposition to the concept of teleology. In this Essay, therefore, we assess the merits and shortcomings of teleology, and whether an object or action always has 'purpose'.

An interesting recent discussion with an old colleague and collaborator from the University of Worcester, Andy Renfree, on the teleology of entropy, got me thinking in a more general way about the concept of teleology and its twin concept determinism. Teleology is defined as the explanation of phenomena by the purpose they serve rather than by postulated causes, or perhaps more succinctly, it is defined as the description of the doctrine of design or purpose in the material world. Determinism is defined as the doctrine that all events, including human action, are determined by causes regarded as external to the will, and that for every event, including human action, there exists pre-existing causes for it that could lead to no other event other than the one that is being examined. From a teleological or deterministic perspective, if you look carefully at all human activities, as scientists do, one can explain all human behaviour as being caused by prior events or circumstances, and all human creations as being purposive. For example, the teleological reason for the existence of a house is to provide shelter for those that live in it. The teleological reason for the sensation of hunger is to ensure that one initiates action to ensure one ingests food to allow the requisite energy is available to maintain human essential functions. Every single human action can be explained in a teleological manner with either a bit of logical thought or careful scientific analysis.

This obviously becomes problematical for many folk as it does not allow for the possibility of randomness or chance, denies the capacity for free will, and has the potential to undermine an individual's sense of personal autonomy, given that this sense of autonomy is underpinned by the perception that they ultimately are in control of their own destinies, and the concepts of teleology and determinism suggest that control of one's destiny and actions lie in prior events and previous activities that have necessitated a change or a particular action which is to be manifested in any action the individual is currently performing, even if often the actions feel spontaneous rather than planned.

Awareness of these universal concepts can either therefore be liberating or stifling for different folk, depending on their world view and the value they put on their requirement for personal autonomy. It has a positive for folk that do acknowledge it though, in that one cannot excuse chance or randomness for any of one's actions and requires one to evaluate each of one's actions in the light of what prior event or events led to them occurring, in a manner that will lead to an improved response to a similar action that occurs at a later stage. Of course, this learning or change of behaviour would itself be teleological and deterministic. As the old proverb goes – for the want of a nail the shoe was lost, for the want of a shoe the horse was lost, for want of a horse the rider was lost, for want of a rider the message was lost, for want of the message the battle was lost, for the want of a battle the kingdom was lost. Behind, or perhaps one should say before, every event there exists a 'nail' that causes it, and life as we know it would not exist if not underpinned by teleology and determinism.

Essay 49. Zeitgebers - External processes that generate structure in our daily lives

The leaves are starting to brown and fall as autumn in the Northern Hemisphere approaches. Apart from changing the climate considerably, the changes in the four seasons on a repetitive and cyclical basis also acts as a Zeitgeber, meaning that it also sets cyclical changes in our physiology and social behaviour. Similarly, the day / night cycle acts as a Zeitgeber, and we set our 24-hour behaviour according to the day / night cycle, usually sleeping in the darkness and eating and working in the daylight hours. These fascinating external 'cyclical controllers', and their complex effects on the body and brain are not well known or described. Therefore, in this Essay we examine the concept of Zeitgebers, what they are, how they work, and their effect on our human physiology, psychology, and social behaviour.

A conversation earlier this week where I discussed with a colleague that I had only been in my current job for ten months and was looking forward to having a full year cycle in my new job complete, so I could be aware of the year-round structure and key dates associated with the work I do, got me thinking of zeitgebers and their influence on our lives. Most of my research work in my career to date has examined our brain and body's physiological system regulatory control mechanisms, to understand what regulates our basic human functions and how they are controlled. Most of this work, like in most laboratories around the world, has examined systems within the body, or a specific organ or physiological system in the body, to try and understand its regulation. But of course, the activities of our body and our behaviour are not just regulated by internal processes, but also by the need to respond to external environmental or social influences, and zeitgebers are one such important external controller.

A zeitgeber is defined as any external environmental or social cue that 'entrain' and synchronizes our body's functions in a rhythmical way, and therefore ultimately controls its function over a time period. Examples of zeitgebers include light, temperature, and social interactions. A potent cyclical zeitgeber is the day/night light cycle which sets our 24-hour (circadian) cycle of physiological activity. At a physiological level, the alternating presence or absence of light which is part of the day / night cycle appears to regulate biological 'clocks' in our body via receptors in the eye which transmit this information from the external environment to key regulatory areas of the brain, which then adjust our body systems level of activity – usually higher in times of light (daytime), and lower in times of darkness (night). There is also a social zeitgeber 'loop' that is induced by the day / night cycle, namely that when it is dark, we lie down and sleep, which in an indirect way also slows down our body's physiological activity levels, and when it is light, we become more active and perform our activities of daily living, including routine exercise, and therefore our body's physiological activity levels increase during the day. Each new day and night cycle cause this increased and decreased physiological activity to be repeated, and therefore becomes a cyclical / rhythmical activity in an ongoing, repetitive manner. Therefore, the day / night cycle ultimately 'enslaves' or 'entrains' our body and social life functions, without us being aware of its supreme influence.

Social activity, such as feeding cycles have also been proposed to another important zeitgeber. Daily scheduled feeding, such as eating three regular meals at the same time point each day, induces cyclical changes in the activity of our physiological systems which are required to absorb and use the ingested food. Scheduled feeding also induces anticipatory habituated changes to allow these feeding bouts to occur, such as planning a space in our workday to have a lunch break, and these social changes which allow an individual to feed at similar time points in the day become potent zeitgebers themselves. Zeitgebers do not just work over daily cycles, but also can operate over a longer (and shorter) ranges of time. For example, seasonal changes in temperature will cause adjustments in our behaviour at different times of the year, and social activities such as long holidays at specific times of year create different patterns of activity and eating patterns during those specific times of year, in a repetitive and cyclical manner at the same time of year over decades of our lives.

There are also likely to be long term zeitgebers over the course of our entire life cycle. For example, social circumstances and how different stages of our life are 'regulated' and 'marketed' by our societal infrastructure and expectations are likely to influence how we behave as children, young adults, middle aged or old folk. How active we are and how we change how we behave as we move through our life span may not be related just to the physical ageing processes slowing down the function of our bodies but may also be related to us 'fitting into' the behaviour and behavioural patterns acceptable for each period of our lives as so eloquently described in the poem by William Shakespeare about the 'seven stages of man'. So, in effect a social zeitgeber may exist which regulates our social and physical behaviour over our entire life cycle, which is not just related to our own body's age-related changes, but also due to society's expectations and behavioural norms for each specific age we pass through during our lifetime.

Zeitgebers don't seem to be just a human specific phenomenon. For many years each Sunday morning when I woke up, I drove to our local village shop to buy the newspapers and supplies and took my dog for the drive. After a while doing this, each Sunday morning he (the dog) would be waiting patiently by the door before I arrived for this weekly drive to the shop, which was always astonishing to me from an academic perspective. This example obviously highlights the importance of the need for an awareness of the passing of time / the presence of internal clocks as being essential for the function of social zeitgebers, but in a typical 'chicken and egg' scenario, it is not clear if the zeitgebers set the internal clocks that allowed my dog to be aware that it was Sunday morning and therefore time to wait by the door for his weekly drive, or if internal clocks set the social zeitgeber activities by supplying the information to the dog that it was time for him to go and wait for the expected drive. Perhaps like everything, both possibilities are to a degree correct, and both the zeitgeber and the internal clock play an interactive role in my dog's routine weekly behaviour, as it does mine.

So going back to my discussion about looking forward in a few months' time to understanding the entire year of my work cycle, the zeitgeber concept would indicate that firstly I / we are perhaps 'entrained' by our work cycles in a zeitgeber manner we don't realize, and secondly that we actually need or want to be so 'entrained', and feel somewhat 'adrift' if we don't have the knowledge and security that come with the awareness of being immersed in the yearly patterns of our work / holiday cycles, and therefore that zeitgebers maintain not just our body's physiological activity, but also our social wellbeing. There is evidence that disruption of zeitgebers / our cyclical routines can lead to psychopathology such as mood disorders and even depression. Equally, there is evidence that psychopathology is also inherent in some of the zeitgeber cycles themselves, for example in the Northern hemisphere there is increased incidence of seasonal affective disorder (depression) during the dark months of winter, and that most folk find the last week before payday in January to be the most depressing time of the year for several obvious reasons. So roll on the completion of my first full year in my current job, so both consciously and perhaps subconsciously I can understand and adjust to the zeitgeber function my work life creates for me, even if this security does come with the worry about who actually is in control of my life, myself or all the zeitgebers that 'entrain' me in either daily, monthly, seasonal, yearly, and even lifelong cycles that one just cannot escape from, and from which it perhaps would not be optimal indeed to do so.

Essay 50. Fractals - The beauty of life as evidence of underlying purposive control design processes

One of the most fascinating contemporary breakthroughs, or perhaps observations, in science, was by Benoit Mandelbrot, who brought to our attention the concept of fractals, which are irregular shapes which when broken up into smaller parts, create smaller similarly irregular shapes that look identical to the larger dimension objects. Examples are all around us, from the coastline of countries, which are similarly 'jagged' when looked at using a 1:100 map as they do on a 1:1000 000 map. Equally, snowflakes, or the ongoing branching of tree branches, or lung alveoli, show fractal properties, as do non-physical activities, such as the beating of the heart. What is even more bewildering about fractals is that they can be modelled using mathematical equations, which indicates that there is 'order' and 'structure' to the observable irregularity present at all magnifications of the object. In this Essay, therefore, we try and makes sense of fractals, and how them having been discovered has altered our understanding of the world and how many structures in it are created.

Reading an excellent research article on the effect of fatigue on the fractal nature of force output by my fellow academic and friend Mark Burnley and seeing the large tracts of snow that covered the United Kingdom the last few weeks got me thinking of fractal theory, a concept which I have become increasingly interested in during the last decade or so of my research career. A broad definition of fractals is that they are rough or fragmented geometric shapes that can be split into parts, each of which is an approximate copy of the original whole. Examples of fractals are all around us, from snowflakes to the branching of a tree or vines, to the coastline of a country, to our own lungs, intestines and blood vessels, to the patterns of weather and tides, all of which exhibit fractal geometry and dimensions. Fractals have become popularized in art and paintings, and many folks will be aware of fractals through curtains, floor mats or wall art that display fractal art in all its beauty.

While fractal theory, and its twin theories chaos theory and complex system theory have been studied for many years, the concept of fractals was popularized in the 1970s by the pioneering work of Benoit Mandelbrot, who coined the word from the Latin term 'fractus', which describes a 'broken stone'. He used this word to describe 'fractured' shapes and geometry that focused on broken, wrinkled, and uneven shapes, which of course is what most shapes around us in nature are. In the 'normal' geometry we learn at school and most remember geometry as – Euclidean geometry – shapes are regular, for example triangles, rectangles, and squares. Fractal geometry is a description and a way of measuring irregular shapes and qualities that have no clear way of being measured using classical Euclidian mathematical techniques, such as degree of roughness, 'brokenness' or irregularity of an object. Mandelbrot first worked in economics, where before his work economists believed that small daily changes in share and stock prices had nothing to do with large / long term changes. But he looked at the patterns of share fluctuations over, first years, then months, then days, then hours, and found astonishingly that the variable curves for each time period of share price data he examined were almost perfectly matched. In other words, despite the share prices fluctuating seemingly randomly when viewed over a set time period, the changes were 'self-similar' whatever the time duration examined was varied. This indicated that some organizational 'pattern' or principle was occurring with the stock prices that 'cut across' / was universal to whatever time frame of change that had occurred. In what he became most well-known for, Mandelbrot showed similar self-similar patterns occurred when examining the coastline of the United Kingdom. The pattern of the entire coastline is never a straight line and is always variable and constantly different when viewed on a map, but when he looked at a section of the coastline compared to the whole coastline, it had a similar looking 'fractal' pattern, and when he looked at an even smaller section of that sub-section, it looked the same / had the same 'pattern'. So, as he described, this is the key feature of fractal shapes, that they are 'self-similar' no matter how much one 'zooms in' on them. As one zooms in on a fractal shape, no new detail emerges and nothing changes pattern-wise, with the same pattern repeating no matter how small an area one zooms in on. Therefore, if one looks at a snowflake or part of a human's lung, then zooms in on a component of each of them, the sub-contents will have a similar pattern and organization that will occur similar to what was seen at the initial scale of viewing of it.

What is perhaps even more interesting than the concept of fractal geometry in physical and anatomy structures is that there appears to be fractal geometry to the patterns or traces of our daily activity and physiological function over time, for example our heartbeat, walking patterns, or our brain's neuronal function. If you graph all these parameters at a high enough data capture rate, they exhibit a variable pattern that seems random, but has a fractal, and therefore ordered structure to them that looks similar if you look at either the entire physiological activity data trace or a component of it. Working with Andre Bester, Ross Tucker and other folk in the lab I worked in at the University of Cape Town several years ago, we showed that the power output trace of cyclists performing a 20-km time trial had fractal characteristics, and Mark Burnley's interesting data described above showed that when extending the knee in an isometric (non-moving) contraction against resistance, the natural variable fluctuations in muscle activity one has when doing such an ongoing muscle contraction also have a fractal dimension. So, during all activities of daily living, while we are not aware of it, our bodies appear to perform activities and have physiological function that is very structured and is performed according to some geometric design principle which seems random and variable when viewed with the naked eye, but is fractal in nature.

From a 'control of life' perspective, the most astonishing thing about fractals to me is that when scientists, mathematicians and computer programmers began working in the field of fractal theory, they found they were able to generate intricate fractal shapes and reproduce the fractal geometry found in nature and our bodies, on their computer screens, using fairly simple non-linear equations and computer coding programs. For those mathematical minded folk, the key component of the computer programs and equations that generate fractal design is that they have feedback components that are iterative – namely when the equation generates an outcome value and it is fed back into the equation in a repetitive (iterative) manner, the equations' outcomes when graphed shows the beautiful fractal shapes that are all around us, in our bodies, and which are evident as the coastline of the United Kingdom and how it developed, for example, or how stock prices fluctuate during a day, month or year. This concept of an iterative equation underpinning life form and function becomes a concern for geneticists, from the perspective that the 'language' of regulation for those working in the gene field is that life is controlled and regulated by individual, or arrays of specific genes activated sequentially in time. However, when looking at life and its regulation from this fractal 'nature' perspective, there would need to be an equation type activity occurring which would ultimately regulate and 'synchronize' the activity of all components of our life and earth structures, and it is of course perhaps impossible to 'find' an equation in any gene structure or physical domain. So, where these 'equation' based life processes come from and how they are controlled are some of life's big questions – which come first, the equation controlling the 'whole' of life, or the specifics of life which then built up to a 'whole' that incorporates the equation. In either scenario, one can't get away from the concept that an equation-related process underpins all current and past life activity, and it is difficult to get one's 'head around' this concept, using the current theories of how life began and is regulated. When I describe these concepts in academic lectures I give, with a half-smile I always end my lectures by saying that God, or whoever created us, must surely have been a mathematician. Each time one sees snow fall, or clouds develop in an otherwise blue sky, or feel the pulse of a patient to determine their heartbeat characteristics, one should and can only marvel not just at the beauty of life itself and its manifest detail all around us, but at the intricate processes and requirements which appear to 'govern' both its development and its very existence. It's going to be fascinating to see how these concepts help us uncover and understand the 'big concepts' in life, which to this point in time have been beyond our capacity to understand, and which remain mysterious, even if they are beautiful mysteries at that.

Essay 51. Holism - The sum of any systems parts creates something more than its component parts

While in recent times his star has burned less bright due to the racist policies of the government of which he was leader of, surely one of the most astonishing individuals to exist on planet Earth was Jan Christian Smuts. Apart from being a war leader and later Prime Minister of South Africa, he was also a Field Marshal in the British Army and in the war cabinets of the United Kingdom in both first and second world wars. Astonishingly, while doing all this, he was an admirer of botany and science, and wrote an incredible book on the general unitary concept of holism in the 1920s, which is still ahead of its time when read today. In this Essay we look at the concept of Holism, which suggests that the 'whole' is always greater than the sum of its 'parts' and is related to the concept of 'Emergence', which suggests similarly that something greater is created by the joining of two or more things, and attempt to describe how such a busy man as Smuts could have delivered to the world such astonishing observations and theories.

A recent and perhaps much needed debate in South Africa on the role of icons of the past in the makeup of its history and culture got me thinking of one of South Africa's greatest statesmen, Jan Smuts, and some astonishing theoretical writing he did that had a major influence on my career and research thinking. While Smuts had blind spots as a leader, such as his lack of effort to solve the race issues which bedevilled South Africa in the 20th Century, he also had an amazing life and was perhaps the ultimate polymath, filling roles such as Prime Minister of his country, Boer War Field General, Oxford trained lawyer, Field Marshal in the British Army, and strategic confidante and 'revered uncle' to Winston Churchill, amongst his other life successes. But what is not well known about Smuts was his interest in nature and the control of life processes, and that he wrote a book called 'Holism' which was published in 1926, that I have read many times and which has pride of place on my bookshelf, and was simply 'way ahead of its time' in the concepts it outlined such as his philosophical response to Darwinism, whose tenets were very much in vogue (and obviously still are) when he wrote it.

Holism, as described by Smuts, and its partner philosophy, Emergence, proposes the idea that all natural systems should be viewed as 'wholes', which while made up of 'parts', have characteristics associated with their whole system that are more than can be explained by simply understanding and examining all their parts. While any system, be it physical, chemical, biological, psychological, or social, can surely have no separate existence without its underlying components, they can and do form more complex behaviour as a collective when the component parts operate as part of the complete system being observed. For example, at the level of physics, particles and how they interact create activity and behaviour which are associated with 'laws' developed by physicists to explain the observed behaviour at this physical level, such as the laws of thermodynamics, Einstein's theory of relativity, and Heisenberg's uncertainty principle. However, this subatomic activity 'creates' activity at a 'higher' level, namely chemistry, which is the study of the substances which are responsible for creating 'matter', which operate and 'work' under a different set of rules and properties, that cannot be explained by looking at behaviour at the subatomic level as physicists do. Similarly, chemical reactions and combinations of matter make up biological process such as occur in our body, which again while composed of chemical matter, operate very differently and appear to have a 'life of its own – the life as we physically know it – as what occurs at the chemical level. Again, psychology and our conscious interpretation of life 'arises' from physical processes, but are different to them, and social interactions occur as a result of our psychological drives and physical activity, but operate again in different ways, and with different properties, that would not be able to be predicted from observing activity at the underlying levels. So, at each 'higher' level, in the best holistic principles, actions occur which cannot be understood by observing and understanding activity at a 'lower' level or hierarchy – though physicists of course believe their level of academic interest is the 'highest' form of understanding and would not appreciate being described as occupying the 'lowest' level of system activity!

Holism and its twin concept Emergence are in opposition to the concept of reductionism, which suggests that to best understand a system one observes, one should simplify the issue and examine one component of the system, and by understanding that one component, one has a better chance of understanding the system in its entirety. The reductionistic approach in science has 'held sway' for at least the last century, which has resulted in the 'primacy of the gene' and the success of molecular biology in understanding how very specific processes in biology occur, has focussed neuroscience on examining how single, or indeed multiple, cells in the brain fire and interact with each other, or how in physics particles interact with each other or other particles at the subatomic level, such as the Higgs Boson, which physicists believe has recently been 'found' to occur as a real entity. But while the reductionist approach is great for demonstrating 'new' activity or processes in the body, it does not help us explain how, for example, all genes in the body are coordinated in a three dimensional and both spatial and temporal manner to create the incredibly complex physical human which we are, it does not help explain how consciousness arises from the neurons whose firing rate is being examined, and it does not explain how the subatomic particles work as a 'gestalt' in both creating physical matter, or heck, whether subatomic particle activity is involved with, or whether it can 'influence', our conscious thoughts and social interactions.

The pendulum of how science is done is now to a degree 'swinging back' to a more 'holistic' / emergent / gestalt (another popular word associated with defining holistic processes) way of attempting to understand these more 'big picture' questions that reductionistic scientific methods will never likely be able to answer (though in science, one can never say never!), and fields such as complex system science, chaos and fractal theory, have attempted to explore and explain the emergent properties of systems, and the 'big' questions that still await explanation. Why the ground-breaking philosophical work of Jan Smuts is so difficult to accept and is largely ignored by most folk in science, is because it is so hard to test and explain, and also generates uncomfortable / very difficult questions for research folk, such as that it is difficult for theories like evolution to 'explain' concepts like emergence, and it brings into play philosophical concepts such as Universals (in the best Platonic tradition), which are of course intangible and create the 'which comes first' in the development of life conundrum – the 'map of how it all works', or its component parts. But that does not mean that surely a future generation will develop the laboratory techniques that will enable us to understand Holism related processes, and perhaps by doing so will help us explain the 'big questions' described above which to date defy explanation, and which are so important to our understanding of 'life' and how it works. A physicist working at the subatomic level will surely show us great things which we can (and do) all marvel at, but until the physicists understand that they are working within the constraints of a 'closed system' approach, and until they understand that biology, and indeed psychology and social behaviour will affect activity at the sub-atomic level in our bodies (dare I say control it?), and work in big cross-discipline teams to develop holistic methods of understanding life's properties, we will surely be 'stuck in first gear' and keep on working in closed silos, which will surely lead to great understanding of each silo, but perhaps not understand how 'it all' fits together to create the life as we know it, and that which we don't.

So, going back to Jan Smuts and his brilliant book describing holism, which he wrote amidst a period when he must have been working huge hours on a variety of 'big issues' that come with governing a country, leading nations in times of war, and influencing the thinking of great leaders, made me think how brilliant such folk are who are able to do so, and think about, so many things at once. Perhaps though, it is the very capacity of such folk such as Smuts to multi-task, and who 'juggle many plates' at any one time, who are the folk that are able to see the 'big picture' and that after a century or more of the specialist, perhaps it is time once more for the concept of the 'renaissance person' / polymath individual to take up a more pre-eminent place in the academic and world stage. Perhaps Smuts developed his innovative ideas from his own work managing large and complex organizational systems, which made him realize that changes in one area of the organization did not affect the 'whole'. Perhaps like everything, life and scientific discovery occurs in cyclical phases, and we are at the cusp of moving from a reductionist to a 'holistic' way of understanding things, as we seek to make use of the astonishing scientific discoveries of the last few decades developed by reductionistic folk working in their labs and computer rooms, in a 'bringing it all together' manner which will help us understand how it 'all' works. But whatever happens going forward, hopefully the brilliant work and thinking of Jan Smuts and others which has in many ways been 'lost in time', will take its rightful place in the pantheon of great academic achievements, as it surely deserves. Whether he deserves to have a statue put up to acknowledge his excellent academic work, in the face of his leadership 'blind spots' and in the context of South Africa's history and current issues, is for another discussion, of course.

Essay 52. Strategy, tactics, and objectives - In the words of the generals, you can't bake a cake without breaking a few eggs

Strategy and tactics are unifying principles that are the bread and butter of any military institutions, and any leader worth their salt in any leadership position in any discipline, be it business, academia, politics, or sport, will have a 'strategy' for what they plan to do, that they are usually very vocal in telling their team about, and not just once, but at every meeting they chair. There are many definitions of strategy, but to me the most relevant is that it is a plan to achieve an objective that uses available resources in the best possible way in the presence of conflicting options. Unfortunately, a number of truly terrible leaders also like to fling the word strategy about, and put down or fire anyone who does not agree with the strategy they propose, while not realising the definition includes 'available resources' and 'best possible way', and is linked to a 'doable' objective, rather than one which is impossible, or does not take into account available resources and burns out their team, or uses a seemingly clever 'lateral' option which is manifestly clear to all that have to put it into practice is not the best one available. In this Essay, therefore, we examine the concepts of strategy and tactics, and, how they are fundamentally linked to objectives which need to be set before any strategy can be set or adhered to, and how errors are so easily made in setting strategy and tactics.

I have always enjoyed reading history, and particularly military history, both as a hobby and as a way of learning from the past to better understand the currents and tides of political and social life that 'batter one' during one's three score and ten years on Earth, no matter how much one tries to avoid them. Compared to folk who lived in the first half of the twentieth century, I perceive that we have lived our contemporary lives in an environment that is relatively peaceful from the context that there has been no world-war or major conflict for the last 70 or 80 years, though the world-wide political fluxes recently, particularly in the USA and Europe / UK, are worrying, as is the rising nationalism, divisive 'single choice' politics, intolerance of minorities, and increasing number of refugees searching for better lives, all eerily reminiscent of what occurred in the decade before the American Civil War and both World Wars. I recently read (or actually re-read – a particularly odd trait of mine is that I often read books a dozen or more times if I find something in them important or compelling from a learning perspective) a book on the Western Allies European military strategy in the Second World War, and of the disagreements that occurred between the United States General (and later President) Dwight Eisenhower and British General Bernard Montgomery over strategy and tactics used during the campaign, and how this conflict damaged relations between the military leaders of the two countries almost irreparably. I also re-read two autobiographies of soldiers involved in the war, the first by Major Dick Winters, who was in charge of a Company (Easy Company) of soldiers in the 506th Parachute Infantry Regiment of the 101st USA Airborne Division, and the second an (apparently) autobiographical book written by Guy Sajer (if that was indeed his name), a soldier in the German Wehrmacht, about his personal experiences first as a lorry driver, then as a soldier on the Eastern Front in the Gross Deutschland Division, and was struck by how different both the two books were in content compared to the one on higher European military strategy, and also how different the experiences were between Generals and foot soldiers, even though they were all involved in the same conflict. All this got me thinking of objectives, strategy, and tactics, and how they are set, and how they impact on the folk that have to carry them out.

Both strategy and tactics are developed in order to achieve a particular objective (also known as a goal). An objective is defined as a desired result that a person or system envisions, plans, and commits to achieve.

The leaders of most organizations, whether they are military, political, academic, or social set out several objectives they would like to achieve, for the greater good of the organization they lead (though it is never acknowledged, of course, that they – the leaders – will get credit or glory for achieving the objective, and that this is often an 'underlying' objective in itself). To achieve an objective, a leader, or group of leaders, set a particular strategy in order to do so. There are several different definitions of strategy, including it being a 'high level' plan to achieve an objective under conditions of uncertainty, or making decisions about how to best use resources available in the presence of often conflicting options, requirements, and challenges in order to achieve a particular objective. The concept underpinning strategic planning is to set a plan / course of action that is believed to be best suited to achieve the objective, and then stick to that plan until the objective is achieved. If conditions change in a way that makes sticking to the strategy difficult, then tactics are used to compensate and adjust to the conditions while 'maintaining' the overall strategic plan. Tactics as a concept are often confused with strategy – but are in effect the means and methods of how a strategy is implemented, adhered to, and maintained, and can be altered in order to maintain the chosen strategy.

What is strategy and what are tactics becomes challenging when there are different 'levels' of command in an organization, with lower levels having more specific objectives that are individually required to achieve the over-arching objective, but which require the creation of specific 'lower-level' strategy, to reach the specific objective being set, even if the objective is a component of a higher-level strategic plan. From the viewpoint of the planners that create the high-level / general objective strategy, the lower-level plans / specific objectives would be tactics. From the viewpoint of the planners that set the lower-level strategy needed to complete a specific component of the general strategy, their 'lower level' plans would be (to them) strategy rather than tactics, with tactics being set at even lower levels in their specific area of command / management, which in turn could set up a further 'debate' about what is strategy and what is tactics at these even 'lower' level of command. Even the poor foot soldier, who is a 'doer' rather than a 'planner' of any strategic plan or tactical action enacted as part of any higher level of command, would have their own objectives beyond those of the 'greater plan', most likely that of staying alive, and would have his or her own strategic plan to both fulfil the orders given to them, but stay alive, and tactics of how to do so. So, in any organization, there are multiple levels of planning and objective setting, and what is strategy and what is tactics often becomes confused (and often commanders at lower levels of command find orders given to them inexplicable, as they don't have awareness of how their specific orders fit into the 'greater strategic plan'), and this requires constant management by those at each level of command.

It is perhaps not being clear about what the specific objectives behind the creation of a particular strategy are which causes most command conflict and is what happened in the later stages of the Second World War as one of the main causes of the deterioration of the relationship between Dwight Eisenhower and Bernard Montgomery. The objective of the Allies in Western Europe was relatively simple – enter Europe and defeat Germany (though of course the war was mostly won and lost on the Eastern Front due to Russian sacrifice and German strategic confusion) – but it was the strategy of how this was to happen which led to the inter-ally conflict, of which so much has been written. Eisenhower was the supreme Allied Commander, and responsible for all the Allied troops in Western Europe, and for setting the highest level of strategic planning. He decided on a 'broad front' strategy, where different Army Groups advanced eastwards across Europe after the breakout from Normandy, in a line from the northern coast of Europe to the southern coastline of Mediterranean Europe. Montgomery was originally the commander of all Allied ground troops in Europe, then after the Normandy breakout became commander of the 21st Army group, which was predominantly made up of British and Commonwealth troops (but also containing a large contingent of American troops), and he favoured a single, 'sharp' method of attacking one specific region of the Front (of course choosing an area for attack in his own region of command). Montgomery's doctrine was that which most strategic manuals would favour, and Eisenhower was sharply criticized by military leaders both during and after the war for going against the accepted strategic 'thinking' of that time. But Eisenhower, of course, had not just military objectives to think about, but also had political requirements too, and had to maintain harmony between not just American and British troops and nations, but also a number of Commonwealth countries' troops and national requirements. If he had chosen one specific 'single thrust' strategy, as Montgomery demanded, he would have had to choose either a British dominated or American dominated attack, led by either a specific British or American commander, and neither country would have 'tolerated' such 'favouritism' on his part, and this issue was surely a large factor when he decided on a 'broad front' strategy. There was clearly military strategic thinking on his part too – 'single thrust' strategies can be rapidly 'beaten back' / 'pinched off' if performed against a still-strong military opposition, as was the case when Montgomery chose to attack on a very narrow line to Arnhem, and this was more than a 'bridge too far' – the German troops simply shut off the 'corridor' of advance behind the lead troops and the Allies were forced to withdraw in what was a tactical defeat for them. Montgomery criticized Eisenhower's 'broad front' as leading to, or allowing, the 'Battle of the Bulge' to occur, when the German armies in late-1944 counter-attacked through the Belgium Ardennes region towards Antwerp, and caused a 'reverse bulge' in the Allied 'broad front' line, but in effect the rapidity with which the Allies closed down and defeated this last German 'counter-thrust' paradoxically provided evidence against the benefits of Montgomery's 'single thrust' strategy, even though he used the German Ardennes offensive to condemn Eisenhower's 'broad front' strategy. Perhaps Eisenhower should have been more clear about the political nature of his objectives and the political requirements of his planning, but then he would have been criticized for allowing political factors to 'cloud' what should have been purely military decisions (at least by his critics), so like many leaders setting 'high level' strategy, he was 'doomed' to be criticized whatever his strategic planning was, even if the 'proof was in the pudding' – his chosen strategy did win the war, and did so in less than a year after it was initiated, after the Allies had been at war for more than five years before the invasion of Western Europe was planned and initiated.

Whatever the 'high level' strategic decision made by the Generals, the situation 'on the ground' for Company leaders and foot soldiers who had to enact these strategies was very different, as was well described in the books by Dick Winters (the book became a highly praised TV series – Band of Brothers) and Guy Sajer. Most of the individual company level actions in which Easy company participated in bordered on the shambolic – from the first parachute drop into enemy held France where most of the troops were scattered so widely that they fought mainly skirmishes in small units, to operations supporting Montgomery's 'thrust' to Arnhem which were a tactical failure and resulted in them withdrawing in defeat, to the battle of Bastogne which was a key component of the battle of the 'Bulge', where they just avoided defeat and sustained heavy casualties, and only just managed to 'hold on' until reinforcements arrived. A large number of their operations described were therefore not tactically successful, yet played their part in a grand strategy which led to ultimate success. The impact of the 'grand strategy' on individual soldiers was horrifyingly (but beautifully from a writing perspective) described and a must read for any prospective military history 'buffs' in Guy Sajer's autobiography – most of his time was spent marching in bitter cold or thick mud from one area of the Eastern Front to another as his Division was required to stem yet another Russian breakthrough, or trying to find food with no formal rations being brought up to them as the Wehrmacht operational management collapsed in the last phases of the war, or watching his friends being killed one by one in horrific ways as the Russian army grew more successful and more aggressive in their desire for both revenge and military success. There was no obvious pattern or strategy to what they were doing at the foot soldier level, there were no military objectives that could be made sense of at the individual level he described, rather there was only the 'brute will to survive', and to kill or be killed, and only near the end, did he (and his company level leaders) realize that they were actually losing the war, and their defeat would mean the annihilation of Germany and everything they were fighting for 'back home'. Yet it was surely the individual actions of soldiers in their thousands and millions that endured and died for either side, that in a gestalt way led to the strategic success (or failure) planned for by their leaders and generals, even if at their individual level they could make little sense of the benefit of their sacrifice in the context of the broader tactical and strategic requirements, in the times when they could reflect on this, though surely most of their own thoughts were on surviving anther terrible day, or another terrible battle, rather than on its 'meaning' or relevance.

One of the quotes that I have read in military history texts that has caused me to reflect most about war and strategy as an 'amateur' military history enthusiast is attributed to British World War Two Air Marshal Peter Portal, who when discussing some what he believed to be defective strategic planning with his colleague and army equal Field Marshal Alan Brooke, apparently suggested that 'one cannot make a cake without breaking some eggs'. What he was saying, if I understood it, and the comment indeed can be attributed to him, was that in order for a military strategy to be successful, some (actually most of the time probably many) individual solders have to be sacrificed and die for the 'greater good' which would be a successfully achieved objective. From a strategic point of view, he was surely correct, and often Generals who don't take risks and worry too much about their soldiers' safety can paradoxically often cause more harm than good by developing an overly cautious strategy which has an increased risk of failure and therefore an increased risk of more soldiers dying. But from a human point of view the comment is surely chilling, as each soldier's individual death, often in brutal conditions, is horrific both to those that it happens to and those relatives, friends and colleagues that survive them. Often, or perhaps most of the time, individual soldiers die without any real understanding of the strategic purpose behind their death, and with a wish just to be with their loved ones again, and to be far from the environment and actions which cause their death. The folk at senior leadership levels setting grand strategy require a high degree of moral courage to 'see it through' to the end, knowing that their strategy will surely lead to many individual deaths. The folks who enact the grand strategy 'in the trenches' need a high degree of physical courage to perform the required actions to do so in conditions of grave danger, that as a small part of the 'big picture' may help lead to strategic success and attainment of the set objectives, usually winning in a war sense. But every side has its winners and its losers, and there is usually little difference between these for the foot soldier or Company leader, who dies in either a winning or losing cause, with little knowledge of how their death has contributed in any way to either winning or losing a battle, or campaign, or war.

Without objectives, strategy and tactics, there would never be any successful outcome to any war, and a lot of soldiers would die. With objectives, tactics and strategy, there is a greater chance of a successful outcome to any war, but a lot of soldiers will still surely die. The victory cake tastes wonderful always, but always, sadly, to make such a 'winners' cake, many eggs do indeed need to be broken. It will long be controversial which is more important in the creation of the cake, the recipe or the eggs that make it up. Similarly, it will long be controversial whether it is relevant if a 'broad front' or 'single thrust' strategy was the correct strategic or tactical approach to winning the war in Western Europe. But the foot solder would surely not care whether his or her death was in the cause of tactical or strategic requirements or happened during a 'broad front' or 'single thrust' strategy, when he or she is long dead and long forgotten, and historians are debating which General deserves credit for planning the strategy, or lack of it, that caused their death. That's something I will ponder on as I reach for my next book on war strategy that fill the bookshelf next to my writing desk, and hope that my children will never be in the position of having to be either the creators, or enactors, of military strategy, tactics, and objectives.

Essay 53. Plato's horse and the concept of universals - Can you have life as we know it without rules that govern it

One of the greatest conundrums in science, and indeed philosophy, is not which came first, the chicken or the egg, but rather what came first, the independent 'representation' or 'map' of the chicken, or the chicken itself. From the time of Plato, the question of 'Universals', which are these 'representations' of all things from which all things are made, has been much greatly pondered on. When we think of a dog, we understand that the term refers to a whole range of different looking and types of dogs, but we instinctively 'know' that a dog is a dog. In this Essay we examine the concept of Universals, and if they exist, where and how are they 'stored' and 'maintained' as unchangeable 'entities' we refer to as reference points when we think of a 'dog', or 'human' or whatever it is that we are thinking about. This is perhaps one of the greatest puzzles of our time, and it is difficult to see how these Universals if they exist will ever be 'found' or be able to be 'examined' by us scientifically. But despite this, they remain as one of the most fascinating concepts I have come across in a lifetime in science.

My young daughter's precious Labrador puppy, Violet, has grown up, and recently turned two. As a family, we usually traditionally have Schnauzers as pets, and it's been strange but nice to have a different breed around the home, and Labradors have great personalities. What struck me forcibly when Violet came into our life, was that while she has a very different shape and form to our two Schnauzers, she is as instantly recognisable as a dog, as all our dogs are. It again struck me when the family watched a programme on the most loved one hundred dog breeds in the UK (for those interested, Labradors came in first), that while each of the different breeds had very different characteristics – think Chihuahua as compared to a Great Dane, or a Pug compared to a German Shepherd – they are were all instantly recognisable by our family members watching it, and I am sure just about all the folk who watched the programme, as being dogs rather than cats, or lamas, or sheep. In the last few years of my academic career (and perhaps at a subconscious level for my entire research career), after having been an Integrative Control Systems scientist for most of my career, trying to understand how our different body systems and functions are controlled and maintained in an optimal and safe manner, I have come to understand, and have been exploring the concept, along with great collaborators Dr Jeroen Swart and Professor Ross Tucker, that perhaps general rules are operating across all body system control mechanisms, whatever their shape or form, and we recently published a theoretical research paper which described our thoughts. In my new role as Deputy Dean of Research at the University of Essex, I am fortunate to be working with the Department of Mathematics, helping them enhance their research from an organisational perspective, and it has been fascinating working with these supremely bright folk and seeing the work they do, and having it reiterated to me that even simple mathematical principles are abstract, and not grounded in anything in the physical world (for example knowing that one plus two equals three does not need any physical activity for it to be always true). All these recent activities have got me thinking of the much-pondered issue of universals, their relationship to rules and regulations governing and maintaining life, and which came first, the rules, or the physical activity that requires rules and regulations to be maintained in order for the physical activity to continue and be both organised and productive.

Universals are defined as a class of mind-independent (indeed human-independent) entities which are usually contrasted with individuals (also known as 'particulars' relative to 'universals'), and which are believed to 'ground' and explain the relation of qualitative identity and resemblance among all individuals. More simply, they are defined as the nature or essence of a group of like objects described by a general term. For example, in the case of dogs described above, when we see a dog, whether it is a Labrador, Schnauzer, German Shepherd, or myriad other breeds, we 'know' it to be a dog, and the word dog is used to cover the 'essence' of all these and other breeds. Similarly, we know what a cat is, or a house, or shoes, despite each of these 'types of things' often looking very different to each other – there are clearly enough characteristics in each to define them by a universal defining name. Understanding universals gets even more complex though than merely thinking of them as being just a name or group of properties for a species or 'type of thing'. Long ago, back in the time of antiquity, one of the first recorded philosophical debates was about universals, and whether they existed independently as abstract entities, or only as a term to define an object, species or 'type of thing'. Plato suggested that a universal exists independent of that which they define and are the true 'things which we know', even if they are intangible and immeasurable, with the living examples of them being copies and / or imitations of the universal, each varying slightly from the original universal, but bound in their form by the properties defined by the universal. In other words, he suggested that universals are the 'maps' of structures or forms which exist as we see and know them, for example a dog, or a horse, or a tree, and they exist in an intangible state somehow in the 'ether' around us, 'directing' the creation of the physical entities in some way which we have not determined or are currently capable of understanding.

In philosophical terms, this theory of universals as independent entities is known as Platonic Realism. After Plato came Aristotle, who felt that universals are 'real entities', like Plato perceived them to be, but in his theory (known as Aristotelian Realism), he suggested that universals did not exist independent of the particulars, or species, or 'things' they defined, and were linked to their physical existence, and would not exist without the physical entities they 'represent'. In contrast to realism, Nominalism is a theory that developed after the work of these two geniuses (Nominalists are also sometimes described as Empiricists) which denied the existence of universals completely, and suggested that physical 'things', or particulars, shared only a name, and not qualities that defined them, and that universals were not necessary for the existence of species or 'things'. Idealism (proposed by folk like Immanuel Kant) got around the problem of universals by suggesting that universals were not real, but rather were products of the minds of 'rational individuals', when thinking of that which they were looking at.

This dilemma of both the existence and nature of universals has to date not been solved, or adequately explained, given that it is impossible with current scientific techniques, or perhaps psychological 'power' in our minds, to be able to prove or disprove the presence of universals, and folk 'believe' in one of these different choices of universals depending on their world and life points of view. Religious folk would suggest that the world is created in God's 'image', and to them God's 'images' would be the universals from which all 'God's creatures' are created. In contrast, with respect to evolution, which is diametrically opposed to the concept of religion, it is difficult to believe in both evolution and the presence of universals, as evolution is based on the concept of need and error-driven individual genetic changes over millennia in response to that need, which led to different species developing, and to the variety in nature and life we see all around us. In the evolutionary model, therefore, the concept of universals (and the creation of the world by a God as posited by many religions) would appear to be counterintuitive.

While a lot of debate has focused on 'things one can see' as the physical 'particulars' which are either a product of universals or not, there are more abstract activities which support the existence of universals independent of the mind or 'things that they are involved with'. For example, the work done by Ross, Jeroen and me developed from the realisation that a core principle of all physiological activity is homeostasis, which is defined as the maintenance by regulatory control processes or structures of physiological or physical activity within certain tolerable limits, in order to protect the individual or thing being regulated from being damaged, or damaging itself. Underpinning all homeostatic control mechanisms is the negative feedback loop, where when a substance or activity increases or decreases too much, initiates other activity as part of a circular control structure which has the capacity to act on the substance requiring control, and normalises or attenuates the changes, and keeps the activity or behaviour within required 'safe levels', which are set by homeostatic control mechanisms.

The fascinating thing is that the same principle of negative feedback control loops occurs in all and any physical living system, and without these negative feedback loops, life could not occur. Whether gene activity, liver function, or whole-body activity, all of which have very different physical or metabolic regulatory structures and processes, all are controlled by negative feedback loop principles. Therefore, it is difficult not to perceive that the negative feedback loop is a type of universal, but one that works by similar 'action' across systems rather than 'creating' a physical thing in its likeness. Mathematics is another area in which folk believe universals are 'at work', given that even the simplest sums, such as one plus two equals three, needs no physical structure or 'particular' for them to always be such, and true. While we all use mathematical principles on a continuous basis, it is difficult to believe that such mathematical principles do not 'exist' in the absence of humans, or any physical shape or forms.

So where does all this leave us in understanding universals and their relevance to life as we know it? Perhaps what one's viewpoint is regarding the existence of universals depends on one's own specific epistemological perspective (understanding of the nature of knowledge and how it is related to one's justified beliefs) and world view. Though I can in no way prove it, I believe in universals and would define myself as a Platonic Realist. This viewpoint comes from a career in science and working with exceptional scientists like Jeroen Swart and Ross Tucker getting to understand the exquisite and universal nature of control mechanisms which keep our bodies working the way which they do. However, I do not believe in any God or religion in any shape or form, and have greater faith in the evolutionary model, which is counter-intuitive relative to my belief in the presence of independent universals. Therefore, the potential similarities and differences between religion and universals, and evolution and universals described above is clearly redundant for my specific beliefs, and there is probably similar confusion in core beliefs for many (particularly research involved) folks. However, it is exciting to think (at least for me) that there may be universals out there that have no link to current activities or functions or species, and which may become evident to humans at some point in the future, by way of the development of new species or new 'things'. Having said that, I guess it could be argued that if universals do not exist, progress and the evolution of ideas will lead us to new developments, species, or ways of life in an evolution-driven, error-associated way. One cannot 'see' or 'feel' a negative feedback loop, or a maths algorithm, or universal for even something as simple as a dog, which is why perhaps to a lot of folks with a different epistemological viewpoint to mine it is challenging to accept the presence, or indeed the necessity, of and for universals. But when I look at our Labrador, and 'know' as such it is a dog as much as a Schnauzer, Chihuahua, or German Shepherd is, I feel sure there is the Universal dog out there somewhere in the ether that will perhaps keep my toes warm when I leave this world for the great wide void which may exist beyond it. And surely, given what a stunning breed they are, the Universal dog, if it exists out there, can only be a Labrador.

Essay 54. Consistency of task outcome and the degrees of freedom problem - The brain is potentially not a micro-manager when providing solutions to complex problems

One of the most fascinating things in science is how the brain 'chooses' to respond to something in the external environment, or to some change in a body fuel, metabolite or cellular activity. There is usually one outcome wanted and required — usually returning the activity to baseline level, or catching a falling cup, or turning a car wheel as a corner in the road starts, amongst millions of other tasks — but each 'outcome' also has not one but many different solutions. For example, to catch a falling cup, one can use many different muscles in different way to align the arm in the right spatial dimension to catch the cup — literally millions of options of different muscle lengths and force outputs when considering each muscle in the arm. Equally, if body temperature increases, one can either take off some clothes, move into cooler surroundings, drink a cool glass of water, or all of the above. In this Essay, therefore, we examine how the brain and body 'chooses' from these millions of tactical options to complete the same task, and how it does not fail due to 'calculation overload' which could occur if each choice had to be assessed before activation, which would surely result in the cup never being caught.

Part of the reason I enjoy cycling as my chosen sport now I am older is not just because it is beneficial from a health perspective, but because the apparent regularity of the rhythmical circular movement required for pedalling creates a sense of peace in me and paradoxically allows my mind to wander a bit away from its routine and usually work-focussed and life task orientated thoughts. I enjoy watching competitive darts, from the perspective of marvelling at how the folk participating in the competitions seem to hit the small area of the board so often they are aiming for with such precision, after rapidly throwing their darts when it is their turn to do so. This week an old colleague and friend from University of Cape Town days, Dr Angus Hunter, published some interesting work on how the brain controls muscle activity during different experimental conditions, a field of which he is a world expert in, and it was great to read about his new research and innovative ideas as always. Some of the most fun times of my research career were spent in the laboratory working with Angus measuring muscle activity during movement related tasks, where one of our most challenging issues to deal with was the variability of the signal our testing devices recorded when measuring either the power output from, or electrical activity in, muscle fibres each time they contracted when a trial participant was asked to do the same task. A large part of the issue we had to solve then was whether this was signal 'noise' and an artefact of our testing procedures, or if it was part of the actual recruitment strategy the brain used to control the power output from the muscles. All of these got me thinking about motor control mechanisms, and how movement and activity is regulated in a way that gets tasks done in a seemingly smooth and co-ordinated way, often without us having to think about what we are doing, while when one measures individual muscle function it is actually very 'noisy' and variable, even during tasks which are performed with a high degree of accuracy, and how the brain either creates or 'manages' this variability and 'noise' to generate smooth and accurate rhythmical or target-focussed activity, as that which occurs when cycling and throwing darts respectively.

Some of the most interesting scientific work that I have ever read about was done by Nikolai Bernstein, a Russian neurophysiologist, who when working in the 1920s at the somewhat euphemistically named Moscow Central Institute of Labour, examined motor control mechanisms during movement. As part of the communist government of the times' centrally-driven plans to improve worker productivity and output, Bernstein did research on manual labour tasks such as hammering and cutting, to try and understand how to optimise it. Using novel 'cyclogram' photography techniques, where multiple pictures were taken of a worker using a hammer or chisel to which a light source had been attached, he was able to produce the astonishing observation that each time the worker hit a nail or cut through metal, their arm movements were not identical each time they performed the action, and rather that there was a great degree of variability each time the similar action was performed, even though usually this variability in action produced an outcome which had a high degree of accuracy. He realized that each complete movement, such as moving the arm towards the target, is made up of several smaller movements of muscles around the shoulder, elbow and wrist joints, which together synergistically create the overall movement. Given how many muscles there are in the arm, working around three joints (and potentially more when one thinks of the finger joints and muscles controlling them), he suggested that there were a very large number of potential combinations of muscle actions and joint positions that could be used for the same required action, and a different combination of these appeared to be 'chosen' by the brain each time it performed a repetitive task. From a motor control perspective, Bernstein deduced that this could potentially cause a problem for the brain, and whatever decision-making process decided on which movement pattern it would use to complete a task, given that it created a requirement for choosing a particular set of muscle synergies from a huge number of different options available, or in contrast not choosing all the other muscle synergistic options, each time the individual was required to perform a single task or continue performing a repetitive task. This would require a great amount of calculation and decision-making capacity on a repetitive basis by the brain / control processes, and he called this the motor redundancy, or degrees of freedom, problem.

Like a lot of work performed in the Stalin era in Russia, his fascinating work and observations did not become known to Western scientists until the 1960s, when he published a textbook of his career in science, which was subsequently translated and taken forward by excellent contemporary movement control scientists like Mark Latash of the University of Pennsylvania State in the USA. Further studies have supported Bernstein's earlier work, and it is astonishing how much variability there is in each movement trajectory of a complex action that is goal orientated. Mark has suggested that this is not a redundancy problem, but rather one of abundancy, with the multiple choices available being of benefit to the body of any individual performing repetitive tasks, potentially from a fatigue resistance and injury prevention perspective, which may occur if the same muscle fibres in the same muscle are used in the same way in a repetitive manner. Interestingly, when a person suffers a stroke or a traumatic limb injury, the quantity of movement variability appears to paradoxically reduce rather than increase after the stroke or injury, and this reduced variability of motor function is associated with a decrement in task performance accuracy and completion. Therefore, the high variability of movement patterns in healthy folk appears to paradoxically make task performance more accurate and not just more efficient.

How control processes choose a specific 'pattern' of muscle activity for a specific task is still not well known. A number of theories have been proposed (generally as a rule in science, the more theories there are about something, the more the likelihood there is that there is no clarity about it) with some quaint names, such as the equilibrium point hypothesis, which suggests that choice at the motor neuron level is controlled as part of the force-length relationship of the muscle; the uncontrolled manifold hypothesis, which suggests that the central nervous system focuses on the variables needed to control a task and ignores the rest (the uncontrolled manifold being those variables that do not affect task required activity); and the force control hypothesis, which suggests that the central nervous system compares the required movement for the task against internal models, and then uses calculations and feedforward and feedback control mechanisms to direct activity against that set by the internal model; amongst others. All these are interesting and intellectually rigorous theories, but don't tell us very much about exactly how the brain chooses a particular group of muscles to perform a task, and then subsequently a different group of muscles, which use a different flight trajectory, to perform the task again when it is repeated. It has been suggested that there are 'synergistic sets' of muscles which are chosen in their entirety for a single movement, and that the primitive reflexes or central pattern generators in the spinal cord may be involved. But the bottom line is that we just do not currently know exactly what control mechanism chooses a specific set of muscles to perform one movement of a repetitive task, why different muscles are chosen each time the same task is performed sequentially, or how this variable use of muscles for the same task is managed and controlled.

We have previously suggested that several other activities in the body beyond that of muscle control have similar redundancy (or abundancy) in how they are regulated, or at least in respect of which mechanisms are used to control them. For example, blood glucose concentrations can be controlled not only by changes in insulin concentrations, but also by that of glucagon, and can also be altered by changes in catecholamine (adrenaline or noradrenaline) or cortisol levels, and indeed by behavioural factors such as resisting the urge to eat. Each time blood glucose concentrations are measured, the concentrations of all these other regulatory hormones and chemicals will be different ratio-wise to each other, yet their synergistic levels at any one point in time maintain the level of blood glucose concentrations at homeostatically safe setpoint levels. The blood glucose level is maintained whatever the variability in the regulatory factor concentration ratios, and even though this variability in choice of control mechanisms similarly creates a potential for high computational load when managing blood glucose concentrations from a control perspective. Similarly, perception of mood state or emotions are thought to have redundancy in what factors 'creates' them. For example, we can fairly accurately rate when we feel slightly, moderately or very fatigued, but underpinning the 'feeling' of fatigue at the physiological level can be changes in blood glucose, heart rate, ventilation rate, and a host of other metabolites and substrates in the body, each of which can be altered in a variable ratio way to make up the sensation of fatigue we rate as slightly, moderately or very high levels of fatigue. Furthermore, fatigue is a complex sensation made up of individual sensations such as breathlessness, pounding chest, sweating, pain, and occasionally confusion, dizziness, headache and pins and needles, amongst others, a combination of which can also be differently factored to provide a similar general fatigue rating by whoever is perceiving the sensation of fatigue. To make it even more complex, the sensation of fatigue is related to inner voices which either rate the sensation of fatigue (the 'I' voice) or make a judgement on it related to social circumstances or family and environmental background (the 'Me' voice), and it is through the final combination of these that an individual finally rates their level of fatigue, which adds another level of redundancy, or abundancy, to the factors underpinning how the 'gestalt' sensation of fatigue is both created and perceived. There are therefore three potential 'levels' of redundancy / abundancy in the signals and factors which either individually or collectively make up the 'gestalt' sensation of fatigue, and a corresponding increased level of computational requirements potentially associated with its final genesis, and how this perceptual redundancy / abundancy is managed by the control mechanisms which generate them is still not well known.

In summary, therefore, the presence of variability during activities of daily living across a number of different body systems is not only 'noise' / artefacts of testing conditions which are challenges for us researchers to have to deal with; it also appears to be part of some very complex control mechanisms which must have some teleological benefit both for optimizing movement and activity, and ensuring the capacity to sustain it without fatigue or injury to the components of the mechanism which produces it. Each time I cycle on my bike and my legs move up and down to push the wheels forward, different muscles are being used in a different way during each rotation of the wheel. Each time a darts player throws a dart, different muscle synergies are used to paradoxically create the accuracy of their throw. There is real 'noise' that a researcher has to remove from their recorded traces after a testing session in a laboratory, such as that caused by the study participant sweating during the trial, which can affect electrophysiological signals, and there is always a degree of measurement error, and therefore some degree of 'noise' is present in the variability of the recorded output for any laboratory technique that measures human function. But, equally, Bernstein's brilliant work and observations all those years ago helped us understand that variability is inherent in living systems, and after understanding this, each time I observe data, particularly that generated during electrophysiological work such as I have used for a number of experiments in my own research career, including electromyography (EMG), electroencephalography (EEG) or transcranial magnetic stimulation (TMS), which has low standard deviations in the results sections of published research articles, I do wonder at the validity of the data and whether it has been 'paint brushed' by the researchers who describe it, as my old Russian neurophysiology research colleague Mikhail Lomarev used to describe it, when he or we thought data was 'suspect'. The inherent variability in brain and motor control systems makes finding statistical significance in results generated using routine neurophysiological techniques more difficult. It also seems to create a huge increase in the requisite control-related calculations and planning for even a simple movement, though as Mark Latash suggested, the brain is likely to not be a micro-manager, but rather some effective parsing mechanism which can both generate and utilize many synergistic movement patterns in a variable manner for any task, while not utilizing much decision-making power using some sort of heuristic-based decision-making mechanism. Most importantly though, it fills one with a sense of awe at the 'magic' of our own body, and for the level of complexity involved in both its creation and operative management, when even a simple movement like striking an object with a hammer, or cutting a piece of metal, can be underpinned by such complex control mechanisms that our brains cannot currently comprehend or make sense of.

In a laboratory in the middle of Russia nearly a century ago, Nikolai Bernstein made some astonishing observations by doing exceptional research on basic motor control, while trying to increase the productivity of Soviet-era industrial work. A century later we are still scratching our heads trying to understand what his findings mean from a motor control perspective. As I type these final sentences, I reflect on this, and wonder which synergistic composition of muscle activity in my fingers are responsible for creating the actions which lead to these words being generated, and realize that each time I do so, because of the concepts of variability, redundancy, and abundancy, I will probably never use an identical muscle sequence when typing other ideas into words at another future point in time. But then again, I guess the words I will be writing in the future will also be different, and daily life, like motor control programs, will always vary, always change, even though the nail on the wall on which the picture hangs becomes a permanent 'item', as will this article become permanent when I hit the 'send' button to publish it. What is never to be seen again though are the traces in the 'ether' of the hammer blow which embedded the nail in the wall, and the exact movement of the individual muscles in the labourer's arms and hands, and in my fingers as I typed which created these words. Like magic their variability was created, and like magic their pattern has dispersed, never to recur in the same way or place, unless some brilliant modern-day Bernstein can solve their magic and mystery, reproduce them in their original form using some as yet to be invented laboratory device, and publish them in a monograph. Let's hope that if they do so, their great work does not languish unseen for 40 years before being discovered by the rest of the world's scientists, as was Bernstein's wonderful observations of all those years ago!

Essay 55. Strategic planning versus instinctive genius - Where would Winston Churchill have been without Alan Brooke?

Surely my most favourite book, and the one I have read more times than any other, is the War Diaries of Field Marshall Alan Brooke, edited by Alex Danchev and Daniel Todman. These diaries were the full and unexpurgated diaries written by Brooke each day of World War 2, and for those that don't know him, he was the Chief of the Imperial General Staff, the highest ranked officer in the British Army, and he worked day and night with Winston Churchill. Astonishingly, Churchill hardly mentioned Brooke at all in his books on war, described by a colleague as Churchill's autobiography yet titled the World at War, which is why Brooke allowed the diaries to be published. Churchill was an instinctive genius, but he was no strategist, and most of the disastrous strategic decisions of the First and early part of the Second World War were his doing. He was fortunate to have Brooke as his counterfoil, who was a true strategic genius, and tempered Churchill's brilliant, yet often ill-thought-out plans. In this Essay, we describe the respective personalities of Brooke and Churchill, and examine which is more relevant in a leadership setting, instinctive genius or well thought out and pragmatic strategic planning.

After a week thinking about strategic planning and how we can improve our organizational matrix at work, last night I took some time off and watched an old Second World War film, the Battle of Britain, which was a good watch, even though it was a long time since it was made. Both the work week and the film got me thinking of strategy planning, its role in organizational and goal achievement success, and associated with this, the relationship between Winston Churchill and Alan Brooke in plotting Britain's 'pathway' to success, or at least the part Britain played in the success, during the Second

World War. Strategy is defined as a high-level plan, usually generated by a team leader, to achieve one or more goals by the team under conditions of uncertainty. Strategic planning usually, but not always, involves all of the setting of goals based on awareness of resources available, determining both the plans and actions required to achieve these goals, and implementing the plans and actions in a way that the goal is reached in the most optimal way. Strategy has also been defined as a 'pattern in a stream of decisions', or as a 'way of shaping the future in order to get to desirable ends with available means'. A key feature of strategic planning is pre-emptively attempting to investigate the future to assess the multiple possible scenarios and outcomes of the different strategic plans which could be chosen to attain the required goal, whatever it is, and deciding selecting one of the plans based on awareness of the environment, skills and limitations both of the team one leads and the adversaries one potentially competes with before achieving the goal. There is always a degree of guesswork involved in any strategic thinking and planning, but at its basic level, order, structure and logic underpin and are essential for any sound strategic plan.

A book / piece of writing that has most influenced my understanding of strategic thinking has been the War Diaries of Field Marshall Alan Brooke (later Viscount Alanbrooke), which I have read probably 20 or 30 times in the last decade after I first became aware of its existence, and I appreciate it even more each time I do so. Alan Brooke, as a General, commanded one of the two Army Corps of the British Expeditionary Force that served in France in the early stage of World War 2, then served as Head of the United Kingdom Home Forces during the dark days of 1940 and 1941 when invasion was a distinct possibility, then was appointed a Field Marshal and Chief of the Imperial General Staff (CIGS), the highest rank obtainable in the British Army (which included all Commonwealth forces) at that time. Brooke served in this role for the remainder of the war, and in which capacity he worked daily with Winston Churchill, plotting the overall war strategy adopted by the British forces, in conjunction with the Chief of the Air Force (Charles Portal) and Navy (first Dudley Pound and after his death, Andrew Cunningham) Staffs. What is interesting about Alan

Brooke is that his strategy, which he developed right at the start of his tenure as CIGS at the end of 1941, was that which was almost completely followed by the Western Allies during the war, and that he is almost totally unknown to history except by a few history buffs and military academics who explore the war period and its strategy and battles with a strong microscope. The latter may perhaps be because the most famous texts describing the course of the war from the British perspective were written by Winston Churchill himself, in a string of books described by several of his contemporaries as an autobiography of Churchill's personal role in winning the war 'dressed up' as the overall (and bestselling) history of World War Two in its entirety.

There is perhaps a reason Churchill did this (write his own history of the war), which is ego-related. While he was a brilliant man, and deserves just about all of the credit he is given for playing his huge part of that epochal period of Britain's history (though of course the war was essentially won by the Russians and their huge manpower sacrifices to do so, which can only have occurred in a totalitarian state as Russia was at the time), his gifts were surely more those of the instinctive genius, who was superb in a crisis, but fickle in setting policy and strategy for either war and political goals both before and during the war. If World War Two had not occurred, Churchill's epitaph would have been a far less significant one, as a political 'will of the wisp' who changed parties frequently, and was responsible for two of Britain's great disasters during the First World War – the Dardanelles Campaign (known to most for the heroic failure of the Australian and New Zealand forces at Gallipoli) and the Antwerp Raid – both brilliant in theory, but almost completely out of touch with the reality of what could be performed with the manpower available and the logistical issues which should have ensured they never even got past the planning phase, and led to both being disastrous campaigns, and Churchill being sacked from the war cabinet for a period of time. In the Second World War, just before he took over as Prime Minister, as Head of the Admiralty he planned and was responsible for the equally disastrous invasion of Norway, which lead to the resignation of Neville Chamberlain, and for some reason, which is still a mystery today, Churchill evaded the responsibility for this disaster, and became Prime Minister despite it.

Though Alan Brooke was not Churchill's first choice as CIGS (he preferred his soldiers to have colourful personalities or to be strong external 'characters' such as Admiral Mountbatten and General Alexander, both of whom history has shown to have questionable strategic ability, although both had unquestionable bravery and charisma), it proved to be his wisest selection of the war. Brooke was not a 'people's person', had a quick brain and spoke quickly and always gave his honest opinion, whether it was welcome or not, and had an explosive temper (his nickname was 'Colonel Shrapnel', though paradoxically his most enjoyable pastime and hobby was birdwatching). Perhaps because of this, Brooke and Churchill did not enjoy each other completely from a social perspective, though each appreciated their respective strengths and skills. What Brooke had was an absolute brilliant strategic brain and could see very quickly both what is now described as the 'big picture', and the 'wood from the trees' in any difficult situation where the outcome and strategy required was not immediately clear. He always thought several 'steps' ahead, and about what outcome an action or plan in one theatre of the war would have on the other war theatres and campaigns in what was a global and total war. He would not agree with any campaign or new battle plan without being very sure there was capacity to wage it, that it had a good chance of being won, and that it fitted into the overall strategy already set to win the war or would help achieve this goal in a very clear way. Churchill, in contrast, while being a capable strategist, thought in a more intuitive way, and had a number of new ideas and plans he wanted to execute on almost a daily basis, some brilliant, most eccentric (such as wanting to invade Norway on a second occasion later in the war despite no chance of air cover for the landings, and invading the northern tip of an island near Sumatra, again with no chance of air cover and with huge logistical obstacles that would prevent it occurring, as just two examples, both of which caused major conflict between Churchill and Brooke and the Air and Navy Chiefs on Brooke's side, with the Military Chiefs eventually vetoing Churchill's plans). But as a partnership they were brilliant, and Churchill, even if often angered by Brooke – once waving his fist in Brooke's face while saying he did not want his long-term strategic plans to always hinder new potentially fruitful areas for fighting in – called Brooke his alter ego, and perhaps knew that he needed someone like Brooke to curb his erratic, even if often brilliant insights and impulsive behaviour. And again, if you sift through the evidence carefully, it was Brooke's strategic plan that 'won the day', even with the American military leaders (though they did hurry some aspects of his plan, such as the timing of the invasion of Normandy), and one can only imagine what could have happened if Churchill had a less brilliant and less tough (Brooke was one of the few people who stood up to Churchill's temper and roared back when roared at by Churchill during late night strategic planning sessions) strategist to temper his erratic brilliance that went with his magnetic and charismatic leadership. The statue of Brooke in London bears the insignia 'Master Strategist', and as Brooke so well described Churchill in his diaries: 'The wonderful thing is that three quarters of the population of the world imagine that Churchill is one of the great strategists of history, a second Marlborough, and the other quarter have no idea what a public menace he is and has been throughout the war! It is far better that the world should never know, and never suspect the feet of clay of this otherwise superhuman being. Without him England was lost for a certainty, with him England has been on the verge of disaster time and again.'

So, what do the Diaries of Alan Brooke, and his successful relationship with Winston Churchill tell us that could help us in our daily work life? Surely, that sound strategic planning is essential to achieve a required goal. Equally surely, that one needs a blend of both creative geniuses and logical strategists, the one that creates the 'spark' which sets things rolling, and the other that 'knows what the one foot is doing at the same time as the other one is moving', as Brooke always liked to say when he was trying to tell someone that they were not thinking strategically. Brooke was by nature a cautious and systematic man (though his diaries were surprisingly emotional, perhaps because of being written usually late at night when tired after a long day 'sparring' with Churchill), and caution and systematic behaviour is perhaps inherently required for / essential in developing a strategic plan, and the capacity to adhere to the plan 'through thick and thin'. But Brooke would not have had the personality that was required to maintain morale in the 'bad days' of the Blitz and early days of the war when most was going wrong for Britain, as Churchill did so well. A team with only creative geniuses will surely be initially successful but will equally surely not maintain its successes. A team with too many strategists will generate a lot of good plans and has the capacity to administratively take them along as delineated, but the plans may ultimately all remain in the cupboard and never see the light of day without the input of the creative 'go-getter'. Churchill used to often say at social events, that by adding together a dashing Army General, an Air Marshal and a Navy Admiral, he had got the sum of all their fears as a combination / outcome of the group – perhaps not realizing how denigrative he was being towards his military leaders by saying this, and / or not being aware of his own weaknesses that he was perhaps 'hiding' by projecting such aspersions on his more strategically minded military leaders (though of course Churchill was a political genius, and often the military leaders did not see the political requirements which often lay behind Churchill's eccentric military ideas). Sadly, for some reason Churchill chose to ignore the contribution of Brooke to a large degree, for reasons perhaps ego related – great men cannot allow anyone else's shadow to cloud their sun – and his huge contribution has all but disappeared with the passing of time. The moral of this is perhaps that if you want to be remembered for posterity, write your history yourself – but thank goodness historical works like Brooke's diary survived to see the 'light of day' and were published many years after the war, which allowed us to learn the rich lessons in them about both strategic planning and the human effort required to maintain that strategy in order to achieve ultimate success.

Essay 56. Leadership - Is Nelson as an admiral better than a fleet of Nelsons as sailors?

I am sure like all of you reading this, I have worked for some brilliant bosses who are true leaders and managers, and who create happy and settled environments for all around them, which are productive and creative. I am sure like all of you reading this, I have worked for some truly terrible bosses who are terrible leaders and awful managers, who create unhappy, mistrustful, tense environments for all around them, which are neither productive nor creative. Astonishingly, given how important leaders are, and how much has been written about good leadership, there are countless definitions of what makes a good leader, which means that there is no good single definition of one. In this Essay, therefore, we examine the concept of leadership, what supposedly makes a good leader, and conversely what makes a poor leader, and pose the question of whether a group of individuals function better with or without a leader when doing their daily work and tasks.

Along with our School of Medicine senior management team, I attended an excellent symposium by Professor Erwin Schwella from Stellenbosch University on leadership skills this week as part of a Leadership course we have developed. On the same day I received a letter from a university I had previously worked at asking why I had left, presumably as part of the routine human resources practice of that University, and my answer to them was that I had left because of what I perceived was poor leadership at the university in question that had created a negative and hostile work environment, where creativity had become difficult to translate into academic output as a result of the leadership-generated negative environmental milieu, amongst other reasons. These two separate events this week got me thinking even more than usual about leadership and what makes a good leader. I have worked to date in a number of different University (and Hospital and Research Institutions) environments, both as a member of different leaders' teams, and as a leader myself at different levels of the university organizational structure. In these different roles I have seen examples of both good and bad leadership, and how the good leaders create an environment where it is exciting to work in and one feels one is part of a team working for the common good and 'doing' something special, and how in contrast bad leaders can tear apart a previously healthy work environment, creating conflict, suspicion and unhappiness, and eventually mass resignations of staff, either due to their personal leadership style or due to the processes they enact that are not well received by the staff they manage. I have been on many leadership and management courses to date, and read a number of books and scientific articles on optimal management and leadership behaviour, and while it is easy to describe the effects of good and bad leadership on teams they manage, incredibly, given how indelibly part of our societal behaviour the concept of leadership is, it appears to be very difficult to 'pin down' exactly what makes a good leader, or indeed, what a good leader is.

A leader is broadly defined as a person who is followed by others, and to lead is defined as to cause others to go with one, by guiding or showing the way or by going in front. A leader cannot exist as an independent entity – essential to a leader is an organization or group of people that either require leadership or look to someone to lead or guide them. Organizations can be formal, such as is often found in work environments, or informal, where a group of people live together and which are often managed by a leader in an informal manner, such as a family, community, or friends interacting together. In the formal environment, the leader would set the strategic plans and goals for the team they manage, attenuate conflict between team members, and ensure the work environment is optimal to allow both maximum productivity of the team and wellbeing of the team they manage. In the informal environment, a leader would make decisions that would optimise the functioning of the group of people attempting to live harmoniously together, whether as a family unit or in a community. There has long been a debate on whether leadership is needed and whether teams, either formal or informal, would function better with or without a leader. When looking at primates and animal organizations, most appear to function with clearly defined leadership and hierarchal roles and environments. While in most animals these leadership roles are strength related, this is not always the case. In most self-organizing groups that have not existed before, leaders are usually self-selected by the groups to manage the group dynamics, but of course one can never be sure whether this occurs due to innate requirements and practices of the group members, or are the result of the previous or current experiences of the members of the group in other areas of their life which are emulated in the creation of a new group structure. Whatever the case, leadership is an inherent characteristic of nearly all human and animal organizational structures, and therefore there must be a teleological reason for having leaders in any organizational team.

As I said above, what makes a good leader is very difficult to define. There are a huge number of different theories on both what makes leaders and what specific 'leadership' attributes they possess (trait theory, basic style theory, situational theory, transactional theory, transformational theory, for example, amongst many others, for those folks that are interested in academic theoretical work on leadership). But, my experience after many years in academia and science is that when there are many different theories on any subject or concept, it means that the fundamental 'basic' mechanisms underpinning the concept have not been elicited to date, or that the concept is so complex and multifactorial that it will probably never be defined or clarified in any single way or by any single theory, and Leadership probably fits into this latter perception. For example, during several leadership courses I have attended in the past, my personality has been assessed by the Myers Briggs method (amongst other assessment methods), and I have a pretty strong 'ENTJ' profile (Extraversion, Intuition, Thinking, Judgement), which apparently is the classical 'leader' personality profile. But, in reality, only between 10 and 20 percent of leaders have ENTJ profiles, and it is only perceived to be the classical leadership profile because a high proportion of folk with ENTJ profiles are in leadership positions compared to how many of them there are in the general population. As much as this is the case, one can also say that

80 percent of leaders have different types of profiles to that of the ENTJ profile, and indeed a percentage of just about all Myers-Briggs profiles are leaders, and probably do as good a job, but in their own way, as compared to us ENTJ folk. Equally, a high percentage of leaders (to a greater degree than in the general environment) have been shown to be sociopaths, or have sociopathic traits, but obviously that does not mean they are good leaders – I think all of us have experienced the nightmare of working for a sociopathic leader at some point in our life – it just means that more of them are leaders than are present in the general population. So, despite a huge amount of research on what makes a good leader, it is still not completely clear from a definition perspective what makes a good or bad leader. Equally, a good leader is only as good as the team he or she leads, and a leader can lead an organization in a magnificent way, but if the wider social environment is negative or dysfunctional, the leader will likely ultimately fail due to external pressures from the wider environment that have a greater negative effect on the organization than that of the positive 'pressures' generated by the leader. Thus, the organization will fail whatever the leader does, or how good they are as leaders, if the organization they are leading is operating in a 'toxic' external / wider environment.

So, going back to my own experience of what makes a good leader – my experiences at my previous places of work, and indeed my own social and family environments, have shown to me from a personal perspective what good and bad leaders are, even if it is hard to define what makes them such, and I am aware that what for me makes a good leader may be an example of a bad leader to others. I left the university whose human resources folk sent me the follow-up letter because of what I perceived to be poor leadership, however well-intentioned it may have been. I currently work at a university that has an extremely charismatic leader who is to me an example of a good leader. However, how one personally becomes a better leader based on the examples one has is not straightforward, as all situations are different, and all environments change constantly. I remember a good friend and academic colleague of mine from Australia, Professor Frank Marino, gave me the advice when I first took up a formal leadership position that the leadership is not about being a 'boss', but creating the best environment or 'playing field' to enable the folk in it to be the most creative they can be, in a strategic and planned way, but doing this in a way that it is not perceived to be either strategic or planned by the folk one is leading, which to me was very good advice, and has been through most of my career to date. One's team will pick up very quickly if one is doing something for selfish reasons, or to further one's own career. One's team will pick up very quickly if one is being unfair or playing favourites, or if one displays evidence of a lack of integrity or honesty. They do respond positively to clear messages and good planning. They do respond positively to enthusiasm and support. They do respond positively to apologies for mistakes and behaviour on 'bad hair days' which all leaders have. Just about every person has periods of their life when they are leaders, and periods when they are in someone else's team, often at the same time, depending on the different roles they play at work, in social, and in home environments. How each person performs as a leader depends on their capacity to learn from their mistakes, improve themselves, and constantly self-reflect on their daily actions and interactions, and who their role models were in the times when they were in another's team, and they will quickly be made aware by the behaviour of their team how they are doing as a leader. But defining the 'true' / absolute leader profile will perhaps always be a quixotic enterprise, and relative to each different environment and society / organizational structure. So, to answer the question of whether a fleet would do better with Nelson as its Admiral, or if the fleet would do better if it was made up entirely of sailors with Nelson's talent, but with no Admiral, is perhaps a question still waiting to be answered, let alone us understanding exactly what traits led to Nelson being so great as a leader in his time and situation, or at least him being perceived as such. Each person must find their own leadership style and manner, and how the 'sailors' in their 'fleet' respond to them is perhaps most important in, and will surely lead to, each well-led team attaining 'victory', whatever this means and is for each different organization and team.

Essay 57. Patriotism, nationalism, and social identity - do the dangers of 'isms' outweigh their positives in society?

I grew up in the 1970s and 1980s in South Africa, where patriotism and a love of the country was deeply embedded in us through school and sports, using tools such as singing the national anthem often, saluting the flag, and listening to the self-praise of the government back then, and them telling us we were the 'chosen people' and we needed to fight anyone who thought otherwise. And fight indeed did several colleagues from school days, real fighting in the scrub and bush of Namibia and Botswana against the ethnic African 'terrorists' that were seeking to destroy our 'own-created' Lord's paradise. It was only when I got to university that I realised the true depth of the depravity of the state of South Africa as it was then, with Apartheid in full swing, people being murdered for having opinions that disagreed with the government, and 80 percent or more of the population being activity supressed and used as cheap labour by the rulers of the day. In this Essay, therefore, we examine the concepts of patriotism, nationalism, and one's own social identity, and assess whether these are either a force for good or bad, or both at the same or different times of a nation's existence.

This weekend I watched a rugby international game between South Africa and Argentina (and one between Wales and Ireland – a busy weekend as an armchair sports fan!), and when the players of each team lined up prior to the start of the game and the national anthems of each team played, I was struck by the passion that was evident both in the players and spectators, with a lot of folk reverently placing their hands over their national badges on their jerseys, and a number of both players and spectators in tears as the anthems were played. Last week I read about an incident at a local rugby derby between two schools, where all of the players, teachers and parents had become involved in a mass brawl pitting the folk identifying with each School against the other. A few weeks ago, the family and I visited Cape Town, and visited an outdoor restaurant high up on beautiful Table Mountain and noted that a colonial era statue next to it looked like it had recently had something flammable poured on it and it had been burnt by someone or some group of individuals. All of these got me thinking of the issues of patriotism, nationalism and social identify, and why folk felt the need to 'believe' in their national or local rugby sides, or why folk felt agitated enough about a statue that they felt the need to deface it, or indeed why such statues and flags were put up in the first place. This got me wondering whether patriotism, and its twin concept, nationalism, are really beneficial, or are perhaps a sign of identity issues either in individual folk, or of groups of folks, or indeed of nations and / or their leaders.

Patriotism is generally defined as a cultural attachment to one's homeland and devotion to one's country. It is thought that the term patriot was generated from an ensemble of the Greek words 'patriotes', which describes 'countrymen', and 'patris', which describes the concept of the 'fatherland'. Nationalism is defined as a belief or political ideology that involves an individual identifying with and becoming attached to their nation. Nationalism is thought to be associated with national identity, in contrast to patriotism, which is suggested to involve social conditioning and personal behaviour that supports a 'Nation's' decisions and actions. Symbolism is important in national identity, with national flags, anthems and monuments being used by national leaders and communities to both generate and enhance national identity and feelings of patriotism.

Two general theories (amongst many) of how Nationalism and Patriotism developed are the primordial and modernistic theories. In the primordial theory, nationalism is thought to be a caused by the ancient evolutionary tendency or 'desire' of humans, wherever this in the human psyche originates from, to organize into distinct groupings based on affinity from birth, or learnt from family and relatives, which create positive psychological 'triggers' in the minds of folk living in a particular nation that result in positive responses to patriotic or nationalistic cues. In contrast, in the modernistic theory, nationalism is thought to be a more recent phenomenon that requires structural conditions of modern society to exist, and perhaps also manipulation by or encouragement by the nation's leaders for it to be able to develop. It has also been suggested that three levels of common requirements exist that are needed for the development of national identity: 1) At an inter-group level, in response to potential competition or conflict, folk organize into groups to either attack other groups or defend their group from hostile 'other' groups; 2) At the intra-group level, folk as individuals gain advantage through cooperation with others in securing resources that are not available through individual effort; and 3) on the individual level, self-interest concerns of folk related to their own perceived personal fitness levels either consciously or unconsciously motivate the need for and creation of a group formation as a means of security. All these different levels of 'need' result in the development of first group and then national identity, and the development of 'boundaries' between one's own group or nation and those 'outside' of the group or nation, and in essence the development of such national (or group, ethnic or religious) boundaries become both protective of and problematical for the group that uses and defines them.

At the heart of both Nationalism and Patriotism is of course one's own personal and social identity. Identity is defined as the distinctive characteristics belonging to any given individual or shared by all members of a particular social category or group. An individual's self-identity develops through identification with 'significant others', primarily parents and other individuals during one's formative years, but also with the 'groups' that one associates with during one's early stages of development in life. The relationship between one's self-identity and social identity is complex, and obviously societies do not exist without the individuals that collectively make them up, so social identity constructs and individual identity are certainly closely linked. A neat way of looking at oneself and social identity is that it is grounded in the past, and defines one's future behaviour and how one acts to others around one, depending on the boundaries generated by the particular environment one's identity develops in. There is a bell-shaped curve of levels of identity in different people, with the majority of folk having moderate 'levels' of personal and social identity, but with some folk having 'high diffuse' social identity who do not relate to any personal or social identity, and others having 'low diffuse' social identity who relate highly to a particular social identity and are defensive of it. Some folk (likely the 'low diffuse' group) appear to gain a sense of positive self-esteem from their social identity groups, whether it is their local rugby or soccer team fan club (some great work has been done looking at this by my old colleagues Dr Matt Lewis, Dr Melissa Anderson and Dr Sandy Wolfson, amongst others), the school they attend, their work community, their ethnic or religious group or national boundary, or indeed these days with enhanced communication capacity, their international work or social structures.

Patriotism and Nationalism can be forces for 'good' in benign societies, but unfortunately, they can also be problematic and indeed frankly dangerous to those not in the 'circle of trust' of the group of folks that define themselves as a particular nation. Both Patriotism and Nationalism can be used by ruling elites to advance their own agenda, and 'manufacture consent' in the folk they rule, for their own gain rather than that of the general good of the society that make up a particular Nation. Nationalism as a concept is inherently divisive, as it highlights perceived differences between groups and people as an inherent requirement of its definition. Nations, or indeed any particular social identity, creates boundaries, with those outside this identity being by necessity external to the national group. It has been suggested that to be successful a nation should coincide with a single / uniform cultural, ethnic or religious group within its boundaries, as this would allow the nation to most easily create its specific identity and 'nationhood', but this would then create the spectre of potential antagonism of a state towards those not associated with the predominant social culture within its boundaries, whether other external nations or states, or minorities within the nation or state that are 'different' to the culture of the nation or state. History abounds with examples of aggressive actions by 'nations' against those even inside their own boundaries which are 'different' to the self-identity propagated by leaders, and indeed the citizens / followers of the leaders of those nations which profess or propose to have a homogenous self-identity and do not tolerate 'otherness' in that self-identity. Because of its propensity to encourage divisions in society and between nations, the 18th century British statesmen, Samuel Johnson, suggested that 'patriotism is the last refuge of the scoundrel', and the writer George Orwell, while viewing patriotism in a relatively positive light as a devotion to a particular place, described nationalism as 'power-hunger tempered by self-deception'.

Clearly, there are potential benefits to both a degree of nationalism and patriotism from the perception of generating a positive ethos amongst the citizens of a particular nation or state towards accepting the norms, standards and beliefs of that particular state, particularly if it has a benign world view and leadership. However, there is also the potential for negative outcomes when the levels of patriotism or nationalism become too 'high', to both those folks outside of a nation's boundaries, or to minorities within the nation's boundaries who are 'different' to the majority of its citizens. As a leader, one would like to engender a sense of pride and belonging in those whom one leads. But it is a fine line between engendering these positive collective attributes and creating a group of individuals whose self-identity is too tightly linked to that of the institution or state which one leads, and who become resistant either to change, or diversity of opinion, or external influence. Symbols such as flags, statues or anthems can be useful in engendering pride, but as in the example of an old symbol being burnt in Cape Town, they can also be hated symbols of oppression in those for whom these symbols were previously used against, or are currently used, to manufacture antipathy towards and boundaries against. It is uplifting to see young folk before a rugby game being proud to represent their country in their chosen sport, but it's unedifying to see participants, coaches and families feel such strong ties to their chosen team that they resort to violence to 'protect' their social, and perhaps self, identities. Patriotism helps retain bonds and family ties, but can be exclusive to those not originating from a particular geographic or social environment. On a personal level, I have noted that after living for extended periods on three different continents, my personal sense of patriotism has been attenuated (but this may just be associated with increased age and a perhaps wider life perspective which age often, but not always, engenders), and this is a negative from the sense that one feels to a degree 'rootless' if one has lived in many different places for long periods of time, but it is also a positive in that one does not 'ally' closely with any group or social infrastructure, which allows one to often 'walk the middle path' in both social and national disputes and debates.

An old Russian colleague, Dr Mikhail Lomarev, whom I worked with at a Research Centre in Washington DC in the USA in 2002 and 2003, not long after the attacks on both New York and Washington DC which occurred in 2001, when noticing how many Americans had flags on their houses, office buildings and cars, and who had lived through years of communism and socialism in his own country in his life, shook his head and said that he believed that the biggest danger in life are the 'isms' – from Fascism, to Communism, to in this case as he termed it American Patriotism, to Nationalism – and the world events of the decade following this discussion may have justified his concerns about the high level of 'American Patriotism' evident then, in some ways. Each 'ism' created a particular worldview and social structure that was perhaps meant initially to both protect and maintain the folk who lived in and through them, but in the end, all became restrictive and damaging either to their own citizens or those around or 'opposed' to them. So, while I enjoyed seeing the young sports folk holding the badge over the left pocket of their blazer at the start of that rugby game, I worried also where such symbolism and national pride leads to, and that the jackboot of authoritarianism, dressed up as nationalism, or even patriotism, lurks not far behind that simple gesture and the tear-stained patriotic faces which resulted from the singing of the national anthems. As much as belonging to a society or a nation, we also are all one and the same living under the same blues skies and the same green hills and valleys, that existed long before we created nations and states, and will exist long after they are changed or gone. Perhaps this – a perception of 'all-worldism' – should be the ultimate 'ism' we should believe in and adhere to, as a first principle above all others.

Section 7.
Human grand unifying themes

7.1. Introduction

In this final section of three Essays, we continue the theme of 'non-physical' unifying theories, by describing what are to me three key theories of life which are of perhaps a higher order magnitude than those described in the previous section, and are my personal favourite Essays, and were the most interesting to write about. The concepts of solipsism, existentialism and the collective unconscious are challenges to both understand and accept at another higher level of complexity, and to me the poetry of life is embedded most deeply, and are most evident, in these final three Essays. I hope you enjoy reading them as much as I enjoyed writing them.

Essay 58. The concept of solipsism and Samuel Beckett's ill seen ill said - Does a world exist out there outside of the mind?

In the modern era of social media, with 'interactions' with colleagues and friends on direct mail, Twitter, Facebook, Instagram, WhatsApp, and a host of other 'apps' where one does not see the other person, but engages with them despite this, one must trust that the person on the other side of your interaction is indeed the person you are speaking to. But who is to say it is not somebody else, or some 'grand controller' who is playing everyone along? Solipsism is the concept that the only thing that one can be completely sure of is what is happening in one's mind, and everything about the outer world needs to be 'felt', 'seen' or 'heard' through the mind and brain's pathways, therefore one can never be completely sure they exist. In this Essay we examine the concept of solipsism and assess whether we can ever be sure that the world 'out there' really exists, or indeed, if we are merely a 'brain in a vat' being fed made up information by a controlling entity who is experimenting, or 'playing' with us as their objects of amusement.

For my current job and career development plans we moved to a small town in rural South Africa, where one feels a million miles away from the big capitals of the world and science and society, and where each morning from the home where we live we look over miles of farm and bush land and feel like we are in a timeless place. This week on Twitter there was a lively and fun debate over some altimetrics – the metrics of one's public interactions and engagement such as the number of Twitter followers, Facebook friends, and LinkedIn contacts, for example – and whether the higher number of these meant you were a 'top' scientist or not, and I guess also whether one's work and its impact had relevance and meaning to, and in, the wider world. I also had a recent Facebook discussion with Andy Schulze, one of my closest friends from the halcyon days of our youth as students at the University of Cape Town, where we all debated life and its meaning on a daily basis, and this conversation with him reminded me of a book that had a great effect on me at that time (and still does), but which provided Andy with much mirth when he read it – Samuel Beckett's 'Ill seen Ill said'. All of these got me thinking of the concept of solipsism, and whether the connections one has both with the physical world and with family, social, work or broader public life makes a greater difference / one's life more relevant than if they did not exist.

Solipsism is the theory that the 'self', or one's mind, is all that one can be sure exists or can be known – in other words that nothing exists outside of what is occurring in one's mind and thoughts. Furthermore, solipsism posits that knowledge of anything outside or beyond one's mind is uncertain, and the external world, other people and what goes on in the minds of others cannot be known and does not exist outside of one's own mind. The word is derived from the Latin words 'solus', which means 'alone', and 'ipse, which means 'self'. There are different types of solipsism which have been suggested to occur over the years. For example, metaphysical solipsism is the 'strongest' version, and suggests that the 'self' is the only existing reality, and that all other existing realities, including the world and other persons in it, are representations of one's own self, and have no independent existence beyond one's capacity to think of them and thereby acknowledge their existence for the time period that one thinks of them. Epistemological solipsism is less 'extreme', and suggests that only the directly accessible and current contents of one's thoughts can be known, and that the existence of an external world is, with the knowledge we have, not possible to verify (rather than not existing at all), as one is required to 'rely' on second-hand / indirect 'knowledge' of the external world which is only perceived through, and is knowledge generated by, sensory structures which transmit images, sounds, smells or vibrations from the external world, which are integrated as a unified but 'second-hand' version of reality in one's own mind. Therefore, given the 'second-hand' nature of this mentally created version of reality, one can never be sure if this reality is real or a 'figment' of one's imagination or the sensory structures that create them. A further version of solipsism is methodological solipsism, which suggests that no knowledge of an external world, or indeed any knowledge, can be absolutely certain, given that even that which we perceive as the brain is actually part of the external world, as it is only through our sensors of the external world that we can 'see' or 'feel' the brain and think on it, and therefore the existence of thoughts rather than the brain per se is all that we can be certain of.

All of these concepts go back to Rene Descartes' (and others') idea of 'Cogito Ergo Sum' – I think, therefore I exist – and therefore, if one does not think, or if one has no thoughts, one does not exist, nor does the external world. This will obviously be a troubling concept for most folk, to whom the external world and people in it surely 'feels' real and surely are 'real'. But, an interesting theoretical example, known as the 'brain in a vat' experimental scenario, perhaps shows best how tricky it is to absolutely refute solipsism as a concept. In this hypothetical scenario, the brain of a brave volunteer is removed from their body by a pioneering scientist and suspended in a vat of life-sustaining fluid, while all the brain's outgoing and incoming neurons are connected by wires to a computer, which provides it with electrical impulses identical to that which the brain would normally receive if it was still in a body. By simulating actions such as walking along with all the sensations and actions associated with walking, as would all the sensors in the body which send information of the external world to the brain, the 'disembodied' brain would continue to have normal conscious experiences without these being related to objects or events in the external 'real' world. Therefore, one cannot ever be completely sure that the reality we 'feel' and 'observe', and life as we know it is, is real, or whether it is a created artificial reality, and we can also never be completely sure whether our brains are indeed in our bodies rather than in a vat of self-sustaining fluid and being manipulated in an artificial way. Another example used to explain solipsism is that of dreams, which often feel 'real' – how sure can we ever be that what we are doing at a certain point in time is certainly reality, rather than being part of an elaborate dream, or vice versa.

These concepts are explored in Samuel Beckett's book, Ill Seen Ill Said (though there are a number of interpretations of what the book was really about, and Beckett was never clear about the meaning of his book), which for its full length (59 pages) was written in a streams of consciousness manner about an old woman sitting at a window in a room, at the end of her life, where nothing actually happens to her, and she never does anything, for the entire content of the book. Furthermore, the book was written from an observer perspective where the observer who 'wrote' the book was never sure anything she did was real or had meaning, or if she even existed. If that sounds crazy, you will understand why my good friend Andy scoffed at its contents (and I had to read it about 10 or 20 times before I finally 'got it', or at least got what I thought it was about, which was eventually 'enough' for the book to make a big impact on my life and way of thinking). The point of the book, or at least what I got out of it, was that one can never be sure if one's existence is real, and that the line between reality and illusion is not clear. Furthermore, the book suggested that at the end of our lives, we can never be completely sure that all of the things we 'did', all of the things we 'saw', and all of the things that 'happened' during our lives, which are at the end of our lives just memories residing in our brains and minds, are 'real', and how much are 'dreams' or just fiction our minds have created. As the pivotal paragraph of his book (at least to me) so eloquently puts it: 'Incontinent the void. The zenith. Evening again. When not night it will be evening. Death again of deathless day. On one hand embers. On the other ashes. Day without end won and lost. Unseen.' The idea of Beckett's is that for the old woman living alone in her house, with no-one to validate her life, there is no way to be sure that she exists, and she passes through her life 'unseen', even if she does indeed exist. Similarly, we 'feel' at a certain point in time when we see or smell or hear some activity around us that this activity, we perceive is real as it happens, but in effect this perception of activities and occurrences are only thoughts, and like Beckett's woman, we have no possible 'certainty' about what is occurring around us beyond these thoughts we have about them. We experience these thoughts ourselves, and our own thoughts exist only in our own minds and for our own reflection alone, in the best solipsistic sense. We are like Beckett's woman, condemned to be sure of our existence and that of the world around us only in an abstract and intangible way, as a collection of thoughts occurring at a certain point in time in our own unique brain.

So how does all this link to the idea of altimetric and Twitter followers, Facebook friends, and the like which are surely concrete 'evidence' that we do exist, that we have connections with the external world, and that we have a record of our past musings and thoughts recorded as our old posts and tweets (and indeed blogs, books, and scientific papers we write). To me the interesting thing of all of these altimetric related 'records' of our existence and 'connectivity' to others, from a solipsistic perspective (rather than as a record of our relative success or failure as a scientist or person, if they can be taken as such, which is a different story), is that as much as they create a record of 'us', we can never be sure if they actually are related to the person that writes them. For example, those that know me may think and be fairly sure that I am indeed the person who wrote this article. But can you be absolutely sure that the articles I write, or the tweets I send, or the pictures I put up on Facebook are really mine, and not generated by either someone else using my name, or by a random computer generating device? This will likely sound absurd to some of you folk, but it goes to the 'nub' of the concept of solipsism, and the issues and problems solipsism raises about 'absolute' awareness, knowledge, and truth. The whole internet experience has also raised other interesting questions and dilemmas in this regard. As we no longer have to 'connect' with the 'external' world in a physical sense, but rather can do it via the electronic / computer channels which we currently use, and which are becoming increasingly both more complex / real-time 'lifelike' and ubiquitous, we can ask ourselves whether Twitter and Facebook interactions are really 'real' life and indicative of contact with the external world, or in contrast are potentially attenuating our links with the 'real' world and replacing them with links that are more ephemeral, and dare I say it, more solipsistic.

When I sit and drink my tea each morning before work while looking out at an endless vista of bush and farmland, it is easy to wonder if the world beyond the horizon really exists. While working on

411

my computer, responding to emails, sending out tweets, or posting Facebook pictures and text, I wonder if the person or people 'out there' they are 'dispatched to' really exist. I go back inside and look at my wonderful children and family, and I wonder whether, like Beckett's old woman, they really exist. Then I realize that my vat of self-sustaining liquid is running short of a few essential nutrients, and I indicate to the scientist conducting the experiment I am part of, from my fluid filled vat, that I need a few energy fuels added to the broth to keep the solipsistic thoughts and doubts at bay. When he/she has done so, I rise from my chair on the balcony in front of the bush and farmland that stretches to the horizon and go back to that reality which is my daily life, which feels so real and so good, and wonder where on earth such crazy thoughts came from. Ill seen, ill said.

Essay 59. The collective unconscious and synchronicity - Are we all created, held together and united as one by mystic bonds emanating from the psyche?

One of the most interesting collection of work and thinking I have ever read is that of Carl Jung, the psychologist who was Sigmund Freud's chosen 'son' until they disagreed sharply on basic theory, with Freud believing that all thought and all 'issues' in a person's life could be traced back to sexual issues, and Jung disagreeing and suggesting that there were a number of other potential causes of 'issues', dreams and odd thoughts one has. Two of Jung's most interesting ideas (at least to me) were those of the collective unconscious and the concept of synchronicity. In this Essay we examine these two concepts, both of which are impossible to currently prove but intuitively feel they make sense and are ideas that will drive future thinking and research development for many years to come.

Earlier this week I thought of an old friend and work colleague I had not been in contact with for many years, Professor Patrick Neary, who works and lives in Canada, and a few hours later an email arrived from him with all his news and recent life history detailed in it and in which he said he had thought of me this week and wondered what I was up to. Yesterday, in preparation for writing this article, I was reading up and battling to understand the concept of the psychological 'Shadow', one of Carl Jung's fascinating theories, and noticed a few hours later that Angie Vorster, a brilliant Psychologist we recently employed as a staff member in our Medical School to assist struggling students, posted an article on the 'Shadow' in her Facebook support page for Medical Students. Occasionally when I am standing in a room filled with folk, I feel 'energy' from someone I can't see, and when I turn around and a person is staring at me. Watching a video last night, in a scene about religious fervour, all the folk in a church were seen raising their hands in the air to celebrate their Lord. Earlier that afternoon I couldn't help noticing that a whole stadium of people watching a rugby game raised their hands in the air, in the same way as those did in the church, to celebrate when their team scored the winning try. Sadly, perhaps because I read too much existentialism related texts when I was young, I don't have any capacity to believe in a God or a religion, but on a windy day, when I am near a river or the ocean, I can't help raising my hands to the sky and looking upwards, acknowledging almost unconsciously some deity or creative force that perhaps created the magical world we inhabit for three score years and ten. All of these got me thinking of Carl Jung, perhaps one of my favourite academic Psychologists and historical scientific figures, and his fascinating theories of the collective unconscious and synchronicity, which were his attempts to explain his belief that we all have similar psychological building blocks that are inter-connected and possibly a united 'one' at some deep or currently not understood level of life.

Carl Jung lived and produced his major creative work in the first few decades of the 20th century, in what some folks call the golden era of Psychology, where he and colleagues Sigmund Freud, Alfred Adler, Stanley Hall, Sandor Ferenczi and many others changed both our understanding of how the mind works and our understanding of the world itself. He was influenced by, and for a period was, a protégé of Sigmund Freud, until they fell out when Jung began distancing himself from Freud's tunnel vision view that the entire unconscious and all psychological pathology had an underlying sexual focus and origin. He acknowledged Freud's contribution of describing and delineating the unconscious as an entity but thought that the unconscious was a 'process' where several lusts, instincts, desires and future wishes 'battled' with rational understanding and logical 'thoughts', all which occurred at a 'level' beyond that perceived by our conscious mind. He went further though, and after a number of travels to India, Africa and other continents and countries, where he did field studies of (so-called) 'primitive' tribes, he postulated that all folk had what he called a collective unconscious, which contained a person's primordial beliefs, thought structures, and perceptual boundary creating 'archetypes' which were all universal, inherent (as they occurred in tribes and people which had not interacted together for thousands of years due to geographical constraints), and responsible for creating and maintaining both one's world view and personality.

To understand Jung's theory of the collective unconscious and its underpinning archetypes, one must understand a debate that has not been successfully 'settled' since the time of Aristotle and Plato. Aristotle (and other folk who became known later as the empiricists) believed that all that can be known or occur is a product of experience and life lived. In this world view, the idea of the 'Tabula rasa' (blank slate) predominates, which suggests that all individuals are born without 'built-in' mental 'knowledge' and therefore that all knowledge needs to be developed by experience and perceptual processes which 'observes' life and makes sense of it. Plato (and other folk who became known as Platonists, or alternatively rationalists) believed that 'universals' exist and occur which are independent of human life processes, and which are 'present' in our brain and mental structures from the time we were born, and that these universals 'give us' our understanding of life and how 'it' works. For example, Plato used the example of a horse – there are many different types, sizes and colours of horses, but we all understand the 'concept' of a horse, and this 'concept' in Plato's opinion was 'free-standing' and exists as a 'universal' or 'template' which 'pre-figures' the existence of the actual horse itself (obviously religion and the idea that we are created by some deity according to his plan for us would fall into the platonic 'camp' / way of thinking). This argument about whether 'universals' exist or whether we are 'nothing' / a Tabula rasa without developed empirical experience has never been completely resolved, and it is perhaps unlikely that it will ever be unless we have a great development of the capacity or structures of our mental processes and function.

Jung took the Platonist view and believed that at a very deep level of the unconscious there were primordial, or 'archetypical' psychological universals that existed, which have been defined as innate, universal prototypes for all 'ideas' which may be used to interpret observations. Similar to the idea that one's body is created based on a template 'stored' in one's DNA, in his collective unconscious theory the archetypes were the psychological equivalents of DNA (though of course DNA was discovered many years after Jung wrote about the collective unconscious and synchronicity) and the template from which all ideas and concepts developed, and which are the frame of reference of how all occurrences in the world around one are interpreted. Some archetypes that he (and others) gave names to include the mother figure, the wise old man figure, the hero figure, the ego, and shadow (one's positive and negative 'sense of self') and the anima and animus (the 'other' gender component of one's personality) archetypes, amongst others. He thought that these were the 'primordial images' which both filtered and, in many ways, created one's 'world view' and governed how one reacted to life. For example, if one believed that one's own personality was that of a 'hero' figure', and 'chooses it' as one's principal archetype, one would respond to life accordingly, and constantly try to solve challenges in a heroic way. In contrast, if one based one's sense of self on a 'wise old man' (perhaps to be gender indiscriminate it should have been described as a 'wise old person') archetype, one would respond to life and perceived 'challenges' in a wise 'old man way' rather than a 'heroic' figure way. How he came to develop these specific archetypes was by examining the religious symbols and motifs used across different geographically separated tribes and communities and found that there were these similar 'images', or 'archetypes' as he called them, that occurred across these diverse groups of folks, and were revered by them as images of worship and / or as personality types to be deified. Jung suggested that from these 'basic' archetypes an individual could create their own specific archetypes as they developed, or one's 'self' could be a combination of several of them – but also that there were specific archetypes that resided in each individual and were similar across all living individuals and these were conservatively maintained across generations as 'universals'.

Jung went even further in exploring the 'oneness' of all folks with his theory of synchronicity, which suggested that events that occur are 'meaningful coincidences' if they occur with no (apparent) causal relationship but appear to be 'meaningfully related'. He was always somewhat vague about exactly what he meant by synchronicity. In the 'light' version he suggested that the archetypes which are the same in all people allow us all to 'be' (or at least think) similarly. In the 'extreme' version of this theory (which was also called 'Unus mundus', which is Latin for 'one world') it is suggested that we all belong to an 'underlying unified reality', and are essentially 'one', with our archetypes allowing our individual 'reality' to emerge as perceptually different to other folk and unique to us, but this archetype generated reality is illusory and 'filtered', and comes from the same 'Unus mundus' in which and of which we all exist, and to which we all eventually return. He based this observation on similar events to those that which I described above as happening to me, where friends contacted him when he was thinking of them, and when events happened to different folk geographically separate that were so similar that to him the laws of chance and statistical probability could not explain them away. While these theories may appear to be somewhat 'wild' in their breadth of vision, it is notable that Physics as a discipline explores this very concept of 'action at a distance' as 'nonlocality' theories, which are defined as the concept that an object can be moved, changed, or otherwise affected without being physically touched by another object. The theories of relativity and quantum mechanics, whether one believes them or not, are underpinned by these concepts, which similarly, as described above, underpin Jung's theory of synchronicity.

It is very difficult to either prove or refute Jung's theories of the collective unconscious, archetypes, and synchronicity, and they have therefore often been given 'short shrift' by the contemporary scientific community. But Jung is not to blame that even today our neuroscience and brain and mental monitoring devices are so primitive that they have not helped us at all understand either basic brain function or how the rich mosaic of everyone's own private mental life occurs and is maintained, and he would say it is the fact that we each 'choose' different archetypes for our own identity and as a filter of life that makes it 'feel' to us as if we are isolated individuals living a discrete and 'detached' life, and perceive that our life is 'different' to all others. It has also been suggested that the reason why we have similar beliefs and make people out to be heroes, or wise men, or mother figures, in our life, is not because of archetypes but rather because we have similar experiences and respond to our environment and the symbolism that is 'seen' during our daily life, is evident in churches and religious groups, in politics and group management activities, and in advertising (marketers have made great use of archetypes to influence our choices by how they create adverts since Jung suggested these concepts – think of the use of snake and apple motifs, apart from the kind mother or heroic father archetypes which are so often used in adverts) on a continuous basis. Jung would answer in a chicken and egg way, and ask where did all these symbols, motifs and group responses originate from if they were not created or developed from something deep inside us / our psyche? His theory of synchronicity has also been criticized by some as being confused with pure chance and probability, or as an example of a confirmation bias in folk (a tendency to search and interpret new information in a way that confirms one's preconceptions), and the term apophenia has been developed to describe the mistaken detection of meaning in random or meaningless data. But how then does one explain my friend writing to me this week when I was thinking about him a day or two before his email arrived, or how when I am battling to understand a psychological concept the psychologist I work with posts an explanation of exactly what I am battling with (even if I have never told her I am working on understanding these concepts this week) on Facebook, or how the 'feeling' that one has that someone is watching one occurs, and when turning around one finds that they are indeed watching you. These may indeed be chance, and I may be suffering from 'apophenia', but the opposite may also be true.

I have been a scientist and academic for nearly 30 years now and have developed a healthy scepticism and 'nonsense-ometer' for most theories and suggestions which seem outrageous and difficult to prove with rigorous scientific measurements (or the lack of them). But there is something in Carl Jung's theories of the collective unconscious, archetypes and synchronicity that strike a deep chord in me, and my 'gut feel' is that they are right, even though with our contemporary scientific measuring devices there is no way they can be either surely proved or disproved. Perhaps this is because I want to and enjoy 'connecting' with folk and is caused by some inherent psychological need or weakness in my psyche (or because I have chosen the wrong 'archetype' / my current sense of self does not 'fit' the life I have chosen, and this creates a dissonance that makes me want to believe that Jung was right – how's that for some real 'psychobabble'!). But this morning my wonderful daughter, Helen (age 8), gave me a card she had made at school after all the girls in her class had been given a card template to colour in, and the general motif / image on the card (and I assume on all the printed cards) was that of a superman – it's difficult not to believe that a chosen 'hero' motif does not provide evidence for an archetype when such is chosen by a school-teacher as what kids should use to describe their father (though surely myself, and most dads, are not deserving of such a description). This afternoon I will take the kids and dogs for a walk around the dam around where I live, and will very likely raise my hands to the water and wind and sky around me when I do so, as much as it is likely that the folk who will be going to church at the same time will be raising their hands to their chosen God, and those going to watch their team's football match this afternoon will raise their hands to the sky when their team scores – all doing what surely generations of our ancestors did in the time before now. While we all appear to act so differently during our routine daily life, there is always a similar response amongst most folk (excluding psychopaths, but that is for another article / another day) to real tragedy, or real crises, or real good news, when it occurs, and so often folk will admit if pushed to that they appeal either to a 'hero' figure to protect or save them in time of danger, or a 'mother' figure to help 'heal their pain' after tragedy occurs, and these calls for 'help' / succour are surely archetype related (and indeed it has been suggested that the image of God has been created as a 'hero' or 'father' figure out of an archetype by religious folk – though equally religious folk would say if there are archetypes, they may have been created in their God's image).

Our chosen archetypes creates a filter and a prism through which life and folks' behaviour might appear different, and indeed may be different, but at the level of the hypothesized 'collective unconscious', in all of us, there is surely similarity, and perhaps, just perhaps, as Jung suggests, we are all 'one', or at least that mystic bonds are indeed connecting us at some deep level of the psyche or at some energy level we currently don't understand and can't measure. How these occur or were generated as 'universals' as per the thinking of Jung and Plato, is perhaps for another day, or perhaps another generation, to explain. Unus mundus or Tabula rasa? Collective unconscious or unique individual identity? Mystic connecting bonds or splendid isolation? I'll ponder on these issues as I push the 'publish' button, and send this out to all of you, in the hope that it 'synchronises' in some way with at least some of you that read it, though of course via Jung's 'mystic bonds' you may already be aware of all I have written.

Essay 60. Existentialism and the absurdist paradigm - Adding complexity to each individual's search for meaning

Most humans would like to, or do, believe in something, whether it is a god or a deity figure, or that there is life after death, or that their daily life has meaning and purpose and that they improve the world with what they do. Very few people would admit they believe in 'nothing', and that life is inherently purposeless. But, in the early and middle parts of the last century, a concept known as existentialism was developed, which suggested that the individual is a free and responsible agent, and while life appears to have purpose, it is essentially meaningless, and the 'silent, cold universe' is 'indifferent to mankind'. Existentialism as a concept has troubled me for most of my life, and 'robbed' me of the ability to believe in anything in my early twenties and gave me a very different life than I would have had if I still 'believed' in anything, which became impossible after reading the books written by its protagonists. In the last Essay of this book, we critically evaluate the concept of Existentialism, to determine whether it can be refuted, whether it is a force for good or bad (or neither), and whether believing in it does as it suggests and 'condemns us to be free'.

A management discussion at work this week on the need to improve perinatal and child mortality rates in our clinical training platform hospitals, and cleaning up my bookshelf and picking up a book I haven't thought about for a long time, got me thinking about Existentialism as a concept, something which occupied a lot of my thoughts and philosophical reading in my twenties, but which I have not thought of for a long time. I became aware of the philosophy of Existentialism while travelling round Europe on a holiday as an early 'twenty-something' with my good friend from my medical student university days, Simon Anderson. After a particularly hedonistic few weeks touring around, and wanting a bit of quiet down time, at a bookshop in England I bought Albert Camus's epochal book depicting existential philosophy but written as fiction – 'The Fall'. I read it seven or eight times sequentially during the rest of the trip, and it changed my life and career choices thereafter.

Existentialism is broadly defined as a philosophical theory emphasizing the existence of the individual as a free and responsible agent determining his or her own development. Existentialism is conceptually underpinned by the Absurdist paradigm, which Camus described as defining the basic paradox or 'confrontation' between an individual's search or desire for significance and meaning in their life on the one hand, and the 'silent, cold universe' on the other. In other words, while it seems like the things we do in our daily lives have meaning, in the context of the universe they are purposeless, and indeed, it is difficult to ultimately define any purpose or meaning to the universe itself – the universe is essentially indifferent towards humankind. The reason for calling this an Absurdist paradigm is thus that it is therefore absurd to ascribe meaning to anything in life, given that our lives are so irrelevant in the context of the universe, and there is no meaning in the world beyond the meaning we ourselves personally give it.

Understanding, or becoming aware of, this Absurdist paradigm can create what is called an 'existential crisis' in the individual when they become aware of it. This existential crisis comes from wanting to have meaning in one's life, yet also having become aware of its meaningless. A person faced with this existential crisis has several ways of resolving the dilemma, including, firstly, one can commit suicide, and end it all, though as Camus suggested this would not counter the absurd, but would merely be playing out a part of the absurdist paradigm itself. Secondly, one can embrace a religious, spiritual or transcendental belief and use this as a life viewpoint that would counter the concept of the Absurd and one's existential crisis and give oneself a sense of 'meaning' again, though doing so would require a 'leap of faith' and a belief in something that is impossible to prove. Thirdly, one can accept the Absurd and continue to live one's life as one wishes in spite of being aware of its absurd nature, which would mean that one would live continuously aware of the inherent meaninglessness of all of one's actions, while still performing them.

Camus believed that by taking this third option, one paradoxically achieved absolute freedom from all societal, moral, or religious restraints, and therefore this option of living with 'doubt' and awareness of life's essential meaningless would allow one to 'create' a life in which one could determine how and be responsible for living life however one chose, and this is essentially what and how an Existentialist life and world view is defined. Therefore, by recognizing and embracing the position of the absurd gives one 'freedom' from all of life's 'constraints', and the ability to choose whatever meaning one wants in life, while understanding it is essentially meaningless whatever one does, and indeed any 'meaning' is created by an awareness of its absurdist condition. Camus insisted that one must maintain an 'ironic distance' between the created meaning and the condition of the absurd, lest the created meaning 'beguile' one into losing one's perspective of the absurd.

In an Existential life, therefore, one is not necessarily 'immoral' but rather 'amoral', and one can build a life however one chooses – we are 'condemned to be free' in all the choices we make because of the inherent Absurd nature of life. This paradoxically creates more responsibility on the individual for each of their choices and actions, given that one cannot assign blame for their outcomes to any external agent or belief, whether religious or secular, and this 'allows' one to create any life one chooses for oneself, and to set any goal one chooses, free of any external pressure or requirements. If one did not maintain an understanding of the Absurd in all of one's choices, this could create a paradoxical feeling of pressure and fear of the responsibilities associated with each choice needed to be made during one's life, without recourse to an external agent which could (and is often used) to absolve us blame for each of these choices and their consequences. So, in effect, an understanding of the Absurd can be liberating rather than depressing, though the opportunity for the latter emotion is obviously high in those contemplating the Absurdist paradigm, as evident in the use of the word's existential 'crisis' or 'angst' in those contemplating Existentialism and the Absurdist paradigm.

So coming back to why the discussion with my colleagues on how we can improve neonatal and child mortality rates generated Existential thoughts in me – the thought of a child dying, and even more so a neonate a few minutes or hours after they are born, has always raised the question large in my mind (apart from the feelings of grief and sadness for both the child and their parents) of what was the ultimate point of their short lives, and how on earth they could have been 'struck down' so soon after starting their lives. In many ways accepting the Absurdist paradigm is the only relief and 'balm' that one can have to attenuate and come to terms with these challenging concepts, and feelings of helplessness that come from not being able to help more these children in their distress. As with the three choices described above, one could commit suicide, but that would be ultimately a selfish act, one could turn to religion for salvation, but then one is confronted by the notion of an angry or uncaring deity for allowing suffering in a small child, or one can acknowledge the Absurd in all of it, and that there is no meaning or reason for these children's death, and yet still in the best Existential tradition, work as hard as one can, and dedicate one's life to trying to improve and enhance the practice associated with the care of such children and the prevention of their deaths to the best of one's ability, even if one has to live with the knowledge that one 'hopes for nothing, fears nothing' and that in the broad context of the universe, a child's death, and our actions in this life, are essentially meaningless, and the Universe surely unaware of the tragedy that occurs each day all around us. A thousand years from now, surely all we do in our lives will be absolutely forgotten and unknown, and potentially the Earth could itself not exist, and we live 'condemned' to be aware of this knowledge. But, paradoxically, with this awareness comes our own individual freedom to choose to live our lives as we wish to live them, and the capacity to choose to be as best we can and to act with the best personal integrity we can without the restraint of any external influence when confronting all life and situations we are involved in. The challenge perhaps to each person is to fill their life to the best of their ability while realizing personal ambition, goals and desires are all 'straw' in the winds of time, and that the concept of 'meaning' in life is potentially 'absurd' – and if one can, then one can indeed call oneself an Existentialist, for what that is worth!

8. Summary

At the beginning of this book, in the introduction section, I described starting this book in my garden shed, listening to birds twittering to each other and watching through my shed window the breath-taking scenery which is an English summer garden, and land beyond, and it is in this similar place and with similar scenery I finish this book, and commend you for completing reading it, if you have managed to do so. Despite being an academic whose job it is to study, deconstruct, and try to understand more about life and how we function as part of it, I am still in absolute awe of all of the beauty of life, nature, the human form and function, and the complex, rhythmical control processes which govern it all. Each cell in our body has thousands of life-giving processes and activity, all of which work perfectly together and in unison with all the other millions of cells in our body. Each of us individuals work in harmony and union (well, mostly in harmony) with millions of other humans who are just like us, both physically, mentally, and behaviourally, and with the millions of species of animals, plants, trees and other organisms we share a life with on this wonderful planet we call Earth. I hope you have, through these essays, seen the poetry which is life, and that life is poetic, rhythmical, mysterious but above all wonderfully brilliant in its complexity, organisation, and structure. We are all part of life's poetry, and we all contribute to it in our own special way. I am not particularly religious, but the poetic beauty of life does make me wonder what a magnificent entity is the 'thing' which created us, this earth and universe, and breathing, feeling, felt life as we know it. Existentialism was the first 'ism' that made a major impact on me, and I always acknowledge that the world is a cold, uncaring place where we exist for a while in and then disappear forever after our time on the earth ends, but like Jung and his concept of the collective unconscious, there does appear to be connections, links, and rhythmic interactions and energy based activity that underpin all life, that we don't understand a fraction of at this point in time, and perhaps the world in its greater spectrum is warm, linked and poetic, rather than cold and uncaring and existential, but it will be for a later generation of scientist, philosopher or academic, or perhaps like Einstein a young person working after hours in a clerk's office, who finally makes sense of it all, can explain how it all fits together, and how, why and for whom the poetry of life is written and created. But for now, after completing this last page, I will go out to the garden, pour a cup of tea, and sit in the beautiful green surroundings, and ponder on the mystery and poetry of life, even if I can't completely explain it. I hope that when you put the book down, after completing it, you will see life in a new light, or have your similar thoughts of its beauty and poetic nature validated, and will sit for a quiet moment and feel a triumphant exhilaration in your soul to be part of something so special, and so glorious. The poetry of life is all around us, waiting to be seen, waiting to be discovered, and waiting to be appreciated. Seek, and ye shall find!

9. Acknowledgments

All my great medical and scientific teachers, colleagues, mentors and friends, too many to mention, who imparted to me most of the knowledge found in this book, or who were with me for parts of the journey of exploration at the school and university desks, the science laboratories, and conversations over coffee when the main topic was always about the meaning of life, and what it is to be 'human', are acknowledged for their part in shaping my mind and thoughts which produced these essays and this book, though of course the faults in it are all mine. Sadly, I don't remember many from school, as I am sure there were many good teachers that had a positive effect on me, but John Eppel and Alan Pass at Clifton Junior School, Tom Stokes and Yvonne Conway at Westville Boys High, and Ant Lovell, Andy Ward, and Klein Strydom at Hilton Boys College, amongst many others, had a major positive impact on my life due to their knowledge and enthusiasm for their subject work and teaching young kids. At university, Johan Koeslag (Physiology), Cedric Wannenburgh (Anatomy – he drew the most amazing illustrations of neural pathways between the brain and body in 'real time' as we watched him lecture – I am sure he and his illustrations in part inspired my love for neurology and all things to do with the brain), Wieland Gevers and Bob Millar (Biochemistry), Pauline Close (Pathology), Richard Kirsch (Medicine), David Dent (Surgery), and several others also had a profound positive effect on my life and career choices, not least as they treated us students as almost colleagues or friends, rather than as students who must bow down before them, as several of our medical school lecturers and Professors demanded of us. In clinical medicine Offie Fehrson was a real role model as a surgeon to me at Edendale Hospital, as was Mahomed

428

Gafoor at Greys Hospital. I had some great colleagues I worked with whom I also hugely respected not just for their friendship but for their clinical skills – Mike Hofmeyr, later a pathologist, Steve Carter, later an orthopaedic surgeon, Gill Watermeyr and Simon Anderson, who later became physicians, Larissa Cronje, later an anaesthetist, Debbie Mountain, later a psychiatrist, and Chris Douie, Malcom Henry, Pete Darazs and Murray Rushmere, who became general practitioners and Murray an alternative medicine therapist, and also Jacqui Bollman, Linda Courtenay, Philip Roberts, Dave Le Fevre, and many others. From sporting days, Phil Lloyd, Tony Hansen, Andrew Schulze, Dave Ketley, Henri Van Der Merwe, Margi Alford, Mark Bosch, Kevin Gaynor, Sandy Inglis, Willem Van Der Merwe Jr, Tommy Mason, Daniel Conradie, Roelof Van Der Riet, Donnie Malherbe, Naas Fischer, Robbie Stewart, Mark Perrow, Graham Monteith, Robbie Clegg, Eugene Van Der Westhuizen, Simon Williams, Craig Bosenberg, Mike Cheeseman, and many others, made positive impressions on me, either for their paddling prowess or for the discussions we had on and off the water, and surely changed me for the better.

In my research learning days Tim Noakes in the early years, Mike Lambert, Kit Vaughan, Kathy Myburgh, Laurie Rauch, Vicki Lambert, John Hawley, Ed Ojuka, Malcolm Collins, Andrew Bosch, Wayne Derman, Martin Schwellnus, Shuaib Manjra, Janine Gray, Viv Russell, Laurie Kellaway, Peter and Judy Belonje, Dan Stein, Mogamat Hendricks, Calvin Hartnick, Morne Du Plessis, Kathy McQuade, and many others were important mentors and friends. Angus Hunter, Liesl Grobler, Julia Goedecke, Yolande Harley, Sacha West, Sharhidd Taliep, Mike Hislop, Karen Sharwood, Amanda Claassen, Ian Roger, Tracey Kolbe-Alexander, Elske Schabort, Andrew Semark, Jacob Manyonyane, Janine Grey, Zuko Kubukeli, Yumna Albertus-Kajee, Jeroen Swart, Sharief Hendricks, Ross Tucker and many other fellow PhD students and lecturers helped me and were great company and have all gone on to have superb academic careers themselves. In later jobs around the word, at the NIH in the USA, Mark Hallett, Mikhael Lomarev, Agnes Floel, Fidias Sarmiento Leon, Julie Duque, and Bernhard Voller; at Northumbria University, Kevin Thompson, Guy Masterman, Pam Briggs, Craig Mahoney, Peter Golding, Peter

Slee, Ian Postlethwaite, Nick Caplan, Mick Wilkinson, Claire Bruce, Glyn Howatson, Emma Stevenson, Caroline Dodd, Linda Allin, Su Stewart, Sarah and Liz Partington, Ian Walshe, Phil Johnson, and John Dean, amongst many others; at the University of Worcester, Andrew Renfree, Louise Martin, Claire Rhoden, Mick Donovan, Julia West, and Annie Lambeth-Mansell; at St Georges University in Grenada, Briana Fahey, Cal McPherson, and Rade Durbaba; at the University of the Free State, Jonathan Jansen, Lis Lange, Gert Van Zyl, Nats Mofolo, Wayne Marais, Angie Vorster, Pieter Du Plessis, William Rae, Lynnette Van Der Merwe, Judy Koetjie, Willem Kruger, Vernon Louw, Sulet Du Plessis, Henri Pieters, Chelepe Mocwane, Nicky Morgan, Benny Malakoane, Rita Nathan, and David Motau, amongst many others; at the University of Waikato in New Zealand, Brett Langley, Stacy Sims, Bob Rhinehart, Joe McQuillan, Marika Avison, Matt Driller, Kim Hebert-Losier and Martyn Beaven; at the University of Essex, Graham Underwood, Dom Micklewright, David Penman, John Preston, Susan Olivier, Ivan Hutchins, Rob Singh, Christine Raines, Jackie Madden, and Anthony Forster; and at the University of Hull, Una McCleod, Paul Hagan, Matt Hardman, Jane Wray, Fay Treloar, Kevin Oxley, Belen Rebello Garcia, Helen Chapman, and many other folks have been great colleagues and folk I have learnt from. So many of my students and junior colleagues have perhaps taught me (either directly or by teaching them) more than I taught them, and there is a long list of such folks who have gone on to have excellent academic careers of their own, including Kevin Thomas, Penny Rumbold, Stuart Goodall, Dan West, Jamie Tallent, Mark Russell, Mark Stone, Sam Urwin, Susan Allsop, Chris Toms, Samantha Jones, and many others. Several folks I have got to know through academic or medical work have also made a big impact, either in 'the flesh' or by reading their work, including Andy Jones, Carl Foster, Jos De Koning, Jack Raglin, Frank Marino, Flavio Pires, Louise Burke, Romain Meeusen, Roger Enoka, Kevin Tipton, Ron Maughan, Stuart Galloway, Dave Roberts, Mark Burnley, Deiary Kader, Lars McNaughton, Steve Olivier, Jimmy Volmink, Jacques Rousseau, Alastair McAlpine, Annie Vanhatolo, Craig and Kirsty Sale, and many others.

An earlier generation of family, friends and relatives were also excellent role models and / or were kind to me and encouraged me to do what I did through my life, from reading books, to doing sport competitively, to doing medicine, and to becoming an academic, and these folks include Don and Wendy Mackenzie, Mike and Di Adrain, Brain and Liz Horner, Simon Pearce, Alan Watkins, Nev Shave, Ruby Shave, David Shepherd, Don Clarke, Portia Redmond, Al and Lynley Clarke, Rose Clarke, Sally John, Gill Kelly, Andy Shave, Chris Surmon, Glynis Eglington, Gary Green, Mark Gibson, Gus Rout, John Adams, Leon Van Rooyen, my parents, and many others. Lastly, personal friends, many of them since childhood, have stood the test of time, stood by me through the good and bad times, and as such have been my greatest 'pillars' in many ways – these include James Adrain, Alan Mills, Brendan Maciver, Myles Swanepoel, Des O'Dell, Peter McElligott, Bruce Adrain, Mike Martin, Justin Mansfield, Lawrence Heathman, Theresa Stromnes, Guy Ross, Andy Church, Peter Theron, Dean Caro, Brenton Mills, Lynne Galpin, Wendy Sanderson Smith, Jo Miller, Julie Scheepers, Janet Keet, Helen Le Page, Kirsty Selley, Helen Hofmeyr, Chris Hofmeyr, Pete Mills, Dawie Senekal, and more recently Paul and Claire Chappell, Barry and Brigid Evans, Leslie Ullrich, Kobus and Megan Louw, Chris Lewis, Rob Dudley, Chris Robertson, Dave Lee, Dave Graham, Frank Travers, Dom Robinson, Danny Turner, Graham Mytton, Koby Bremer, Guy Caris, and many others. My thanks go to all of these, and all the other unnamed folk, who even with a one-day interaction, or an even briefer meeting, have altered my thinking and viewpoints, or at least made my life richer for the interaction.

Finally, thank you to UK Book Publishing, who took me under their wing and published the book / took me through all the difficult final hurdles needed to publish the book. Thanks also to all editors and designers there, Ruth Lunn and Jay Thompson, amongst others, who did such a great job getting this book finally published in a readable manner.

10. Selective Further Reading

Essay 1. Memes and genes

Wikipedia. 2021. Memes. https://en.wikipedia.org/wiki/Meme

Darwin C. 1991 (1859). The origin of species. Prometheus Books, New York, USA

Dawkins R. 2006. The Selfish Gene, 3rd Ed, Oxford University Press.

Johnston R. 2005. Third nature: The co-evolution of human behaviour, culture and technology. Nonlinear Dynamics Psychol Life Sci. 9:235-280

Noble D. 2008. Genes and causation. Phil Trans Royal Soc 366:3001-3015

Kurbel S, Kurbel B. 2019. Memes: Food for attitudes and behaviour crucial for our survival. Bioessays 41:e1900075

McNamara A. 2011. Can we measure memes? Front Evol Neurosci 3:1-7

Essay 2. Testosterone and its androgenic-anabolic derivative

Wikipedia. 2021. Testosterone. https://en.wikipedia.org/wiki/Testosterone

Giammanco M, Tabacchi G, Giammanco S, Di Majo D, La Guardia M. 2005. Testosterone and aggressiveness. Med Sci Monit 11:136-145

Hislop M, St Clair Gibson MI, Noakes TD, Marais AD. 2001. Effects of androgen manipulation on postprandial triglyceridaemia, low-density lipoprotein particle size and lipoprotein(a) in men. Atherosclerosis 159:425-432

Piacento D, Kotzalidis GD, Del Casale A, et al. 2015. Anabolic-androgenic steroid use and psychopathology in athletes. A systematic review. Curr Neuropharmacol 13:101-21

Probst F, Goole J, Lory V, Lobmaier JS. 2018. Reactive aggression tracks within-participant changes in women's salivary testosterone. Aggress Behav 44:362-371

St Clair Gibson A. 2001. Impartiality, research and the nandrolone debate. SA J Sports Med 8:24

Essay 3. Energy flow in the body

Wikipedia. 2021. https://en.wikipedia.org/wiki/Vitalism

Becker RO, Selden G. 1985. The body electric: Electromagnetism and the foundation of life. William Morrow & Company Inc. Publishers, New York, USA

Billot M, Daycard M, Wood C, Tchalla A. 2019. Reiki therapy for pain, anxiety and quality of life. BMJ Support Palliat Care 9:434-438

Coulter I, Snider P, Neil A. Vitalism – A worldwide view revisited: A critique of vitalism and its implications for integrative medicine. 2019. Int Med 18:60-73

Guo B, Powell A. 2001. Listen to your body: The wisdom of the Dao. University of Hawaii Press, Hawaii, USA

Kirschner M, Gerhart J, Mitchison T. 2000. Molecular "vitalism". Cell 100:79-88

Leskowitz E. 2020. A cartography of energy medicine: From subtle anatomy to energy physiology. Explore S1550: 1-13

Essay 4. The brain, the mind and me

Wikipedia. 2021. https://en.wikipedia.org/wiki/Brain

Gross CG. 1998. Brain, vision, memory. Tales in the history of neuroscience. MIT Press, Cambridge, Massachusetts

Horgan J. 1999. The undiscovered mind: How the brain defies explanation. Phoenix Publishers, London, UK

Kandel ER, Schwartz JH, Jessell TM. 1991. Principles of neural science. 4th Ed. McGraw-Hill Publishers, New York, USA

Le Doux J. 1998. The emotional brain. The mysterious underpinnings of emotional life. Weidenfeld and Nicolson Press, London.

Mabandla M, Kellaway L, St Clair Gibson A, Russell V. 2004. Voluntary running provides neuroprotection in rats after 6-hydroxydopamine injection into the medial forebrain bundle. Metabolic Brain Disease 19:43-50

Sohn Y, Voller B, Dimyan M, St Clair Gibson A, Hanakawa T, Leon-Sarmiento FE, Jung HY, Hallett M. 2004. Cortical control of voluntary blinking: A transcranial magnetic stimulation study. Clinical Neurophysiology 115:341-347

Solms M, Turnbull O. 2002. The brain and the inner world. An introduction to the neuroscience of subjective experience. Other Press, New York.

Essay 5. The Libet awareness of initiation of action study

Wikipedia. 2021. https://en.wikipedia.org/wiki/Free_will

Deeke L. 1987. Bereitschaftspotential as an indicator of movement preparation in supplementary motor area and motor cortex. Ciba Found Symp 132:231-250

Ferris P. 1997. Dr Freud – A life. Counterpoint Press, Washington DC.

Hallett M. 2016. Physiology of free will. Ann Neurol 80:5-12

Libet B, Gleason CA, Wright EW, Pearl DK. 1983. Time of conscious intention to act in relation to onset of cerebral activity (readiness potential). The unconscious initiation of a freely voluntary act. Brain 106:623-642

Essay 6. Self-talk and mentors

Wikipedia. 2021. https://en.wikipedia.org/wiki/Internal_monologue

Athens L. 1994. The self as soliloquy. Sociol Quart 35:521-532

Morin A. 2003. Inner speech and conscious experience. Sci Consc Rev 3:1-6

Peters S. 2012. The chimp paradox. Vermilion Publishers, London

St Clair Gibson A, Foster C. 2007. The role of self-talk in the awareness of physiological state and physical performance. Sports Med 37:1029-1044

Essay 7. Control of movement and action

Wikipedia. 2021. https://en.wikipedia.org/wiki/Motor_control

Balshaw TG, Pahar M, Chesham R, Macgregor LJ, Hunter AM. 2017. Reduced firing rates of high threshold motor units in response to eccentric overload. Physiol Rep 5:e13111

Latash M. 1998. Progress in Motor Control 1: Bernstein's traditions in movement sciences. Human Kinetics Publishers. Champaign, Il, USA

Latash M, Zatsiorsky VM. Classics in movement science. Human Kinetics Publishers. Champaign, Il, USA

St Clair Gibson A, Lambert MI, Noakes TD. 2001. Neural control of force output during maximal and submaximal exercise. Sports Med. 31:637-650

Essay 8. Information processing in the brain and body

Wikipedia. 2021. https://en.wikipedia.org/wiki/Information_theory

Fries P, Reynolds JH, Rorie AE, Desimone R. 2001. Modulation of oscillatory neuronal synchronization by selective visual attention. Science 291:1560-1563

Montague PR, McClure SM, Baldwin PR, Phillips PEM, Budygin EA, Stube GD, Kilpatrick MR, Wightman MR. 2004. Dynamic gain control of dopamine delivery in freely moving animals. J Neurosci 24:1754-1759

Palmer GS, Hawley JA, Dennis SC, Noakes TD. 1994. Heart rate responses during a 4-d cycle race. Med Sci Sports Exerc 26: 1278-1283

Scott SH. 2004. Optimal feedback control and the neural basis of volitional motor control. Nat Rev Neuro 5:532-546

St Clair Gibson A, Lambert EV, Rauch LHG, Tucker R, Baden DA, Foster C, Noakes TD. 2006. The role of information processing between the brain and peripheral physiological systems in pacing and perception of effort. Sports Med 36:705-722

Essay 9. Cell function and metabolic flux control

Wikipedia 2021. https://en.wikipedia.org/wiki/Cell_(biology)

Adachi Y, Kindzelskii AL, Ohno N, Yadomae T, Petty HR. 1999. Amplitude and frequency modulation of metabolic signals in leukocytes: Synergistic role of IFN-y in IL-6 and IL-2 mediated cell activation. J Immunol 163:4367-4374

Hawley JA, Lundby C, Cotter JD, Burke LM. 2018. Maximizing cellular adaptation to endurance exercise in skeletal muscle. Cell Metab 27:962-976

Ye J, Medzhitov R. 2019. Control strategies in systemic metabolism. Nat Metab 1:947-957

Zotter A, Bauerle F, Dey D, Kiss V, Schreiber G. 2017. Quantifying enzyme activity in living cells. J Biol Chem 292:15838-15848

Essay 10. The core requirement and skill of decision-making in life

Wikipedia 2021. https://en.wikipedia.org/wiki/Decision-making

Boksem MAS, Tops M. 2008. Mental fatigue: Costs and benefits. Brain Res Rev 59:125-139

Damasio A. 2000. The feeling of what happens. Body emotion and the making of consciousness. Vintage Press, UK

Micklewright D, Parry D, Robinson T, Deacon G, Renfree A, St Clair Gibson A, Matthews WJ. 2015. Risk Perception influences athletic pacing strategy. Med Sci Sports Exerc 47:1026-1037

Parvizi J, Damasio A. 2001. Consciousness and the brainstem. Cognition 79:135-160

Renfree A, Martin L, Micklewright D, St Clair Gibson A. 2014 Application of decision-making theory to the regulation of muscular work rate during self-paced competitive endurance activity. Sports Med 44:147-158

Essay 11. Passion and desire

Wikipedia 2021. https://en.wikipedia.org/wiki/Passion_(emotion)

Busby DM, Chiu H-Y, Leonhardt ND, Iliff E. 2019. Sexual passion in committed relationships: Measurement and conceptual issues. Fam Process 58:734-748

Gathorne-Hardy J. 2005. Kinsey: A biography. Pimlico Publishers, London, UK.

Masters SH, Johnson VE. 1966. Human sexual response. Bantam Books, Boston, USA

Seschadri KG. 2016. The neuroendocrinology of love. 20:558-563

Weinrich JD. 1988. The periodic table model of the gender transpositions: Part II. Limerent and lusty sexual attractions and the nature of bisexuality. J Sex Research 24:113-129

Winterson J. 1987. The Passion. Penguin Books, London, UK

Essay 12. The Stanford marshmallow test

Wikipedia 2021. https://en.wikipedia.org/wiki/Stanford_marshmallow_experiment

Freud S. 2001. The standard edition of the complete psychological works of Sigmund Freud vol XX1 – The future of an illusion, civilization and its discontents, and other works. Vintage Press, London, UK

Kluwe-Schiavon B, Viola TW, Sanvicente-Vieira B, Lumertz FS, Salum GA, Grassi-Oliveira R, Quednow BB. 2020. Substance related disorders are associated with impaired valuation of delayed gratification and feedback processing: A multilevel meta-analysis and meta-regression. Neurosci Biobehav Rev 108:295-307

Richardson RD. 2007. William James – In the maelstrom of American modernism. First Mariner Books, USA

Essay 13. The Milgram electric shock experiments

Wikipedia 2021. https://en.wikipedia.org/wiki/Milgram_experiment

Baker N. 2008. Human Smoke: The beginnings of world war II – The end of civilization. Pocket Books Publishers, London, UK

Burger JM. 2009. Replicating Milgram: Would people still obey today? Am Psychol 64:1-11

Carlson S, Shoda Y, Ayduk O, Aber L, Schaefer C, Sethi A, Wilson N, Peake PK, Mischel W. 2018. Cohort effects in children's delay of gratification. Dev Psychol 54:1395-1407

D'Ippolito M, Purgato A, Buzzi MG. 2020. Pain and evil: From local nociception to misery following social harm. J Pain Res 13:1139-1154

Rhodes R. 1999. Whey they kill: The discoveries of a maverick criminologist. Vintage Books, New York, USA

Russell NJC. 2011. Milgram's obedience to authority experiments: Origins and early evolution. Br J Soc Psychol 50:140-162

Stein DJ. 2000. The neurobiology of evil: Psychiatric perspectives on perpetrators. Ethn Health 5:303-315

Essay 14. Courage under fire

Wikipedia 2021. https://en.wikipedia.org/wiki/Courage

Brown G. 2008. Wartime courage: Stories of extraordinary courage by exceptional men and women in World War two. Bloomsbury Publishing PLC, London, UK

Grant US. 1886. Personal Memoirs. Penguin Books, New York, USA

Harper G, Richardson C. 2016. Acts of Valour: The history of the Victoria Cross and New Zealand. Harper Collins Publishers, Auckland, New Zealand

Mackenzie C. 1962. On moral courage. Collins Clear-Type Press. London, UK

Mobbs D, Adolphs R, Fanselow MS, Feldman Barrett L, LeDoux JE, Ressler K, Tye KM. 2019. Viewpoints: Approaches to defining and investigating fear. Nat Neuroscience 22:1205-1216

Tancer B. 2013. Click: What we do online and why it matters. Harper Collins Publishers, London, UK

Wilson CM. 1945. The anatomy of courage: The classic WW1 account of the psychological effects of war. Constable and Robinson Ltd Publishers. London, UK

Essay 15. Self-identity, life transitions, and the ageing process

Wikipedia 2021. https://en.wikipedia.org/wiki/Self-concept

Marcia JE. 1966. Development and validation of ego-identity status. J Pers Soc Psych 3:551-558

Partington E, Partington S, Fishwick L, Allin L. 2005. Mid-life nuances and negotiations: Narrative maps and the social construction of mid-life in sport and physical activity. Sport Ed Soc 10:85-99

Rochat P. 2003. Five levels of self-awareness as they unfold early in life. Conscious Cogn 12:717-731

Shakespeare W. 1623 (2016 Ed). As you like it. Digi-Reads.Com Publishers

Siekanska M, Blecharz J. 2020. Transitions in the career of competitive swimmers: To continue or finish with elite sport? Int J Environ Res Public Health 17:6842

St Clair Gibson A, Lambert MI, Noakes TD. 2004. Age-related decrements in cycling and running performance. SA J Sports Med 16:8-11

Essay 16. Death and our own dying

Wikipedia 2021. https://en.wikipedia.org/wiki/Death

Balasubramanian C, Subramanian M, Balasubramanian S, Agrawal A, Raveendran S, Kaliaperuma C. 2018. "Thanatophobia": Physician's perspective of dealing with patients with fear of death. J Nat Sci Biol Med 9:103-104

Greer DM, Shemie SD, Lewis A, Torrance S, Varelas P, Goldenberg FD et al. 2020. Determination of brain death / death by neurologic criteria: Th world brain death project. JAMA 324:1078-1097

Martial C, Cassol H, Laureys S, Gosseries O. 2020. Near-death experience as a probe to explore (disconnected) consciousness. Trends Cogn Sci 24:173-183

Essay 17. The capacity for maximum physical performance in humans

Wikipedia 2021. https://en.wikipedia.org/wiki/VO2_max

Enoka RM, Stuart DG. 1992. Neurobiology of muscle fatigue. J Appl Physiol 72:1631-1648

Gandevia SC. 2001. Spinal and supraspinal factors in human muscle fatigue. Physiol Rev 81:1725-1789

Ikai M, Steinhaus AH. 1961. Some factors modifying the expression of human strength. J Appl Physiol 16:157-163

Kay D. Marino FE, Cannon J, St Clair Gibson A, Lambert MI, Noakes TD. 2001. Evidence for neuromuscular fatigue during high-intensity cycling in warm, humid conditions. Eur J Appl Physiol 84:115-121

Noakes TD. 1997. 1996 J.B. Wolffe Memorial Lecture. Challenging beliefs: ex Africa semper aliquid novi. Med Sci Sports Exerc 29:571-590

St Clair Gibson A, Lambert ML, Noakes TD. 2001. Neural control of force output during maximal and submaximal exercise. Sports Med 84:115-121

Winchester R, Turner LA, Thomas K, Ansley L, Thompson KG, Micklewright D, St Clair Gibson A. 2012. Observer effects on rating of perceived exertion and affect during exercise in recreationally active males. Percep Mot Skills 115:213-227

Essay 18. The sensation of fatigue

Wikipedia 2021. https://en.wikipedia.org/wiki/Fatigue

Borg GA. 1973. Perceived exertion: A note on 'history' and methods. Med Sci Sports 5:90-93

Eston RG, Williams JG. 1988. Reliability of ratings of perceived effort regulation of exercise intensity. Br J Sports Med 22:153-155

Hampson DB, St Clair Gibson A, Lambert M, Noakes TD. 2001. The influence of sensory cues on the performance of effort during exercise and central regulation of exercise performance. Sports Med 31:935-952

Marcora SM, Staiano W, Manning V. 2009. Mental fatigue impairs physical performance in humans. J Appl Physiol 106:857-864

St Clair Gibson A, Baden DA, Lambert MI, Lambert EV, Harley YXR, Hampson D, Russell V, Noakes TD. 2003. The conscious perception of the sensation of fatigue. Sports Med 33:167-176

Swart J, Lindsay TR, Lambert MI, Brown JC, Noakes TD. 2012. Perceptual cues in the regulation of exercise performance – physical sensations of exercise and awareness of effort interact as separate cues. Br J Sports Med 46:42-48

Tucker R. 2009. The anticipatory regulation of performance: the physiological basis for pacing strategies and the development of a perception-based model for exercise performance. Br J Sports Med 392-400

Essay 19. The self as soliloquy

https://en.wikipedia.org/wiki/Internal_monologue

Aitchison C, Turner LA, Ansley L, Thompson KG, Micklewright D, St Clair Gibson A. 2013. Inner dialogue and its relationship to perceived exertion during different running intensities. Percept Mot Skills 117: 1053-1072

Athens L. 1994. The self as soliloquy. Sociol Quart 35:521-532

Gammage KL, Hardy J, Hall CR. 2001. A description of self-talk during exercise. Psychol Sport Exerc 2:233-247

Morin A. 2003. Inner speech and conscious experience. Sci Consc Rev 3:1-6

Schomer HH, Connolly MJ. 2002. Cognitive strategies used by marathon runners in each quartile of a training run. SA J Res Sport Phys Ed Rec 24: 87-99

Van Raalte JL, Brewer BW, Rivera PM, Petitpas AJ. 1994. The relationship between observable self-talk and competitive junior tennis players match performance. J Sport Exerc Psych 16:400-415

Essay 20. Teleoanticipation

Wikipedia 2021. https://en.wikipedia.org/wiki/Forecasting

Catalano JF. 1974. End-spurt following simple repetitive muscular movement. Percep Mot Skills 39:763-766

Church RM, Meck WH, Gibbon J. 1994. Application of scalar timing theory to individual trials. J Exp Psychol Anim Behav Process 20:135-155

Kvist A, Lindstrom A, Green M, et el. 2001. Carrying large fuel loads during sustained flight is cheaper than expected. Nature 411:752-753

Micklewright D, Angus C, Suddaby J, St Clair Gibson A, Sandercock G, Chinnasamy C. 2012. Pacing strategy in children differs with age and cognitive development. Med Sci Sports Exerc 44:362-369

St Clair Gibson A, Noakes TD. Evidence for complex system integration and dynamic neural regulation of skeletal muscle recruitment during exercise in humans. Br J Sports Med 2004; 38; 797-806

Thompson KG. 2015. Pacing: Individual strategies for optimal performance. Human Kinetics, Champaign, USA

Stepp N, Turvey MT. 2010. On strong anticipation. Cogn Syst Res 11:148-64

Ulmer H-V. 1996. Concept of an extracellular regulation of muscular metabolic rate during heavy exercise in humans by psychophysiological feedback. Experentia 52: 416-420

Essay 21. Elite athlete performance and super-achievers in sport

Wikipedia 2021. https://en.wikipedia.org/wiki/High_performance_sport

Collins D, MacNamara A. 2012. The rocky road to the top: why talent needs trauma. Sports Med 42:907-914

Freud S. 1915. Papers on metapsychology. In: The standard edition of the complete psychological works of Sigmund Freud Vol XIV: On the history of the psycho-analytic movement, papers on Metapsychology and other works. Vintage Press, London, UK, 2001

Freud S. 1923. The Ego and the Id. In: The standard edition of the complete psychological works of Sigmund Freud Vol XIX: The Ego and the Id and other works. Vintage Press, London, UK, 2001

Hauck ER, Blumenthal JA. 1992. Obsessive and compulsive traits in athletes. Sports Med 14:215-227

Mondin GW, Morgan WP, Piering PN, Stegner AJ, Stotesberry CL, Tine MR, Wu M-Y. 1996. Psychological consequences of exercise deprivation in habitual users. Med Sci Sports Exerc 28:1199-1203

Raglin JS. 2012. Addiction to physical activity. In: Rippe J (Ed). Encyclopedia of Lifestyle Medicine and Health 1:9-11

Essay 22. Anxiety, stress and the highly sensitive person

Wikipedia 2021. https://en.wikipedia.org/wiki/Anxiety

Allen SF, Wetherell MA, Smith MA. 2020. Online writing about positive life experiences reduces depression and perceived stress reactivity in socially inhibited individuals. Psychiatry Res 284:112697

Aron EN. 1999. The highly sensitive person – How to thrive when the world overwhelms you. Harper Collins Publishers, London, UK

Crocq M-A. 2017. The history of generalized anxiety disorder as a diagnostic category. Dialogues Clin Neurosc 19:107-116

Goodwin G. 2015. The overlap between anxiety, depression, and obsessive-compulsive disorder. Dialogues Clin Neurosc 17:249-260

Grimen HL, Diseth A. 2016. Sensory processing sensitivity: Factors of the highly sensitive person scale and their relationships to personality and subjective health complaints. Percep Mot Skills 123:637-653

Essay 23. Chronic fatigue syndrome

Wikipedia 2021. https://en.wikipedia.org/wiki/Chronic_fatigue_syndrome

Afifi TO, MacMillan HL, Boyle M, Cheung K, Taillieu T, Turner S, Sareen J. 2016. Child abuse and physical health in adulthood. Health Rep 27:10-18

Baumeister RF, Bratslavsky E, Muraven M, Tice DM. 1998. Ego depletion: Is the active self a limited resource? J Pers Soc Psychol 74:1252–1265

Freud S. 1923. The Ego and the Id. In: The standard edition of the complete psychological works of Sigmund Freud Vol XIX: The Ego and the Id and other works. Vintage Press, London, UK, 2001

Sharpe M. 2011. Chronic fatigue syndrome: Neurological, mental or both. J Psychosom Res 70:498-499

St Clair Gibson A, Lambert MI, Collins M, Grobler L, Sharwood KA, Derman EW and Noakes TD. Chronic exercise activity and the fatigued athlete myopathic syndrome. International SportMed Journal 2000; 1(3)1-10

St Clair Gibson A, Grobler LA, Collins M, Lambert MI, Sharwood K, Derman EW, Noakes TD. 2006. Evaluation of maximal exercise performance, fatigue, and depression in athletes with acquired training intolerance. Clin J Sport Med 16:39-45

Toms C, Robson-Ansley P, St Clair Gibson A. 2010. Chronic fatigue syndrome: a hormonal origin? A rare case of dysmenorrheal membranacea – alternative pathology. Archives of Gynecology and Obstetrics 282: 467-468

Wojcik W, Armstrong D, Kanaan R. 2011. Chronic fatigue syndrome: Labels, meanings and consequences. J Psychosom Res 70:500-504

Yancey JR, Thomas SM. 2012. Chronic fatigue syndrome: diagnosis and treatment. Am Fam Physician 86:741-746

Essay 24. Athlete collapses

Wikipedia 2021. https://en.wikipedia.org/wiki/Heat_exhaustion

Hauck ER, Blumenthal JA. 1992. Obsessive and compulsive traits in athletes. Sports Med 14:215-227

Holtzhausen LM, Noakes TD, Kroning B, de Klerk M, Roberts M, Emsley R. 1994. Clinical and biochemical characteristics of collapsed ultra-marathon runners. Med Sci Sports Exerc 26:1095-1101

Noakes TD, Mekler J, Pedoe DT. 2008. Jim Peters' collapse in the 1954 Vancouver Empire Game marathon. S Afr Med J 98:596-600

Roberts WO. 1989. Exercise associated collapse in endurance events: A classification system. Phys Sportsmed 17:49-59

Schuler J, Langens TA. 2007. Psychological crisis in marathon and the buffering effects of self-verbalizations. J Appl Soc Pyschol 37:2319-2344

St Clair Gibson A, De Koning JJ, Thompson KG, Roberts WO, Micklewright D, Raglin J, Foster C. 2013. Crawling to the finish line – why do endurance athletes collapse? Implications for understanding of mechanisms underlying pacing and fatigue. Sports Med 43:413-424

Winchester R, Turner LA Thomas K, Ansley L, Thompson KG, Micklewright D, St Clair Gibson A. 2012. Observer effects on the rating of perceived exertion and affect during exercise in recreationally active males. Percept Mot Skills 115:213-227

Essay 25. Athlete pre-screening for cardiac and other clinical disorders

Wikipedia 2021. https://en.wikipedia.org/wiki/Sudden_cardiac_death_of_athletes

Brosnan M, La Gerche A, Kalman J, Lo W, Fallon K, Maclsaac A, Prior D. 2014. The Seattle Criteria increase the specificity of preparticipation ECG screening among elite athletes. Br J Sports Med 48:1144-1150

Corrado D, Basso C, Thiene G. 2012. Sudden cardiac death in athletes: what is the role of screening? Curr Opin Cardiol 27:41-48

Halkin A, Steinvil A, Rosso R, Adler A, Rozovski U, Viskin S. 2012. Preventing sudden death of athletes with electrocardiographic screeing: what is the absolute benefit and how much will it cost? J Am Coll Cardiol 60:2271-2276

Lee IM, Sesso HD, Oguma Y, Paffenbarger RS. 2004. The 'weekend warrior' and risk of mortality. Am J Epidemiol 160:636-641

Noakes TD, Opie LH, Rose AG. 1984. Marathon running and immunity to coronary heart disease: fact versus fiction. Clin Sports Med 3:527-543

Solberg EE, Bjornstad TH, Anderson TE, Ekeberg O. 2012. Cardiovascular pre-participation screening does not distress professional football players. Eur J Prev Cardiol 19:571-577

Essay 26. Anterior cruciate knee ligament injuries

Wikipedia 2021. https://en.wikipedia.org/wiki/Anterior_cruciate_ligament_injury

Failla MJ, Arundale AJH, Logerstedt DS, Snyder-Mackler L. 2015. Controversies in knee rehabilitation: anterior cruciate ligament injury. Cl J Sports Med 34:301-312

Solomonow M, Barratta R, Zhou BH, Shoji H, Bose W, Beck C, D'Ambrosia R. 1987. The synergistic action of the anterior cruciate ligament and thigh muscles in maintaining joint stability. Am J Sports Med 15:207-213

St Clair Gibson A. 2002. Neural control mechanisms and anterior cruciate ligament injury. SA J Sports Med 9: 17-22

St Clair Gibson A, Lambert MI, Durandt JJ, Scales N, Noakes TD. 2000. Quadriceps and hamstrings peak torque ratio changes in persons with chronic anterior cruciate ligament deficiency. J Orthop Sports Phy Ther 30:418-427

Essay 27. Low carb high fat Banting diets and appetite regulation

Wikipedia 2021. https://en.wikipedia.org/wiki/William_Banting

Burke LM, Ross ML, Garvican-Lewis LA, Welvaert M, Heikura IA, Forbes SG, Mirtschin JG, Cato LE, Strobel N, Sharma AP, Hawley JA. 2017. Low carbohydrate, high fat diet impairs exercise economy and negates the performance benefit from intensified training in elite race walkers. J Physiol 595:2785-2807

Burke LM. 2021. Ketogenic low-CHO, high-fat diet: the future of elite endurance sport? J Physiol 599:819-843

Noakes TD. 2013. Low-carbohydrate and high-fat intake can manage obesity and associated conditions: occasional survey. S Afr Med J 103:826-830

Noakes TD, Creed S-A, Proudfoot J, Grier D. 2013. The real meal revolution: Changing the world one meal at a time. Quivertree Publications, Cape Town, South Africa

Schutz Y, Montani J-P, Dulloo AG. Low-carbohydrate ketogenic diets in body weight control: A recurrent plaguing issue of fad diets? Obes Rev 2021 2:e13195

Webster CC, Murphy TE, Larmuth KM, Noakes TD, Smith JA. 2019. Diet, diabetes status, and personal experiences of individuals with type 2 diabetes who self-selected and followed a low carbohydrate high fat diet. Metab Syndr Obes 12:2567-2582

Essay 28. Doping and drugs in sport

Wikipedia. 2001. https://en.wikipedia.org/wiki/Doping_in_sport

Albergotti R, O'Connell V. 2013. Wheelmen: Lance Armstrong, the Tour de France, and the greatest sports conspiracy ever. Headline Publishing Group, London, UK

Lentillon-Kaestner V. 2013. The development of doping use in high-level cycling: From team-organized doping to advances in the fight against doping. Scan J Med Sci Sports 23:189-197

Lucia A, Earnest C, Arribas C. 2003. The Tour de France: A physiological review. Scand J Med Sci Sports 13:275-283

Ljungqvist A. 2017. Brief history of anti-doping. Med Sport Sci 62:1-10

Morente-Sanchez J, Zabala M. 2013. Doping in sport: A review of elite athletes' attitudes, beliefs, and knowledge. Sports Med 43:395-411

Pope HG Jr, Katz DL. 1988. Affective and psychotic symptoms associated with anabolic steroid use. Am J Psychiatry 145:487-490

Pope HG Jr, Katz DL, Champoux R. 1988. Anabolic-androgenic steroid use among 1,010 college men. Phys Sportsmed 16:75-81

St Clair Gibson A. 1994. Anabolic steroids - a contemporary perspective. South African Medical Journal 84: 468-469

Vernec A, Slack A, Harcourt PR, Budgett R, Duclos M, Kinahan A, Mjosund K, Strasburger CJ. 2020. Glucocorticoids in elite sport: Current status, controversies and innovative management strategies – A narrative review. 54:8-12

Walsh D. 2012. The program: The seven deadly sins – My pursuit of Lance Armstrong. Simon and Schuster, London, UK

Essay 29. Anorexia nervosa and the eating disorders

Wikipedia 2021. https://en.wikipedia.org/wiki/Anorexia_nervosa

Batista M, Antic LZ, Zaja O, Jakovina T, Begovac I. 2018. Predictors of eating disorder risk in anorexia nervosa adolescents. Acta Clin Croat 57:399-410

Castellini G, Lo Sauro C, Lelli L, Godini L, Vignozzi L, Rellini AH, Faravelli C, Maggi M, Ricca V. 2013. Childhood sexual abuse moderates the relationship between sexual functioning and eating disorder psychopathology in anorexia nervosa and bulimia nervosa: a 1-year follow-up study. J Sex Med 10:190-200

Davis C, Kaptein S. 2006. Anorexia nervosa with excessive exercise: A phenotype with close links to obsessive-compulsive disorder. Psych Res 142:209-217

Guisinger S. 2008. Competing paradigms for anorexia nervosa. Am Psychol 63:199-204

Laghi F, Pompili S, Zanna V, Castiglioni MC, Criscuolo M, Chianello I, Mazzoni S, Baiocco R. 2017. How adolescents with anorexia nervosa and their parents perceive family functioning? J Health Psychol 22:197-207

Moskowitz L, Weiselberg E. 2017. Anorexia nervosa / Atypical anorexia nervosa. Curr Probl Pediatr Adolesc Health Care 47:70-84

Vansteelandt K, Pieters G, Vandereycken W, Claes L, Probst M, Van Mechelen I. 2004. Hyperactivity in anorexia nervosa: A case study using experience sampling methodology. Eating Behav 5:67-74

Westmoreland P, Krantz M, Mehler PS. 2016. Medical complications of anorexia nervosa and bulimia. Am J Med 129:30-37

Essay 30. Muscle dysmorphia and the Adonis complex

Wikipedia 2021. https://en.wikipedia.org/wiki/Muscle_dysmorphia

Choi PYL, Pope HG Jr, Olivardia R. 2002. Muscle dysmorphia: a new syndrome in weightlifters. Br J Sports Med 36:375-377

Foster AC, Shorter GW, Griffiths MD. 2015. Muscle dysmorphia: Could it be classified as an addiction to body image? J Behav Add 4:1-5

Kaplan RA, Rossell SL, Enticott PG, Castle DJ. 2013. Own-body perception I body dysmorphic disorder. 18:594-614

Kelly MM, Didie E, Phillips KA. 2014. Personal and appearance-based sensitivity in body dysmorphic disorder. Body Image 11:260-265

Pope CG, Pope HG, Menard W, Fay C, Olivardia R, Phillips KA. 2005. Clinical features of muscle dysmorphia among males with body dysmorphic syndrome. Body Image 2:395-400

Steele IH, Pope Jr HG, Kanayama G. 2019. Competitive bodybuilding: Fitness, pathology, or both? Harv Rev Psychiatry 27:233-240

Tod D, Edwards C, Cranswick I. 2016. Muscle dysmorphia: Current insights. Psychol Res Behav Man 9:179-188

Essay 31. Narcissistic personality disorders and sociopathy

Wikipedia 2021. https://en.wikipedia.org/wiki/Psychopathy#Sociopathy

McGrath J, Bates B. 2013. The little book of big management theories: And how to use them. Pearson Publishers, Harlow, UK

Caligor E, Levy KN, Yeomans FE. 2015. Narcissistic personality disorder: Diagnostic and clinical challenges. Am J Psychiatry 172:415-422

Decety J, Chen C, Harenski C, Kiehl KA. 2013. An fMRI study of affective perspective taking in individuals with psychopathy: Imagining another in pain does not evoke sympathy. Front Hum Neurosci 24:489

Viding E, McCrory E, Seara-Cardoso A. 2014. Psychopathy. Curr Biol 24:871-874

Woody GE, McLellan AT, Luborsky L, O'Brien CP. 1985. Sociopathy and psychotherapy outcome. Arch Gen Psychiatry 42:1081-1086

Essay 32. Rites of passage ceremonies, initiation, and hazing

Wikipedia 2021. https://en.wikipedia.org/wiki/Hazing

Diamond AB, Callahan ST, Chain KF, Solomon GS. 2016. Qualitative review of hazing in collegiate and school sports: Consequences from a lack of culture, knowledge and responsiveness. Br J Sports Med 50:149-153

DiRosa GA, Goodwin GF. 2014. Moving away from hazing: The example of military initial entry training. Am Med Ass J Ethics 16:204-209

Jeckell AS, Copenhaver EA, Diamond AB. 2018. The spectrum of hazing and peer sexual abuse in sports: A current perspective. Sports Health 10:558-564

Mann L, Feddes AR, Doosje B, Fischer AH. 2016. Withdraw or affiliate? The role of humiliation during initiation rituals. Cogn Emot 30:80-100

Essay 33. The Kübler-Ross five emotional stages of grief

Wikipedia 2021. https://en.wikipedia.org/wiki/Five_stages_of_grief

Kübler-Ross E, Kessler D. 2014. On grief and grieving: Finding the meaning of grief through five stages of loss. Simons and Schuster, London, UK

Lowrie D, Ray R, Plummer D, Yau M. 2018. Exploring the contemporary stage and scripts for the enactment of dying roles: A narrative review of the literature. J Death Dying 76:328-350

Raju B, Reddy NK. 2018. Perspectives of gliobastoma patients on death and dying: A qualitative study. 24:320-324

Sacks O. 2015. On the move: A life. Picador Publishers, London, UK

Essay 34. Research and public engagement

Wikipedia 2021. https://en.wikipedia.org/wiki/Research

Greenland S, Senn SJ, Rothman KJ, Carlin JB, Poole C, Goodman SN, Altman DG. 2016. Statistical tests, P values, confidence intervals, and power: A guide to misinterpretations. Eur J Epidemiol 31:337-350

Hopkins WG, Marshall SW, Batterham AM, Hanin J. 2009. Progressive statistics for studies in sports medicine and exercise science. Med Sci Sports Exerc 41:3-13

Mishra P, Pandey CM, Singh U, Keshri A, Sabaretnam M. 2019. Selection of appropriate statistical methods for data analysis. Ann Card Anaesth 22:297-301

Pyke M. 1961. The boundaries of science. Harrap and Co Publishers, London, UK

Smith CS, Pell JP. 2003. Parachute use to prevent death and major trauma related to gravitational challenge: systematic review of random controlled trials. BMJ 327:1459-1461

St Clair Gibson A. 1996. Medical research - inferential errors. SA Med J 1996; 86: 514

Essay 35. Universities

Wikipedia 2021. https://en.wikipedia.org/wiki/University

Caulfield T, Ogbogu U. 2015. The commercialization of university-based research: Balancing risks and benefits. BMC Med Ethics 16:70

Digby A. 2013. Black doctors and discrimination under South Africa's apartheid regime. Med Hist 57:269-290

Shek DL. 2010. Nurturing holistic development of university students in Hong Kong: Where are we and where should we go? 10:563-575

Spires ES, Monroy-Hernandez A. 2016. Shifting stakes: Understanding the dynamic roles of individuals and organizations in social media protests. PLoS One 11:e0165387

Westhues K. 1998. Eliminating professors: A guide to the dismissal process. Kempner Collegium Publications, New York, USA

Essay 36. The Harvard psilocybin, marsh chapel and concord prison experiments

Wikipedia 2021. https://en.wikipedia.org/wiki/Harvard_Psilocybin_Project

Carhart-Harris RL, Goodwin GM. 2017. The therapeutic potential of psychedelic drugs: Past, present and future. Neuropsychopharmacol 42:2105-2113

Devonis DC. 2012. Timothy Leary's mid-career shift: Clean break or inflection point? J Hist Behav Sci 48:16-39

Doblin R. 1998. Dr Leary's Concord prison experiment: A 34-year follow-up study. J Psychoactive Drugs. 30:419-426

Horgan J. 2003. Rational Mysticism: Dispatches from the border between science and spirituality. Houghton Mifflin Publishers, New York, USA

Wark C, Galliher JF. 2010. Timothy Leary, Richard Alpert (Ram Dass) and the changing definition of psilocybin. Int J Drug Policy 21:234-239

Essay 37. Technology and the university environment

Wikipedia 2021. https://en.wikipedia.org/wiki/Technology

Macznik AK, Ribeiro DC, Baxter GD. 2015. Online technology use in physiotherapy teaching and learning: A systematic review of effectiveness and users' perception. Med Educ 15:160

Mak HC. 2017. Harnessing MOOCs for the practice of science. Cell Syst 27:157

Pei L, Wu H. 2019. Does online learning work better than offline learning in undergraduate medical education? A systematic review and meta-analysis. Med Educ Online 24:1666538

Shaw R. 1988. Small group teaching. J R Coll Gen Prac 38:175

Wakefield A, Cartney P, Christie J, Smyth R, Cooke A, Jones T, King E, White H, Kennedy J. 2018. Do MOOCs encourage corporate social responsibility or are they simply a marketing opportunity? Nurse Educ Prac 33:37-41

Essay 38. Scientific conferences

Wikipedia 2021. https://en.wikipedia.org/wiki/Academic_conference

Dominic C, Bhalla G. 2021. A framework for student-led education conferences. Clin Teach 18:104-108

Lortie C. 2020. Online conferences for better learning. Ecol Evol 10:12442-12449

Swash M, Lees AJ. 2019. Medical Conferences: Value for money? J Neurol Neurosurg Psychiatry 90:483-484

Oswald A-MM, Ostojic S. 2020. Curating more diverse conferences. Nat Rev Neurosci 21:589-590

Essay 39. Contemporary medical training and societal medical

Wikipedia 2021. https://en.wikipedia.org/wiki/Medicine

Benatar S. 2016. Politics, power, poverty, and global health: Systems and frames. 5:599-604

Cottrell E, Alberti H, Rosenthal J, Pope L, Thompson T. 2020. Revealing the reality of undergraduate GP teaching in UK medical curricula: A cross-sectional questionnaire study. Br J Gen Prac 70:644-650

Homberg A, Hundertmark J, Krause J, Brunnee M, Neumann B, Loukanova S. 2019. Promoting medical competencies through a didactic tutor qualification programme – A qualitative study based on the CanMEDS physician competency framework. BMC Med Educ 19:187

Patel M. 2016. Changes to postgraduate medical education in the 21st century. Clin Med 16:311-314

Van Der Merwe JW, Rugunanan M, Ras J, Henderson BD, Joubert G. 2016. Patient preferences regarding the dress code, conduct and resources used by doctors during consultations in the public health sector in Bloemfontein, Free State. S Afr Fam Prac 1:1-6

Essay 40. A career in medicine

Wikipedia 2021. https://en.wikipedia.org/wiki/Sisyphus

Papadimos TJ. 2014. Eluding meaninglessness: A note to self in regard to Camus, critical care, and the Absurd. Perm J 18:87-89

Papakostas YG. Papakosta VM, Markianos M. 2008. The notion of 'Sisyphus task' in medicine: A reconstruction. Psyckiatriki 19:330-336

Stolarski A, Moseley JM, O'Neal P, Whang E, Kristo G. 2020. Retired surgeons' reflections on their careers. JAMA Surgery 155:359-361

West CP, Dyrbye LN, Shanafelt TD. 2018. Physician burnout: Contributors, consequences and solutions. J Intern Med 283:516-529

Essay 41. Psychology

Wikipedia 2021. https://en.wikipedia.org/wiki/Psychology

Ferris P. 1997. Dr Freud: a life. Counterpoint Publishers, Washington DC, USA

Gillis LS. 1977. Guidelines in Psychiatry. Juta and Co Publishers, Cape Town, South Africa

Le Doux J. 1998.The emotional brain: The mysterious underpinnings of emotional life. Weidenfield and Nicolson Publishers, London, UK

Lieberman EJ. 1985. Acts of will: The life and works of Otto Rank. University of Massachusetts Press, Amherst, USA

Weiten W. 1989. Psychology: Themes and variations. Brooks / Cole Publishing Company, Belmont, USA

Essay 42. History and historical revisionism

Wikipedia 2021. https://en.wikipedia.org/wiki/Historical_revisionism

Churchill W. 1959. The second world war. Pimlico Publishers, London, UK

Colville J. 1985. The fringes of power: Downing Street diaries 1939-1955. Phoenix Publishers, London, UK

Danchev A, Todman D. 2001. The War Diaries of Field Marshal Lord Alan Brooke 1939-1945. Phoenix Publishers, London, UK

Kennedy J. 1957. The business of war: The war narratives of Major-General Sir John Kennedy. Hutchinson Publishers, London, UK

Essay 43. What is normal - Can normative data ever exist in a world of individual differences and qualia

Wikipedia 2021. https://en.wikipedia.org/wiki/Normality_(behavior)

Briese E. 1998. Normal body temperature of rats: The setpoint controversy. Neurosci Biobehav Rev 22:427-436

Koeslag JH. 1993. What is normal? S Afr Med J. 83:47-50

Pogrel MA. 1991. What are normal esthetic values. J Oral Maxillofac Surg 49:963-969

Schaefer JH. 1954. Hemoglobin: Normal values. Calif Med 80:32-33

Essay 44. Entropy - The forgotten universal principle

Wikipedia 2021. https://en.wikipedia.org/wiki/Entropy

Cohen IR, Marron A. 2020. The evolution of universal adaptations of life is driven by universal properties of matter: energy, entropy, and interaction. F1000Res 9:626

Jeffery KJ, Rovelli C. 2020. Transitions in brain evolution: Space, time and entropy. Trends Neurosci 43:467-474

Kleidon A. 2010. A basic introduction to the thermodynamics of the earth system far from equilibrium and maximum entropy production. Philos Trans R Soc London B Biol Sci 365:1303-1315

Popper K. 1974. Unended quest: An intellectual autobiography. Routledge Classics Publishers, London, UK

Essay 45. Homeostasis and the constancy principle

Wikipedia 2021. https://en.wikipedia.org/wiki/Homeostasis

Carpenter RHS. 2004. Homeostasis: A plea for a unified approach. Adv Physiol Educ 28:180-187

Lambert EV, St Clair Gibson A, Noakes TD. 2005. Complex systems model of fatigue: Integrative homoeostatic control of peripheral physiological systems during exercise in humans. Br J Sports Med 39:52-62

Modell H, Cliff W, Michael J, McFarland J, Wenderoth MP, Wright A. 2015. A physiologist's view of homeostasis. Adv Physiol Educ 39:259-266

St Clair Gibson A, Swart J, Tucker R. 2018. The interaction of psychological and physiological homeostatic drives and role of general control principles in the regulation of physiological systems, exercise and the fatigue process – The Integrative Governor Theory. Eur J Sport Sci 18:25-36

Sturis J, Van Cauter E, Blackman JD, Polonsky KS. 1991. Entrainment of pulsatile insulin secretion by oscillatory glucose infusion. J Clin Invest 87:439-445

Woods SC, Ramsay DS. 2007. Homeostasis: Beyond Curt Richter. Appetite 49:388-398

Essay 46. The negative feedback loop

Wikipedia 2021. https://en.wikipedia.org/wiki/Negative_feedback

Guyton AC. 1987. Human physiology and mechanisms of disease (4th Ed). WB Saunders Publishers, Philadelphia, USA.

Hoermann R, Midgley JEM, Larisch R, Dietrich JW. 2015. Homeostatic control of the thyroid-pituitary axis: Perspectives for diagnosis and treatment. Front Physiol 6:177

Igoshin OA, Brody MS, Price CW, Savageau MA. 2007. Distinctive topologies of partner-switching signalling networks correlate with their physiological roles. J Mol Biol 369:1333-1352

Noble D. 2006. The music of life: Biology beyond genes. Oxford University Press, Oxford, UK

Novak B, Tyson JJ. 2008. Design principles of biochemical oscillators. Nat Rev Mol Cell Biol 9:981-991

Saunders PT, Koeslag JH, Wessels JA. 1998. Integral rein control in physiology. J Theor Biol 194:163-173

Saunders PT, Koeslag JH, Wessels, JA. 2000. Integral rein control in physiology II: A general model. J Theor Biol 206:211-220

Turrigiano GG. 2008. The self-tuning neuron: synaptic scaling of excitatory synapses. Cell 135:422-435

Yang J, Clark JW, Bryan RM, Robertson C. 2005. Mathematical modelling of the nitric oxide / cGMP pathway in the vascular smooth muscle cell. Am J Physiol Heart Circ Physiol 289:886-897

Essay 47. Metabolic activity setpoint regulation in the body

Wikipedia 2021. https://en.wikipedia.org/wiki/Teleology

Briese E. 1998. Normal body temperature of rats: the setpoint controversy. Neurosci Biobehav Rev 22:427–436

Buchman TG. 2002. The community of the self. Nature 420:246–251

Glass L. 2001. Synchronization and rhythmic processes in physiology. Nature 410:277-284

Kawano F, Nomura T, Ishihara A, Nonaka I, Ohira Y. 2002. Afferent input-associated reduction of muscle activity in microgravity environment. Neuroscience 114:1133-1138.

Parvizi J, Damasio A. 2001. Consciousness and the brainstem. Cognition 79:135-159

St Clair Gibson A, Goedecke JH, Harley YX, Myers LJ, Lambert MI, Lambert EV. 2005. Metabolic setpoint control mechanisms in different physiological systems at rest and during exercise. J Theor Biol 236:60-72

Essay 48. Teleology and determinism

Wikipedia 2021. https://en.wikipedia.org/wiki/Teleology

Hallett M. 2007. Volitional control of movement: The physiology of free will. Clin Neurophysiol 118:1179-1192

Hudson M, McDonough KL, Edwards R, Bach P. 2018. Perception teleology: Expectations of action efficiency bias social perception. Proc R Soc B Neursci Cogn 285:20180638

Kampourakis K. 2020. Students' "teleological misconceptions" in evolution education: Why the underlying design stance, not teleology per se, is the problem. Evo Edu Outreach 13:1-12

Wisniewski D, Deutschlander R, Haynes J-D. 2019. Free will beliefs are better predicted by dualism than determinism beliefs across different cultures. PLoS One 14:e0221617

Essay 49. Zeitgebers

Wikipedia 2021. https://en.wikipedia.org/wiki/Zeitgeber

Hofman MA. 2004. The brain's calendar: neural mechanisms of seasonal timing. Biol Rev Camb Philos Soc 79:61-77

Lewy AJ, Emens J, Sack RL, Hasler BP, Bernert RA. 2003. Zeitgeber hierarchy in humans: resetting the circadian phase positions of blind people using melatonin. Chronobiol Int 20:837-852

Mistleberger RE, Skene D, 2004. Social influences on mammalian circadian rhythms: Animal and human studies. Biol Rev Camb Philos Soc 79:533-556

Rensing L, Ruoff P. 2002. Temperature effect on entrainment, phase shifting, and amplitude of circadian clocks and it molecular bases. Chonobiol Int 19:807-864

Reppert SM, Weaver DR. 2002. Coordination of circadian timing in mammals. Nature 418:935-941

St Clair Gibson A, Goedecke JH, Harley YX, Myers LJ, Lambert MI, Lambert EV. 2005. Metabolic setpoint control mechanisms in different physiological systems at rest and during exercise. Journal of Theoretical Biology 236:60-72

Essay 50. Fractals

Wikipedia 2021. https://en.wikipedia.org/wiki/Fractal

Bassingthwaighte J, Hunter P, Noble D. 2009. The cardiac physiome: Perspectives for the future. Exp Physiol 94: 597-605

Briggs J. 1992. Fractals: The patterns of chaos – Discovering a new aesthetic of art, science and nature. Simon and Schuster, New York, USA

Costa MD, Goldberger AL. 2015. Generalised multiscale entropy analysis: Application to quantifying the complex volatility of human heartbeat time series. Entropy 17:1197-1203

Gleick J. 1987. Chaos: Making a new science. Penguin Publishers, New York, USA

Hu K, Ivanov PC, Chen Z, Hilton MF, Stanley HG, Shea SA. 2004. Non-random fluctuations and multi-scale dynamics regulation of human activity. Physica A 337: 307-318

Mandelbrot BB. 1975. Stochastic models for the earth's relief, the shape and the fractal dimension of the coastlines, and the number-area rule for islands. Proc Nat Acad Sci 72:3825-3828

Sardar Z, Abrams I. 1998. Introducing chaos. Icon Books, Cambridge, UK

Tucker R, Bester A, Lambert EV, Noakes TD, Vaughan CL, St Clair Gibson A. 2006. Non-random fluctuations in power output during self-paced cycling. Br J Sports Med 40: 912-917

Essay 51. Holism

Wikipedia 2021. https://en.wikipedia.org/wiki/Holism

Balague N, Torrents C, Hristovski R, Kelso JAS. 2017. Sport science integration: An evolutionary synthesis. Eur J Sport Sci 17:51-62

Delker RK. Mann RS. 2017. From reductionism to holism: Toward a more complete view of development through genome engineering. Adv Exp Med Biol 1016:45-74

Desmond C, Seeley J, Groenewald C, Ngwenya N, Rich K, Barnett T. 2019. Interpreting social determinants: Emergent properties and adolescent risk behaviour. PLoS One 14:e0226241

Fesce R. 2020. Subjectivity as an emergent property of information processing by neuronal networks. Front Neurosci 14:548071

Smuts JC. 1926. Holism and evolution. MacMillan Publishers, New York, USA

Steyn R. 2015. Jan Smuts: Unafraid of greatness. Jonathan Ball Publishers, Cape Town, South Africa

Wolkenhauer O, Green S. 2013. The search for organizing principles as a cure against reductionism in systems medicine. FEBS J 280:5938-5948

Essay 52. Strategy, tactics, and objectives

Wikipedia 2021. https://en.wikipedia.org/wiki/Strategy

Bradley OM. 1951. A soldier's story. Random House Publishers, New York, USA

Breuer WB. 1995. Feuding allies: The private wars of the high command. Castle Books, Edison, New Jersey, USA

Dixon N. 1976. On the psychology of military incompetence. Pimlico Publishers, London, UK

Eisenhower DD. 1948. Crusade in Europe. John Hopkins University Press, Baltimore, USA

Grant US. 1885. Personal Memoirs. Penguin Books, New York, USA

Roberts A. 2008. Masters and Commanders: How Roosevelt, Churchill, Marshall, and Alan Brooke won the war in the west. Penguin Books, London, UK

Essay 53. Plato's horse and the concept of universals

Wikipedia 2021. https://en.wikipedia.org/wiki/Universal_ (metaphysics)

Avena-Koenigsberger A, Goni J, Sole R, Sporns O. 2015. Network morphospace. J R Soc Interface 12:20140881

Lim WA, Lee CM, Tang C. 2013. Design principles of regulatory networks: Searching for the molecular algorithms of the cell. Mol Cell 49:202-212

Russell B. 1946. History of western philosophy: And its connection with political and social circumstances from the earliest times to the present day. Routledge Publishers, UK

St Clair Gibson A, Swart J, Tucker R. 2018. The interaction of psychological and physiological homeostatic drives and role of general control principles in the regulation of physiological systems, exercise, and the fatigue process – The integrative governor theory. European Journal of Sport Science 18:25-36

Essay 54. Consistency of task outcome and the degrees of freedom problem

Wikipedia 2021. https://en.wikipedia.org/wiki/Degrees_of_ freedom_(mechanics)

Guimaraes N, Ugrinowitsch H, Dascal JB, Porto AB, Okazaki VHA. 2020. Freezing degrees of freedom during motor learning: A systematic review. 24:457-471

Latash M. 1998. Neurophysiological control of movement. Human Kinetics. Champaign, USA

Latash M. 1998. Progress in motor control volume one: Bernstein's traditions in movement studies. Human Kinetics Publishers, Champaign, USA

Latash M. 2012. The bliss of motor abundance. Exp Brain Res 217:1-5

Essay 55. Strategic planning versus instinctive genius

Wikipedia 2021. https://en.wikipedia.org/wiki/Strategic_thinking

Bryant A. 1957. The turn of the tide: Based on the war diaries of Field Marshal Viscount Alan Brooke. The Reprint Society Publishers, London, UK.

Colville J. 1976. Footprints in time: Memories. Williams Collins Publishers, London, UK

Danchev A, Todman D. 2001. The War Diaries of Field Marshal Lord Alan Brooke 1939-1945. Phoenix Publishers, London, UK

Fraser D. 1982.Alan Broooke. Harper Collins Publishers, London, UK.

Ferguson B. 1957. The business of war: The war narrative of Major-General Sir John Kennedy. Hutchinson Publishers, London, UK

Wilson CM (Lord Moran). 1966. Churchill at war 1940-1945. Constable and Robinson, London, UK.

Essay 56. Leadership

Wikipedia 2021. https://en.wikipedia.org/wiki/Leadership

Clark A. 1961. The donkeys. Pimlico Publishers, London, UK

Cruikshank A, Collins D. 2016. Advancing leadership in sport: Time to take off the blinkers? Sports Med 2016:1199-1204

Ferguson A, Moritz M. 2015. Leading. Hodder and Stoughton Publishers, London, UK

Ford K, Menchine M, Burner E, Arora S, Inaba K, Demetriades D, Yersin B. 2016. Leadership and teamwork in trauma and resuscitation. West J Emerg Med 17:349-356

McGrath J, Bates B. 2013. The little book of big management theories: And how to use them. Pearson Education Publishers, Harlow, UK

Essay 57. Patriotism, nationalism, and social identity

Wikipedia 2021. https://en.wikipedia.org/wiki/Patriotism

De Zavala AG, Cichocka A, Eidelson R, Jayawickreme N. 2009. Collective narcissism and its social consequences. J Pers Soc Psychol 97:1074-1096

Gangl K, Torgler B, Kirchler E. 2016. Patriotism's impact on cooperation with the state: An experimental study on tax compliance. Polit Psychol 37:867-881

Hoyt CL, Goldin A. 2016. Political ideology and American intergroup discrimination: a patriotism perspective. J Soc Psychol 156:369-381

Roos J. 2012. Nationalism, racism and propaganda in early Weimar Germany: Contradictions in the campaign against the 'black horror on the Rhine'. Ger Hist 30:45-74

Willis-Esqueda C, Delgado RH, Pedroza K. 2017. Patriotism and the impact of perceived threat and immigration attitudes. J Soc Psychol 157:114-125

Essay 58. The concept of solipsism and Samuel Beckett's ill seen ill said

Wikipedia 2021. https://en.wikipedia.org/wiki/Solipsism

Beckett S. 1981. Ill seen, ill said. John Calder Publishers, London, UK

Hogan AM, Winter DC. Changing the rules of the game: How do we measure success in social media? 2017, Clin Colon Rectal Surg 30:259-263

Lawson-Frost S. 2017. Dismissing the moral sceptic: A Wittgensteinian approach. Philosophia 45:1235-1251

Patthi B, Prasad M, Gupta R, Singla A, Kumar JK, Dhama K, Ali I, Niraj LK. 2017. Altmetrics – A collated adjunct beyond citations for scholarly impact: a systematic review. J Clin Diagn Res 11:16-20

Russell B. 1946, History of western philosophy: And its connection with political and social circumstances for the earliest times to the present day. Routledge Publishers, London, UK

Essay 59. The collective unconscious and synchronicity

Wikipedia 2021. https://en.wikipedia.org/wiki/Collective_ unconscious

Bennet EA. 1954. The collective unconscious. Proc R Soc Med 47:639-641

Donati M. 2004. Beyond synchronicity: The worldview of Carl Gustav Jung and Wolfgang Pauli. J Anal Psychol 49:707-728

Mills J. 2019. The myth of the collective unconscious. J Hist Behav Sci 55:40-53

Jung CG. 1961. Memories, dreams, reflections. Fontana Press

Mattoon MA. 2005.Jung and the human psyche: An understandable introduction. Routledge Publishers, London, UK

Essay 60. Existentialism and the absurdist paradigm

Wikipedia 2021. https://en.wikipedia.org/wiki/Existentialism

Bolmsjo I, Tengland P-A, Ramgard M. 2019. Existential loneliness: An attempt at an analysis of the concept and the phenomenon. Nurs Ethics 26:1310-1325

Camus A. 1942. The Outsider. Penguin Books, London, UK

Camus A. 1957. The Fall. Penguin Books, London, UK

Galdston I. 1961. Existentialism and Psychiatry. Bull N Y Acad Med 37:835-47

Popa G, Hanganu E. 1979. The faces of death. J Med Ethics 5:71-72

Sartre J-P. 1938. Nausea. Penguin Books, London, UK

Readers' Notes

Printed in Great Britain
by Amazon

77849045R00271